ADVANCE PRAISE

"In *Complex Integration of Multiple Brain Systems (CIMBS) in Therapy*, Beatriz and Albert Sheldon provide an innovative model in which insights from neuroscience are embodied in an effective and compassionate form of psychotherapy. At the core of their therapy is a deep respect for our need as a species to be safe and to trust. Their insightful treatment model documents that the journey to optimized mental health may efficiently be reached through a treatment model informed by an appreciation of the brain circuits that evolved to support our biological imperative to trust and to be socially connected."

—**Stephen W. Porges, Ph.D.,** Distinguished University Scientist, Founding Director, Traumatic Stress Research Consortium, Kinsey Institute, Indiana University Bloomington

"Psychotherapeutic insights and practices are being revolutionized by neuroscience, epigenetics, and the growing recognition that we have multiple evolved processing systems many of which are not fully conscious and can be in conflict. In this intriguing book on interacting brain systems Beatriz and Albert Sheldon attempt to bridge recent findings from evolutionary neuroscience into therapeutic insights and practices. They indicate how therapists can help clients become familiar with old and new brain processes and help them cultivate motives and competencies that enable a better interaction and integration of mental processes. Therapists will find many new ways of thinking about psychological processes and ways of engaging with client complexity. An easy to understand, unique, and deeply informative book for all therapists."

—**Paul Gilbert, Ph.D.,** Professor, Centre for Compassion Research and Training, College of Health, Psychology and Social Care, University of Derby, author of *Human Nature and Suffering* and *The Compassion Mind*

"Wow, what a book. This extraordinary summary of clinically relevant brain science is clearly written, thoroughly practical, and infused with caring for the people we work with. It provides a necessary foundation for early career therapists while also offering many fresh insights for experienced clinicians. The overall approach is truly brilliant. Highly recommended."

—**Rick Hanson, Ph.D.,** author of *Buddha's Brain:*
The Practical Neuroscience of Happiness, Love, and Wisdom

Complex Integration of
Multiple Brain Systems
in Therapy

THE NORTON SERIES ON INTERPERSONAL NEUROBIOLOGY

Louis Cozolino, Ph.D., Series Editor
Allan N. Schore, Ph.D., Series Editor, 2007–2014
Daniel J. Siegel, M.D., Founding Editor

The field of mental health is in a tremendously exciting period of growth and conceptual reorganization. Independent findings from a variety of scientific endeavors are converging in an interdisciplinary view of the mind and mental well-being. An interpersonal neurobiology of human development enables us to understand that the structure and function of the mind and brain are shaped by experiences, especially those involving emotional relationships.

The Norton Series on Interpersonal Neurobiology provides cutting-edge, multidisciplinary views that further our understanding of the complex neurobiology of the human mind. By drawing on a wide range of traditionally independent fields of research—such as neurobiology, genetics, memory, attachment, complex systems, anthropology, and evolutionary psychology—these texts offer mental health professionals a review and synthesis of scientific findings often inaccessible to clinicians. The books advance our understanding of human experience by finding the unity of knowledge, or consilience, that emerges with the translation of findings from numerous domains of study into a common language and conceptual framework. The series integrates the best of modern science with the healing art of psychotherapy.

A Norton Professional Book

Complex Integration of Multiple Brain Systems in Therapy

BEATRIZ SHELDON & ALBERT SHELDON

FOREWORD BY DANIEL J. SIEGEL

W. W. NORTON & COMPANY
Independent Publishers Since 1923

The cover image for this book was created through a joint effort by Richard Strickland and Nicola Swaine. The design is a visual representation of the complex processes of activation, facilitation and differentiation of emotional brain systems that will be described in detail in Chapters 8 and 11.

This book is intended as a general information resource for professionals practicing in the field of psychotherapy and mental health. It is not a substitute for appropriate training, peer review, and/or clinical supervision. Standards of clinical practice and protocol vary in different practice settings and change over time. No technique or recommendation is guaranteed to be safe or effective in all circumstances, and neither the publisher nor the author(s) can guarantee the complete accuracy, efficacy, or appropriateness of any particular recommendation in every respect or in all settings or circumstances. In particular, the use of these treatments with patients who have "borderline," dissociative, bipolar or psychotic disorders is strongly discouraged.

The names of all patients mentioned have been changed and identifying details changed or omitted, and some patients are composites. Any URLs displayed in this book link or refer to websites that existed as of press time. The publisher is not responsible for, and should not be deemed to endorse or recommend, any website other than its own or any content that it did not create. The author, also, is not responsible for any third-party material.

Illustrations by Nicola Swaine
Copyright © 2022 by Beatriz Sheldon and Albert Sheldon
Foreword copyright © 2022 by Mind Your Brain, Inc.

For information about permission to reproduce selections from this book, write to Permissions, W. W. Norton & Company, Inc., 500 Fifth Avenue, New York, NY 10110

For information about special discounts for bulk purchases, please contact W. W. Norton Special Sales at specialsales@wwnorton.com or 800-233-4830

Manufacturing by Sheridan Books
Production manager: Gwen Cullen

ISBN: 978-0-393-71327-5

W. W. Norton & Company, Inc., 500 Fifth Avenue, New York, N.Y. 10110
www.wwnorton.com

W. W. Norton & Company Ltd., 15 Carlisle Street, London W1D 3BS

1 2 3 4 5 6 7 8 9 0

Dedicated to our patients and our trainees. Their contributions to the paradigm and treatment approaches of Complex Integration of Multiple Brain Systems are beyond description.

CONTENTS

FOREWORD

··

BY DANIEL J. SIEGEL

This is a mind-opening book that will take you on a journey into the depth and details of neural integration as a core source of health and healing, resourcing and resilience building. Filled with solid scientific foundations, practical clinical applications, and numerous illustrative case examples—often in the form of therapeutic session transcripts—this compilation of the life's work of a devoted and disciplined psychologist and psychiatrist reveals the step-by-step details a therapist, new or experienced, will need to lay the groundwork for an exciting new approach to the psychotherapeutic process.

I was honored when our illuminating authors, Beatriz and Albert Sheldon, contacted me years ago to discuss their approach to psychotherapy. They offered both exciting ways of looking into the structure and function of the brain and conscientious attention to the details of the communication between clinician and client as they meticulously studied both the videos and transcripts of therapy sessions to uncover the exciting steps of the change process. Their work reveals how careful attention to the therapist-client relationship, and the ways the therapist helps the journey of growth, involve a fundamental process that an exploration of the nature of the mind and mental health supports: When we differentiate and link aspects of a complex system, we enable the natural self-organization of that system to move toward harmony. When either differentiation or linkage are hampered, the result is an impediment to self-organization in the form of chaos, rigidity, or both.

The name we can use for this mathematical finding of complex systems' self-organization is quite simple: integration. When we integrate, we are linking differentiated parts; such integration creates a synergy in which the "whole is greater than the sum of the parts" and the integrity of the individual components is not comprised in their being linked, in their joining to form a larger whole.

In the cross-disciplinary framework known as interpersonal neurobiology (IPNB), we use the approach of consilience (*Consilience*: E.O. Wilson, 1998) to seek out the common ground or universal principles discovered by independent pursuits of knowledge. From an IPNB perspective, integration is the heart of health (*Mind* or *The Developing Mind*, Siegel, 2017/2020). The mind can be seen as having at least four facets: subjective experience, consciousness, information processing, and self-organization. Each of these may be emergent properties—a fundamental aspect of complex systems—of energy and information flow. In this way, the mind is both fully embodied, including the flow of energy in the nervous system, the embodied brain; and it is fully relational, involving the flow of energy between individuals within interpersonal relationships, and between us and all of nature, with the planet as a whole. This is the embodied *and* relational nature, the inner *and* inter locations, of the human mind. A healthy mind is one that cultivates integration within and between.

In the *Complex Integration of Multiple Brain Systems,* as both a text and as an approach, you will find a powerful way in which you can learn to deepen an understanding of integration in the mind, and how to cultivate this in your clients—and in yourself. I have found this book to be deeply informative, engaging, and highly rewarding. It is a consilient approach to IPNB, and its disciplined way of drawing on basic brain science and then applying these findings to useful ways of carrying out steps toward differentiating and linking, toward integration, are original, creative, and effective. Our articulate and in-depth guides, companions in creating this CIMBS approach in their professional as well as their personal lives, bring a love for this exciting new way of working with people that you can feel on each page. This is an inspiring work of heart built on the solid science foundation of the head.

The book is organized in an effective and accessible manner that allows a clinician totally unfamiliar with the brain to ease into this approach by building a scaffold of knowledge that then can support you in the application of these practical steps in your therapeutic work. As the authors suggest, take your time: Learning new information and new ways of doing things requires reflection, practice, and repetition. You'll be gaining new skills and knowledge in each step of the way. What initially may feel new and unfamiliar, perhaps even odd or uncomfortable, will soon come to be familiar, and have more clarity and details that you'll find will begin to build a solid foundation for your integrative healing work.

Health and healing are derived from the root idea of wholeness; to integrate is to make whole by linking differentiated elements into a coherent, functional whole with more capacities, more resilience, more health.

I welcome you to the exciting world of neural integration and the many ways we can apply these strategies for the benefit of the well-being of all the people with whom we work. It is an honor to welcome you to the Sheldon's powerful strategy for helping bring health into our lives. Enjoy!

HOW TO READ THIS BOOK

This book contains many new or unfamiliar concepts, perspectives, and types of knowledge. Much of the knowledge in this book may be inconsistent or incongruent (Chapter 13) with your intuition, experience, or training. Some of what you will learn is likely to be disorienting to your way of seeing the minds of others or your own. It certainly is disorienting for our patients and trainees alike. That is a good thing; for it can stir up your curiosity. Your skepticism and doubt are welcome, as they invite all of us to pay more attention. Novelty is where we learn the most. We hope we are providing enough intriguing and practical information to motivate you to exert the effort to absorb unfamiliar knowledge. However, our minds need time and energy to absorb novel information rather than dismiss it. So we encourage you to read some, ponder more, put the book down, and pick it up later. Our intention is that this book will help you make your own surprising discoveries.

If you choose to experiment with a brain systems approach to psychotherapy, there are many paths you can explore. Each chapter is intended to give you some new ideas, understandings, perspectives, and opportunities to add to your therapeutic practice. There will be many examples of interventions you can try. You could start with Chapter 9 or Chapter 2, or somewhere in between. For those readers who want to experiment or practice with this therapeutic paradigm right away, we suggest starting with Chapter 2 as a demonstration, to get a taste of an actual session. Then we recommend that you jump ahead to Chapter 5 on the Therapeutic Attachment Relationship and/or Chapter 6 on Initial Directed Activation. Those chapters contain practical and straightforward interventions and protocols with which to experiment, a kind of quick-start manual. Your next steps could be Chapter 4, "A Different Frame of Mind," and Chapters 8 and 11 on Differentiating. If you find those experiments useful or productive, you can explore the underlying neurobiological principles in Chapter 3 or Chapter 15 which elaborates on neuroplasticity and neurotransmitters. Many of the chapters illustrate approaches to Facilitating resilient emotional brain systems in order to develop Fail-Safe Networks.

Enjoy! This is a ride on a multidimensional neurobiological paradigm.

PREFACE

PURPOSE

Our purpose in writing this book is to translate our clinical research and successful training courses onto the page in an approachable, intriguing, yet comprehensive manuscript.

We want to share the results of our research with others. We are scientists, and we value new scientific data. We believe others are curious about our successful, unanticipated, and sometimes anomalous results. We have been repeatedly encouraged to share our clinical research with a wider audience.

At the same time, we are practical, empirical therapists. So we know that other therapists would like to have some new practical approaches to enhance treatment with their patients. We hope to inspire others to experiment with new frames of mind, perspectives, and interventions. We have found significant benefit in our practices and in the practices of our trainees.

Our purpose is to intrigue, challenge, and invite new learning for each reader. Our hope is to inspire therapists to develop new practices to become increasingly expert and competent in their work. We hope to help readers believe in themselves in new ways. We have found that as that occurs, they can let go of their control and trust their patients and the therapeutic process. This allows more room for uncertainty and releasing the self-organizing aspects of the patient's brain and mind.

We hope to open readers' minds to be receptive to their patients' novel experiences. Our other goal is to help therapists develop new mental search patterns that will enable them to detect important nonverbal and nonconscious information with which to guide and fine-tune the therapeutic process. Although we use some vocabulary that may not be familiar to you, it will be defined in the first couple of chapters and the glossary at the end. When we review video recordings of our trainees' sessions, we notice many beneficial phenomena that they did not recognize at the time, but that they are able to see with practice.

Patient and therapist factors are much more important than the therapeutic modality in a successful outcome of psychotherapy. Our purpose is to show the reader how to change those patient factors and therapist factors from the first moment of each and every therapy session. Our intention is to show readers many new and different resources to enhance their therapeutic success. We believe that therapists have more to offer their patients than they realize. Our paradigm can help therapists harness and focus their own energy and intention to be more effective.

LIMITATIONS AND CHALLENGES

It has been very challenging for two nonwriting clinicians to put down in words what we have discovered, practiced, and taught experientially. A contrasting therapeutic paradigm is difficult to describe. Our successful teaching does not easily translate onto the page. We have tried to copy and paste our teaching into this book, and we needed a different approach for print.

It is hard to trust what you cannot see. So many beneficial nonconscious activations are transpiring that you have not been trained to observe or value. Learning something counterintuitive takes effort. We intend to desensitize the reader to the discomfort of experimenting with something quite different.

We will give you a range of new perspectives to help you discover and discern what was previously invisible. It is challenging to persist with new interventions or perspectives when you are getting little or no verbal or conscious feedback that your patient is benefiting from your intervention. We know it takes practice to enhance trust in yourself, your patient, and the therapeutic process.

Changing emotional patterns in your patients' minds is challenging. We hope to provide you with new sources of energy, focus, and inspiration to meet those challenges with confidence and calm.

SCOPE

Complex Integration of Multiple Brain Systems (CIMBS) is a distinct therapeutic paradigm that we have developed over the past 25 years as a result of our academic (neuroscience), scientific, and clinical research.

Research in CIMBS is a creative and systematic work that we undertook to increase our knowledge of the inner workings of the nonconscious emotional processing of the human BrainMind. Through this work we have established new facts, solved new and existing clinical problems, and developed new effective, efficient, and reproducible psychotherapeutic treatments.

Our CIMBS research has included:

- *Academic research* studying and integrating neuroscience literature by Siegel, Panksepp, Porges, Davidson, Grawe, Damasio, LeDoux, and others.
- *Scientific research,* formulating hypotheses and testing them to see whether we could confirm or falsify them. We have gathered reliable data and shared them with hundreds of colleagues to confirm the facts and hypotheses.
- *Clinical research* as physician-therapists, personally assessing patients to evaluate interventions that treat emotional disorders (mitigate symptoms and previous trauma) and harness the wisdom and energy of internal adaptive emotional capabilities to help patients thrive.

The clinical scientific data that we have collected and recorded prioritizes psychophysiological phenomena that are readily revealed in CIMBS psychotherapy demonstrations. The video recordings of therapy sessions can be reviewed in minute detail for evidence of effectiveness of the interventions, testing hypotheses, and studying the psychophysiological phenomena from multiple perspectives and by many different observers.

GENESIS OF THIS BOOK

We started experimenting with different approaches to the therapeutic process more than 25 years ago. We have struggled to find ways to share the results of our clinical research with a wider audience. In 1996, Albert submitted an article describing his research on clinical approaches to enhance the patient's autonomous authority to the *International Journal of Intensive Short-Term Dynamic Psychotherapy.* Our mentor, Habib Davanloo, and the other editors found the research and the article interesting. However, they chose not to publish it because it was too different from other articles in the journal.

In 2002, Beatriz added her perspective to the written attempts to share the results of our clinical research. She recognized that this clinical research was more distinctive than Albert appreciated. She pointed out how the process was impacting multiple nonconscious functions of the patient's brain. She believed it would be necessary to explore some novel ways of describing and explaining the research in these clinical experiments. She suggested writing an article about the clinical discoveries from a multiple brain systems perspective in 2003. Our second writing attempt became an article that we sent to several readers from different therapeutic backgrounds. They responded that the research and the concepts were too unfamiliar and hard for them to grasp.

We stopped trying to write and turned to other avenues. We began showing the video recordings of the research at grand rounds and therapy conferences. The presentations with video recordings demonstrating the research were more successful. The participants were able to experience the therapeutic process and ask questions about the evidence that was presented. We thought, "A picture is worth a thousand words."

However, many viewers did not recognize or appreciate what they were observing for two reasons. Some of the participants could not discern what we were doing or how it was being effective. Most of our clinical work is directed at nonconscious emotional systems that are contained deep within the brain, and therefore their manifestations are subtle, with little or no verbal content. Many of the participants also did not have mental search patterns to observe the psychophysiological phenomena that were guiding the therapist and the therapeutic process. They could not discern the empirical evidence of the clinical progress that was unfolding in the session.

We successfully refined our teaching by sharing our research in experiential weekend training courses. A picture is primarily perceived by visual brain systems; however, an experience is perceived by all of the conscious and nonconscious brain systems. If a picture is worth a thousand words, then an experience is worth more than a thousand pictures. Experiential learning is mostly nonconscious, and there are often no words that can describe the visceral experiences. We have since limited our teaching focus to eight different two-day training courses. We have published these courses as DVDs and virtually as streaming videos (Sheldon & Sheldon, 2014, 2015, 2016a, 2016b, 2017a, 2017b, 2018).

The requests from our students and trainees have been the final genesis of this book. They have repeatedly asked for a comprehensive written summary of our therapeutic paradigm that would provide them another avenue for learning. Even our eight different weekend courses could not provide a sufficiently broad overview of this therapeutic paradigm we call CIMBS.

We have made a special effort to use precision in our terminology to meet our trainees', students', and readers' need for clarity and orientation. We have used common language terms as much as possible even as we are using them with specificity. We have tried to avoid psychological (psychotherapy) jargon and acronyms. Precise terminology can help the reader distinguish one system, phenomena, or intervention from another. We have included a glossary of terms and phrases that have specific definitions to help you better understand their depth of meaning. Although it will take some effort to become familiar with these terms and definitions, our trainees have found they provide greater insight and confidence in their therapeutic treatment.

ACKNOWLEDGMENTS

Our greatest acknowledgment is to each other. We have shared 20 years of learning, discussions, and sitting for hours looking at minute details in our research. There have been many challenging questions and disagreements to inspire us to grow as human beings and as a couple. We have shared difficult and exhilarating times together in this process of researching psychotherapy from many different perspectives, from innumerable coffees in bed interviewing each other, trying to understand what it is that we do, to hours and hours watching each other's videos second by second. The therapeutic paradigm we call Complex Integration of Multiple Brain Systems has been a brainchild for us. Further research will enable the paradigm to keep evolving.

We are so profoundly thankful for the presence of Richard Strickland, our local editor and longtime friend. His background as a science editor, author, and college professor has been very helpful for us. His abilities to ask cogent questions, rearrange the pieces of the puzzle that have become our book, and his knowledgeable editing skills have made this book more accessible and rich. Without his hours and hours of painstaking and loving work, this book would not have evolved to what it is right now—a readable book rather than a brick. He has been the midwife of our brainchild. We are forever indebted to him.

Nicola Swaine has been our dedicated illustrator, drawing all of the figures and images in the book. She has the enthusiasm and ability to be inspired by our ideas and approach so we could experiment together with different drawings to try to communicate nonverbally. She worked hard to bring these concepts to life visually. Her illustrations are important to us, for much of this knowledge will be unfamiliar to many readers.

Daniel Siegel has been a constant source of inspiration and guidance. As you will see throughout the book, his understanding of the importance of differentiation of systems, neural integration, and self-organizing phenomena have guided our own research and teaching. He encouraged us to write this book and initiated our introduction to Deborah Malmud at Norton.

We have learned the most from our patients. Their authentic vulnerability and courage have inspired and instructed us. They have approached our scientific experiments together as co-investigators. They have willingly participated in our clinical research and given us verbal and visceral feedback on their experiences. Many of our patients have given us permission and have been honored to have verbatim transcripts of one of their sessions included in this book. We are grateful for their direct contributions to us and our readers. We have been deeply changed by our shared journeys. We are pleased to pass along this knowledge to a wider audience.

Dr. Habib Davanloo, McGill University, Montreal, Canada, was a mentor for each of us at different points in our training and careers (see introduction). We are grateful for his dedication to teaching and his scientific approach. He taught us to video record our therapy sessions so we and others could review and learn from them. We learned to work in the present moment and the therapeutic relationship in order to facilitate changes within each session. He encouraged us to teach and share our competence with other colleagues.

Many colleagues have helped us along in our journeys of research and teaching. Jon Frederickson helped us recognize how our work was more different from all other modalities than we realized at first. He also played a big role in helping us find our voice in learning how to teach others. Ellen Beauchamp, Zandra Zimmerman, Judith Kaftan, Deb Haynes, Gina Delmastro, Nasrin Rousta, Barbara Jo Hinsz, Sean Hatt, Stephanie Neill, Janel Fox, Jess Bolton, Christy Sweaney, Jordon Wolfe, and many others supported and challenged us along the way.

Dr. Sallie Sheldon is a research biologist and college professor who encouraged us over the past 25 years in our research endeavors. She taught us how much effort it takes to develop new mental search patterns. She also helped us believe in the paradigm we were developing and directed us to teach our own short courses rather than trying to fit into other therapy presentations.

The Bush Medical Fellowship gave Albert funds in 1992 for a sabbatical to do clinical psychotherapy research. They also gave encouragement to make discoveries without being limited by others' ideas or priorities. Dr. Michael Feldman and the Park Nicollet Clinic also supported Albert during his time away from his psychiatry practice.

The University of Washington, Seattle, is in our backyard. The Department of Psychiatry and Behavioral Health has been an arena in which to teach and train our young colleagues. The Whiteley Center at the University of Washington, Friday Harbor Labs on San Juan Island provided us a retreat center where we could spend time away to focus completely on writing this manuscript.

Erika Morales has transcribed audio recordings of many of our training courses and brainstorming sessions. She worked to understand what we meant even when our words may have been confusing.

We are so grateful to Deborah Malmud and W. W. Norton for working with us to bring this project to fruition. She has been patient and supportive of us as we struggled to find our voice and how to write about and share our knowledge and research with a larger audience.

Our families and friends have been a source of constant encouragement and support.

Complex Integration of Multiple Brain Systems
in Therapy

The Origins of Complex Integration of Multiple Brain Systems

We work in an office with 10 other psychotherapists. Several years ago, one of our new colleagues observed how patients leaving our offices seemed to be in a more positive, happy, upbeat frame of mind than those from any of the other offices. One of our other colleagues who overheard this comment in the lunch-room said in a loud and somewhat playful voice, "Then you are doing it wrong!" And we have heard similar reactions from some others with whom we shared our work.

Over the years, we have developed a unique and in some ways contrarian paradigm of psychotherapy, which we call Complex Integration of Multiple Brain Systems (CIMBS). We have had what we consider to be great success with it. We are teaching other psychotherapists with very rewarding results. The most consistent benefits are immediate results that can be observed in a brief (20-minute) period of time, patients discovering things about themselves that they never knew before, and leaving the session with an increased experience of their own competence to face their distress, symptoms, and personal challenges. CIMBS is made up of many distinct concepts, frames of mind, perspectives, treatments and approaches. The purpose of this book is to share the breadth and depth of our clinical research and teaching experiences with readers (such as you). We have found so much benefit in our practices and in the practices of our trainees that we wanted to share our knowledge and experiences with a wider audience.

We propose CIMBS as a new neuroscientific and therapeutic paradigm for psychotherapy. The term "paradigm" has a controversial place in science, stimulated by the seminal work of Thomas Kuhn (1970). In his telling, it refers to "the entire constellation of beliefs, values, techniques, and so on shared by members of a given community." Kuhn argues that science proceeds through a progression of "normal science"—in which scientists operate under an existing paradigm—and "revolution," in which problems with an existing paradigm prompt the search for and eventual replacement with a new one. As we demonstrate in this book, the tenets of CIMBS are broad, deep, and far-reaching. We believe that they have the potential to advance psychotherapy by offering an improved and comprehensive alternative to the existing accepted therapeutic models. Time will tell if what we claim is borne out in the years to come.

FOUR DISTINCTIVE FEATURES OF CIMBS

We have trained hundreds of experienced colleagues in the past 10 years. We have asked them what stands out most that differentiates our therapeutic approaches from all the other therapies they have studied and practiced. The following are the four aspects that they found most distinctive about our therapy.

1. We have sought to operationalize recent neuroscience research from Siegel, Panksepp, LeDoux, Davidson, Grawe, Damasio, Porges, and others in practical ways. CIMBS is based on the knowledge that our brain and mind are made up of multiple distinct brain systems (Chapter 1). This understanding has enabled us to make sense of anomalous and counterintuitive phenomena. This has felt like having X-ray vision to see the inner workings of these different brain systems. Knowledge of these distinct systems has inspired strategies and interventions to enhance their competence, harness their innate wisdom, and facilitate integration. Our paradigm emphasizes facilitating nonconscious competencies of multiple brain systems rather than directly remediating the disorder, problem, or complaint that brought the patient for treatment. As we facilitate nonconscious competencies, we also make at least some of them more conscious—moving things from below the waterline above it on the metaphorical iceberg. The processes of CIMBS simultaneously mobilize multiple different types of neuroplasticity that are readily accessible for therapists in order to increase their efficacy (Chapter 15). These processes can release the nervous system's natural

tendency to evolve into higher levels of complexity, also called spontaneous self-organization.

2. CIMBS provides a different way of working with trauma. When our patients become anxious, defensive, and/or uncomfortable, we carefully redirect the process to harness their underlying competencies. This shift of focus embodies much more than different intentions, priorities, or interventions. These innovative strategies are informed by a different therapeutic *frame of mind*. In this frame of mind, the therapeutic energy is directed at the root of the patient's emotional resources that originate in the brainstem as noted in the research by Panksepp, Damasio, and Porges. When we encounter implicit constraints or triggers from previous trauma, we embrace their discomfort, release it, and direct our attention and energy to hidden resources that are otherwise out of a patient's awareness. We use a shorthand expression, "Go the Other Way" (Chapter 4), to describe this frame of mind when we teach.

For example, when a patient states, "I am a very anxious person. I am incapable of being aware of anything or being in charge of my life," the therapist Go(ing) the Other Way will respond, "And right now you are being capable of being aware of your anxiety. You are being capable right now." The patient can then learn to self-regulate their emotions effectively, even when triggered. The patient is exposed to a more complex experience of themselves. The processes of Go the Other Way open up a different (new) universe for our patients. These new discoveries from the base of the brain take time to emerge. Our patients commonly say such things as, "I did not know that about myself." One of our colleagues shared the following story: "I had a client who wanted the work to go faster. Albert said something I have never forgotten that displays this concept. He said, 'Tell your client that the way to speed things up is to slow things down.' I did. We did. And progress sped up considerably."

3. The patient-therapist relationship is fundamental to all forms of therapy. We have developed enhancements to this alliance that we call the Therapeutic Attachment Relationship (Chapter 5). We find it difficult to adequately convey the differences in our approach to the relationship. Yet our approaches to the Therapeutic Attachment Relationship have been the most compelling distinction for our trainees and weekend training participants. We utilize carefully targeted interventions to activate the patient's innate nonconscious attachment capabilities and patterns from the first moment of every session. In addition, we actively

direct the process and reinforce novel adaptive experiences for the patient. The Therapeutic Attachment Relationship can become a new way of being with your patients. You become the therapeutic instrument (no tools or techniques required).

4. Our therapy primarily takes place in the Transpiring Present Moment. *Transpiring* refers to the uniquely unfolding emotional responses to therapeutic interventions. *Present* refers to the experience of right now, rather than some recent or past experience. *Moment* is a period of time that is long enough to contain a conscious or emotional experience (7–10 seconds). Our minds prefer to be in our thoughts, memories, or plans. Psychophysiological phenomena and shifts reveal to us the evidence of the uniquely transpiring activations of conscious and nonconscious neural circuits (see chapters 7, 8, 10, and 14). Psychophysiological phenomena are observable physical movements and behaviors. Common examples are facial and mouth movements, tone of voice, eye contact, tears, and body posture. Attention to these phenomena can help you discover immediate nonconscious evidence of your patient's transpiring responses to therapeutic interventions. Narrowing the focus on transpiring activations becomes a more precise and energizing therapeutic instrument. The transpiring principle is the key difference from several other forms of present-moment psychotherapy.

Our practice is unconventional, and it may be difficult for a newcomer to grasp. Some therapists feel uncomfortable at first when they participate in our two-day training courses. Our therapeutic approaches are outside of their previous experience and training. Those novel approaches can mobilize feelings of curiosity, anxiety, confusion, or annoyance. After they have a few hours to experience and integrate this new learning, however, most therapists become fascinated, excited, and curious about what they are discovering. Only a few find the differences too uncomfortable and end up disliking the approaches we teach.

We have been collaborating with our illustrator, Nicola Swaine, to provide you with unique figures and drawings to bring our chapters to life. The illustrations are our best attempts to help you, the reader visualize (see) the brain systems perspectives, treatments, and inner (nonconscious) workings of the brain and mind. The drawings are intended to give you a felt sense of the brain systems we are describing and to help you more readily remember each system after you put this book aside.

We think it will help you if we explain how CIMBS originated. It is a product of our two unique life histories, both of them off the beaten path of mainstream psychotherapy training. And of course it involved a bit of serendipity, a chance meeting that changed the course of our lives.

WHO ARE WE?

For several years, each of us individually attended week-long annual international meetings on Intensive Short-Term Dynamic Psychotherapy organized by Dr. Habib Davanloo at McGill University in Montreal, Canada. But we never got to know each other until fortune sat us down side by side. One year, Albert was unable to arrive at the meeting until the second day, when the only empty seat in the full conference room was next to Beatriz, whose friend had to leave early because of an emergency. Over the course of the next four days, we stayed seated beside each other and found ourselves comparing notes about our different viewpoints on what was being presented. We have been working together ever since. But for you to really understand how we came to our present therapy practice, we want to tell you our individual life stories.

Pioneer (Beatriz)

I was born in Mexico, and I have always had a game-changing personality. In college I sliced and stained rat brains in the Neurology Department of the University of Mexico while my family and friends went off to play. I aspired to become a neurosurgeon. After finishing a psychology degree, I earned a scholarship to go anywhere in the world for graduate school. But my family was against it—in the 1970s, a Mexican woman did not leave her family, her country, and her fiancée to study abroad. Everyone told me that I would just get married, have children, and never finish my career. Nonetheless, I enrolled at McGill University in Montreal to earn a master's degree in educational psychology. My knowledge of English was limited, so essays and tests were very hard. I sweated bullets and shed tears, but I stayed. Looking back, I don't think I would do it again. It was very courageous and a little bit crazy.

Instead of studying therapies in vogue at the time—cognitive-behavioral therapy, psychodynamic psychotherapy, solution-focused psychotherapy, and so on—I took the road less traveled. I saw Dr. Habib Davanloo of the the

McGill Psychiatry Department demonstrate videos of Intensive Short-Term Dynamic Psychotherapy, a new innovation. I was impressed and wanted to study with him. Unfortunately the program only accepted male psychiatrists. I camped outside Dr. Davanloo's office for three days, asking him to hear my plea that, as a female from another discipline, I could help him disseminate his new psychotherapy more broadly. If he would just teach me, he would not regret it!

He finally accepted me into the Intensive Short-Term Dynamic Psychotherapy program. Much of the training took place in a room with a closed-circuit TV. When it was my turn, Dr. D and the other seven (male) psychiatrists sat in the next room and watched my therapy sessions. If I did something "wrong," a little bell would sound, and they would call me out of the room to help me. It was very stressful, but I learned and became good at it.

After moving to Vancouver, BC, and establishing a successful therapy practice, I continued going back to Montreal for training. Over the next 15 years, I taught Intensive Short- Term Dynamic Psychotherapy and joined the West Coast international Intensive Short Term Dynamic Psychotherapy Institute faculty, where I was labeled "the therapist to call when you are stuck with a patient."

But I was increasingly aware that something was missing in my understanding and treatments. I felt that there were more healing possibilities for my patients that I could not access. Some of my former patients returned for more help. They were successful, assertive, and strong, but they were still having problems with self-esteem and intimate relationships. So I started experimenting with being more connected in the therapeutic relationship. I would declare out loud my positive feelings toward my patients, and in return would welcome their positive feelings, hence making the caring relationship explicit. I called it "caring out loud." In order to experiment with building self-esteem in the present moment, I would declare, "We are caring for you right now," "We are esteeming you," and "You are valuable to be valued."

I noticed that my colleagues were uncomfortable with this practice. They feared that I could be overstepping therapeutic boundaries and making my patients dependent on me. "You don't say those things out loud," one colleague told me. "That is wrong!" But the opposite was happening. My patients were beginning to form intimate relationships in their everyday lives. They were needing our once-a-week relationship less and less. I knew I was onto something. Little did I know that my practice would be included in the principles of CIMBS.

Lost in Translation (Albert)

I had a wealth of curiosity, clinical experience, intellectual resources, and therapeutic motivation to bring to our first meeting in Montreal. My life's journey had been off the beaten path since before high school. Various quirks of fate and my responses kept taking me further and further afield from the paths of my friends and peers in school. Rather than following my natural bent toward economics, language, and philosophy, I studied the natural sciences. I chose to go to medical school in order to learn skills that would enable me to participate intimately in multiple cultures around the world. While in medical school, I became interested in the doctor-patient relationship, and I chose to go into family practice, while 95% of my classmates chose to specialize.

I really got off the beaten path early in my career as a primary physician. I worked with Doctors without Borders on the Altiplano in rural Bolivia, South America. My patients spoke only their indigenous language, Aymara, and came from a culture that viewed illness in a very different manner than we do. As a consequence, I discovered that when I asked (in Spanish) my Aymara translator questions to learn about the patients' concerns or symptoms, the answers that came back had no relevance to the intentions of my questions. The medical history and description of symptoms was either misleading or useless. Verbal communication was essentially impossible.

I soon realized that I would have to rely completely on my clinical observations and the physical exam. Lab tests were virtually unavailable. I learned that by fine-tuning the physical exam, I was able to test a wide range of my patients' biological capacities. These tests mobilized innate physiological shifts that revealed the underlying functioning of different biological systems in the body. A simple example is testing the knee-jerk reflex to discern the functioning of the quadriceps and hamstrings. Subtle or not-so-subtle physiological phenomena became the key to understanding patients' illnesses and what might be helpful in treating them. If the physiological responses to biological tests are the only language that is reliable, you naturally become adept at seeing subtleties, just as a deaf person learns to rely on vision to make sense of what is happening around them. I learned to read the story the patient's body tells.

My strong interests in science, relationships, and healing kept propelling me forward into new experiences and out of my comfort zone. My years of primary care practice helped me develop relational skills to have a healing bedside manner. I learned to be comfortable with my patients' pain and the incoherence of their illnesses. I came to trust my observational skills and the wisdom of what we describe later as nonconscious phenomena in the body. It took time for me to become comfortable when I needed to cause my patients pain, such as by setting a broken bone. As a primary care physician, I enjoyed my relationships with my patients, and became so interested in their mental health that I chose to further specialize in psychiatry. Although I trained in a biological psychiatric residency, I chose to prioritize developing my skills as a psychotherapist. I pursued multiple types of training after residency, including cognitive-behavioral therapy, psychodynamic, psychoanalytic, hypnosis, systems-centered, group, interpersonal, and some forms of experiential therapy.

During this exploration process, I attended a course on Intensive Short-Term Dynamic Psychotherapy presented at McGill by Dr. Davanloo. I was intrigued by his scientific approach to therapy. Rather than talking about his therapy, he showed us video recordings of sessions. I was able to see how active interventions were having immediate beneficial impacts on his patient right in front of my eyes. I wanted to be able to learn how that worked and how I could integrate that learning into my own practice as a therapist. I joined a small training group that met for a week four times a year with Dr. Davanloo in Montreal. At roughly the same time, I started a psychotherapy research project when I was awarded a Bush Medical Fellowship. I chose to study the precise details of the psychotherapeutic process carefully.

My experiences in South America inspired me to focus my research on subtle psychophysiological phenomena that were giving me nonverbal, nonconscious clues about the functioning of the patient's emotional nervous system. Studying the video recordings of therapy sessions in slow motion or with the sound turned off highlighted the importance of these psychophysiological phenomena. These clues became the evidence that could suggest hypotheses about the inner workings of the mind. These hypotheses were tested, and the psychophysiological responses were empirical evidence that were used to confirm or falsify the hypothesis.

I discovered, explored, and experimented with some of the principles, perspectives, and approaches that later formed the nuclei of this book.

More Than Meets the Eye

It was at this point that the two of us had our chance (or fated?) meeting in Montreal. We immediately noticed that we shared a common outlook. For example, we observed that much more was going on in the video recordings of sessions than was being addressed in the presentations. There were times when the presenter seemed to be locked into his method of addressing the trauma and not paying attention to other adaptive capacities of the patient. We invited each other to explore those aspects and look at our own sessions before we attended the next annual meeting in Montreal.

Over the next couple of years, we would again rendezvous in Montreal to continue the discussions that occurred during our first chance meeting. Those discussions and brainstorming sessions took our work onto a novel trajectory. Some of those sessions were stormy, as we both had strong opinions and a wealth of experiences to back up our viewpoints. We came to learn that our disparate viewpoints all had merit and that there was so much more to learn. This was when we came to fully appreciate the importance of parallel processing (Chapters 1 and 2). We discovered that we were both comfortable being naive outsiders. We were curious about the failures of ourselves and others that pointed to new possibilities.

First, we started off on a journey of discovery and research. We had large volumes of data from video recordings of our colleagues' and our own therapy sessions. We decided to sit down and explore the subtle and disparate evidence hidden under the surface in those sessions. We both had the patience to spend up to four hours studying the video of a 40-minute session. Each time we rewound a vignette, we saw something new and interesting to explore. We would sometimes watch our videos without sound to focus on the minute changes in the body of the patient. Then we would watch again, with the sound on, to see which of many variables may have caused those changes. It was there and in subsequent meetings that we discovered that even if the patient was triggered, other processors were acting in parallel that were not being triggered. That was very intriguing.

By this time, Albert was already exploring approaches different from those of his training group in Montreal. Dr. Davanloo recognized that Albert was becoming masterful in his therapy and encouraged him to teach what he was learning. The discoveries already contained some of the CIMBS principles, but Albert did not realize it. He did not recognize how distinct these principles were from the training in Montreal. Beatriz encouraged him to branch out: "Follow your genius and take your own path."

And follow our "geniuses" we did. We once more stepped out of the comfortable path. Those hours and hours watching our videos changed the trajectory of our lives and our careers. We shared our love and passion for therapy and for each other. We found the courage and vision to contribute to the discipline of psychotherapy by researching new ways to treat trauma. Those discussions and brainstorming sessions gave our work a completely different trajectory. "Changing the world one therapist at a time" became our motto.

Paint It Red

Over time, we learned that our therapeutic approaches were becoming increasingly different from mainstream psychotherapy. We did not know how different until we started to share our work with our colleagues. Albert tried to demonstrate these discoveries at psychiatric grand rounds at the University of Washington in Seattle and University of British Columbia in Vancouver. It did not work. Only a minority of the people in attendance were able to appreciate what was being presented. Many were not able to see it, while others were skeptical, dismissive, or even angry with the novelty (intensity and complexity) of the therapeutic interactions. Some protested that facilitating the patient's capabilities (Go the Other Way) was superficial rather than delving into the trauma.

We realized that the unaccustomed differences of this therapy (it did not have a name yet) stirred up a lot of emotions in the observers. We presented at several mainstream psychotherapy conferences. We were frustrated that many of the principles, perspectives, and therapeutic approaches we were sharing did not come across. In the postmortem discussions, Beatriz summarized our learning: "We have to paint it red." She meant that we needed to make our evidence so clear that it could not be missed. We resolved not to give up. We followed our own inner direction and the consistent evidence found in our video recordings.

We later expanded the practice of showing video recordings to include live demonstrations, with participants from the audience. By chance one day, we were teaching when the video projector suddenly stopped working. Beatriz courageously and creatively stepped into the fray, armed with her trust in the process. Like a magician, Beatriz asked for a volunteer to come to the front to participate in a live demonstration. Looking back on it, that was crazy! She was putting us in a vulnerable position.

One of the skeptics in the group volunteered. To our great satisfaction and relief, the volunteer had a deep and novel experience of himself during the live therapy demonstration. We all could observe how this man's psychophysiology changed in a short time, even without his conscious cooperation. The live demonstration gave everyone in the room a moving experience in a matter of 30 minutes. Beatriz's trust in the power of the principles and perspectives stood her in good stead. Ever since then, we have conducted multiple live demonstrations in each of our training courses. Live demonstrations and experiential practices are now our primary ways of teaching. Personal experience is the best way to explore nonconscious emotional processing.

A couple years later, we decided that we were having so much fun together that it would be even more fun to get married. We share so much together now. We practice, teach, research, write, and live together. It is a bit much sometimes!

The writing in this book is intended to provide a mix of principles and practice. We are pragmatic researchers and teachers. We have experimented using these approaches and interventions with hundreds of colleagues and many hundreds of patients over 15 years. We will emphasize simple and practical approaches and interventions to both illustrate the principles and to give you ideas about how you might apply those approaches in your own work with patients. In the following chapters, we seek to illustrate and illuminate the many discoveries we have made in our exploration of psychotherapeutic processes. We encourage you to trust the process just as we do. You too will discover that you have so much more to offer your patients.

Beatriz is not a native English speaker. She sometimes uses words or expressions that are not proper English. Some of her language might be a little quirky. Certainly her patients, trainees, and friends can speak to that. We have chosen to leave most of that intact because sometimes her turn of phrase is more memorable.

Many of our senior trainees are gratified to discover how much more rewarding their therapy has become since they started to apply the knowledge and interventions they now know. They are surprised how differently they feel at the end of their work day. They no longer look forward to retirement, but rather want to delay it. "This therapy gives me life and keeps me young. There is some alchemy here that transcends the trauma, the resistance, the terror, shame, and guilt. I wish everybody could do this. I am so grateful for the freedom that it offers my patients. I feel this synergy of connection with myself and my patients when I utilize this knowledge." We share these experiences from a number of colleagues to inspire rather than try to convince you of the value of our research and knowledge. We invite you to explore and make your own discoveries inside yourself and with the people in your life.

There are a number of case studies and transcripts throughout the book. Many of the concepts and the neurobiology will be unfamiliar on an emotional and nonconscious level. It takes lots of repetition for it to sink in, just as it does with our patients.We struggle with the need for repetition, the need to let new concepts sink in deeper, and the need to give the reader a felt sense of the experience. It is hard to judge the right amount, since we anticipate a wide range of readers. We don't think there is a correct answer for the best amount of detail. We would rather have a little too much than not enough. You do not need to read it all. Some readers will skim it, some will skip over it, and others will go back and read it again and get more and more out of it. It is one thing to understand what you are reading, and something else entirely to literally (pun intended) get it on a visceral level in your heart and guts. Finding the right level of detail and repetition has been one of the biggest challenges in writing a book about this nonconscious, nonverbal, unfamiliar, and counterintuitive paradigm.

If you find this material interesting and want to take advantage of the many novel learning opportunities, we suggest that you take your time reading it. We have learned from colleagues who have taken our online training courses that they get much more out of the course if they consume it in small bites. They watch videos for 15 to 20 minutes and then sit with what they have seen and experienced. They compare what they previously understood with this new information. Later they study some more. Often they find it helpful to look at parts they have already studied before and realize that there was additional valuable information that they could not grasp the first time through.

No book, no matter how detailed or well written, can by itself teach someone how to perform psychotherapy. We attempt to offer a reference document for interested readers who seek an introduction to CIMBS, and for serious readers to refer to as part of a broader exposure that includes video recordings and live training sessions. You can gain much deeper insight into CIMBS in action by viewing selected video-recorded sessions and online training courses via our website (www.complexintegrationmbs.com). Visual and auditory observation add tremendously to your ability to perceive the psychophysiological evidence of the patients' conditions and the therapists' manner and techniques.

CHAPTER 1

Discovering Emotional Brain Systems

···

A man with a thick Canadian Maritime accent (sometimes called a brogue) stepped forward at one of our two-day training courses for fellow psychotherapists. He was volunteering for one of the live therapy demonstrations with participants. Beatriz expressed her concern. "His accent is so thick, I can barely understand what he is saying. I'm not sure I can do it." Albert reassured her: "This is perfect. You can do it. You can show everybody how to work with this patient with little or no verbal content. The lack of verbal content will mobilize neuroplasticity, and he will have a deeper experience." The volunteers for these demonstrations are usually either the skeptics or those who are really intrigued. This man was a skeptic. Albert continued, "The demonstration will show him and the others the universal effectiveness of this process even for participants who doubt it." And so she agreed to proceed.

When the demonstration began, Beatriz jumped right in. She activated the Therapeutic Attachment Relationship, then facilitated his desire to learn more about himself and to be fully present to himself. Little by little, he became more engaged. When he seemed to withdraw, she went the other way, seeking out his capabilities underneath his constraints. There were increasing glimmers of smiles, pleasure, and animation. Beatriz kept reinforcing and reactivating his Play, Seeking, and Connection brain systems. His voice became much louder, and his articulation was more precise and intelligible. What was most remarkable

were the changes on his face. Fear had frozen his face before, and now the activations had released his facial animation.

The next day, he was a different man. We could all see that he looked like he
had had a face lift. His voice was deeper, more resonant, and more understandable. He spoke personally to Beatriz and shared some of his conscious learning since the therapy demonstration the previous day. He reported that he had
already known that he had some blocks and resistance to showing his feelings
and expressing himself openly. He went on to say that he had discovered a profound sense of innate self-worth and how he had repressed his deep positive
feelings his whole life. He had experienced a different dimension of himself. "I
didn't know that I didn't know something so important about myself."

This anecdote illustrates the rapid and dramatic power of the therapeutic
paradigm we call the Complex Integration of Multiple Brain Systems, CIMBS.
The fact that it had such a significant and immediate impact with a resistant and
constrained patient is noteworthy. How did Beatriz do this? There are 50 different answers to that question. Every one of them is practical and meaningful.
We will take the entire book to spread them out and paint them red (see Introduction) so you can see for yourself. In this chapter and Chapter 3, we introduce
the foundational concepts and principles of CIMBS and provide background on
their psychological and scientific origins. We introduce key terminology you
encountered in this story—terms such as Activating and Facilitating, Therapeutic Attachment Relationship (Chapter 5), Go the Other Way (Chapter 4), and,
of course, brain systems, which we introduce below. In Chapter 2, we present a
short case study of a patient's therapy session as a beginning illustration of how
CIMBS operates in practice.

We use a combination of case stories and clinical transcripts to illustrate the
interventions and the therapeutic processes. The case stories without a transcript
are composites of several patients with similar emotional patterns. Case studies
include word-for-word transcripts that have had minimal editing to highlight
relevant principles. Our patients have been pleased and even honored to have
brief transcripts of their sessions included in our book to illustrate the therapeutic process explicitly with all of its strengths and weaknesses. All of them have
had previous therapy, and they know firsthand the value added by working with
concepts entailed in CIMBS. They feel that their voices add another perspective
that can help the reader/therapist appreciate the benefit of this paradigm.

This contrasting paradigm is neither a technique nor a protocol. We want to add to your knowledge, understanding, and practice with new principles, perspectives, and approaches to your work and your self. Complex Integration of Multiple Brain Systems is the heading we use to bring together a carefully researched collection of independent, unique, and interrelated psychotherapeutic principles, perspectives, and approaches that has the potential to change your way of being as a therapist, the variety of things to which you pay attention, and the depth of your understanding. CIMBS can bring a new sense of hope and expectancy to each and every encounter with your patients.

ON THE SHOULDERS OF GIANTS

In our first years of working together, we knew that we were creating new approaches to therapy. We were encouraged by the results we were getting. But we felt the need to explore the biological and behavioral research done by others that could help to explain and support what were were observing. We sought to develop a rational and scientific underpinning for our methods so that we could understand—and explain to others—what worked for us and why. In 2003, we took a sabbatical and embarked on a research journey into the recent neuroscience literature in order to see how it could explain the success of our therapy and perhaps further refine our approaches to our patients.

One of the motivators in our research has been the periodic therapeutic problem of feeling stuck and not being sure what was getting in the way of our progress. With some patients, it became apparent that we were doing too much of the work. With other patients, we had reached a plateau of progress and were not moving forward. Sometimes we had what looked like a breakthrough session, and then there was little carry-forward. Our neuroscience explorations addressed these challenges and others directly. The two biggest neuroscience concepts for us have been brain systems (LeDoux, 1996) and the linkage and complex integration of different domains (Siegel, 1999). For example, integration between the left and right hemispheres of the brain can release the unpredictable but self-organizing nature of the brain. This self-organizing property is also called the "nonlinear dynamics of complex systems" (Siegel, 1999). Hence the name for our therapy paradigm: Complex Integration of Multiple Brain Systems.

The Brain Has Systems; Our Journey

On vacation kayaking the fjords of British Columbia, Albert read *The Emotional Brain* by neuroscientist Joseph LeDoux, whose research focused on the neurological basis of emotional reactions (in animals). LeDoux's book introduced us to the concept of brain systems. LeDoux proposed that there may be many different brain systems and not just one emotional brain system: "Since different emotions are involved in different survival functions—defending against danger, finding food and mates, caring for offspring and so on—each may well involve different brain systems that evolved for different reasons. As a result there may not be one emotional brain system, but many" (LeDoux, 1996, p. 103).

LeDoux has done most of his research with the fear system in the brains of rats and cats. Each emotional brain system "can be thought of as consisting of a set of inputs, an appraisal mechanism, and a set of outputs. The most practical working hypothesis is that different classes of emotional behavior represent different kinds of functions that take care of different kinds of problems for the animal and have different brain systems devoted to them" (LeDoux, 1996 p. 127). This definition is what we use when we think, write, and teach about brain systems. The concepts of brain systems are unfamiliar to most therapists, so we recommend you go back and read this paragraph again to familiarize yourself with emotional brain systems.

Eureka! We had a name. We resolved to call our therapy Brain Systems Psychotherapy. LeDoux's proposal was an important conceptual opening for us, in which we cross-pollinated the fundamentals of neuroscience research and psychotherapy experience. It helped us understand emotional phenomena and reactions that had made no sense before as we were watching our videos one second at a time. Now they not only made sense, they gave us new avenues to explore. Those explorations have brought us to this time where we keep the presence of distinct brain systems in our minds all the time.

TERMINOLOGY

The therapeutic dimensions of CIMBS include a wide range of practical treatments, along with multiple orientations, frames of mind, and therapeutic processes. We use the term *process* in two specific and distinct ways. First, the therapeutic process is a dynamic series of emotional and relational interactions between the patient and the therapist. This is in contrast to *content*, which refers to the words or stories that are being discussed. The contrasting paradigm of CIMBS is predominantly focused on the dynamic processes that are transpiring within the patient and between the patient and therapist. Second, brain systems (see below) operate like the processors in your computer. The brain systems take raw inputs from the body and environment and focus that energy into emotions, motivations, inhibitions, and enhancers. Brain systems do the work of the mind (Siegel); they process energy and information.

We use the conventional term *patient* to describe persons who come to us for help because they are suffering. The word *patient* is the present participle of the Latin verb *patior*, which means to suffer. The complement to the patient who suffers is the healer, who tries to relieve the suffering. Our patients seek us out to be relieved of their symptoms and suffering so that they can feel better about themselves and move forward in their lives. They need our help to change and get unstuck. However, change even for the better makes us anxious (Cozolino, 2016). Change triggers a conflicted mix of emotional reactions. Some patients are particularly afraid to feel anxiety or conflict. They have often spent a life-time trying to avoid their anxiety. They do not have an internal experience of safeness in order to embrace and learn from their anxiety. Our approach to this problem is to Activate and Facilitate their capabilities to feel safe, cared for, and connected so that they can tolerate the inevitable anxiety (and pain) that comes with change and healing.

Brain Systems

The brain is made up of a hierarchy of individual neurons, circuits, and systems. The electrical signals in the nervous system are transmitted along nerve fibers by cells called *neurons*. The signals are transmitted from one cell to the next across gaps called *synapses* by chemicals called *neurotransmitters*. Thousands of neurons that interconnect to perform a function are called a *neural circuit*, and multiple circuits then coalesce into brain systems. A distinct *brain system* is made up of many interconnected neural circuits dedicated to meeting our survival and emotional needs. Neurons, circuits, and systems that are utilized frequently typically become insulated with myelin, which speeds the activity of those circuits up to 100 times faster. Multiple interconnected systems form an integrated *complex network*.

Our brain consists of many types of systems— such as sensory, emotional, and homeostatic—that operate outside of our awareness. Sensory brain system examples include vision, taste, and hearing. Homeostatic brain system examples are hunger, thirst, and body temperature regulation. In this book, we concentrate on the emotional brain systems, which we define in detail below. An emotional brain systems perspective can help you understand how trauma, neglect, and/ or abandonment could cause dysfunctions in the interactions between different systems of the mind, causing your patient to become symptomatic. According to neurologist Helen Mayberg, many mental health disorders could be the result of imbalances in the functioning of brain systems. "Depression is unlikely a disease of a single gene, brain region, or neurotransmitter system. Rather, the syndrome is conceptualized as a systems disorder with a depressive episode viewed as the net effect of failed network regulation under circumstances of cognitive, emotional or somatic stress" (Dichter, Felder, & Smoski, 2008).

The wiring of brain systems goes a long way to help us understand how mental health disorders arise. Adaptive neural circuits, which are the foundations of the emotional brain systems, develop naturally early in life through a combination of genetic drives and nonconscious learning (defined below) to support our survival and enhance our ability to thrive. Maladaptive circuits can develop in threatening situations in which the developing child needs to suppress one or more of the highly evolved brain systems—such as Care or Connection, which we introduce below—in order to survive. Those circuits are beneficial at the time; however, when they become rigid and reflexive, their habitual behavior patterns prevent the functionality of Care, Connection, or other essential brain systems.

Why use the term *brain systems* rather than more familiar psychological terms such as emotions, affects, cognitions, insights, behaviors, defenses, implicit memories, somatic experiences, or motivations? We have found that *brain systems* is a more precise, neurobiological, universal, and neutral term. Although it is not a familiar term to most people or therapists, we believe that once you read and digest our definitions and explanations, you will find it a useful scaffold on which to place large volumes of disparate and conflicting information.

Neuroplasticity

Neuroplasticity, or neural plasticity, refers to the ability of the brain to change over the life span. Neuroplasticity enables the brain to reassign jobs. Our mind literally has the ability to change the structure of the brain (Schwartz & Begley,

2002). The formation of new synaptic connections is one form of neuroplasticity. Synapses may strengthen or weaken over time (LeDoux 2002, p. 223). "Directed, willed mental activity can clearly and systematically alter brain function" (Schwartz). Nature has endowed the human brain with malleability and flexibility that lets it adapt to the demands of the world in which it finds itself (Davidson). The activation of neural circuits in a very targeted, structured, intensive, and enduring manner will facilitate the malleability of the brain (Grawe).

In CIMBS psychotherapy, we have endeavored to simultaneously mobilize and harness many different forms of neuroplasticity. For example, we use more precise repetitions in our work to utilize the wisdom of constraint-induced neuroplasticity (Chapter 15). Recent research on neurotransmitters has inspired us to differentiate six different dopamine networks to energize our therapy and enhance our patients' long-term learning. Our exploration of internal positive and negative feedback loops has helped us be more precise in our interventions (Chapters 8, 9, 11, 12).

Activating, Facilitating, Differentiating

We employ three powerful treatment methods in cooperation with each other to work with multiple brain systems. The term *Activating* refers to the specific and precise use of verbal and nonverbal (embodied) interventions to arouse one or more neural circuits or brain systems. *Facilitating* refers to the therapist's continued interventions directing attention and energy, which we find increases functioning in distinct neural circuits and/or brain systems. Facilitating includes external energy and positive reinforcement from the therapist. Facilitating new adaptive emotional experiences can add efficiency and effectiveness to your work, remediating your patients' symptoms and difficulties. *Differentiating* brain systems is a combination of activating, explicitly identifying, and disentangling distinct neural circuits. The disentangling refers to interrupting rigid, habitual, maladaptive emotional behavior patterns that interfere with the capabilities of specific systems. In later chapters we explore these three related approaches in great depth.

Multiple Brain Systems, Integration, and Complexity

Daniel Siegel (1999), author of *The Developing Mind*, has been the neuroscientist who has influenced our research, clinical practice, and teaching the most. He helped us understand the interactive attachment system as it develops in infancy. He emphasized the importance of the mindful brain (Siegel, 2007). Siegel (2019) has developed a comprehensive definition of the mind that is congruent with our research and understanding: "The mind is an emergent process of a complex system that is self-organizing, embodied, relational and regulates the flow of energy and the flow of information." But most of all, he introduced to us the importance of the interwoven concepts of integration, complexity, and self-organizing patterns of differentiated systems. "As complex systems, we have a natural tendency to move toward maximizing complexity as we self-organize across time" (Siegel, 2010a).

When sufficiently differentiated, emotional brain systems can both operate independently and coordinate with other brain systems, via reciprocal feedback, to sustain adaptive emotions and behaviors. Each of the emotional brain systems is capable of learning and being molded by life experiences. Some of the brain systems can modulate the functions of other systems to maintain homeostasis and emotional equilibrium by means of neural circuits such as internal negative feedback loops. We call this complex coordinated behavior Integration. The power of neuroplasticity gives our psychotherapy the ability to facilitate the growth of new adaptive circuits that will organize into resilient emotional brain systems. *Resilient* refers to brain systems that are able to process large volumes of energy and information smoothly. Integrated resilient brain systems enable our nervous system to function flexibly and optimally. Multiple integrated resilient brain systems will release the BrainMind's (see below) capacity for self-organization at a higher level of complexity. That is why we refer to our therapy and our therapeutic outcomes as Complex Integration of Multiple Brain Systems (CIMBS) Psychotherapy.

The concept of integrated systems achieving complexity and flexibility helped us to make sense of what we were observing in our research and clinical practices. These concepts helped us trust the therapeutic and empirical process in new ways. Our work and teaching changed radically. We use Siegel's ideas about the integration of differentiated systems, emerging complexity, and releasing the BrainMind's capacity for self-organizing throughout this book.

BrainMind

The book *Affective Neuroscience* by neuroscientist Jaak Panksepp (1998), along with his subsequent research on the neural mechanisms of emotion, gave us a much clearer understanding of brain systems. In 2012, Panksepp & Biven coined the term BrainMind to assert that there is no useful distinction between the brain and the mind in affective neuroscience. There are many brain systems in our BrainMind. They operate on different scales. The autonomic nervous system is large-scale and impacts the whole body. For example, it controls heart rate, breathing, digestion, and immune functions. The sensory brain systems such as hearing and vision are more circumscribed.

Panksepp described brain systems as a variety of basic emotional circuits that are anatomically situated in brain regions. They are highly evolved, distinct neural circuits of such universal importance for survival that they were built into the brain independently to help us meet our needs to survive and thrive. He described and explored three levels of emotional processing in the central nervous system (see Figure 1.1). Each level of processing occurs in different brain structures. The brain systems that perform primary-level and secondary-level emotional processing are what he calls nonconscious (see below). The conscious brain systems operate at the tertiary level. The brain structures that reside in each processing level are listed in Figure 1.1. Each distinct neural circuit takes in information from the body and environment, appraises that information based on its specializations, and sends outputs to other parts of the body and/or brain. The energy of each brain system communicates with higher, lower, and the same levels of processing.

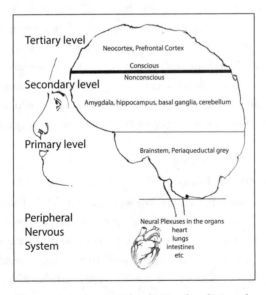

Figure 1.1: Four Levels of Mental and Neural Processing

Nonconscious—Unconscious

The term *unconscious* is ambiguous and has different meanings depending on the context and who is using the term. It has been used as a psychological term to refer to thoughts and feelings that cannot be deliberately brought to consciousness yet have important influences on our behavior and well-being. It has also been used to describe trancelike phenomena and other altered states of consciousness. Unconscious is used as a physiological or neurological term to describe people who are in a coma or not conscious due to some medical or biological state, such as during general anesthesia or after a head injury.

Antonio Damasio is a neurologist who has studied and written extensively about consciousness. He introduced us to the terms *core consciousness* and *nonconscious*. The concepts of core consciousness have been very useful to us in our clinical experiments in exploring and differentiating distinct conscious brain systems. *Nonconscious* is a more precise term than *unconscious*, and we use the term *nonconscious* in this book. It refers to the vast amount of processes and contents of the BrainMind that can never be known, although their effects can be clearly observed. Highly evolved hidden wisdom and know-how are contained in the primary-level brain systems and the peripheral nervous system. Patterns that were acquired through experience lie dormant, and many that never become explicitly known are found in the secondary-level processing regions of the BrainMind such as the basal ganglia. Nonconscious refers to almost everything that the brain does. Nonconscious brain system activations generate some behaviors and feelings that can become consciously known. For example, we cannot be conscious of all the muscle movements, nerves, and coordination that enable us to ride a bike. However, we are conscious of the sensations, choices, and effort involved in riding.

Powerhouses of the Mind

In his book *The Archaeology of Mind* (Panksepp & Biven, 2012), Panksepp described emotional brain systems as "jewels" and "powerhouses of the mind." Mammalian brain systems generate affective variations of world events in the form of nonverbal feelings. Brain systems are molded though life experiences. "Each of these systems controls distinct but specific types of behaviors associated with many overlapping physiological changes. When these systems are stimulated in humans, people always experience intense emotional feelings, and presumably when the systems are normally activated by life events, they generate abundant memories and thoughts for people about what is happening to them" (Panksepp & Biven, 2012, p. 2).

The expression "powerhouses of the mind," however, does not do justice to the various capabilities that have evolved in each of the emotional brain systems. Each of these emotional brain systems generates energy. For example, they give you the energy to care for your infant. They concentrate the energy they generate in order to do the work of caring. Each emotional system takes in information from other parts of the nervous system to be able to respond to the uniqueness of the present situation. The care you provide for your child is specific and compelling. You may find yourself doing things for your child that you have never seen or learned before. Each emotional brain system has outputs and sends energy to other brain systems to enhance surviving and thriving.

All of our brain systems have distinct capabilities. *Capabilities* refer to the innate, highly evolved emotional resources that help us survive and empower us to face the challenges of our lives. You can trust that they are present even when underdeveloped or constrained. For example, our Assertive brain system has the potential to provide us with the energy and wisdom to go after our needs and wants even in dangerous situations. The therapeutic process can stimulate each brain system to reveal their present competence. *Competencies* refer to the actual and visible activations of these innate capabilities to whatever extent they are developed. Experience and training have the potential to enhance the competencies of each brain system.

EMOTIONS AND BRAIN SYSTEMS

We humans have a panoply of emotions. There are many names and approaches to describing and distinguishing between the different emotions. There is often disagreement about which emotions are distinct rather than a mix of other emotions. Much has been written about emotions in neuroscience, psychotherapy research, and psychotherapy practice, and for the general public. We have found it very useful to focus on the underlying distinct brain systems that generate these emotions in order to appreciate their unique energy, wisdom, and potential. We believe that the activation of distinct brain systems is what generates the internal experience and observable behavior that we associate with emotions.

Brain Systems Generate Emotions

Emotion researchers and investigators have two divergent explanations for how emotions happen in humans. The larger, more traditional group views emotions as arising from the neocortical cognitive readout of physical actions of the body (prime examples of these investigators are James, Lange, LeDoux). In other words, the thinking part of the brain (frontal area) receives information from the body and formulates the relevant feelings. For example, "I feel fear when I run away from danger." The other group (Cannon, MacLean, Panksepp) views emotions as emerging directly from nonconscious subcortical structures much deeper in the brain. They have extensive neuroscience research that shows distinct emotions are occurring even when the neocortex has been damaged or is not functioning. In other words, multiple emotions can be happening out of our awareness. For example, "I do not know why I moved away from that object (e.g., a snake) that I did not consciously see."

Our clinical research and experience keeps validating the principles that emotions emerge directly from multiple nonconscious brain systems. Most of our emotions never become conscious, even though they play significant roles throughout every moment of our lives, even when we are asleep. This evidence has helped us harness the evolutionary wisdom and energy of multiple distinct nonconscious brain systems.

The terms *affect* and *emotion* are sometimes used synonymously. Affects are neurobiological phenomena that generate a specific kind of brain activation that mobilizes us to respond to some stimulus or threat. There are three categories of affects: homeostatic, sensory, and emotional (Panksepp, 1998). When the homeostatic affect for hydration mobilizes thirst, an animal will seek out water without any necessary conscious choice. It is automatic. When our sensory affect of sight sees a snake, we automatically go on danger alert without conscious awareness. When our sensory affect of taste detects bitterness, we automatically spit out whatever is in our mouth. When our emotional affect of care sees our infant, we automatically direct our energy and attention to comfort and connect with our child.

It is easier to understand the nonemotional affects because they are neutral and obvious. Emotional affects are more complicated because we have lots of associations, feelings, memories, and learning about emotions and the terms used identify the emotions. We have gone to some pains to be specific and precise about 20 distinct emotional brain systems, which are the focus for this book and a brain systems approach to neurobiology and psychotherapy.

Nonconscious Emotional Learning and Emotional Brain Systems

It can be difficult to wrap your mind around the distinctions between your personal experience of emotions, your nonconscious emotional learning, and your nonconscious emotional brain systems. We will do our best to use these distinctions precisely. Let's look at them from the top down.

Emotions refer to our conscious feelings of visceral activation that inspire us to movement and determination. We have a felt sense of our emotions that is unique to each of us and often unique to the context and relationships. Our gut feelings or heartfelt experiences are literal and metaphorical examples of our conscious emotions. Our conscious emotions arise from our present-moment experience that is being simultaneously processed by our bodies, our nonconscious emotional brain systems, and our nonconscious emotional learning. For example, physical closeness with my child stimulates my heart neural plexus, which then activates my primary-level Care brain system in the brainstem. Activation of my Care brain system is then colored by my nonconscious emotional learning from my early life, and if the activation of closeness and care are strong enough to cross a threshold into consciousness, I can then actually feel the emotion of care for my child.

Nonconscious emotional learning refers to your lifetime of experiences that have affected the development of each of your emotional brain systems. Most of this learning was processed at the level of the basal ganglia, including such structures as the hippocampus, amygdala, and cerebellum. Much of this learning starts in utero and takes place in infancy and early childhood. Not only is the learning nonconscious, it is also nonverbal and does not have any explicit associated memory. We believe that each of the emotional brain systems contains its own distinct emotional learning. For example, the Play brain system will learn from an event differently than the Care brain system does. This will become clearer from examples in the case studies.

Emotional brain systems refers to the distinct, innate neurobiological systems that evolved to enable a person or animal to survive and thrive in a wide range of environments and circumstances, and under significant stressors. These systems operate as generators of energy, processors of information, and sources of highly evolved neurobiological wisdom. Emotions reflect the wisdom of the ages. These systems have become more specialized and precise in primates and other higher mammals, enabling them to thrive and live complex social lives.

Nonconscious emotional brain systems operate like the hardware in your computer. They function automatically without any direction from you, their operator. Your nonconscious emotional learning is similar to the learning in your mind that enables you to read the words on this page or to understand the words spoken by your family members. Even though you were born with an auditory brain system, it takes years of development and nonconscious learning to recognize spoken words. Your nonconscious emotional learning is similar to your computer software, also called the operating system, which gets updated periodically and sometimes dramatically. Your conscious experience of emotions is similar to your personal computer documents. Those documents depend on the hardware to function, and they are affected and altered by the software. Your emotions may range from rigid, unchanging visceral patterns to infinitely flexible, constantly novel, multidimensional, creative, and complex responses.

In the following section, we outline the 20 emotional brain systems we have found to be most important and valuable to us as therapists. We have found that training our colleagues to be able to focus their energy and attention on any one or more of these emotional brain systems has greatly enhanced the progress of their psychotherapy. We capitalize the proper names of the emotional brain systems, such as Care, Play, Shame, and Grief, and we lowercase words that refer to the emotions such as shame, guilt, fear, or anger.

MEET THE BRAIN SYSTEMS

We have settled on 20 emotional brain systems that have been most practical in our teaching, research, and practice. One could certainly make a case for more or fewer systems. Our book is dedicated to focusing on both conscious (Chapters 7–9) and nonconscious emotional brain systems (Chapters 10–13). Jaak Panksepp and Lucy Biven gave us a much clearer understanding of the importance and relevance of nonconscious primary-level brain systems to our therapy. Nonconscious emotional brain systems are particularly important because they "generate affective valuations of world events in the form of nonverbal feeling states or the passions of the mind" (Panksepp & Biven, 2012). It is important to note that all primary-level brain systems contain drives, goals, and motivations. The secondary-level brain systems inhibit or enhance those drives. They protect us from danger, and they help us sustain adaptive behaviors and emotions.

Participants in our training courses are intrigued by the transformative benefits that often occur in our 20-minute live therapy demonstrations. They say, "It looks like magic." (Remember the man with the brogue). It looks like we are pulling a rabbit out of a hat. But we have no magic. Actually, we are enabling our patients to release the "rabbits" hidden deep inside their nonconscious brain systems. That is the magic that each of us has within our BrainMinds.

We have organized the brain systems we have selected into the following hierarchy (see Figure 1.2):

- Five conscious tertiary-level brain systems (abbreviated Tertiaries; Chapters 7–9)
- Eight nonconscious secondary-level brain systems (Secondaries; Chapter 13)
- Seven nonconscious primary-level brain systems (Primaries; Chapters 10–12)

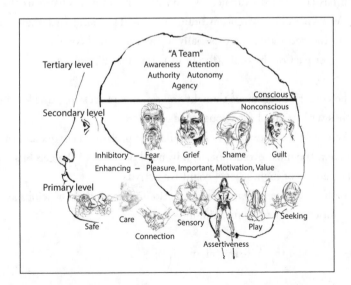

Figure 1.2: Multiple Brain Systems: Tertiaries, Secondaries, and Primaries

Conscious Tertiary-Level Brain Systems: The A-Team

Our original research sought to improve our understanding of the inner workings of our patients' conscious BrainMind capabilities. We discovered that some patients had a good capacity to attend to our work, yet had little capacity for self-awareness. Some were able to exercise their authority, but did not have a sense of their own autonomy, and hence always deferred to others' wants. Some lacked a sense of agency and so could not implement their wants and desires. Careful attention to different conscious capabilities greatly enhanced our effectiveness. After 15 years of clinical experimentation, we settled on five distinct conscious capabilities that have pragmatically worked for us as therapists. We have labeled them the A-Team: the Awareness, Attention, Authority, Autonomy, and Agency brain systems. There are sure to be others. We have found that the more our patients have distinct access to each of those capabilities, the more successful the treatment throughout each session.

Over the course of a lifetime or through therapy, the competencies of the tertiary-level brain systems can develop and become resilient (Chapter 2). There is some overlap between these conscious brain systems as they can work in parallel, support, and sustain each other. Richard Davidson's (2012) brain imaging research has confirmed evidence of the different brain mechanisms that make up the Awareness and Attention brain systems. He found that they primarily operate in the neocortex and especially in the prefrontal cortex.

The upper part of the brain (forebrain) contains (Figure 1.1):

- The center of conscious thought and sensory processing, divided into lobes with areas of functional specialization.
- The cerebral cortex, and in particular the prefrontal cortex and the neocortex, the most evolutionarily advanced portions of the cerebrum and the centers of highest-level cognitive activity.
- The tertiary level of emotional functioning, extended consciousness, cognitions, executive functioning.

We present to you the A-Team (Figure 1.3):

1. The *Awareness brain system* is our conscious ability to mindfully observe our internal and external experiences. You can observe that your patient

will be able to carefully reflect on and describe their authentic internal experience that is congruent with your observations. For example, "I am aware that I am safe and yet my body feels unsafe."

2. The *Attention brain system* is our ability to carefully and intentionally focus our conscious mind moment by moment. For example, your patient is able to mindfully direct their conscious focus toward their internal experience or any topic. For example, "I have many thoughts and feelings going through my mind; however, I am harnessing my attention to focus on myself right now."

Figure 1.3: The A-Team: Tertiary-Level Brain Systems (Tertiaries)

3. The *Authority brain system* enables us to discern and be open to our own unique wants, desires, preferences, and choices. Your patient is able to speak spontaneously and strongly about their own truths and wants. For example, "I am feeling a pull to my usual worries, and it is important that I choose [spoken with emphasis] to step out of my comfort zone right now."

4. The *Autonomy brain system* enables us to experience ourselves as separate from other people, their expectations, and judgments. Your patient is readily able to speak up and assert their unique desires and override any tendency to please you or others. For example, "I know that I am used to meeting others' expectations, yet I have a right [said emphatically] to do what I want to do."

5. The *Agency brain system* refers to our ability and trust that we can make things happen in our life. Your patient becomes more animated as they express (embody) their desires. "I know it will be difficult to make these changes, and I trust in my own capability [said passionately] of following through to improve my life."

SECONDARY-LEVEL BRAIN SYSTEMS

Nonconscious Secondary-Level Brain Systems: Survival Guardians

The secondary level of emotional processing is an area of great interest and importance to psychotherapists and other care providers. Patients seek out help because they are suffering. This is the region of the BrainMind where much of their suffering develops and remains entrenched. The secondary-level emotions of fear, grief, shame, and guilt are normal and adaptive. Anger is a special emotion that is explored in depth in Chapter 10. Anger can be a dimension of any of the primary-level brain systems. Or it could be reactive/defensive anger and rage that arises out of fear and shame (secondary-level emotional learning). Early developmental trauma, neglect, abandonment, and abuse can cause maladaptive emotional learning within the secondary-level brain systems. Your patients' symptoms of depression, anxiety disorders, chemical dependencies, compulsive behaviors, sexual problems, self-destructive tendencies, and relationship difficulties are the tip of the iceberg. The rest of the iceberg is contained in the secondary and primary levels of emotional processing (Figure 1.4).

The secondary-level brain systems operate in the region of the basal ganglia, especially in the amygdala, hippocampus, and cerebellum (see Figure 1.2; Panksepp, 1998). This region is responsible for activation and coordination of emotions, social actions, and movement.

- The amygdala functions as an organ of appraisal for danger, safety, and familiarity in approach-avoidance situations.
- The hippocampus stores both explicit and implicit learning and is vital for conscious, logical, and cooperative social functioning.
- The cerebellum is adjacent to this region at the back of the brain. Through experiential learning, the cerebellum coordinates sensory input, physical movements, and emotional balance.

Secondary-level brain systems modify or modulate the strengths and activations of both primary-level brain systems and tertiary-level brain systems. They can be categorized as either enhancing or inhibiting our actions and behaviors. Inhibitory neural mechanisms protect us from some danger. Enhancing neural mechanisms strengthen adaptive motivations, behaviors, or emotions. Inhibiting and enhancing mechanisms have been installed by evolution and are therefore present in all of us. For example, the Fear brain system has innate circuits that make us freeze (inhibit our movement) when we see a snake. On the other hand, innate feelings of pleasure or importance provide nonconscious positive feedback (enhancement) to our adaptive behaviors.

Writing about processing in secondary-level brain systems has been the most challenging for us. The wisdom of primary-level and tertiary-level brain systems is fairly straightforward and understandable, but the mental processing at the secondary level is

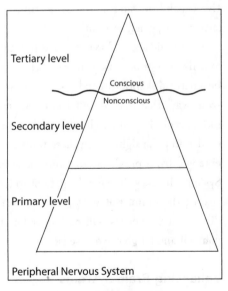

Figure 1.4: Consciousness and Symptoms Are the Tip of the Iceberg

confusing, contradictory, and often counterintuitive. Exploring and utilizing distinct secondary-level brain systems requires more mental effort.

Most of us have had experience with our patients becoming bogged down with the emotions of fear, grief, shame, and guilt. There certainly are other inhibitory secondary-level brain systems that deserve attention yet are not within the scope of our exploration. It takes intention and practice to override our patients' and our own habitual patterns to try something different to help release our patients from their emotional constraints. Constraints are nonconscious limitations or restrictions on the range of responses of the mind to present-moment experiences. They can prevent adaptive actions and complex responses. From a brain systems perspective, this means there is lack of differentiation (impaired integration; Siegel, 2010a) between primary- or secondary-level brain systems.

We have developed distinctive approaches to addressing the troubling emotions of fear, grief, shame (pain), and guilt. Together with our patients, we dive to the bottom of the iceberg. We have found that when we embrace the whole iceberg, deeper and more effective healing is possible (see Baby Blues, Chapter 2). Your patient can harness the power of four levels of emotional processing. This is bigger than words can readily describe. This will activate multiple adaptive capabilities and at the same time release the constraints hidden in their shame, fear, grief, or guilt.

As we said above, having access to multiple levels of emotional processing can look like magic because you are working with nonconscious processes. There can be a natural skepticism and discomfort when you intervene, because you may do so in ways that may at first feel counterintuitive. When you direct your vision more precisely, you will be able to discover brain system dynamics that had been hidden in plain sight. With these tools and others, you can help your patient disentangle from previous emotional learning held within Secondary-Level Brain Systems. It takes time for the patient to trust something new, especially if it goes against the grain. But with gentle persistence, it is possible that your patients' distress and defenses will no longer be obstacles or distractions. You can trust yourself and let go of your sense of duty to accomplish something.

Enhancing Brain Systems

Enhancing brain systems help us maintain and strengthen emotions and actions that are adaptive. They help us develop positive feedback loops so that adaptive emotions and actions become self-sustaining. They reinforce our innate capabilities. They enable our capabilities to become increasingly competent. For example, with the help of secondary-level brain systems, the experience of delight can be sustained and integrated with other brain systems so that delight can become a trait (Hanson, 2016).

There is a natural balance between the inhibitors and enhancers of the secondary-level brain systems that help us to be both precise and graceful at the same time. Our BrainMind uses a mix of inhibitors and enhancers to enable us to learn how to walk as toddlers. When we lean too far one way, our inhibitors detect the error and suppress that circuit. When we move just right, our enhancers reinforce that circuit. It is helpful to tease these influences apart so that you can activate the four enhancing brain systems independently and have the benefit of these separate sources of energy and information.

Each of the enhancing brain systems evolved to add energy to adaptive actions and emotions. They also can focus the energy more precisely so that it will be more effective and enable us to do more work. Each of these systems is associated with a characteristic neurotransmitter (denoted below in parentheses). The four enhancing secondary-level brain systems we explore briefly here, and later in Chapter 14, are the Pleasure, Importance/Salience, Determination, and Valuable/Internal-Reward brain systems.

1. The *Pleasure brain system* (opioids; Panksepp & Biven, 2012) activates in response to stimuli that enhance our survival. For example, consuming healthy food activates neural circuits that alert us that we like what we are eating. Your patient will often have a smile or twinkle in their eye when they experience pleasure. This positive feeling directs us to go forward with the same action. "What are you experiencing that tells you it feels good to be assertive?"

2. The *Importance/Salience brain system* (dopamine; Grawe, 2007) responds to adaptive behaviors by providing positive feedback to sustain actions that are important to our well-being. Your patient readily stays present and focused on your therapeutic work even when they are uncomfortable. Their sense of importance keeps their eye on the prize. Saying "How do you know that this matters to you?" invites the patient to become aware of their internal sense of importance. "I feel clear and committed to my struggle."

3. The *Motivation/Determination brain system* (dopamine; Schwartz & Begley, 2002; Grawe, 2007) provides energy to help us persevere when we meet obstacles or other difficulties. It provides a sense of wanting or desire to pursue that which is within our reach. This energy helps us climb over (override) our fears, shame, or other inhibitions. Your patients' bodies tend to lean forward, and sometimes they will set their jaw when this brain system is activated. You could focus on this source of energy with an invitation such as, "Do you feel a drive for our connection?"

4. The *Valuable/Internal-Reward brain system* (acetylcholine, glutamine, dopamine; Grawe, 2007; Panksepp & Biven, 2012) provides us with internal positive feedback even when there is no obvious benefit or pleasure in our actions. Learning to walk takes time and much trial and error, and yet it is unconditionally rewarding to the individual. There is inherent frustration, and the benefits will not be experienced for months or years. Nature evolved this enhancing brain system to give us the innate incentives to learn what is ultimately valuable for us to survive and thrive in our lives. Your patient's body can reveal a sense of incentive, animation, and anticipation. For example, the patient may be excitedly ready to start the session. "How do you experience this feeling of satisfaction inside yourself right now as you assert yourself?" "How do you feel your sense of accomplishment in your progress?"

Certainly, other enhancing brain systems play important roles in helping us survive and thrive in our lives. Examples could include empathy, confidence, pride, and competence. We have selected the four enhancing brain systems that we have found most effective in our practice and that we believe have the most neuroscience research to support them. These systems can operate independently, although they usually work in concert with each other to help maximize adaptive behaviors and intentions. You will see how we harness the patient's enhancers to help them override emotional constraints in subsequent chapters.

Inhibiting Brain Systems: The Gatekeepers

The four inhibiting secondary-level brain systems that we have found most important are the Fear, Grief, Shame, and Guilt brain systems. Panksepp (1998) calls them the defensive emotions that evolved to help us survive dangers. We call them the "Gatekeepers of Survival" (Figure 1.5). It is important to notice that these inhibiting brain systems are also modulators, for although they have an inhibitory bias, they also support and modify adaptive actions that arise from the Care, Safe, and Connection brain systems. They are listed in order of their emotional and probable evolutionary development:

1. The *Fear brain system* (LeDoux, 1996; Panksepp, 2012) activates in response to physical (not Safe) danger. The nonconscious physiological experience is: "Pull back from the danger—come back to safe." Severe threats to well-being activate hardwired circuits in the brain and produce responses that help us survive (LeDoux, 2002). Fear can be both an adaptive response aimed at survival in the face of life-threatening

Figure 1.5: Gatekeepers: Secondary Brain Systems (Secondaries)

circumstances, and also may create devastating psychiatric problems, including severe affective disorders. Fear occurs when we are unsafe, and it mobilizes fight, flight, or freeze reactions. Your patient's frozen face or tight voice reveal the activation of their Fear brain system (Porges, 2009), which can be activated by a present-moment threat or a previously learned threat. For example, "That dog is threatening me" or "I am terrified of dogs."

2. The *Grief brain system* (Panksepp & Biven, 2012) activates in response to the danger of loss of Care from others. The nonconscious physiological experience is: "Stop the aloneness—come back to Care." Grief can be consciously experienced as mental suffering, sorrow, or painful regret. Your patient's face reveals grief with through sad facial expressions and/ or tears. Grief is an adaptive emotion, although when constrained it can become maladaptive and even turn into depression.

3. The *Shame brain system* (Schore, 1994) activates in response to relational (no Connection) danger. The nonconscious physiological experience is: "Stop the action that upsets my caregiver—come back to Connection." Shame is characterized by behaviors of withdrawal and feelings of distress, powerlessness, and worthlessness. Shame also triggers visceral sensations of nausea, gagging, and/or an inward collapse. Your patient's slumped posture, with the head down and avoidance of eye contact, reveals shame. Shame is the toddler's psychophysiological adaptive freeze reaction when their enthusiastic running into the street causes their parent to cry out in distress. However, the overuse of shame as a disciplinary tool predisposes children to long-term difficulties with emotional regulation, high anxiety, and internalized feelings of worthlessness.

4. The *Guilt brain system* (Schore, 1994; Cozolino, 2016) activates in response to social (not belonging to the group) danger. Guilt is an emotional experience characterized by feeling distress when we believe we have done something that compromises standards of conduct for the group, clan, or family. The physiological experience of the Guilt brain system is a suffocating, heavy feeling in your chest and an incessant throb in your heart pushing you to make repairs. Your patient's constrained yet erect posture, pained expression, and emotional vocal tones can help you distinguish guilt from shame. Guilt and shame are both social emotions, so there is often a visible overlap in their psychophysiology. However,

each arises from distinct neural circuits in the BrainMind. Guilt becomes maladaptive when it becomes self-hatred, meaning, "I am inferior."

> *Canst thou not minister to a mind diseased,*
> *Pluck from the memory a rooted sorrow.*
> *Raze out the written troubles of the brain,*
> *And with some sweet oblivious antidote*
> *Cleanse the stuff'd bosom of that perilous stuff*
> *Which weighs upon the heart?*
> Shakespeare, Macbeth, *Act 5, Scene 3* (quoted in LeDoux, 2002)

These four secondary-level inhibiting brain systems are disproportionately powerful. Shakespeare understood this. The activations of these brain systems will overrule all other impulses to protect survival. For example, the shame reaction freezes the child's exuberant play. Early trauma can foster survival patterns (habits) to adapt to that environment. For the sake of survival, they often become entrenched and inflexible. In later life, those closed patterns are unable to adapt to new information and therefore are now maladaptive. These entrenched survival patterns often play a significant role in human suffering and hence in our patients' lives.

Survival habit patterns are difficult to change or treat. Survival trumps everything else.

Let's explore another example: A mother is busy at the stove boiling water, when her child approaches seeking care and embraces her leg. The mother says, with tension in her voice because she is afraid to put her child in danger, "Not right now. I am busy!" The child's Shame brain system feels the danger of her tension and inhibits the impulse of his Connection brain system. The Shame brain system activates the psychophysiology of shame, with sensations such as nausea or hesitation. The child's nervous system experiences adaptive shame and inhibits the embrace. After the mother puts the water aside, she picks up her child, embraces him, and makes a repair. Everything is okay; he is learning adaptive shame nonconsciously. His BrainMind learns that sometimes his love impulse is dangerous, for whatever reason. He learns how to regulate his Connection brain system in context.

However, if the mother is constantly depressed, she is likely to push the child away. Rather than saying, "Not right now—it's dangerous," she is more likely like to say, "You are a bother. I do not have time for you." She might even say, "You are a bad child for bothering me." Because of her own issues, she confounds the adaptive shame inhibitions by shaming the child. If he is repeatedly burdened by her shaming, he could develop core shame (Cozolino, 2016). As a result, he starts to feel bad about himself, unworthy, and wrong. That can become part of his personality structure and could affect him for the rest of his life. Healthy inhibitory shame is flexible and contingent. Maladaptive and core shame are inflexible and generalize inappropriately (see Baby Blues in Chapter 2).

It is often difficult for our patients to get their minds around the fact that the emotional learnings contained in these secondary-level brain systems are often illogical, counterintuitive, and sometimes maladaptive. Emotional learning serves to increase survival. It was adaptive when the learning took place and may be maladaptive in adulthood.

NONCONSCIOUS PRIMARY-LEVEL BRAIN SYSTEMS: THE MAGNIFICENT SEVEN

The next lower region, called the brainstem, is located underneath the basal ganglia. The brainstem contains structures called the periaqueductal gray matter, midbrain, pons, and medulla oblongata. The periaqueductal gray matter is central to the primary-level emotions described below. The other structures play significant roles in psychophysiological phenomena such as facial expressions, tears, coughing, and posture. All the nerves connecting the brain with the rest of the body pass through the brainstem, and thus it acts as a central switchboard. We will briefly mention psychophysiological phenomena you can observe in your patients to alert you to the presence of these brain systems. More elaborate descriptions come later in Chapter 10 on the primary-level brain systems. Processing in these primary-level brain systems is nonconscious (Chapters 10–12).

We focus on seven nonconscious brain systems that originate in this portion of the brain and that have been delineated by Jaak Panksepp in his extensive affective neuroscience research. We have relabeled several of his names for those brain systems to make them more practical and understandable to our patients and trainees.

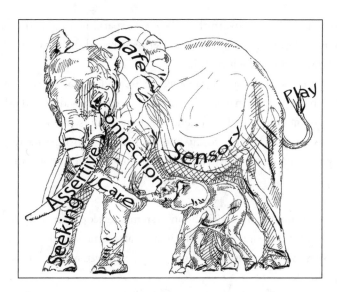

Figure 1.6: Primary-Level Brain Systems: Magnificent
Seven, Powerhouses (Primaries)

We have chosen the figure of an elephant to illustrate the fact that each of these primary-level brain systems is present in every mammal (Figure 1.6). Each of these primary brain systems is highly evolved for the same reason that the tusk, eye, trunk, and ear of the elephant are also highly evolved. Later, in Chapter 10, we use the parable of the blind men and the elephant to help you discover these nonconscious primary-level brain systems with your own hands. The figure can also remind you that there is always an elephant in the room, challenging yet worthy of your attention.

In addition to defining each of the brain systems, we also describe the patient's somatic experience of the system when it is functioning well. We refer to this as the embodied experience of the brain system.

1. The *Safe brain system* is much more than the absence of fear or anxiety. The patient's embodied experience of safety is a deep sense of calm and fullness, expansive, solid, and grounded. Your patient sits upright, with an open posture, and the voice is animated.
2. The *Care brain system* inspires us to invest enormous amounts of attention, energy, and interest in another being or ourselves. The patient's embodied

experience of care is warmth in the chest, sparkling eyes, and spontaneous smiles. Patients will have tenderness around their eyes, in their voice, and around their mouth.

3. The *Connection brain system* mobilizes us to gradually and viscerally develop deep emotional attachments to our care providers and others. The patient's embodied experience of connection is one of feeling closeness, wanting proximity to this specific person, and "I matter to them; they matter to me." Your patients are able to sustain an unconditional eye gaze, especially in moments of silence.

The Safe, Care, and Connection brain systems develop immediately at birth. Together they facilitate and sustain the infant's attachment to the care providers. Our approach to the activation of those three brain systems is addressed explicitly in Chapter 5.

4. The *Seeking brain system* happens when we are free to explore our environment and meet our needs in thousands of different ways. The patient's embodied experience of seeking is the felt sense of interest, curiosity, expectancy, excitement, and anticipation. Your patients might hold their heads up or tilt their heads as if looking to discover something new or from a different viewpoint.

5. The *Play brain system* motivates us to interact with others in a funny, joyous, rough-and-tumble, laughing, spontaneous, quirky, and exploratory fashion. The patient's embodied experience is one of lightness, uplifting, tingling, an internal giggle, and feeling delight. Your patients are smiling with their eyes, and they laugh and interact readily.

6. The *Assertive brain system* empowers us to pursue our needs, satisfy our wants, and thrive in the world. The patient's embodied experience is strong (especially in the paraspinal muscles), powerful, and capable. "I feel like I have a rod up my back." Your patients start to hold themselves more erect and assert themselves with their hands and arms.

7. The *Sensory brain system* processes and integrates the information and energy that comes in from the peripheral nervous system. Patients develop a felt sense of themselves and their bodies. Your patients readily identify internal physical sensations.

ORGANIZATION OF THE BOOK

In the folllowing chapters, we seek to illustrate and illuminate the many discoveries we have made in our exploration of psychotherapeutic processes. We encourage you to Trust the Process.

We have found it very difficult to translate our work with nonconscious emotional processing and experiential teaching onto the written page. Numerous readers have helped us find better ways to share our discoveries with you. Hopefully some of those attempts will resonate with you sufficiently that you decide to experiment with one or more of the principles or approaches contained in this book. We have chosen the following sequence of chapters as a result of successful experiments with different teaching approaches for the past 15 years. In Part I, after the three introductory chapters, we have three chapters that give the reader some practical applications for these concepts. Part II has an introductory chapter. The three conscious brain systems (Chapters 7–9) come next in order to emphasize how working with these systems enhances collaboration and harnesses the processing power of differentiated conscious brain systems. Next the focus is on Facilitating seven nonconscious primary-level brain systems because they produce their own energy, process information and experiences uniquely, and release the natural potential for self-organizing phenomena in the BrainMind. We have placed the brain systems of Fear, Grief, Shame, and Guilt last because we have found that when we focus on Facilitating and Differentiating the five conscious brain systems and the seven primary-level brain systems, the constraints within the secondary-level brain systems tend to drop away naturally.

Part I Overview
Paradigm of a Multiple Brain Systems Therapy
In Chapter 1, we have mapped out the fundamental concepts of brain systems that underly the practice. Various components make up the structure and format of this paradigm. We have defined terms and listed the 20 brain systems we have found most useful in therapy.

Chapter 2 provides a clinical illustration of the application of this paradigm of therapy. We introduce the goals of developing resilient brain systems and a Fail-Safe Complex Network of multiple integrated brain systems.

Chapter 3 introduces the principles and approaches that constitute the paradigm of CIMBS and that we use when applying the components presented in Chapter 1. The chapter starts with a clinical case story that illustrates some of the counterintuitive experiences that inspired us to develop new ways of understanding the inner workings of our patients' minds. There is a brief example of how we practically apply each of the principles.

Chapters 1 and 3 highlight the neurobiological foundations on which we stand every day. This knowledge is based on solid science; you do not need to take our word for it. Chapters 4, 5, and 6 introduce you to practical applications of this knowledge. We have found these processes effective and efficient. Try them out for yourselves.

Initial Practices of CIMBS

Chapter 4 explores a different approach to trauma and the patient's symptoms. It describes and illustrates a process we call Go the Other Way. When we meet symptoms, reactions, and/or trauma that arise in the session, we direct our attention and energy to the patient's underlying resources and competencies rather than dwelling on their distress. This chapter introduces the reader to how we provide our patients with continuous experiential (nonconscious) learning.

Chapter 5 describes and illustrates our approach to the patient-therapist relationship. Our goal is to develop a Therapeutic Attachment Relationship. We explore a variety of interventions we have developed to activate the nonconscious attachment brain systems in our patients from the first moment of each session.

Chapter 6 describes a series of interventions designed to activate multiple conscious and nonconscious brain systems at the start of therapy. The Initial Directed Activation invites patients into what we refer to as the Transpiring Present Moment (see Chapter 2) inside themselves. It consists of a brief meditation, explicit invitations to specific brain systems, and a precise focus on a patient's relationship with themselves.

Part II: In-Depth View

Conscious Brain Systems, the Tertiaries

Chapter 7 explores the conscious Awareness, Attention, Authority, Autonomy, and Agency brain systems in greater depth, including brain system dysfunctions such as hypoactivity or hyperconnection to illustrate other approaches to managing those challenges. We explore several approaches to Activating conscious brain systems to utilize their wisdom, energy, and processing capabilities.

Chapter 8 explores the purpose and processes of Facilitating, Differentiating, and Training conscious brain systems. Differentiating brain systems disentangles rigid, maladaptive emotional habit patterns that interfere with the capabilities of specific systems. Repeated Activation, Facilitation, and Differentiation of distinct brain systems (Training) will enable them to become resilient brain systems. Further clinical examples illustrate this practice and the development of internal positive feedback loops.

Chapter 9 takes us to our goal of Integrating conscious brain systems. Sustained simultaneous activations of differentiated brain systems is a process we call parallel processing, which refers to the often incoherent experience of each brain system operating independently. Simultaneous activations will enable the process of Integrating of differentiated systems to unfold. This can give rise to a Fail-Safe Complex Network of brain systems. If one or more of the brain systems gets triggered or shuts down, the integrated network continues to function normally.

Nonconscious Primary-Level Brain Systems, the Primaries

Chapter 10 explores the Safe, Care, Connection, Seeking, Assertive, Play, and Sensory brain systems in greater depth. This chapter illustrates a variety of approaches to Activating these nonconscious brain systems. Clinical examples give the reader some practical approaches to discern and explore each system.

Chapter 11 explores the purpose and process of Differentiating primary-level brain systems. We use clinical examples to illustrate Facilitating, explicitly identifying, and disentangling distinct neural circuits that make up the Primaries. These approaches of Differentiating the nonconscious brain systems harness our patients' innate yet heretofore unknown capabilities. This part of therapy is quite energizing to the patient and the process. It can be a kind of physiotherapy for the mind.

Chapter 12 takes us to our goal of Integrating primary-level brain systems. Clinical examples illustrate practical ways of sustaining simultaneous activations of differentiated Primaries. Simultaneous activations enable the processes of Integrating to unfold at all four levels of the nervous system. The addition of the integrated primary-level brain system adds a whole new level of flexibility and complexity to the brain. We could again call this integration a Fail-Safe Complex Network.

Secondary-Level Brain Systems, Constraints and Adaptive Learning

Chapter 13 takes a more precise look at the eight nonconscious secondary-level brain systems that guide, constrain, and enhance our primary-level brain systems. The Shame, Fear, Guilt, and Grief brain systems are the inhibitors. The Pleasure, Value, Salience, and Motivation brain systems are the enhancers. Each of them has both innate and learned capabilities. Psychophysiological phenomena and shifts reveal the activations of these nonconscious brain systems. These systems often contain maladaptive constraints from previous trauma, neglect, or abuse.

Chapter 14 explores how attending to the patient's psychophysiology can provide empirical evidence of the functioning of nonconscious brain systems. You can learn how to observe and discern many psychophysiological phenomena. A psychophysiological perspective can enable you to fine-tune your therapy based on nonconscious patient factors. We refer to this process as physiopsychotherapy. Practical homework exercises between sessions will facilitate new adaptive neural circuits and lead to further integration of a full spectrum of brain systems.

Chapter 15 explores Neuroplasticity, and the final chapter includes reminders of the distinct neurobiological principles that make up this paradigm. This chapter will also highlight some of the most effective approaches with which to operationalize the power and flexibility of therapy utilizing multiple brain systems.

CHAPTER 2

Resilient Brain Systems and Fail-Safe Complex Networks

∙∙

CASE STUDY: BABY BLUES

Ann first came to therapy after being depressed for a year. She came to Albert for treatment to get off her medications so that she could get pregnant safely. She successfully got off her meds and became pregnant. Her pregnancy and delivery went smoothly. She came back six weeks postpartum for follow-up. During the first few minutes of the session, she described fatigue and difficulty taking care of her infant. She complained that she was unhappy, anxious, and unable to rest even when her baby was asleep. She was troubled that she was withdrawing from her daughter and at times not wanting to take care of her or even play with her. Ann was afraid of developing postpartum depression.

Because this treatment process is primarily experiential rather than verbal or cognitive, the following transcript contains the music, score, and lyrics of the session, so to speak. The "music" refers to the descriptions of the nonverbal body movements, facial expressions, voice tones, and other psychophysiologi-cal phenomena that reveal the emotional activations of both participants. The "score" refers to the therapist's inner thoughts and moment-to-moment decision points to promote the ebb and flow of the brain system activations and therapeu-tic intentions. The therapist's inner observations will help you see through the eyes of the therapist the distinct psychophysiological phenomena that provide evidence of the functioning of the primary- and secondary-level brain systems. The "lyrics" are the unedited words that were spoken in the session.

Please interrupt any effort your brain is making to figure out what is happening in the session. Rather than figuring out what the therapist is doing or what the patient is saying and experiencing, trust your capacities for observing with different lenses and from different vantage points. Use your beginner's mind. Let yourself be moved in our unique way by this therapy session.

The following is an 8-minute vignette from Ann's first session after her baby, Dawn, was born. Albert offers comments about his observations as a therapist.

> **Albert:** We can see you are working to care for yourself and care for Dawn.
> **Ann:** It takes work. I feel conflicted all the time!
> **Albert:** Mmm, this is interesting. Are you curious about it?
> **Ann:** I mostly feel sad.

I could see tears beginning to well up in Ann's eyes.

> **Albert:** Ann, what do you see in my eyes right now?
> **Ann:** You are smiling.
> **Albert:** What else?
> **Ann:** You like me?
> **Albert:** Yes! I care for you. I am caring for you.

I saw a puzzled look on Ann's face. She started crying softly. Then she quickly swung her head away with an expression of disgust.

> **Ann:** I feel nausea and want to run away!
> **Albert:** How wonderful that you are being aware of the feelings of nausea and running away. You are aware of these feelings and you are <u>not</u> running away. You are being capable of being aware. Are you curious about that?
> **Ann:** Not really. I just want to run away and hide.
> **Albert:** Curious, isn't it? Any idea of what is bringing up this feeling of nausea at this present moment?
> **Ann:** I don't want you to care for me. I am not a good person.

Albert: What do you see in my eyes?
Ann: You still like me?

Ann looked at me sideways. Her quizzical expression had returned. I raised my arms toward her and opened my hands in a welcoming gesture.

Albert: Together we can care for you in your struggle.
Ann: I feel resistance.

Ann at first nodded her head, then gave me the sideways puzzled look again.

Albert: Good awareness! You are aware of your resistance. Are you curious about it?
Ann: I am beginning to be curious.
Albert: Do you *want us* to care for you in your struggle?
Ann: It feels bad. I feel wrong to tell you that I want to be cared for.

Ann's expression shifted. She seemed to be stunned by her conflicting feelings. I said nothing, but once again I gave her an affectionate gaze, and I raised and opened my hands toward her.

Ann: This is what happens with my baby. Weird; she loves me and I feel unworthy. I feel bad and I put her down. This a very strange experience. I feel like it is totally natural for a mother to receive the love of her baby.

At first, as she spoke, Ann was sighing and wiping tears from her eyes. Then her voice strengthened, and she became more animated.

Albert: It is interesting, isn't it? There are some aspects of this intense love, this beautiful love, that stir up shame and unworthiness. As if there is something wrong to receive the love of your baby.

It is wonderful. It is out in the open. You know it, and can describe it, so that it does not become an obstacle to loving Dawn—to loving yourself, to allowing yourself to be loved by Dawn.

Do you want to allow yourself to be loved by us, just at this little moment in time?

I placed my hands on my chest in a hugging gesture. Ann sobbed openly. Then I swung my hands to the side, as if to sweep the shame away. Ann sighed in response and turned her face away.

> **Ann:** I feel resistance, like what is the catch? What do you want from me? And then I know it is not true.
> **Albert:** It is irrational, but it is your reality. It is your truth. Things have happened in your development that have created these connections. Unfortunately we cannot erase them, we can just override them.
> **Ann:** Okay, let's override it!

As Ann spoke, her voice again became stronger, and she sat up straighter in the chair. I addressed her emphatically and swept the shame away to her left with my hands. Then I again raised open hands toward her, gave her a warm, open gaze, and leaned slightly forward toward her.

> **Albert:** We are overriding it! The shame is over there, so it does not become an obstacle. It is a very significant discomfort. It does not have to be an obstacle between you and receiving our caring. Together we can care for you in your struggle, and in your desire to receive our caring.
> **Ann:** It feels dangerous and wrong. I feel nausea. I feel resistance.
> **Albert:** And you are overriding those feelings to stay connected. Well done!
> **Ann:** I feel relieved, and hopeful too, that maybe I can actually love my baby.
> **Albert:** It is interesting, isn't it? It is a paradox, but it is true. Do you want to continue receiving our caring?
> **Ann:** Okay, let's do it!

Ann was a stew of conflicting body language. She still had the puzzled look, but she nodded and held our gaze of connection even as she cringed and squirmed. I used an animated voice and continued to show the affectionate expression and the open-hand gesture. She leaned toward me slightly, and gradually turned to face me directly for half a minute before squirming and looking away.

> **Albert:** Well done! It is hard work and you are doing it! You are being capable of staying here receiving my caring. You are being capable.
> **Ann:** That is probably what my depression is really about.

Albert: How do you know that?

Ann: Because it feels the same way. It feels painful. I feel depressed. . . . But it feels like I really want to love her.

Albert: That is great. That is what is underneath your depression: your want, your desire, and your capacity to love and to allow yourself to be loved. It releases pain, but we are facing that.

Ann began to cry again, and her voice was tight. She placed her hand on her heart, and I responded with a hand gesture of release over my torso.

This session was a turning point for Ann. She did not develop postpartum depression. Albert saw her for several more sessions. She was able to release more grief from her past traumas. She developed an increasingly secure attachment with her daughter, and even more importantly, a more secure attachment with herself. When Albert saw her for 10-year follow-up, she remained free of depression. Her daughter was flourishing independently.

Baby Blues: Debriefing

Ann's story is a case study that illustrates several key aspects of CIMBS therapy. Below, Beatriz and Albert discuss and analyze a video recording of Ann's session in their characteristic manner. This session with Ann gives a brief example of how CIMBS therapy operates in practice. Beyond that, the analysis below is a deep dive into what it is like to experience a CIMBS session. We wished to demonstrate some of the concepts and principles we outlined in Chapter 1—to paint them red. We look at the brain systems that Albert chose to Activate and how they operated in this particular patient. We also highlight the therapeutic interventions and approaches that Albert used in the session and their effects. In later chapters, we will examine each of these interventions and approaches in greater detail.

We follow the video analysis by answering a couple of typical questions that occur when we show video recordings of therapy sessions in our training courses. After this debriefing, we elaborate on some key CIMBS therapeutic interventions and strategies that emerge from Ann's case study: Activating, Facilitating, Differentiating, and Go the Other Way.

The rest of the chapter is dedicated to defining and developing our concept of resilient brain systems and how they could transform your patient and their therapy. Developing and integrating multiple capabilities can achieve an outcome that releases the self-organizing capacities (Siegel, 1999) of our BrainMind. When multiple resilient brain systems operate together, they create what we call a Fail-Safe Complex Network, which can thrive and survive even in the most adverse of emotional environments. This is the outcome we seek from Complex Integration of Multiple Brain Systems.

Baby Blues: The Postgame Show

Albert: As soon as the session began, I could see that Ann was overwhelmed with conflicting emotions. She was clearly struggling to fully care for her daughter. So for my Initial Directed Activation (Chapter 6), I focused on activating her Care brain system. I said, "We can see you are working to care for yourself and care for Dawn." This assertion explicitly alerted Ann that she possessed adaptive caring capacities, and that they were present right now. I also wanted to establish a positive Therapeutic Attachment Relationship with her through both physical and verbal expressions of caring.

Ann reacted with sadness, and she cried. So I reinforced the activation by smiling, giving her a caring look, and when she recognized it, verbally confirming it. Her reaction was to say, "I feel nausea and want to run away," and to turn her head in disgust.

Beatriz: I can see that Ann's nausea and urge to run away were caused by Shame and Fear, respectively. Those are nonconscious secondary-level brain systems, and they were entangled with Care, a nonconscious primary-level brain system. Those Secondaries were constraining her ability to receive caring from you, as well as to express caring for her daughter. But you didn't explore what those constraints felt like or where they were coming from. Instead, you probed the inner capabilities that could help her cope with the constraints.

You told her, "How wonderful that you are being aware of the feelings of nausea and running away . . . and you are not running away." You helped make her aware of her nausea and avoidance constraints, and that activated her Awareness brain system. And you further pointed out that despite her revulsion, she was not running away. She was seeking help. That was an act of caring—for her daughter, and for herself. So after you Activated her Care system, you connected it to her Awareness system to get them working together. Further Activation of her Care brain system would help her viscerally experience her capabilities rather than trying to explain them to her.

Albert: Yes, and I followed up by asking, "Any idea what is bringing up this feeling of nausea at this present moment?" I did that to Activate her Seeking brain system (curiosity) to help her override the overwhelming feelings. After I asked why she was feeling nausea, she said she didn't want me to care for her, that she was not a good person. She was revealing an absence of self-worth that surprised me. And when I showed her again that I cared for her and invited her to share in that caring, she said, "I feel resistance."

I replied, "Good awareness! . . . Are you curious about it?" And she said, "I am beginning to be curious." This was a great opportunity now to connect her Awareness and Seeking brain systems after both had been activated. And it seemed that her Fear system was starting to calm down a bit. She was beginning to be able to explore her difficulties rather than being overwhelmed and avoiding them.

Beatriz: Yes, I can see that at that point, Ann was no longer being as overwhelmed by the caring feelings coming her way. She was not moving her head away with an expression of disgust. She was actually looking at you sideways, which was good. It meant that her constraints were less dominant. The emotional energy was shifting from protection and avoidance to approach and discovery.

Albert: The next step was very important. When I said, "Together we can care for you in your struggle," I followed up with, "Do you *want us* to care for you in your struggle?" When Ann's emotional energy shifted towards more openness, I saw an opportunity. By asking whether she was willing to join me in caring, I activated two more brain systems: the Motivational (want) and Authority (choice) brain systems. And I explicitly used the word "us," to take advantage of the positive Therapeutic Attachment Relationship I had been developing with her. Developing explicit collaboration is particularly important with this level of emotional activation and constraints. I embodied the attachment relationship with my silence and the look of caring in my eyes.

Beatriz: I can see that this became a turning point in the session. Ann repeated how it felt bad to be cared for, and to feel the love of her baby. But then she said, "This a very strange experience. I feel like it is totally natural for a mother to receive the love of her baby." And as she said this, her voice grew louder and more animated. She was entering a state of disequilibrium and novelty, in which transpiring changes can take place. Ann was actually experiencing her inner entanglement. When she heard herself say, "My baby loves me and I feel unworthy," she consciously realized how her Shame was conflicting with her Care. Just for this moment, her entanglement was being differentiated.

Albert: I wanted to reinforce Ann's conscious Awareness of this differentiation process. So I said, "It is interesting, isn't it? . . .This intense love, this beautiful love stirs up shame. As if there is something wrong to receive the love of your baby." I made a hugging gesture, and Ann started crying freely.

Beatriz: It looks like all these activations reduced the constraints on her Grief brain system and she was able to release her tears. This was an important release for her. Probably she was experiencing grief over her inability to receive her baby's love, along with some grief from the past that we don't know about. We could speculate that her grief comes from feeling unworthy of care. You spotlighted her grief for her, you connected her Grief and Awareness, when you said, "It is wonderful. It is out in the open." In cases like Ann's, we also need to activate the Care and Connection brain systems again and again so that they develop strength and become resilient brain systems.

Albert: Yes, and that is why I continued by saying, "Do you want to allow yourself to be loved by us, just at this little moment in time?" She said she still felt resistance, and I saw her look away again, but she also said she recognized the contradictory nature of her desire to love and be loved, yet feeling blocked. That was a valuable awareness, and I validated it verbally. "It is irrational, but it is your reality. It is your truth. Things have happened in your development that have created these connections." Then it was time again to Go the Other Way. I told her, "Unfortunately we cannot erase [these conflicts], we can just override them."

Beatriz: That was great! I could see Ann sit up straighter and speak more firmly as she asserted, "Let's override it!" These were significant psychophysiological shifts telling us that her Authority and Assertive brain systems were being activated. She was in a state of novelty and discovery. It is vital for our patients to have these kinds of new adaptive experiences in order to change the brain.

Albert: I wanted to support those brain system activations, so I made the arm gesture of sweeping the conflicts to the side, and I declared to her, "We are overriding it!" Then I made caring gestures with my eyes and my arms, and told her, "It does not have to be a barrier between you and receiving our caring." Not surprisingly, she reported that she felt the nausea and resistance all over again.

Beatriz: Yes, the resistances came back, as expected. But I could see that she was nodding and keeping the eye connection, even as she squirmed, cringed, and looked puzzled. She was successfully overriding those resistances. The drives of the Care, Connection, and Assertive (primary-level) brain systems were activated, and they were overcoming the Shame and Fear (secondary-level) brain systems that were inhibiting those drives. She was in a moment of struggle. This was the perfect moment to Go the Other Way to help her to see her capabilities at this moment in time rather than exploring the "dangerous or wrong" feelings.

Albert: At this point I thought the best thing to do was just to keep reinforcing the shifts that she was experiencing. I said, "You are overriding those feelings to stay connected. Well done!" I was very encouraged when she replied, "I feel relieved, and hopeful too, that maybe I can actually love my baby." I asked her whether she wanted to keep receiving caring. She fidgeted, but she also shifted her body slightly towards me, looked me straight in the eye, and said, "Okay, let's do it!" Then she squirmed and looked away again. I continued, "Well done, it is hard work and you are doing it! . . . You are being capable."

Beatriz: What you did really helped Ann start to build the resilience of her Care and Connection brain systems and to continue Differentiating her Care and Connection brain systems from her Shame and Fear brain systems. I can see that her struggle is mostly visceral and only partly conscious. You kept your focus on creating an experience for her rather than just giving her explanations or descriptions.

Albert: There was one more round of emotions in this session. Ann's voice tightened again. She cried and put her hand on her heart, and she said, "I feel depressed. . . . But it feels like I really want to love her." I reflected back to her that she had it right: "That is great. That is what is underneath your depression: your want, your desire, and your capacity to love and to allow yourself to be loved. It releases pain, but we are facing that."

Beatriz: I can sees that this was a visceral breakthrough for her. For just this moment, she was able to stand up to the Shame and Fear that kept her from bonding with her infant and placed her on the verge of a postpartum depression. She was releasing pain and grief from some implicit emotional learning. She was having a complex experience.

Baby Blues: Questions and Answers

Ann's story has been very useful for us to present as a CIMBS case study to our colleagues. When we first showed this session to a child psychiatrist, for example, she was immediately excited. She likened this session to heart surgery, in which one operation (session) can save the life of an infant from great suffering. This child psychiatrist went further by saying, "In one session you stopped the possible development of postpartum depression and helped the mom to develop a secure attachment relationship with her baby. This changed the developmental trajectory of this child and future generations by stopping the intergenerational attachment dysfunction."

When we have presented Ann's case in our training sessions, it has stimulated many interesting questions, such as the following:

Question: Were you surprised by Ann's resistance to attaching to her infant?

Albert: Yes, I was quite surprised. She was very excited and well prepared to become a mother. The strength of her resistance in the face of her powerful maternal attachment drive was most surprising of all. I will never look at postpartum depression as only a function of hormonal imbalances, anxiety, and sleep deprivation again. Her feeling unworthy and resistant to her daughter's love helps me understand the intergenerational transmission of depression and insecure attachments.

Question: How do you make sense of Ann's feelings of shame, grief, and danger in relationship to being cared for by Albert? [We suggest that you stop reading for a second and ponder your own answer before you read ahead.]

Beatriz: That was quite an array of emotional resistances, wasn't it? We can all see how it was easier for her to give in to the resistance rather than to stand up to those feelings of grief, shame, and fear. There are a number of explanations for her resistances from a brain systems perspective. The simplest answer is that her Shame brain system was entangled with her Care brain system. In other words, when she started feeling cared for, Shame was triggered (as well as nausea) and the experience "felt wrong" (guilt). That does not explain her feelings of pain or danger, though. We could speculate that the pain came from her Grief brain system. Her grief may be the result of her own feelings of insecurity and/or loss of attachments. The fear could be the result of feelings of abandonment from her own infancy. What is important to see here is that Ann is feeling the constraints from three distinct brain systems: Shame, Fear, and Grief. These facts can help us understand how difficult it is to change those implicit emotional learnings.

Question: How come you did not address her crying, her sadness directly?

Albert: I felt the tears were a mix of emotions: tears of intimacy and connection with the therapist, tears at feeling understood and acknowledged, and tears of grief from previous losses. The fact that she was experiencing the grief was healing, because crying is a healing process. It helps to release grief.

Beatriz: Albert very much paid attention to the crying, but he did not try to make sense of it. He sustained the care and connection, and that is what released the grief. Stopping to analyze or explain grief often stops the visceral release. We believe that helping the release of the grief is very beneficial. It is likely that some of the sources of these tears are from deeper nonconscious experiences. Sustaining the care and connection is a way to keep strengthening those capacities so that the healing tears can be released. Albert is trusting her capacity and her spontaneous self-organization (Siegel, 1999, p. 214).

Albert met with Ann to obtain her permission to print the transcript above. She was moved to tears by reading and reflecting on the session. She was inspired and pleased to revisit her experiences, so Albert asked her to write down her thoughts. These are Ann's exact written words after reviewing the transcript from the session after her baby was born:

"I was honored when Dr. Sheldon asked if he could include one of my therapy sessions in his book. When I read the document transcribing key portions of that session, tears filled my eyes. I felt immense gratitude for the very special growth that occurred in that session: from feeling blocked and unable to connect on a deep heartfelt level with my newborn baby daughter, to feeling freed to love her and care for her deeply as her mother. It seemed remarkable that I could clear such a seemingly complex block in just one therapy session. Dr. Sheldon and I spent several moments sharing this sense of gratitude reflecting on that past session, because what else could be more impactful than a mother being able to love her child completely, unconditionally, and without old trauma getting in the way? Sitting in our chairs several feet apart, but close enough to make eye contact, our feet both firmly grounded, hands on our legs, sitting and sharing space in a sort of silence that I had grown very accustomed to in therapy with Dr. Sheldon. After several moments, a deeper wisdom surfaced, and I realized that although this session seemed miraculous and one of a kind, it was in fact, not at all. There was a much deeper context that had set the framework within which this 'leap' could be made in my psyche. I told Dr. Sheldon this really wasn't an isolated phenomenon. It was the painstaking practice we had done together in therapy prior to this session, which consisted of session after session untangling my feeling of shame from all my other feelings, creating new healthier neural pathways to replace the old trauma pathways, and growing my self-worth. All the practice we had previously done with shame and my self-worth had given me a set of tools I was familiar with, so when life presented this new situation where shame and unworthiness were triggered, I was able to process it and overcome the trigger.

What made this session remarkable, was when I overcame the trigger of shame and unworthiness, I was able to connect with and integrate into my life unconditional love for my new baby. At the time of this session, I had just given birth to my first baby, so everything in my body, mind and spirit were primed toward protecting, caring for, keeping alive, and nurturing my newborn baby. You can imagine how surprising and perplexed I felt when the old feelings of shame and unworthiness had surfaced, causing me to feel so uncomfortable with my baby needing me and loving me! I felt profoundly unworthy of her love—the shame was acute. Even now while writing this, I can sense the feeling of shame in my body like a hand pressing hard against my chest, a stone dropping in my stomach, and hands tight around my neck restricting my voice. But something new and wonderful happened in this session, that shined a very bright light and helped me move out of sorrow to—unconditional love for my baby. Deep within my being, something very maternal overpowered that force of shame. My baby was much more important than the grip shame had on me and the stories it told me about myself. It didn't matter if I felt unworthy; what mattered was being her mom and giving her everything she needed to flourish. The light of love was so bright, that the darkness of shame could not exist with it in the same moment, or at least was greatly minimized for the moment. When that pure, selfless love came into my being and I connected with it, my heart opened and shame released its hold. I was free to love my new baby, and free to allow my new baby to love me. Becoming a parent truly propelled my own personal healing, and I would often return to this unconditional love for my children in my recovery as time went on to redirect myself out of depression."

Baby Blues: Lessons Learned

What are the main messages that we can draw from this session and our analysis of it? Below we describe three prominent therapeutic processes we use as interventions to work with brain systems: Activating and Facilitating, Differentiating, and Go the Other Way. Each is useful in its own right, and they are more effective when used together.

All three of these processes are most effective, however, when employed within a strong Therapeutic Attachment Relationship (Chapter 5). Albert used his assertive emotional connection with Ann as an active agent empowering his interventions to reveal and to activate her problematic brain systems. Albert actively projected caring, using not only his words, but also his eyes and his body language. The emotional power of this relationship helps the therapist bring sometimes counterintuitive emotional constraints out into the open.

Ann's visceral experience of shame, fear, and grief, for example, stood out in marked contrast to her genuine connection with and care for her baby daughter. Ann discovered something unexpected about her inner workings that she did not know, and that was the opposite of what she believed about herself and her intentions. These reactions of her BrainMind were counterintuitive, maladaptive, and irrational. She was in a state of what we call Static Contradiction (Chapter 3). From past dysfunctional emotional learning, her different brain systems were in a tug-of-war with each other, resulting in emotional gridlock and leaving her feeling baffled and stuck. How do we go about getting someone like Ann unstuck?

PSYCHOPHYSIOLOGICAL PHENOMENA: THE TRANSPIRING PRESENT MOMENT

Ann's case gives an example of how we identify brain systems that are creating problems for the patient, and the way we recognize which brain systems may be constraining or entangled with others. Therapeutic interventions can be more precise and effective when you pay close attention to subtle observable cues that you can read in your patient. We were able to identify Ann's relevant brain systems not just from her words, but also from her body language: tears, nausea, looking disgusted or surprised, looking at Albert sideways, and then a strengthening voice.

Psychophysiological phenomena are observable physical movements and behaviors that arise from the activations of distinct neural circuits and brain systems. These kinds of cues and shifts provide visible evidence of activations of conscious and nonconscious neural circuits in response to your interventions. Common examples are facial and mouth movements, tone of voice, eye contact, tears, and body posture. Different brain systems have distinct psychophysiological signatures. For example, the Assertive brain system empowers an erect physical posture and a stronger, emphatic voice. Chapter 14 discusses psychophysiological phenomena in greater detail.

Attention to these phenomena could help you discover immediate empirical evidence of your patient's transpiring responses to therapeutic interventions. The psychophysiological phenomena you are observing could come from two sources. One source is sensory information coming in from the body at this transpiring moment in time, and the other is emotional processing from previous learning or trauma.

We use the term *transpiring* to refer exclusively to phenomena that arise from activations that initially start in the peripheral nervous system in response to the environment. If those activations are strong, they will be processed in the primary-level brain systems (see Figure 1.2). And if the activations of the Primaries are strong enough, then they will also be processed by the secondary-level brain systems. All of this processing occurs nonconsciously. If the activations are stronger still, they can pass a threshold to be processed within the tertiary-level brain systems. They may become conscious at that point. We use the phrase Transpiring Present Moment to draw attention to the spontaneous, present-moment emotional and physical responses that are transpiring in response to the therapist and therapeutic process

We distinguish transpiring phenomena (arising from the peripheral nervous system) from psychophysiological phenomena that originate at the secondary

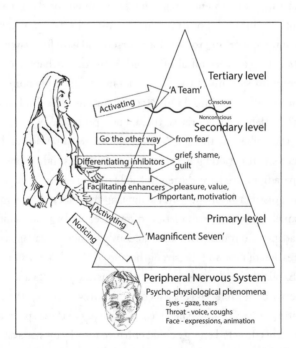

Figure 2.1: Psychophysiological Phenomena in the Transpiring Present Moment

level of emotional processing. The latter phenomena may arise from baseline emotional tendencies such as a mood, previous implicit learning, trauma history, and/or recent events. For example, your patient may come to the session in tears about a fight with their spouse. These tears are psychophysiological phenomena that come from a mix of sources. They might come from emotions of anger, frustration, fear, grief, shame, or impotence. You did not cause your patient to cry, and the tears did not originate in your office. These are not considered Transpiring Present Moment psychophysiological phenomena (Figure 2.1).

Activating and Facilitating

Activating refers to the specific and precise use of verbal and nonverbal (embodied) interventions to arouse one or more neural circuits or brain systems. Activating mobilizes the system to utilize its wisdom, energy, and processing capabilities. Activating also tests the functioning of a distinct circuit or system. For example, responses could be hyperactive, moderate, or hypoactive. Activating also describes our intentions to encourage the development of the innate capacities of our patient's BrainMind. For example, the way Albert began Ann's session— "We can see you are working to care for yourself and care for Dawn"—is part of an intervention we call the Initial Directed Activation (Chapter 6). Identifying the operative brain systems through psychophysiological phenomena holds the key to making an effective Initial Directed Activation. This kind of intervention is designed to initiate a collaborative therapeutic process.

Facilitating describes the therapist's ongoing directed attention and energy used to possibly increase functioning in distinct neural circuits and/or brain systems. In the CIMBS paradigm, we have chosen to Facilitate the resources and motivational energy of each distinct brain system. Facilitating harnesses the energy of specific systems; a small amount of stimulation often releases large amounts of energy. Facilitating adaptive circuits will simultaneously inhibit maladaptive neural circuits. The creation of new and the strengthening of already present neural circuits takes time. Explicitly Facilitating impoverished neural circuits and brain systems is not easy because they tend to resist such effort (Grawe, 2007). We capitalize the terms Activating or Facilitating when we are referring to these specific therapeutic interventions. This directed energy could enhance the circuit's or system's capacity to be more effective in performing its functions. Those interventions could help override the maladaptive shame, anxiety, fear, and so on, right there in front of your and (more importantly) your patient's eyes, as you saw happening with Ann's shame and fear. This ability is reproducible, and our trainees have found it very useful in their therapies, because it helps to override the patient's defenses and resistances without having to wrestle with them, thereby saving time and energy.

Differentiating

Differentiating refers to dynamic therapeutic processes that enable the therapist and patient to see and experience the distinct nature of one or more neural circuits and/or brain systems. Differentiating is especially important when one brain system is entangled or hyperconnected with another (see Chapter 7). For example, in Ann's case, the Shame and Fear brain systems were hyperconnected with the Care brain system. You saw how Albert was Differentiating those brain systems in an experiential way. Differentiating includes training distinct emotional and physiological neural circuits that are stimulated at this moment. This is akin to working with your trainer to isolate specific muscle groups to enhance your fitness. Differentiating also refers to mindful collaborative mental states of curiosity, seeking, and multiple awarenesses. Differentiating is essential in order to access the unique power and information of each brain system. The processes of differentiating are particularly important in mindful learning (Langer, 2016). We explore several approaches to differentiating conscious brain systems in Chapter 8 and in nonconscious brain systems in Chapter 11.

Go the Other Way

Go the Other Way refers to a process in which the therapist actively focuses attention on the patient's present-moment capabilities and competencies rather than on their distress or symptoms. These important interventions are often counterintuitive to both the patient and therapist. But setting aside the pain of past trauma and seeking instead to locate and strengthen adaptive brain system capabilities and turn them into competencies helps patients get unstuck.

For example, when Ann stated, "I feel nausea," Albert responded, "How wonderful that you are *aware* of feeling nauseated." Again, when Ann said, "I feel nausea and want to run away," Albert replied, "How wonderful that you are being aware of the feelings of nausea and running away. You are *aware* of these feelings and you are *not* running away. *You are being capable* of being aware." Albert placed his focus on the competence of the Awareness brain system rather than the distress of the nausea. This therapeutic paradigm prioritized activating and differentiating the competences of Ann's Care and Connection brain systems rather than trying to directly remediate her shame, fear, and grief. We explain and illustrate Go the Other Way in depth in Chapter 4 and throughout the book.

RESILIENT BRAIN SYSTEMS AND FAIL-SAFE COMPLEX NETWORKS

Ann's case illustrates how, when brain systems can be influenced to work together and become integrated, the patient immediately benefits. The fundamental strategies of CIMBS seek to enable these abilities. Albert helped Ann to integrate her Care and Awareness brain systems, so that she was able to begin overcoming the constraints of Shame and Fear that were troubling her. The next several sessions helped her consolidate the differentiations of her Care and Connection brain systems from her Shame, Fear, and Grief brain systems. Albert also continued Activating, Facilitating, Differentiating, and Integrating Ann's Seeking, Motivation, Authority, Agency, and Assertive brain systems. Working to Activate and Differentiate these brain systems has the goal of improving their resiliency. And when multiple resilient brain systems become integrated, they can form a Fail-Safe Complex Network.

In the following sections, we explore the principles of developing resilient brain systems and Fail-Safe (emotional) Networks. Utilizing these principles can help you and your patient access the innate competencies of multiple distinct brain systems operating simultaneously. Each of the brain systems has innate wisdom and generates energy, power, and drive to meet our needs to survive and thrive (Panksepp & Biven, 2012). When we tap into multiple brain systems, even more energy is available for change. Your potential as a person and as a therapist can be enhanced as you focus on the presence and importance of multiple brain systems. We explore other underlying principles of this paradigm in Chapter 3.

Resilient Brain Systems

We would all like to feel better, be happy, and have better relationships, fulfilled lives, and an internal sense of well-being. Those qualities are observable and even palpable in our friends or patients. From a brain systems perspective, those qualities result when differentiated brain systems are resilient and functioning optimally. We tend to think that those qualities are a function of circumstance, good fortune, and real effort. But those qualities are best achieved when we have resilient brain systems that are flexibly interwoven (wired together) and integrated with each other.

For example, when the Care brain system is strong, differentiated, and integrated with other systems, it will empower your patient to pursue their deep desire for care, no matter what kinds of trauma they have faced in the past. Building resilient brain systems helps your patient interrupt or override trauma-based symptoms and patterns of behavior.

A resilient brain system enables a person to move through the world with more focus and energy to prosper. This brain system is functioning at its best and will continue to improve as a result of further experiential emotional learning. It will get stronger in the gym of life. Your patients can then keep their focus, even in the midst of multiple external stressors and internal stressors such as anxieties, defenses, and grief. Facilitating the development of resilient brain systems could harness various forms of neuroplasticity to increase the efficiency and efficacy of your therapy.

In contrast, a nonresilient brain system can easily become overwhelmed or overreactive. Those reactions can lead to a cascade of physiological stress responses. For example, when a post-traumatic stress disorder patient hears a loud noise, his reactive Fear brain system might trigger a shutdown of other brain systems (Figure 10.9). His overreaction might prevent his Awareness, Safe, or Connection brain systems from moderating his terror reaction. He will not be able to discern that the noise was a car backfiring and not a source of danger.

Resilient brain systems ideally possess the following characteristics:

- They are highly developed and distinct.
- They are capable, reliable, and competent.
- They process large amounts of energy and information without getting overwhelmed, triggered, or shut down.
- They operate smoothly, independently, and autonomously even in times of crisis.
- They are differentiated from other systems and do not depend on other networks to function well.
- They can generate large amounts of energy.
- They have well-developed positive feedback loops to sustain life-enhancing activations.

• They access evolved natural wisdom and are continually learning
and developing.

How do we build resilient brain systems? The simple answer is, observe clues
from Activating one of the brain systems, name that brain system out loud, and
consistently repeat the activation. This requires being explicit and repetitive.
Let's look at it more slowly using the clinical example of Ann to illustrate these
concepts and interventions.

We use the term *explicit* in two distinct ways. One form refers to interventions that explicitly label the brain system or the intention of the therapeutic
intervention. For example, "Together we can care for you in your struggle."
The other form refers to two different kinds of stored learning: implicit and
explicit. Implicit learned memory develops before birth and is mostly nonconscious. Explicit (declarative) learned memories are conscious, and they become
available later (about age 3), after the hippocampus develops sufficiently to install
conscious memories.

Albert first observed that Ann's Care brain system was having difficulty processing the flow of emotional energy and information. Second, he named the
Care brain system out loud to her, saying, "Yes! I care for you. I am caring for
you." He made explicit assertions about the brain system he observed, such as,
"Together we can care for you in your struggle." He also used his body language
for emphasis. Finally, he kept repeating the activation of the brain system. He
kept mobilizing her capacity for collaboration with such invitations as, "Do you
want to allow yourself to be loved by us, just at this little moment in time?" "Do
you want to continue receiving our caring?" And he also reinforced her progress:
"Well done! It is hard work and you are doing it. You are being capable of staying
here receiving my caring. You are being capable."

To an outside observer, this process can look repetitive, but the patient experiences each repetition differently, as the activated brain system becomes stronger and more resilient. Even if the intervention is identical, it is being directed
at a BrainMind that is constantly changing. It is hard to appreciate the nonconscious learning that is taking place under the surface. It takes time and practice
to trust that learning (Chapters 8 and 11).

At the end of the session, you can discuss with your patient what emotional
learning they would like to take home and practice frequently before the next
session. This is similar to the exercises your physical therapist gives you to

perform after your treatment to further your progress. These new neural circuits will need outside repetition and reinforcement, or they will be deleted (pruned) by the brain when it does its usual housekeeping during sleep.

This repetition keeps activating and facilitating that specific brain system. As you saw, this process of activating Ann's Care brain system uncovered emotions of shame, embarrassment, grief, pain, guilt, and fear. Most of those inhibiting emotions were previously nonconscious. The contrast between her adaptive maternal care for her infant—plus her natural care for herself—and the shame, embarrassment, grief, pain, guilt, and fear provided Ann with novel emotional learning. Her Care brain system was becoming more capable and distinct, so that it could tap into evolutionary wisdom and generate more energy to override the shame, embarrassment, grief, pain, guilt, and fear emotions. And that is how a brain system becomes resilient.

Observing and Facilitating Competence: Become an External Generator

As Albert sustained the activations of Ann's Care brain system, he was being what we call an *external generator*. The adaptive energy generated by the activation of any brain system will be transient. If we do not intervene, the patient's brief surge of emotion and wisdom will dissipate in a matter of moments. This is consistent with the second law of thermodynamics, which states that the natural tendency of any isolated closed system is to degenerate into a more disordered state. So we invite you to help the patient to step over their natural tendency to behave in familiar ways, and to override that pattern. Your precisely focused energy can keep Activating and Facilitating, again and again, a brain system that would otherwise come to rest and lose its power. You can direct the energy of your curiosity (Seeking), delight (Play), and Care brain systems to keep stimulating their activations in your patient.

As Albert kept praising Ann's progress, he became an external generator that kept sending energy into her isolated brain system, which would otherwise have wound down. With time and practice, that system will become stronger and start to develop internal positive feedback loops, so it becomes self-sustaining. Self-sustaining resilient brain systems are naturally competent. They will keep evolving throughout the life span, developing even greater competence. For example, patients with depression are unable to sustain positive activations such as play, so they do not experience delight even when they are doing adaptive things in their lives. The therapist's presence as an external generator can help patients experience the pleasure of play, feel delight, and discover how play can become an important part of their life. Play will become an emotional competency and a source of connection, discovery, or safety.

Fail-Safe Complex Network

The Complex Integration of Multiple Brain Systems means that several or more systems are independently interconnected. Our basic premise is that a network made up of multiple resilient and integrated brain systems can process large amounts of emotional energy and information. Using an electric power grid analogy, these systems all function in parallel (see Figure 2.2). When one or more of these brain systems shuts down or gets triggered, the other integrated brain systems are able to assume the load of energy and information. Simple networks that are wired together in series (see Figure 2.3) will shut down if one of its systems fails (think old-fashioned Christmas lights). The Complex Integration of Multiple Brain Systems can provide your patients with a Fail-Safe Complex Network.

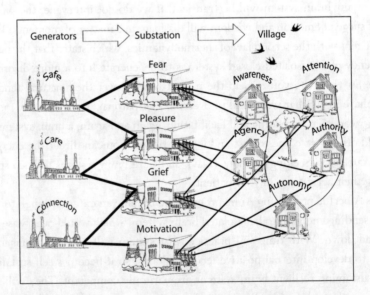

Figure 2.2: Three Levels of Mental Energy and Information Flowing in Parallel in a Fail-Safe Complex Network With Parallel Processing

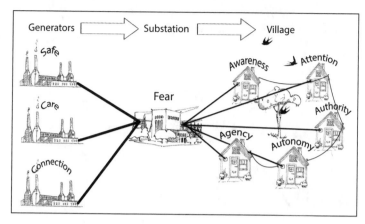

Figure 2.3: Mental Energy and Information Flowing in Series, in a Network Vulnerable to Interruption

An example of a nonintegrated network—one that does not have multiple resilient networks—could be a depressed patient who chronically feels bad about himself and his life. He is unable to do things that could help him feel better or move forward in his life. Let's look at his functioning from a brain systems perspective. He does not have access to his Authority brain system, because his Fear brain system is often triggered, so he does not know that he is capable (Figure 2.4). He does not have access to his Autonomy brain system, so he is constantly trying to meet other people's needs and expectations, disregarding his own needs. His Assertive brain system is so entangled with fear and shame that his natural assertive impulses are shut down before they even reach consciousness. He has difficulty experiencing his Play or Connection brain systems.

According to chaos theory, the most stable network systems are those that are differentiated, open, and connected. That is, various parts of the system are quite different, but they are all connected to each other and open to input (Siegel, 1999).

Our nervous system evolved independent brain systems to help us survive in a wide range of life circumstances. Imagine a soldier in battle who is terrified by all of the danger around him. When he sees that his comrade has been wounded on the battlefield, he chooses to step into increasing personal danger to rescue his comrade. His commitment to his squad, his higher cause, and his care for his friend give him the courage to override the terror that would otherwise compel

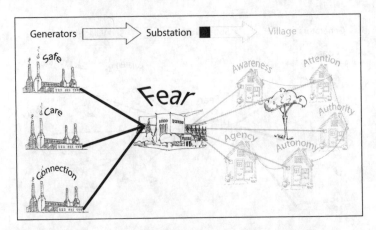

Figure 2.4: Network Shut Down by Fear Reaction

him to shut down, freeze, or flee. His Connection and Care brain systems are able to override his Fear brain system.

A Fail-Safe Complex Network includes one or more of the following characteristics:

- It contains multiple independent integrated resilient brain systems.
- Each system stands on its own and is ready to activate in an instant.
- Emotional tasks are handled simultaneously, differentially, and in parallel by each distinct brain system.
- Each system is flexible and able to support other systems through positive feedback mechanisms to sustain adaptive responses. Positive feedback loops sustain and add energy to the activation of another system.
- The systems operate out of awareness, do not depend on conscious management, and yet readily respond to conscious choices.
- The network is dynamic, free to learn in all circumstances and handle a unique crisis in a novel way.

Emotional states can monopolize other brain resources (LeDoux, 1996). In the presence of a threatening stimulus, the Fear brain system can take over all the other systems. Survival trumps all other functions. Due to previous trauma or neglect, your patient's hyperactive Fear, Shame, and/or Grief brain systems can dominate their existence. The patient can thus become stuck, feeling anxious, unworthy, or depressed. In the example of Baby Blues, Ann's Shame, Guilt, and Grief brain systems threatened to take over her life. This conflict caused her to feel exhausted, depressed, and unable to function normally. She could have become seriously depressed without our interventions. Such a depression would have interfered with the development of a secure attachment with her infant.

Our clinical example illustrated how Ann and Albert collaborated to activate and facilitate her Care, Connection, Authority, and Awareness brain systems. She was able to intentionally override her resistance. She modulated her Fear, Shame, and Guilt brain systems. Their effort enabled her to interrupt her slide into depression and to move forward in her emotional development. She took charge rather than being controlled by her fear, shame, or grief.

Each resilient brain system in a Fail-Safe Complex Network can function smoothly on its own, even in a crisis. The Complex Integration of Multiple Brain Systems provides each of us with multiple backup systems to see us through any stressful situation. This flexibility and complexity provide us with a Fail-Safe Network of brain systems. Our patients become able to complete therapy trusting their own competence. They will continue to face problems and stresses, but now they have access to their power, flexibility, and internal wisdom to learn, change, and ultimately thrive. In the following chapters, we illustrate various approaches and interventions to help you and your patient develop a Fail-Safe Network of brain systems.

CHAPTER 3

Research and Principles

··

"UNWORTHY"

Some years before meeting Beatriz and developing the practice of CIMBS, Albert made a number of surprising discoveries with a series of patients. The following patient we will call Patrick is a composite of several of those discoveries. These discoveries provided a big impetus in the direction that their therapy would one day grow.

Patrick had struggled with depression for 20 years. At his first session, Albert sat directly in front of him with a focused but soft eye gaze. The intensity of this gaze seemed to heighten the anxiety that he could see Patrick was clearly already feeling. Albert began by asking Patrick directly whether he was willing to work together with him on his depression. He responded with ambivalence. Albert continued, "I welcome your ambivalence and your anxiety. We can work together on that if you are willing."

Patrick was able to describe a range of his reactions to these invitations. He said he felt a "wall inside himself" that he never knew was there. He said he was surprised at his strong resistance. He found it difficult to open up and be authentic. Albert asked again, "Are you willing to let go of your wall, even just for a moment?" Patrick said that it made him feel fearful and unsteady, but he agreed to cooperate in managing his fear and lowering his wall. When Patrick briefly mentioned his relationship with his partner, Albert gently steered the conversation back to his relationship with him instead. Albert pressed him to keep his awareness in the present moment and not let his attention wander from the immediacy of how the two of them were relating.

Just then, Patrick's energy shifted dramatically. He spoke of the pain of his isolation and inability to trust anyone. He uncovered some anger. "It feels weird—I am sitting here, just talking about my anger. Usually I get really mad and act it out." More emotions began to pour out: gratitude, sadness, and then painful sobbing. Albert pointed out the very close connection he was having with him and with himself.

Patrick suddenly felt very intense nausea, as though he would vomit, and started looking for the wastepaper basket. He spontaneously said, "I am *unlovable and unworthy.*" Albert was caught off guard and troubled by his intense nausea. He had never seen anything like that before and didn't know where it had come from. He just continued offering the positive feelings of care and connection, and eventually Patrick felt calmer. Patrick expressed surprise at the way he resisted the intimacy he actually longed for. At the end of the session he commented, "I didn't know that I didn't know how unworthy I feel inside." At the second session he reported that he was exhausted after the first session, but that he also was inexplicably improved.

For Albert, in retrospect, this was a Eureka! moment. At first he did not understand what had provoked the sudden nausea, nor did several colleagues with whom he shared the video recording of the session. None of them had ever seen such a visceral reaction, and they had no explanation. It was Beatriz who helped Albert realize that his practice had taken him and his patient into unknown territory. This was no longer the dynamic short-term psychotherapy that he and his colleagues were studying in Montreal.

MAKING SENSE OF THE COUNTERINTUITIVE

This session told us, in the early days of our collaboration, that even before we knew it, we were already on the road less traveled. It woke us up to how our practice had already departed from the mainstream, and it showed us that we were encountering a range of therapeutic experiences that we knew nothing about. Years of research following that evolved into the paradigm of CIMBS that we describe in this book. If we saw Patrick today, we would have a much clearer understanding of where his nausea came from. Albert was using what we call today the Therapeutic Attachment Relationship, and he was concentrating on the Transpiring Present Moment. He was activating several brain systems, including Awareness and Authority, and he was helping Patrick turn hidden capabilities into competencies. These are powerful instruments and can release intense reactions. When Albert saw his patient Ann (Chapter 2) 10 years later, he was prepared when she also had nausea in response to loving her daughter and feeling care for herself. Over years of experience, we have developed a wide range of additional therapeutic principles. In this chapter we offer these principles to our fellow therapists to help them in similar situations.

WHAT MAKES PSYCHOTHERAPY WORK

Psychotherapy is an interpersonal treatment based on psychological principles, with a trained therapist and a patient who is seeking help. Therapy is (ideally) individualized for this patient and their problems. There are common rituals and procedures used by all psychotherapists. Examples include reducing the sense of alienation by developing an alliance, maintaining the patient's hope for improvement, providing new learning experiences, arousing the patient's emotions, and enhancing the patient's sense of self-efficacy (Wampold & Imel, 2015).

The relative efficacy and success of therapy depends on a mix of three important components: (1) patient factors, (2) therapist factors, and (3) treatment methods (Lambert, 1992). Approximately 50% of the explainable variance in psychotherapy outcomes is attributable to patient factors such as nature of symptoms, reactance/resistance level, stages of change, and coping styles. Thirty percent of therapy outcomes depend on therapist factors, such as the person of the therapist, ability to customize treatments to patients' particulars, and the therapeutic relationship, such as alliance, collaboration, goal consensus, empathy, cohesion, positive regard, and attunement. Fifteen percent of outcomes result from the specific treatment method (Norcross, et al., 2009). Clearly the therapeutic relationship and the ability of the therapist to fine-tune the therapy to the patient factors produce the most robust therapeutic benefits.

This chapter focuses on the results of our empirical research to improve our therapeutic efficacy. Much of that research focused on how to better utilize patient and therapist factors in therapy. We describe how we fine-tuned our treatment methods to adapt to the patient factors that are present at this moment in the therapy session. Along that journey, we uncovered a number of neurobiological principles that have come to guide our understanding and direct our therapeutic processes. Last, we explore the therapist's experiences of utilizing these principles and approaches.

Trial and Error Detection

We started our research 20 years ago to learn about ways to improve our skills and our therapeutic process. Our first step was to explore our therapeutic errors. What kind of errors were we making and in what context? Examples of errors in this context are: misattunement—not accurately reading the patient's emotional state; too narrow a perspective—focusing on one emotion and neglecting others that are also present; or getting entangled with old habits and missing opportunities to provide new learning. We undertook a practical and empirical process of studying video recordings of our psychotherapy sessions. We did this alone, together, and with colleagues. We often saw the same errors. We made a wide range of observations. What was distinct about our approach to this research was that we worked very slowly. We would look at a 20-second vignette five times in a row. Slow motion enabled us to observe phenomena that were invisible at normal speed. We made precise transcripts to tease apart small details. The elimination of sound reduced the distractions of the verbal content and helped us to focus on nonverbal psychophysiological phenomena.

Expert musicians, athletes, surgeons, and therapists deliberately practice and train their skills throughout their career (Rousmaniere, 2017). If you want to improve your skills as a musician, athlete, surgeon, or therapist, it helps to be able to detect your errors.

We discovered that we were often missing nonverbal clues and cues. These errors were missed opportunities. Clues were often psychophysiological phenomena such as breath holding, hand movements, eye gaze, facial movements, and so on. Some clues were obvious, and others were subtle. Beatriz saw some clues that Albert did not see, and vice versa. We realized that our minds deleted some clues because they made no sense. These errors were not mistakes or misperceptions; they were the result of insufficient training. We had not developed the necessary mental search patterns to see some clues that later became obvious with practice. A mental search pattern is how our BrainMind recognizes a word, object, or movement that we have seen before, and we can rapidly identify it. For example, you can see a red sphere and readily identify it as an apple rather than some other object such as a rubber ball.

The way that errors can be caused by the absence of search patterns was illustrated by Albert's sister, an aquatic research biologist. She used university students to help in her summer research projects studying underwater weevils (tiny insects, 3 mm long). In order to train them to count organisms, she gave them small containers of water with underwater plants and weevils. She asked them to count the weevils in each container. At first they could not find any. The error was their inability to see the weevils. She redirected them to go back and look again and for longer periods of time. After many trials over the course of three days, they finally had the ah-ha moment of seeing the weevils for the first time. Once they had developed the search pattern for the weevils, they were always able to see them, even the following summer.

Developing new search patterns became an exciting journey for us into an unknown jungle. We opened ourselves up to large amounts of information that we had been unable to see or value previously. We had never explored the jungle with this quality of curiosity, scientific intention, and willingness to be wrong. We trusted that if we kept looking, our minds would discover new things that we had never seen before. We discovered that what we had known and valued prior to this research was just the tip of the iceberg. The iceberg under the surface contains all the neural circuits and activations in the nonconscious Brain-Mind that we had not been able to see or appreciate previously (see Figure 1.4). In this context, a *neural circuit* is a series of neurons that operate together to perform a particular function, such as the knee-jerk reflex.

GATHERING DATA

We entered into a scientific exploration, gathering data. We found that the most useful and reliable data come from psychophysiological phenomena. These phenomena provide visual and auditory evidence of present-moment activations of nonconscious emotional circuits (reflexes, habits) and brain systems that are present in all mammals. The more we looked, the more data we uncovered, the more weevils we discovered. It is exciting to discover so much hidden in plain sight once you have developed a broader array of mental search patterns.

We found ourselves looking at the data from a variety of perspectives:

• The initial phenomena that reveal how the system is operating at baseline. For example, how rapidly is the patient breathing when we are sitting quietly together?

- The dynamic phenomena that respond to our interventions, such as when we ask the patient what they are experiencing and they hold their breath for a moment.
- Looking at the phenomena from the perspective of different brain systems. For example, we typically looked for evidence of how the Safe or Connection brain systems were functioning. Was the patient's change in breathing a result of feeling unsafe, or because of disorientation from the connection with the therapist, or both?

When we looked at the same phenomenon from different perspectives, we learned so much more. The principle of multiple brain systems grabbed us and would not let us go.

Sometimes the meaning of the data we gathered was obvious, but often it was not. We developed hypotheses to test our ideas about these phenomena: What caused the changes in breathing? What else had changed in the patient, and were the changes caused by our interventions? We experimented with a variety of interventions to test our hypotheses. The psychophysiological phenomena were the most reliable evidence of how the patient's BrainMind was responding to the interventions. For example, if we sensed that the patient felt unsafe, we tested that hypothesis explicitly: "To what extent do you feel safe right now?" Often the patient responded with a puzzled look, perhaps saying, "I think I am safe," with a quiet voice and constrained breathing. Their psychophysiology revealed nonconscious fear as their conscious mind declared they were not aware of any danger.

This research provided new information and different training for us as therapists. Looking at videos in slow motion is similar to playing scales on your musical instrument, kind of boring and enlightening at the same time. Gathering all these data helped us improve our therapeutic understanding of subtle phenomena that are transpiring all the time. Our intention was to use that information to be better able to fine-tune and customize our therapy to achieve successful outcomes.

PATIENT FACTORS

Recall that patient factors accounted for 50% of identifiable successful psychotherapy outcomes in multiple studies (Lambert, 1992). Examples of patient factors include self-awareness, motivation to change, fear, shame, cognitive limitations, psychosis, and personality patterns. Although these factors are not usually what patients complain of when they seek therapy, they can significantly affect the progress and success of therapy.

Patients come to therapy instead to address a behavioral presenting problem such as depression, panic attacks, chemical dependencies, or relationship difficulties. Often there are several presenting problems. Therapists sometimes limit their treatment to the presenting problems and miss out on many other therapeutic opportunities. The presenting problems can be viewed as the symptoms on the surface, the tip of the iceberg (Cozolino, 2016). We have found it useful to uncover the roots of the presenting problems that arise from the patient's nonconscious emotional learning. However, even more important are the discoveries of a patient's underlying capabilities and competencies (see Chapter 4), of which the patient has no awareness. These discoveries are also patient factors. Our successful treatment depends on gathering empirical information about these nonconscious capabilities as well as the patient's emotional constraints (recall Ann's inability to care for her infant in the Baby Blues case study in Chapter 2).

We don't view the constraints as psychological problems or pathology; we view them as normal developmental adaptations of a patient's BrainMind that helped them survive trauma and get along in their often difficult and/or traumatic early life. These adaptations are the nonconscious implicit learning contained in the secondary-level brain systems (Figure 1.2). In Chapter 1, we defined enhancing and inhibiting secondary-level brain systems, and explained how inhibitory systems could intervene to shield a patient from trauma or danger. But then in later life, when the original source of trauma or danger is far in the past, the same protective systems could constrain other brain systems and impede the patient from responding in a healthy and functional manner to new challenges of life. We can see that the constricted adaptions are in need of liberation (Siegel, 2010a).

For example, in the case study at the start of this chapter, Patrick developed a wall to protect himself. That was an adaptation to protect him from his intrusive and controlling mother. However, this protective wall prevented growth and making meaningful connections with others as well as taking in new relevant information. When we approach these adaptations without judgment, we can fine-tune our responses to these patient factors. Patrick's Fear brain system was slow to accept the safeness of this new connection with Albert. The therapist can adjust to this patient factor to fine-tune the therapy for a more successful outcome.

The principles, strategies, and knowledge of CIMBS can help you uncover patient factors that were previously hidden or invisible. We believe that working with conscious and nonconscious brain systems has enabled us to efficiently change patient factors and thus work directly with the most important component of successful psychotherapy outcomes. We will endeavor to highlight opportunities to discover and work directly with these factors in your patient throughout the book. We will repeat the use of the term *patient factors* to alert you to that perspective to enhance your own psychotherapy outcomes.

Static Contradiction

In our research, we have learned that some patients have constraints that operate like obstructions. For example, if the patient's Connection brain system is obstructed by the Shame brain system because of sexual abuse, then all attempts at connection will be blocked or obstructed at the nonconscious secondary level of emotional processing. In the example of Baby Blues, Ann was not able to appropriately care for and attach to her newborn infant. Her drive for Care and Connection clashed with her Fear, Shame, and Grief brain systems. Ann: "It feels wrong to love my baby! Weird; she loves me and I feel unworthy. I feel bad and I put her down. This a very strange experience!" Here the inhibition was so strong that it contradicted the underlying emotional and neurobiological drive to connect.

To get a picture of how this might occur in the BrainMind, imagine your right arm and hand pushing against your left arm and hand with full force, and your left hand and arm pushing back with full force as well (Figure 3.1). Energy is spent and nothing moves. It remains static as both forces nullify each other. We refer to this clashing of brain systems as a Static Contradiction. The Shame brain system is contradicting the Connection brain system. The Shame brain system is unable to appropriately modulate the Connection brain system, so no work can be done and no learning can take place. We believe that the constant isometric clash of these contradictory forces creates psychic pain, panic, depression, grief, anxiety attacks, and so on. Perhaps multiple Static Contradictions between the Primaries and the Secondaries lead to the structural problems that can cause personality disorders, core shame, chronic depression, and other mental disorders.

Static Contradictions are patient factors that tend to become entrenched and resist change. Here is where therapists often get stuck and feel frustrated.

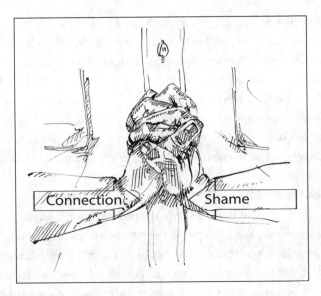

Figure 3.1: Static Contradiction

Their static nature has become a kind of painful equilibrium of opposing forces. Our BrainMind can create distortions and even delusions to maintain a congruence with the present constraints or contradictions. It takes carefully focused energy to intervene successfully to take the patient out of this nonconscious, painful, congruent equilibrium. After years of trial and error and careful research, we have arrived at several practical approaches to address these Static Contradictions and dislodge this impasse (see Chapters 3–6). It is possible to change patient factors effectively and efficiently. Often when we show the video of a session to the referring psychiatrist or therapist who had struggled to help the patient previously, they exclaim, "This is not the same patient! She seems so easy!"

Therapists can become intimidated by the patient's obsessive ruminations, ambivalence, and high levels of anxiety or emotionality. The nonconscious shame and fear can suck all the energy out of the room. Therapists can become discouraged, angry, or confused. It is difficult to direct the therapeutic process when we are overwhelmed with these patient factors. The key here is to bring these nonconscious patient factors out into the open where we can both address them together. We propose that you work with these factors directly, rather than trying to work around them. Although this is uncomfortable for both patients and therapists at first, it will change the nature of your patient's constraining emotional patterns. It is possible that you can avoid getting stuck with your patient's constraints and uncover resources that were invisible before. At the same time (and this is exciting!), this opens up the process to reveal the patient's previously undiscovered competencies and capabilities.

Let's look at the example of Patrick to illustrate how patient factors are revealed. His resistance (Fear and Shame) to being open and authentic (Connection) came to the surface as the session unfolded. He was able to develop greater self-awareness (Awareness, Attention) of his defensive wall, and he was able to release the constraints of some of his underlying Grief. He discovered his nonconscious resistance (Shame) to the intimacy (Care, Connection) he seeks (Assertive, Agency), and he viscerally released emotions of nausea and tears (Shame, Grief).

Our active interest in embracing the full range of patient factors has enhanced our effectiveness and made our job more interesting and engaging. We encourage you to continue to use your own training and therapeutic method as you experiment with these different approaches to addressing patient factors.

THERAPIST FACTORS

Patients seek out a therapist to get help with the struggles they have in their lives and within themselves. The therapist provides an emotionally charged, confiding relationship in a healing setting. Outcome research indicates that the therapeutic relationship is the most important treatment instrument that the therapist has to offer (Cozolino, 2016; Miller & Rollnick, 2013; Norcross et al., 2009).

Therapist factors refers to the person of the therapist, the real relationship between the patient and therapist, and the manner in which the therapist utilizes the therapeutic relationship to heal the patient and address the symptoms. The research of Norcross and Miller lists the therapist factors found in successful outcomes: empathy, genuineness, respect, openness, congruence, collaboration, alliance, goal consensus, cohesion, and positive regard.

In our research, we experimented with a variety of approaches to enhance the therapist's ability to be a more effective presence in the treatment process. We have found that the most effective therapeutic learning takes place in the present-moment therapeutic relationship. We have developed a combination of elements that come together under the heading of the Therapeutic Attachment

Relationship, which we explore more fully in Chapter 5. These elements seek to help the therapist more actively participate in the Activating, Facilitating, and Integrating of the patient's emotional experiential learning in the sessions. The Therapeutic Attachment Relationship activates the attachment brain systems that can release neurotransmitters such as oxytocin, endogenous opioids, and serotonin. Those neurotransmitters can help calm the Fear, Shame, Grief, and/ or Guilt brain systems that might immobilize the patient in a freeze, flight, or fight reaction. "Even though psychotherapy may appear to focus on thoughts, . . . the aim of treatment is to positively change the patient's affective experience" (Panksepp & Biven, 2012).

Deliberate practice is more important than new knowledge to improve therapist factors. Remember how much time it takes to develop new search patterns. For the past 10 years we have been developing a variety of training approaches to teach therapists how to be more effective. New therapists are procedure oriented and want to be told what to do. Experienced therapists are more comfortable with the ambiguity of the process. We all need help learning to trust ourselves, our patient, and the process (see Trust the Process below). Two examples of this deliberate practice are working with a mentor or training group to practice new interventions, and reviewing video recordings of treatment sessions. The therapist factors that come up most often in our training groups are not trusting that they know what to do, and being afraid to be outside of their own comfort zone. The therapist's hesitation is often the limiting treatment factor rather than the patient's resistance or defensiveness. Anything you do to address your therapist factors will add to your success with whatever therapeutic method or techniques you utilize.

TREATMENT STRATEGIES

Providing treatment and developing treatment strategies are more complicated in psychotherapy than other forms of medical care. The nature of the dysfunctions in the patient's BrainMind can be difficult to discover. The dysfunctions of your patient's BrainMind are often multiple and contradictory. Therefore it is challenging to choose treatments that can address these complications. By contrast, when a patient arrives for urgent medical care with pain in the belly, the physician makes an assessment about the nature of the dysfunction that is causing the patient's pain. They make a diagnosis and consider treatment to resolve the dysfunction. If the diagnosis is an infected appendix, the treatment strategy is usually surgical removal of the appendix.

The CIMBS paradigm contains a wide array of treatments and treatment strategies designed to enhance adaptive functioning and address underlying dysfunctions. *Strategy* refers to a plan to achieve one or more goals under conditions of uncertainty. One of the strategies is to discern the functioning of distinct brain systems in order to make more precise assessments of the inner workings of your patient's BrainMind. Those assessments of the functioning of distinct brain systems will enable you to customize your treatment to this patient at this moment in time. The most important distinction in our treatment and treatment strategies is that we invite you to focus most of your energy and time Facilitating the functionality of each of your patient's brain systems.

The treatment strategies of this paradigm seek to harness the full range of the patient's conscious and nonconscious brain systems in order to change the neural structures in their BrainMind. You can accomplish this primarily by Facilitating and Differentiating adaptive (positive, self-affirming) neural circuits and brain systems. These treatments need to be experiential, embodied, and repeated many times in order for them to develop new adaptive neural circuits. We know that Facilitating adaptive circuits will also inhibit maladaptive (negative, destructive, toxic, dysfunctional) neural circuits (Grawe, 2007). This combination of Facilitating and Differentiating multiple brain systems and inhibiting the constraints of maladaptive circuits develops resilience in each system. The simultaneous facilitation of multiple systems leads to integration, self-organization, increased complexity, and Fail-Safe Complex Networks. The structural changes to the BrainMind from these treatments have been confirmed by multiple brain scan studies (Grawe, 2007; Schwartz & Begley, 2002; Davidson, 2012).

In the following section, we list and explore the neurobiological principles that we have found most useful in formulating our therapeutic strategies, and in guiding the tasks and interventions to implement those strategies. We introduce basic therapeutic approaches we have developed to apply these principles in psychotherapy. Utilizing any of these principles can become a source of guidance with your patients. Chapters 7 through 15 explore additional treatment strategies in greater depth such as:

- Activating, Facilitating, and Differentiating specific brain systems (Chapters 8, 11).

- Leveraging the competencies of underdeveloped and/or previously unknown brain systems (Chapters 8, 11).
- Simultaneously Activating and Integrating multiple brain systems to harness the multidimensionality of the BrainMind (Chapters 9, 12).
- Releasing the BrainMind's capacity for complexity and self-organization (Chapters 9, 12).
- Utilizing the evolved wisdom of the secondary-level brain systems such as Motivation, Value, and Grief (Chapter 13).

PRINCIPLES AND APPROACHES

We have used our study of neurobiology research to formulate a number of what we call therapeutic principles that guide our evaluations and interventions. Each principle contains knowledge that could empower successful changes for your patient and your therapeutic process. We have tested these principles hundreds of times with a wide spectrum of patients. We have found them to be valid and reliable. These principles have enabled us to deeply trust ourselves, our patients, and our therapeutic processes. They can also feel like an internal gyroscope that helps us keep our balance in the (sometimes) stormy seas of therapy. Since these principles are based in neurobiology, they apply to all humans at all times. These principles are informed by the recent neuroscience research of Damasio, Davidson, LeDoux, Panksepp, Porges, Grawe, Siegel, and others.

We use the term *approaches* to refer to numerous interventions and interactions that we use to apply our principles to the therapeutic processes. Each of these approaches is a form of treatment. Therapeutic approaches also provide training for our patients. For example, we can train our patient's nonconscious capabilities by bringing them into explicitly into awareness: "What are you experiencing as you assert your want right now?" These approaches will be best illustrated by examples and clinical illustrations of actual transcripts of therapy sessions in subsequent chapters.

Principle 1: Multiple Distinct Brain Systems

Our nervous system is made up of a number of distinct emotional and nonemotional brain systems. Multiple brain systems provide us with specificity, flexibility, and reliability. There are at least 20 emotional brain systems that we consider relevant to psychotherapy. Accessing the presence of this spectrum of brain systems can provide you and your patient with many autonomous sources of energy, emotional wisdom, and paths to explore (see Figure 1.2).

Approaches: Activate specific brain systems; in the Baby Blues example, Albert kept focusing on Care and Seeking to mobilize those innate capabilities. Repeating and sustaining multiple brain systems.

Principle 2: Brain Systems Can Change and Adapt Appropriately

Healthy, functioning brain systems are open and balanced in relationship with each other. Open systems are flexible and can take in new learning (Siegel, 2007). They both operate in the present and have access to previous emotional learning. This knowledge can direct the therapist to test and observe which brain systems are open and which are closed. An open brain system is capable of learning and taking in new information. A closed brain system is unable to learn, inflexible and unchanging. You can also test the functional capacity of each system. For example, you can test whether the system is operating at partial or moderate capacity (see Chapter 7). Dysfunctional systems can be hyperactive, hypoactive, and/or hyperconnected. For example, a hyperactive system is one that does not downregulate appropriately when it is not needed. The Fear brain system is hyperactive in post-traumatic stress disorder (PTSD) patients. The patient overreacts to loud noises or other minor stresses.

Approaches: Test the operational capacity of the brain system by activating it explicitly. "Do you want us to care for you?" Keep stimulating systems that are slow to respond. Downregulate hyperactive systems; Differentiate entangled systems.

Principle 3: Resilient Brain Systems Are Powerful

As we outlined in Chapter 2, resilient brains systems are strong and flexible, and they can process large amounts amount of energy and information without getting overwhelmed, being triggered, or shutting down. When a brain system is resilient (for example, the Attention brain system), it can function smoothly on its own, even in a crisis. If your patient is getting emotionally overwhelmed, we can hypothesize that there are some brain systems that are not resilient. It is important not to underestimate the potential resilience of nonconscious brain systems.

Approaches: Develop resilient brain systems by Activating each brain system one by one. Uncover the competence of each system. Keep reinforcing each brain system until the patient develops their own positive internal positive feedback neural circuits.

Principle 4: Differentiated Brain Systems Process Energy and Information in Parallel

Each distinct brain system is capable of uniquely processing present-moment experience (Figure 2.2). In order for that to occur, each system needs to be differentiated from the others. Differentiated systems enable the patient to be present to a spectrum of emotions and respond choice-fully rather than being limited to an old reflexive reaction pattern. Differentiated systems retain their flexible functionality, no matter what the trauma has been. For example, the therapeutic relationship will differentially activate the Shame, Safe, Care, and Connection brain systems. In the clinical case study in Chapter 2, Ann was finally able to feel care and connection even as she was triggered with fear and shame.

Approaches: Differentiating occurs when the therapist isolates and exercises distinct neural circuits and brain systems. Differentiating changes the nervous system's previous emotional coordination patterns. Several types of differentiating are described in detail in Chapters 8 and 11.

Principle 5: Integrating Systems Can Release Self-Organizing System Capabilities

When two or more differentiated brain systems are activated simultaneously, they will naturally link together and operate in coordination with each other. This process of linkage between systems is called Integration. The Integration of differentiated systems is fundamental to releasing the BrainMind's capacity for self-organizing (Siegel, 1999). This is how we arrived at calling our therapeutic paradigm the Complex Integration of Multiple Brain Systems (CIMBS). In Chapter 2 we referred to the flexibility and complexity of multiple integrated resilient systems as a Fail-Safe Complex Network. This level of complexity can help your patients to pursue their deep desire for connection and to achieve the kind of stress tolerance, internal wisdom, creativity, and choices of which our BrainMinds are capable. This is especially important for patients who have suffered severe trauma or neglect. This could provide you with different approaches to working with trauma.

Approaches: Maintain and sustain the activations of multiple distinct systems in parallel.

Principle 6: Change Requires Energy

Therapeutic change requires work. Unless they are in crisis, our patients arrive in their usual equilibrium with patterns of defenses, behaviors, and coping mechanisms. A person in this kind of equilibrium tends to stay in the same state unless we exert focused energy to overcome their inertia. Where are we going to find the energy to do this work? The energy in our paradigm comes from two main sources:

- The brain systems: Each brain system is like a spring that generates its own energy flow. It is important to recognize that this energy is distinct from the emotional energy that arises from stories of the past, trauma, or recent events.
- The therapist: When we learn to channel our energy, it is powerful. Your focused energy (see Chapters 5 and 6) will potentiate change in your patients.

Approaches: Activating each brain system taps into the sources of energy that power the patient's BrainMind. Watching the body's psychophysiology will provide evidence of what is being uniquely experienced in the Transpiring Present Moment.

Principle 7: The Therapist Is an Effective Therapeutic Instrument

The therapist can use their energy to activate and reinforce the mobilization of the patient's brain systems. A careful focus on the Therapeutic Attachment Relationship will activate the nonconscious attachment brain systems: Safe, Care, and Connection. These activations will develop a strong alliance and uncover constraints from early life attachment neglect and trauma. The Therapeutic Attachment Relationship provides emotional regulation.

Approaches: CIMBS therapy is done almost exclusively within the Therapeutic Attachment Relationship.

Principle 8: Sustained Experiential Learning Changes the Structure of the Brain

Experience can change the brain, but neural circuits need to be active in order to change. Novel experiences change the brain faster due to the activation of multiple brain systems and the release of the neurotransmitter dopamine. In order to interrupt maladaptive patterns (triggers), we need to facilitate other adaptive patterns (Grawe, 2007). Repeated activations of related neural circuits gradually recruit adjacent neurons to enhance that circuit. Brains have a strong confirmation bias; that means that the brain will tend to revert to established patterns of thinking and feeling unless actively retrained. New circuits will be deleted (pruned) if they are not refreshed and reinforced.

Approach: We stimulate these changes with processes we call Differentiating and physiotherapy for the BrainMind (Chapters 8, 11, and 14). For example, explicit and repeated activation of specific circuits such as the Connection or Care brain system will recruit adjacent neurons to enhance those systems.

Principle 9: The Brain Changes Through Processes of Neuroplasticity

The mind has the capacity to change the structure of the brain through the processes of neuroplasticity. There are a variety of forms of neuroplasticity: novel experiential learning (Davidson, 2012; LeDoux, 1996; Siegel, 2007), self-efficacy (Davidson, 2012; Schwartz & Begley, 2002; Siegel, 2007), compensatory reorganization (Doidge, 2007), and emotional memory reconsolidation (Ecker et al., 2012). With those instruments in hand, you and your patient can direct the processes of neuroplasticity to enhance the efficiency and effectiveness of your therapy.

Approaches: Take the patient out of their emotional habit patterns into novel adaptive experiences (see Go the Other Way in Chapter 4, Integrating in Chapters 9 and 12, and Neuroplasticity in Chapter 15).

Principle 10: Adaptive Present-Moment Experiences Can Update Traumatic Implicit Learning

The implicit trauma memories are stored at the secondary level of the brain, in the hippocampus and amygdala (see Figure 1.1; Panksepp & Biven, 2012). Since this learning developed early and promoted survival, it resists change. Survival trumps everything. Trauma can be reworked by activating other brain systems in parallel. The activation of primary-level brain systems in the Transpiring Present Moment will differentiate innate competencies from traumatic emotional learning. Focusing on competencies reduces the effort to remediate emotional learning from developmental trauma and neglect. This often feels like an update of previous traumatic learning.

Approaches: 80% or more of the energy of the therapist is directed toward enhancing the patient's capabilities in the present moment. In Chapter 4, we go into detail about how we use Go the Other Way as an approach to pursue this principle.

Principle 11: Primary-Level Brain Systems Are Powerhouses

As we described in Chapter 1, Jaak Panksepp and Lucy Biven (2012) identified seven primary-level nonconscious brain systems, which he calls the "powerhouses" of the BrainMind. Each of us has untapped capacity and potential contained in our nonconscious primary-level brain systems. Activating and Differentiating these nonconscious brain systems can harness limitless energy, wisdom, and processing capacity of the BrainMind.

Approaches: Explicitly calling out these brain systems, for example the Care brain system, "We are here to care for you"; or the Assertive brain system, "Your assertions are important"; or the Seeking brain system, "Are you curious about your anxiety?"

Principle 12: Psychophysiological Phenomena Are Sources of Empirical Evidence

Psychophysiological phenomena provide visible and auditory evidence of the activations of nonconscious brain systems. These phenomena are happening all the time, yet they are usually fleeting. It takes time to develop search patterns for these phenomena. Attention to these phenomena can help the therapist discover immediate evidence of the nervous system's responses to therapeutic interventions. Having this information enhances the precision of therapy.

Approaches: The therapist can learn to detect meaningful yet subtle shifts such as eye gaze, voice prosody, or facial expressions (see Chapter 14).

THE THERAPIST'S EXPERIENCE OF CIMBS

Our primary goal when training therapists is to introduce them to their own innate capabilities and potentials that are underdeveloped or previously unknown. We believe that the release, practice, and exercise of these competencies can greatly enhance your experiences as a person and as a therapist. We have trained both novice and experienced therapists in how to utilize one or more of these principles or approaches for the first time within an hour. We have observed thousands of times (in our courses) how this training can have a profound effect on both therapists and their colleagues in the role of patient. They often discover some important capability within themselves that they never knew before. When you access these competencies inside yourself, you will naturally discover them in your patients as well. When you explicitly practice these principles and approaches repeatedly, you will discover their precision and power.

Complex Integration of Multiple Brain Systems includes many practical, efficient treatments. For example, when you utilize the principle of bringing your patient into direct contact with one of their nonconscious capabilities (e.g., the Assertive brain system), you will be able to see psychophysiological evidence of immediate physical benefit (e.g., they spontaneously sit up). Or when you focus on the patient-therapist relationship that is unfolding right now, you might notice how unsafe they feel with the caring you are offering. You could then focus your process on activating their Care, Safe, and Connection brain systems. Activating other brain systems could reduce the feelings of being unsafe and enable the patient to receive the care that they always desired. Each of these beneficial therapeutic outcomes can provide you with evidence that your patient's BrainMind is becoming increasingly capable and flexible.

A therapist who was coming to the completion of her own therapy gave this description: "I am surprisingly aware of an enormous sense of abundance of resources inside of me. There are all these challenges in my life and I feel so confident, capable, and trusting in myself. I feel in charge of myself and comfortable letting go of things I used to try to control. I know that I will be able to recognize when I am triggered and be able to regain my emotional balance quickly. I have a good capacity to be present to myself, trust in myself, believe in my wisdom."

Some trainees who only take one course from us will reach out to us months and years later, telling us how grateful they are and what a difference that weekend course has made in their practices. Other trainees keep returning for additional training for years. They keep discovering more dimensions in themselves, in their patients, and in their therapy. They are still excited and interested to learn more. CIMBS is a dynamic emergent psychotherapy. We are still discovering new aspects as we teach and in our attempts to translate this experiential learning into this book.

Success Stories

Here are testimonials from three experienced therapists after attending one of our weekend courses on the tertiary-level brain systems:

- I always have felt stuck with certain types of patients, and I couldn't figure out why we were stuck. I kept on thinking that they were too defiant, defensive, ambivalent, not ready to do therapy, etc. But after the workshop, I realized that it was none of the above. It was me. I did not know how to get them unstuck. After I learned how to work with their Authority, Autonomy, and Agency brain systems, my patients began to really move and grow.
- I realized that even though my patients knew what they wanted (they had their Authority), they had difficulty executing what they wanted. Their Agency brain system was not working. I took it for granted that if they knew what they wanted, they then would be able to satisfy their wants. It was a discovery to me that Authority and Agency are two separate brain systems. Now I knew how to work with the distinction!
- After a few sessions activating the competency of the Authority brain system and differentiating it from constraints, it was like we found the "capacity-to-do-life" button! And changes starting happening very rapidly. I didn't know that I didn't know, and now I know!

CHALLENGES FOR THE THERAPIST

The parable of the blind men and the elephant is found in ancient texts from India (Figure 1.6). Each of the blind men discovers distinct aspects of this animal that he has never encountered before. Each man argues with the others for the importance of his point of view. Someone finds the ear, and someone will feel the leg, or the tail. Each one is valid, and each can learn more from the other perspectives. We all have limitations of perception when we are exposed to novelty.

It can be difficult to appreciate the value and effectiveness of the principles and approaches that we describe in this book. By way of analogy, to see a 3D picture, you have to concentrate and soft-focus your eyes in order to see the extra images jump off the page into multiple dimensions. Once the image is visible, the discovery seems simple, and so it is with CIMBS principles. Discovering how simple each principle and approach is does not take its power away, however. We use a simple exercise to give our course participants this experience. They break into pairs (dyads) and then take turns slowly repeating a series of short assertions four times in a row, such as, "Our attention is unconditional"; "We have no expectations." Each time the assertion is said, the recipient feels it differently. It is almost as if it is being processed by a deeper level of the nervous system.

Our trainees report that they discovered challenges they were not aware of until they experimented with the principles and frames of mind of the CIMBS therapeutic paradigm. They say things such as, "This approach is more intimate than anything I have done before." "It is hard for me to let go of the control and ways of intervening that I have been used to for years." "It is uncomfortable yet exhilarating to be so emotionally and physically involved in the therapy with my patients." "The focus of the energy within this paradigm is intense and unfamiliar." "It is hard to give up the clinical detachment I learned in order to step into the intimacy of the Therapeutic Attachment Relationship with my patients."

In this paradigm, the therapist operates more like a fellow explorer with the patient in an unfamiliar jungle. The therapist has lots of experience in other jungles, and has confidence in their own and their patient's competence. But this jungle is new to both of them. The patient will be the one making discoveries during their exploration, and the therapist helps them realize they have found something novel and important that they would have missed without that perspective.

What are you discovering from what you have read so far? What resonates with you or inspires you? What stirs your curiosity, doubt, or skepticism? We repeatedly give our trainees the invitation, "Let yourself be moved." We are naturally more open to new learning when we have been activated. Stepping out of our usual emotional patterns is inherently uncomfortable. This is a heads-up that you are likely to find some aspects of CIMBS weird, counterintuitive, inscrutable, and/or troubling. Grasping something new takes more time and effort. Novelty is often difficult and annoying. However, the stress of novelty can take you out of your usual thought patterns and habits into new possibilities. Complex Integration of Multiple Brain Systems could help you discover unknown gems and precision instruments within your grasp with which to enhance your therapy.

We caution you to practice any new approaches with your most stable and high-functioning patients. We recommend that you first try out new approaches and interventions with your friends or colleagues to discover how they feel for you and how your partner experiences your approach without the pressure of a therapy session. We also encourage you to explore these processes with a mentor, consultant, or trainer. Surprisingly, even mindful meditation has been known to lead to dissociation, depression, psychosis, and suicidality in susceptible patients.

New participants in our trainings sometimes ask us which patients they should exclude from these treatments. On the one hand, the neurobiological principles contained here apply to everyone. This knowledge can be useful in understanding patients with serious mental health difficulties such as psychosis, dementia, or delirium. On the other hand, we discourage the use of these treatments with patients who have borderline, dissociative, bipolar, or psychotic disorders.

PATIENT'S EXPERIENCE AT COMPLETION

The following are two testimonials from patients who describe what was unique and effective in their experience of this therapeutic paradigm. We encourage you to note what is distinctive about their experiential learning.

Samantha: I have had previous therapy for 15 years before. This therapy is the weirdest of all and surprisingly the most effective and efficient. What was surprising at every turn is that we were always looking at what was working and the positives inside of me. Capacities that I did not know I had. Once we found my capacities, we expanded on them and made them stronger. Previously I was preoccupied with what was broken inside of me and what we needed to repair. I was always talking about stories from the past in order to understand what had happened to me. In this therapy we did not try to understand the past. We didn't even talk about the past! We worked with my trauma without talking about the past. When we found a trigger like terror, we built paths around the terror. I know that the terror is still there but now I have choices. For the first time I can let my hypervigilance relax. The trauma has become part of my history and is no longer present. I feel safe inside of me.

Jonathan: I understand myself better, not from explanations or insights but from the experience of my inner sensations that are happening right now. I am in charge of my life. I can hold on to the good things that are happening and feel the fullness of me. I am enough; nothing to change, nothing broken. For the first time I know I can complete therapy and I will be fine. We built an outrigger to my canoe. I know I can take the big waves of life without capsizing. I don't need therapy anymore. I feel I became so lovable. . . . Go figure.

TRUST THE PROCESS

We encourage you to take this assertion to heart: Trust the Process. Your attention to patient factors will give your work precision. Your therapist factors will focus your energy to work more efficiently. Utilizing many distinct treatment factors will provide your work with flexibility. The principles are neurobiological knowledge you can count on. Trust the Process also refers to the fact that most of the changes and learning that take place by applying these principles occur in the patient's nonconscious levels of emotional processing. You will not necessarily be able to receive verbal feedback or confirmation of the progress you are making. Trust the Process can help you stand on the foundations of principles and intentions and let go of control (see Introduction to Part II). Trust the Process is initially hard for all therapists when they enter into an unpredictable emotionally-laden relationship. We go into greater depth with applications of these principles in the second half of this book.

By way of illustration, recall the training session we described in Chapter 1 with the man with the brogue. We all witnessed a dramatic positive response in a participant who had started as a skeptic. From some perspectives, the successes of that brief session are remarkable. What enabled Beatriz to be so effective in a short time is that she was able to maintain access to many of her own internal emotional competencies when there was virtually no verbal or conscious content to help her direct the session. She was able to trust herself and her intentions. She trusted that her patient's nonconscious capabilities would spontaneously arise and provide the patient and herself with the energy and direction to help him make new discoveries about his own inner self.

With practice you can become highly proficient at using these principles and learn to be increasingly responsive to your patient's needs. Proficiency at any skill is composed of three essential elements: a full understanding of the intellectual concepts within the skill; repeated practice until the embodied aspects of the skill become second nature; and finally, such familiarity with the experience that you can respond instinctively, effectively, and creatively, through both conscious and nonconscious abilities, to the situation.

By way of analogy, consider a professional jazz musician improvising or jamming with fellow players. The musician must have a deep understanding of musical theory; he or she must have highly developed physical skills with the instrument; and finally, there is a less tangible skill, the ability to instinctively create novel melodies and rhythm, mostly reflexively, in harmony with others. That ability is developed only after long hours of attention, practice, and experience.

You can reach similar therapeutic proficiencies through a combination of study of the principles and approaches described in this book and devotion to clinical practice. This book outlines the foundations and strategies of CIMBS. Utilizing these principles and strategies will provide you with deeper understanding, new skills, and creative therapeutic interactions with your patients. For example, the skills of reading your patients' psychophysiological cues and understanding what they are telling you will fine-tune your interventions. That recognition, connected with your intellectual understanding, will lead you to a robust ability to respond intuitively and effectively to your patients' signals and their therapeutic needs.

It takes practice to Trust the Process. We invite you to consider practicing one of the principles or approaches with a colleague or friend to see what happens. For example, you might sit in front of your friend and say one of the therapeutic assertions four times slowly, such as, "You are worthy of our attention." We invite you to trust yourself, your patient, and the process:

1. You have much to offer your patients (more than you realize).
2. There are many beneficial nonconscious activations transpiring below the tip of the iceberg.
3. You can sustain and observe mixed experiences to enhance their complexity.

Chapter 4 will school you in the therapeutic approach we call Go the Other Way. The interventions attempt to operationalize some of the principles we have introduced here. We invite your curiosity. It can be counterintuitive at first. So suspend judgment until you explore it further and see how others have benefited from this approach.

A Different Frame of Mind: Go the Other Way, Changing Patient Factors

Beatriz's new patient, Roberta, was 10 minutes late for the first appointment. So Beatriz decided to text her, thinking maybe she was lost. Roberta texted Beatriz back saying that she was in the parking lot and did not know how to get into the building. That had never happened before. People come up the walk and open the door. Beatriz exited the building to find Roberta wide-eyed, terrified, standing by her car. Beatriz invited her in. Once in the office, Roberta was unable to write her address and telephone number on the intake form. The attempt to get her history was unsuccessful because Roberta kept losing her train of thought. So Beatriz abandoned the intake process and proceeded to start therapy. After the Initial Directed Activation (Chapter 6), Beatriz asked her what she was aware of. Roberta replied, "I feel calm. My body is calm." Beatriz thought that her lack of self-awareness would be challenging. Beatriz's first instinct was to ask Roberta about her anxiety, but instead she decided to Go the Other Way. Rather than addressing the anxiety directly, she chose to activate and pay attention to Roberta's underlying capabilities and competencies in order to reduce the anxiety. Even though Roberta was not consciously present with herself, Beatriz trusted Roberta's ability to become aware of herself. So Beatriz began by focusing on her Awareness brain system:

Beatriz: What are you aware of in your torso right now?

Roberta: I feel heaviness in my chest.

Beatriz: Good awareness! What else are you aware of?

Roberta: My heart is pounding and I feel shaky.

Beatriz: Good awareness! You are being capable of being aware of yourself and your sensations. How is it for you that I am saying that you are being capable right now?

Roberta: Capable is not who I am.

Beatriz: Right now you are *being* capable [with special emphasis on the word *being,* pronouncing it *beeing,* adding another *e* to accent the present capacity] of the task at hand. You are *being* capable of being aware of your sensations and describing those sensations to us. You are *being* capable.

Roberta [Body relaxing a little, taking a deep breath and shrugging her shoulders at the same time]: That's nothing.

Beatriz: And you are *being* capable at what we are here to do. You are *being* capable of *being* aware of you. This is success already! Do you want to pay attention to you being capable right now?

Roberta [*scrunching her face and smirking a little bit*]: You are weird.

Beatriz [*smiling*]: Yes, this is a weird therapy. What are you aware of right now?

Roberta [*surprised look*]: My anxiety is less? I am always embarrassed to be so anxious and clumsy, and so I hide that I'm anxious.

Beatriz: Good awareness again! You are capable of noticing that your anxiety is less. I wonder what happened here that reduced your anxiety? [Go the Other Way again, paying attention to the capability of the awareness brain system rather than the shame about the anxiety.]

Beatriz continued paying attention to Roberta's capabilities, such as her authority to override the fear and her shame about her anxiety. Roberta's psychophysiology changed by the end of the session. She was observably less anxious; her shoulders were down, her face more relaxed, and she was not wide-eyed anymore. She reported lightness in her chest and easier breathing. The reduction of anxiety rendered her more capable of accessing her intelligence and wisdom, and therefore less clumsy. She became more interested and curious about her anxiety, and she was then able to differentiate herself from her anxiety. They were able to change some of the patient factors by paying attention to her capabilities. In our view, Go the Other Way enabled Beatriz to skip what would have been a difficult and frustrating dance for therapist and patient in which the therapist is trying to work with Roberta's anxiety while Roberta is trying to hide it and avoid her shame.

ORIGINS OF GO THE OTHER WAY

After years of practice as psychotherapists, we struggled to find solutions to the obstacles we faced with some of our patients. The problems ranged from a lack of progress to feeling stuck, getting bored, and sensing that we were missing something very important. We consulted with others, underwent more training, studied video recordings of our sessions, and showed our work to other therapists and colleagues. We researched and experimented with a wide array of interventions, perspectives, and principles to learn how to enhance our effectiveness. We developed the interventions that make up the processes of Go the Other Way in our attempts to improve our efficiency and effectiveness with our patients' nonconscious constraints.

The expression *Go the Other Way* developed spontaneously within our small training groups. In the process of training the participants to be more engaged with their patients, we found ourselves directing them to look underneath the discomfort, the avoidances, or the symptoms, rather than addressing the discomfort directly. So we found ourselves saying, "Go the other way." Rather than asking about the discomfort or symptoms, we encouraged the therapist to focus on the patient's present-moment competence of which the patient has no awareness.

Go the Other Way is a treatment strategy that inspires a wide array of interventions to enliven therapy and give your patients some immediate benefit in the session. Go the Other Way is readily reproducible even in a novice's hands, as we have seen hundreds of times at our beginner workshops. These approaches can easily be taught to other therapists in a short time. They in turn have been able to use these approaches with their own patients and to observe results within the session and between sessions.

Our demonstrations of Go the Other Way or presentations of videos at training sessions for therapists can be a bit disorienting for some of the participants. It can feel counterintuitive to focus the therapeutic energy on subtle capabilities when the patient's symptoms and distress look so imposing, even overwhelming. Most therapists have been taught a variety of techniques to directly address the patient's anxiety and distress. Go the Other Way can feel wrong until you observe how effective it is in harnessing the patient's underlying capabilities, dislodging nonconscious constraints, and developing new competencies.

Training Group Example

The following is an example from a small training group to illustrate and bring to life the Go the Other Way approach. The advantage of this vignette is that it can give you explicit information about both the patient's and the therapist's actual experience in this process.

The small training group consists of five therapist trainees and one trainer. During the three-hour meeting, there is an initial discussion about one or more specific principles (Chapter 3), followed by a practice exercise. One trainee is in the position of the therapist. The primary goal is to give the therapist an opportunity to practice and experience some new therapy principles and approaches. This live exercise is not intended to be therapy, although it is often therapeutic. Another trainee is in the position of the patient. Since the goal is not therapy, the trainee in the patient's chair is encouraged to be curious about their inner experiences when they are on the receiving end of these interventions. As you will see, the patient's experience is often quite different from what the therapist thought was happening.

The exercise is basically a 15-minute live therapy session that is video recorded. The trainer, acting as a sort of therapist-whisperer, sits behind the therapist trainee to whisper interventions to help guide them in the process if needed. The therapist-whisperer is the trainer's role that Beatriz developed for training therapists to utilize new approaches and interventions. The therapist trainee then repeats the intervention to the patient trainee. After the session is finished, all members of the group discuss their experience and their observations. Then the group reviews the video of the session in which they just participated. The different viewpoints on this process are quite illuminating. Everyone is able to compare both the therapist's and patient's inner experiences with their own observations. The patient trainee is free to speak about their inner experiences that were not visible or articulated during the exercise itself. There are often interesting discoveries on the part of both the therapist and the patient.

There are several advantages to training therapists in this fashion. They are given a great deal of support to practice and learn rather than perform. No matter what happens, there is minimal shame about doing it "wrong," since there is no right way. The new discoveries are naturally exciting, and the participants often describe looking forward to practicing what they have learned the next day. Small-group training is a deliberate practice in the same way that professional musicians, athletes, and surgeons learn to enhance or develop new skills.

In the following vignette, the primary goal was to help the trainees practice keeping the therapeutic process in the Transpiring Present Moment. Sarah was in the therapist's chair, Jane in the patient's chair, and Albert was the therapist whisperer. The psychophysiological activations of the patient and the embodied interventions of the therapist are nonverbal and thus in italics. The internal thoughts of the trainer are included to help you understand the decision-making processes of directing the therapeutic process.

Sarah began with the Initial Directed Activation (Chapter 6), and then she responded to what unfolded:

> **Sarah:** We are here to pay close and caring attention to you. We are here to help you feel safer inside of yourself. We are interested and curious in whatever you are experiencing . . . without judgment . . . without expectations . . . and without agenda. All of you is welcome. [*She opens her hands and arms toward Jane.*] It is important that you are present, and aware and attentive to yourself right now.
>
> **Jane** [*Starts crying and looks uncomfortable*]
>
> **Albert** [*Whispering intervention*]: Whatever you are experiencing is welcome. We are here to connect with you together. [*He encourages Sarah to reach her arms out toward Jane as she repeats that assertion. She does so.*]
>
> **Jane** [*Nods, more tears, but more direct eye contact*]
>
> **Albert** [*Internal thoughts*]: More eye contact—there is a shift in the energetic balance. [*Whispering intervention*]: We care for you and what you are experiencing.

Sarah repeated the intervention and maintained an *intimate eye gaze* and *sat in silence* to let the intervention sink in deeper.

> **Jane** [*Sits up more and holds her head higher*]: I am anxious. I am not sure what these tears are about.

Albert [*Internal thoughts*]: Another shift in the energetic balance; she sat up more. She appears less anxious and yet she is consciously aware of her anxiety. Let's reaffirm her conscious capability and the competency of her Awareness brain system. [*Whispering intervention*]: Great awareness. We want to strengthen your ability to be present to yourself.

Sarah repeated the intervention. She *leaned a little closer* to Jane (and *held her hands over her chest* to embody the intervention).

Jane [*Her eyes clear and there is a hint of a smile, and a puzzled expression*]: I am not sure what is happening in me.
Sarah: What is happening right here that is bringing these emotions to the surface? [*She raises her arms up* and *opens her hands to embody the intention to hold Jane's attention on the present-moment experience.*]
Jane: I feel held by you and that you really want to connect with me. All of me. [*Her eyes are misty.*]

We spent a couple of minutes discussing the process to let the experience settle in. We looked at the video recording of the session together to explore in greater depth the mix of phenomena that were unfolding. Sarah commented that without the assistance of the whispered interventions, she would have asked Jane about her tears and tried to comfort her. She asked Jane directly if she felt that her tears were being dismissed or minimized by the process. Jane's response was surprising to both of them. She said, "On the contrary! If you had focused on my tears I would have felt that you thought that you needed to take care of me. I would have felt even worse about myself than I did already. It would have been a repetition of what I suffered

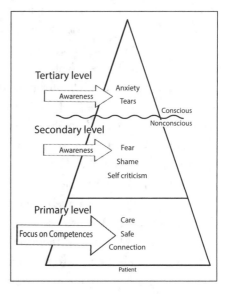

Figure 4.1: Go the Other Way, Simplified

with my mother. It was really helpful when you chose to Go the Other Way and believed in my ability to manage my emotions. I had a new experience when you trusted my capability and did not treat me as if I was fragile or incapable. I have always been easy to tears. I was surprised to discover that it was your care and our connection that were bringing the tears to the surface. They were tears of connection, being acknowledged, seen! I learned something I did not know about myself."

Interesting, isn't it? Most of us have been trained to focus on our patients' problems. There is a natural human tendency to try to reduce our patients' discomfort, so it takes more effort to Go the Other Way and embrace their competencies (Figure 4.1).

UNLOCKING THE CAPABILITIES OF MULTIPLE BRAIN SYSTEMS

At first glance, the strategies and interventions that make up Go the Other Way can look like a simple protocol and/or technique. But Go the Other Way is much more than just a range of suggested interventions. It s a different way of being with our patients. This way of being can become a different frame of mind within yourself as the therapist and with your patient. Go the Other Way seeks out the energy and wisdom of highly evolved distinct brain systems hidden underneath the systems we see operating on the surface that produce the visible symptoms our patients present.

Neurobiological research informs us that each of our brain systems is always active at some level. Think of the fact that the auditory brain system is always on, even when you are sleeping. It is difficult to trust that there are these other brain systems operating in parallel underneath the surface when, for example, our patient is on the verge of a panic attack. The therapist can be on the lookout to discover and bring into the open capabilities and wisdom that are operating in the present moment in parallel when the emotions of fear, shame, or grief may dominate the patient's awareness.

In this frame of mind, the therapist knows that there are other capable brain systems that can be brought to the forefront. We often lose sight of our patients' competencies when they are overwhelmed by their difficulties. Even when they have been underdeveloped because of neglect or trauma, those capabilities are still there. We can Activate, Facilitate, and reinforce them by being the external generator at first and then helping the patient to become their own internal generator to sustain their own capabilities (Chapters 8 and 9).

Our patients' difficulties are the tip of the iceberg. Our patients' capabilities, constraints, and competencies are the iceberg itself. When we work with Go the Other Way, we could say that we are mainly doing therapy to the Primaries (see Figure 4.2) underneath the emotional learning of the Secondaries. Could we then say that we are doing therapy to the brainstem? Major, often untapped emotional resources are present and available in the brainstem noted in the research by Panksepp, Damasio, Porges, such as the Care, Play, Seeking, and Assertive brain systems. This way of being enables us to directly approach the primary-level brain systems (bottom of the iceberg) and more readily override the secondary-level fear, shame, defenses, or terror.

Go the Other Way can enable us to discern what is happening under the surface explicitly, and to focus the energy to directly change some of the patient factors. It also provides us an avenue to access traumatic, emotionally encoded memories and rework those memories in a more adaptive way. Go the Other

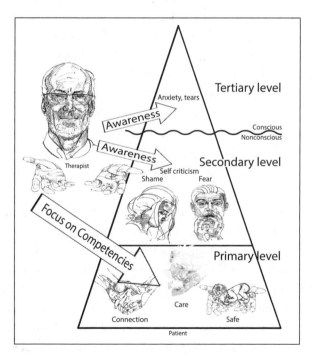

Figure 4.2: Go the Other Way, Complete

Way is a different approach to working with trauma that seeks to harness the powerhouses of the BrainMind and our nervous systems' capabilities for neuroplasticity.

Recall that in the Baby Blues case study (Chapter 2), Albert helped Ann orient to the capabilities of her Awareness and Attention brain systems that were hidden underneath her nausea and impulse to flee. When we harness these resources, we can more readily override a patient's emotional constraints from previous learning and trauma. In other words, we don't need to dig through the fear, shame, trauma, or defenses. We can arrive at the bottom of the iceberg sideways (Figure 4.1).

The interventions of Go the Other Way shift the energetic equilibrium and emotional balance in the patient and the therapeutic process within a moment. The interventions are often counterintuitive and disorienting, so they take practice.

We want to make distinctions between equilibrium and balance. Balance is an even distribution of weight enabling someone or something to remain upright and steady. You might be walking with a crutch or holding onto a railing to maintain your balance. For example, your present emotional balance could mean holding onto your fear from childhood to protect yourself from the pain of attachment and abandonment. Balance is akin to riding a bicycle with slight adjustments left and right to keep upright.

Equilibrium is a state in which multiple sources of energy are in some kind of sustainable harmony with each other. Our minds develop a kind of emotional equilibrium based on the energy of multiple systems. The energy from five to ten distinct systems could be playing a role in your present emotional equilibrium. A unicycle is a better metaphor for equilibrium because you can be unstable in 360 degrees.

We all have different types of emotional equilibrium based upon our temperament, developmental learning, and various contexts. We tend to keep those equilibriums unless there is sufficient energy to move us out of that state. Newton's first law of motion states that "an object at rest will tend to remain at rest." Go the Other Way can be one of the sources of energy to release the constraints of the present equilibrium, the status quo, into new phases of growth and discovery. This shift of energy will create a state of disequilibrium. Moments of disequilibrium are also states of novelty and potential neuroplasticity.

You can see how potentially beneficial it could be to facilitate moments of disequilibrium for your patients. However, there are costs as well as benefits to changing the patient's present equilibrium. Some of the costs are obvious. It takes work and energy to make changes. It is disorienting to get off the familiar emotional bicycle and learn to ride a unicycle. It is so much easier to go down the old paths (six-lane highways) rather than striking out on new paths that have not been cleared. Some of the costs are surprising. Often patients can feel dizzy, light-headed, or unsteady and have brief spells of changes in motor skills. This can be unsettling at first, so Trust the Process and let the new learning unfold slowly. When we Go the Other Way, we will be stepping over invisible fences that are full of alarms and shocks. Examples of these invisible fences are feelings of betrayal, guilt, shame, disgust, unworthiness, wrongness, fear, pain, grief, and terror. Even when we know what we are up against (riding a unicycle), we need to keep going the other way, keep getting on the bike in order to allow the internal emotional balance mechanisms in the basal ganglia and cerebellum to change their settings. The old patterns of holding onto the previous emotional learning are no longer useful. We are installing a new operating system, and lots of old learning (documents) will either no longer function or need to be updated.

Go the Other Way has been one of our most effective and efficient therapeutic approaches because it can dislodge the Static Contradictions out of their own equilibrium and change the emotional balance in which our patients are often stuck. In other words, we are providing more and different sources of energy that could break the stasis of the obstruction or inhibition and release the innate power of the brain systems. These kinds of interventions provide different avenues to access deeply encoded traumatic memories by providing an adaptive experience in the present moment to reconsolidate those memories. When the patient has a new experience in the present moment, it allows the rigid past to become reorganized in a more flexible and resilient fashion.

PETER GROWING WINGS: A DIFFERENT FRAME OF MIND

The CIMBS therapist deeply trusts and believes in the inborn evolutionary capabilities of the patient's BrainMind. It's like telling a caterpillar, "You will become a butterfly," and the caterpillar says, "You're crazy. That's so foreign, so alien, I can't do that." And yet, the therapist knows there are these capabilities that have been shut down, shamed, or turned down. The therapist can come to trust these neurobiological truths. The patient is capable of growing wings. The therapist's energy of unconditional trust can mirror back the neurobiological knowledge that is a part of every mammal. It has been rewarding to experience clinical and teaching sessions where the patient is stunned by discovering some new capability—a capability that we know they have—and the patient declares, "I didn't know that I didn't know."

One of our trainees, Don, asked Beatriz to see one of his patients for a consultation. Don had been working with this young man, Peter, for two years with little progress and wanted to see if there was something more he could do. Peter had attention deficit disorder with extreme distractibility. Peter had difficulty paying attention in the session, and as a result the therapy was slow and frustrating for both of them.

Various difficulties occurred when Peter was small that interfered with the development of his Attention and Awareness brain systems. Peter's single mother was very sick when he was a toddler. Much of Peter's survival energy may have been directed at keeping his mother calm and not angry at him. Peter and his therapist accepted that he had attention deficit disorder and did their best to work around it.

Beatriz approached Peter with a different frame of mind. Instead of giving in to Peter's distractibility, she trusted the underlying potential of Peter's Attention brain system. Beatriz repeatedly focused on developing this system. First Beatriz invited Peter's explicit collaboration to actively join in to do this difficult work. She activated his Authority and Awareness brain systems by asking him:

- "Do you want to pay attention to yourself?"
- "Do you want to be aware when your mind starts to wander?"
- "When your mind starts to wander, do you want to harness your attention in order to not let it wander?"
- "Do you want to keep harnessing your attention for one more round?"

Peter was able to assert his wants and realized that his authority enhanced his capability of paying attention. No one had invited his authority before, let alone trusted that he was capable of exercising his authority to harness his attention. He became actively engaged in the session. His anxiety dropped markedly and interfered less with his attention and awareness. When Beatriz and Peter's therapist, Don, later looked at the video recording of the session, he remarked, "Peter looks like a different patient right now!

NOVEL UTILIZATION OF THE THERAPIST'S ENERGY: THE THREE FORCES

To summarize the key features described above that make Go the Other Way a unique therapeutic frame of mind, we have identified three forces that enable Go the Other Way to be effective in therapy. When we utilize any one of these three forces, it can look as if we are pulling a rabbit out of a hat. And we are, because we are actually releasing the potential (magic) in each brain system. You don't need to exert all three forces; just one or two will suffice for some shift of energy to happen. Let us remind you that this magic happens in the Transpiring Present Moment activation of the brain systems. This is how we are able to release the hidden potentials:

Force 1: The therapist focuses energy and interest on finding other brain systems that might be operating at the same time outside of the patient's awareness.

Force 2: The therapist harnesses the energy of the underlying emotional capabilities of those brain systems and directs the therapeutic process toward opening the scope of attention to provide adaptive learning. The patient begins to discover a new self that has been operating underneath their awareness.

For example, remember the vignette with Roberta:

Beatriz: Good awareness! You are being capable of being aware of yourself and your sensations. How is it for you that I am saying that you are being capable right now?

Roberta: Capable is not who I am.

Beatriz: Right now you are being capable and successful at doing the task at hand, being aware of yourself and your sensations and capable of describing those sensations to us. You are *being capable.*

Or the vignette with Jane:

> **Jane** [*Sits up more, and holds her head higher*]: I am anxious. I am not sure what these tears are about.
>
> **Albert** [*Internal thoughts*]: Another shift in the energetic balance; she sat up more. She appears less anxious and yet she is consciously aware of her anxiety. Let's reaffirm her conscious capability and the competency of her Awareness brain system. [*Whispering intervention*]: Great awareness. We want to strengthen your ability to be present to yourself.

It is easier and more familiar for our patients to talk about their trauma, fears, or negative thoughts than to become aware of their capabilities. But when we Go the Other Way, we press patients to expand their awareness of these hidden capabilities.

Force 3: The therapist becomes the external generator.

The therapist sustains the dynamic process (potential) that is transpiring in the present moment by activating, sustaining, and developing positive feedback loops for those capabilities (see Chapters 8, 11). These adaptive emotions and actions will become self-sustaining with ongoing practice. For example:

> **Beatriz:** And you are *being* capable at what we are here to do. You are *being* capable of *being* aware of you. This is success already! . . . Do you want to pay attention to you being capable right now? . . . And we are staying here paying attention to you as you are being capable.

In the accompanying tables, we provide some examples of brain system capabilities and therapist interventions to help you put Go the Other Way into practice. Table 4.1 lists key brain systems that we engage while we Go the Other Way, along with their emotional capabilities, condensed from the descriptions in Chapter 1. Table 4.2 presents examples of therapist responses to patient prompts directed at specific brain systems when following the principles of Go the Other Way. (Note that most of the therapist's interventions are assertions of the patient's present-moment competencies.) Table 4.2 gives examples from just a few of the brain systems at each level of the BrainMind.

TABLE 4.1: Examples of Underlying Emotional Capabilities of Different Brain Systems

Brain System	Emotional Capability
Awareness	Ability to mindfully observe our internal and external experiences
Attention	Ability to intentionally focus our conscious mind moment by moment
Authority	Knowing our wants, desires, preferences, and choices
Autonomy	Following our wants, choices, and desires separate from other people's expectations and judgments
Agency	Ability and trust that we can make things happen in our life, being in charge of our lives
Safe	Ability to feel a sense of being calm, full, solid, and grounded
Care	Ability to invest attention and energy in another being
Connection	Ability to develop emotional attachment
Seeking	Ability to have the felt sense of curiosity, interest, excitement, and anticipation
Play	Ability to interact with others in a funny, laughing, teasing, spontaneous fashion
Assertive	Ability to pursue our needs and satisfy our wants
Sensory	Ability to have a felt sense of our sensations and emotions

TABLE 4.2: Brain System Competency Responses

Brain System	Patient Prompt	Therapist Response
Conscious Brain Systems		
Awareness	I am anxious.	Good awareness. You are capable of being aware of your anxiety!
Attention	My mind wanders all the time.	You are paying attention to your mind's tendency to wander. You are capable of harnessing your mind to keep paying attention to the inner workings of your mind.
Authority	I never know what I want, yet I want to get better. [Sits up straighter in the chair]	Good. How are you experiencing that want inside yourself? Your wants are important to us. Your wants matter.
Enhancing Nonconscious Secondary Brain Systems		
Pleasure	I am feeling very anxious and my chest is very tight. I feel very uncomfortable. [small smile]	There is a small smile. Is there some small pleasure right now?
Importance/Salience		How important are you to yourself?
	I never feel important.	Right now you are paying attention to yourself. You are paying attention to your feelings and thoughts. That attention means you are being important to you right now. And you are being important to us right now.

Inhibiting Nonconscious Secondary Brain Systems		
Fear	I am feeling terrified, as if something bad is going to happen!	How safe do you know you are, right here? How safe do you know you are right now?
	In my head, I know I am safe.	So you know you are safe. This is the adult present in you, even as your body feels terrified. Both feelings are happening at the same time. Here we can pay attention to the knowledge that you are safe even when your body feels terrified.
Grief	I am very sad. My life is awful. [Open hands on cheeks]	[Imitating the hands on the cheeks] I sense there is also feelings of compassion towards yourself?
Primary Nonconscious Brain Systems		
Seeking		As we pay attention to you, you notice your anxiety rising up. How interesting! This is very interesting, isn't it? Are you curious about that?
Sensory	I feel nausea, and like I need to duck.	Good awareness. What else are you aware of?
	I sense I want to smile, but not wanting to let you see my smile.	This is success. You are capable of being exquisitely sensitive to your sensations.

THE DISCOMFORT ZONE

Go the Other Way is especially useful when patients become symptomatic, constrained, or distressed in the session. Go the Other Way is a novel experience that will often take them out of their comfort zone. You could view your patient's depression, dissociative patterns, or anxiety disorder as a kind of emotional equilibrium that they have lived with for years. Part of their BrainMind will endeavor to maintain that balance because it is familiar, even though it may be at a significant cost. How many times have you heard one of your patients say that they don't want to give up their depression? So when you disrupt this balance by focusing on your patient's competencies, their nervous system will react in both adaptive and maladaptive ways. It is often surprising and counterintuitive that focusing on your patient's competencies is often a source of discomfort.

Go the Other Way can release the patient's constraints experientially in order to remediate their difficulties. This release can tip the balance in the patient's BrainMind out of rigidity and/or chaos, as might be created, for example, by Static Contradictions, into new phases of integration that are more flexible and adaptable (Siegel, 2019). For example, the neural circuits of anxiety in Ann (Baby Blues, Chapter 2) or Jane in the vignette above were what Beatriz calls six-lane highways. These deep neural circuits had been exercised and traveled so many times that they were fast (by myelination) and made strong by the processes of neuroplasticity. These neural circuits took up a disproportionate area of real estate in the patient's BrainMind. Those circuits were the ones that were most easily activated, and thus became repeatedly reinforced.

While noticing these hyperactive brain systems, the therapist can more quietly activate other compensating brain systems. With the Go the Other Way frame of mind, the therapist's task can be to notice these other competencies (brain systems) and bring them out into the open. The therapist might say, "I see you are feeling anxious, and I also see a small smile. Are you feeling a little bit of pleasure too?" It could be that the patient is not aware that his Pleasure brain system is activated simultaneously, because the anxiety is overwhelming.

Your presence as a guide on this new path can help your patients override the fear, grief, shame, or guilt that keeps them contained in their usual patterns and habits. Knowing that you are embarking on a journey of discovery helps you normalize the discomfort that naturally occurs outside of the patient's comfort zone. New avenues and experiences are sources of valuable data. Even as they explore new experiences, emotions and patterns from the past will be present at the same time. The contrast between the previous emotional learning and the present-moment experiences can be both healing and enlightening. For example, shame often occurs with this discomfort. Novel learning can help the therapist avoid their own shame about having caused patients' discomfort.

NEW ADAPTIVE EMOTIONAL PATTERNS INHIBIT PROBLEMATIC EMOTIONAL HABITS

"The task of psychotherapy is very often to inhibit something problematic because 'getting rid of' or 'eradicating' simply doesn't work. The main task of the therapist, then, consists of activation and facilitation" (Grawe, 2007). The problematic patterns are often obvious, and we have all learned a variety of therapeutic modalities (Gestalt, cognitive-behavioral therapy, psychodynamic, emotion-focused therapy, etc.) to remediate those problems. We are proposing that you try something else by activating and facilitating your patients' conscious and nonconscious brain systems to inhibit those problems within their BrainMind in the present moment. We have found that to be remarkably powerful, and it can look like magic in a 20-minute therapy demonstration (see Chapter 1).

Patient Example: Penny

To illustrate this therapeutic approach, we use the transcript of the first session of a depressed young woman we will call Penny. This is an actual transcript with all of its strengths and weaknesses. She was referred to Beatriz when her psychiatrist was unable to bring her into remission after eight months of psychotherapy and medication. We will start at minute three of the session with the Initial Directed Activation (see Chapter 6). The complete session can be viewed from our website (http://www.complexintegrationMBS.com) as part of the Primary-Process Brain Systems workshop.

In this transcript, words that are underlined are spoken with emphasis and importance. At one point we include Beatriz's inner thoughts before she speaks. At the end, Albert presents an extensive postsession analysis as we would when showing the video to trainees.

Beatriz: We are here to pay close, caring attention to you. And it is important that you go inside of you, paying attention to all of your sensations
inside of you. [*She places both hands on her own chest.*] These sensations
are very important because your sensations in this present moment will
guide our therapy today, with no judgments or expectations. They will
help you to get to know yourself better in the present moment of you.

[There is a long pause. Beatriz keeps *her hands on her chest, with an intimate eye
gaze. Penny is nodding slightly, quite still, with a frozen facial expression, making eye
contact, and her eyes wide open.*]

Beatriz: What are the sensations that you are aware of?

Penny: I am not sure what you are talking about. [*Her voice is tense, almost
inaudible, and she talks barely moving her lips, with tears in her eyes.*]

Beatriz [*internal thoughts*]: She is so anxious that she is having trouble
understanding the invitation. It will be important to make the invitations
more concrete.

Beatriz: Are you aware of breathing?

Penny [*Silence. She gives a slightly bigger nod, yet her body remains stiff, with
shallow breathing, hunched posture, and soft crying.*]

Beatriz: You are <u>being</u> capable of being aware of your sensations. [*She has an
excited voice and is smiling.*]

Penny [*Still silent. She nods more strongly, eyes full of tears, with downturned
mouth, stiff body, hunched over, still unable to talk.*]

Beatriz: What else are you aware of? [*She places both hands on her chest.*]

Penny: My palms are clammy. [*Her voice is audible for the first time! She weeps
soft tears.*]

Beatriz: Good <u>awareness</u>! That is <u>very good</u> awareness. [*Her voice is louder
and more excited; her face and body are more animated.*]

Penny: And my mouth is dry. [*She is whispering, but her body becomes less stiff.*]

Beatriz: Your mouth is dry, good awareness. It is good you are <u>being</u> capable of <u>being</u> aware. What else are you aware of?

Penny: My ears hurt. Like they are numb. [*Her vocal tone is stronger and
deeper.*]

Beatriz: This is very good. You are being <u>aware of yourself right now.</u>

Penny: My stomach is so tight. [*She chuckles. Her voice is stronger. She stops crying, and her body posture is more upright.*]

Beatriz: Tell me about the chuckles. [*Her voice has a lilt, with surprise around the eyes.*]

Penny: I don't know . . . [*She looks puzzled, but her body and breathing are more relaxed. Her voice is stronger, and she is smiling.*]

Beatriz: There are some chuckles here.

Penny: Yes . . . ? [*She is smiling and frowning at the same time.*]

Beatriz: This is important. Tell us more.

Penny: As in why? . . .

Beatriz: As in . . .

Penny: Because there is a little bit of this that is kind of . . .fun! [*She smiles, bounces in her chair slightly, and chuckles again.*]

Beatriz: Exactly, yes! Tell me more!

Penny: And . . . playful! [*She is smiling, with shiny eyes, an upright posture, and increased eye contact.*]

Beatriz: Yeah, exactly, say more! [*She is showing excitement and smiling, with a louder voice.*]

Penny: Like now my feet are numb. . . . It's kind of silly. Why, I wonder? I am curious. [*Her voice is louder. She is laughing openly. Her eyes are more open. She is looking more surprised and swallowing awkwardly.*]

We will share more of this session in Chapter 9.

Albert's Commentary

When Penny first presents in near panic, Beatriz has a decision point, whether to focus on the panic or Go the Other Way and focus on Penny's underlying emotional capabilities. She trusts the competencies of Penny's Awareness and Attention brain systems and directs her energy there. Beatriz's verbal and non-verbal interest and encouragement are the external generators that sustain the activations of Penny's Awareness and Attention brain systems. Beatriz uses both the observable and reported psychophysiological phenomena as evidence to provide her immediate feedback on the success of her interventions. There is a significant energetic shift when Penny chuckles. Beatriz knows that the release of her laugh reveals activations of Play, Pleasure, and possibly Seeking brain systems. Penny's verbal responses, "This is kind of fun!" and "I am curious" indicate a significant differentiation of her Fear brain system from her Awareness, Pleasure, Play, and Seeking brain systems. Beatriz's strategy of Go the Other Way has helped her utilize a combination of three forces to release some of the constraints, harness the power of multiple brain systems, and shift the energetic balance in Penny's BrainMind. If you would like a deeper analysis of Penny's session, please read the box.

ANALYSIS

Right at the very beginning of the session, Penny is clearly uncomfortable. Her Fear brain system is so activated that it appears to be obstructing the adaptive actions of being able to be aware of herself. Notice how Beatriz is not asking her about her anxiety but is Going the Other Way as she focuses her energy (Force 1) on developing Penny's capacity for self-awareness. "Are you aware of breathing?" She gets a slight nod from Penny.

Beatriz harnesses the competency of Penny's Sensory brain system (Force 2) when she asserts, "You are being aware of your sensations." And her nonverbal enthusiasm and reinforcement sustain the dynamic process that is transpiring in the present moment (Force 3). This effort proves successful, as Penny's self-awareness expands, and she is able to observe, "My palms are clammy. . . . And my mouth is dry." This ability to speak out loud is a psychophysiological shift that indicates a release of some constraints and change in her internal balance. This is observable evidence of progress. Penny is now working with her own internal potential for dynamic learning. Don't forget that Beatriz is maintaining the activation of the Care, Connection, and Safe brain systems by continuously attending to the Therapeutic Attachment Relationship (Chapter 5).

Beatriz continues to Go the Other Way for the next several minutes. She focuses her energy to keep harnessing the potential of Penny's Awareness brain system (Force 2). This time she adds the Valuable/ Internal Reward brain system into the mix by saying, "Good awareness! That is very good awareness." Beatriz's voice is louder. She is excited, and her face and body are more animated. In this way, she is being an external generator (Force 3) to sustain the adaptive activations. Beatriz's ongoing focus on Penny's present-moment capabilities of awareness and attention are differentiating her competence from her pattern of panic (Static Contradiction). The increasing flow of information, dynamic learning potential, from Penny's BrainMind is revealed as she can feel and describe the numbness in her ears and the tightness in her belly.

An emergent phenomenon happens: Penny chuckles! Her voice is stronger. She stops crying and her body posture is more upright. There is a significant psychophysiological shift from when she started six minutes earlier. This is a precious opportunity for Beatriz to Go the Other Way and seize this moment. She seeks to catch the activation as it flies before it is constrained (Force 1). If we do not notice these subtle cues, they will fade away in a matter of seconds. She grabs the chuckles to harness the energy of her Play brain system (Force 2) by saying, "Tell me about the chuckles." At the same time she becomes the external generator (Force 3) by saying, "Exactly, yes! Tell me more!" to help sustain the discovery of Play underneath this heavy burden of Fear/panic. This is evidence that there has been a significant shift of energy. For this moment, the door is open, and Penny's authentic, playful, curious self is emerging.

Beatriz's strategy of Go the Other Way has helped her carefully direct the therapeutic process. She has utilized a combination of three forces to shift the energetic balance in Penny's BrainMind. There is clear evidence that she has been successful. Penny sits up, speaks more loudly and deeply, establishes a direct eye gaze, and chuckles. Penny's nonverbal communication is revealed through her smiles, shiny eyes, upright posture, and increased eye contact. Her verbal responses, "This is kind of fun!" and "I am curious," indicate a significant differentiation of her Fear brain system from her Awareness, Pleasure, Play, and Seeking brain systems. The simultaneous activations of differentiation release self-organizing capabilities of her BrainMind and facilitate new learning and integration.

We could look at this process from the perspectives of the Go the Other Way neurobiological principles. Beatriz trusted in the potential capabilities of Penny's brain systems. So even though Penny was near panic, Beatriz sought out her capability of becoming aware of herself. This was clearly a novel experience for Penny, and she discovered competencies that she had never known before. When we showed this session to the referring psychiatrist, she said, "This is not the same patient!" These new experiences reduced emotional constraints that were some of the sources of the Fear and near-panic that she presented with at the beginning of the session.

CHALLENGES

The approach of Go the Other Way is different from what we all learned in training and what we have observed in everyday life. Developing new skills requires deliberate practice. Not only are you trying a new intervention, you are interrupting your usual responses or reactions. In the small training group example above, Sarah had to deal with the discomfort of interrupting her usual treatment response to Jane's tears and trying a new intervention at the same time. We are naturally clumsy at first and develop grace with time and experience. Novelty and new learning are also exciting. Newness mobilizes curiosity (Seeking brain system, Chapter 10), and releases the neurotransmitter dopamine in both you and your patients (Chapter 15). Our trainees experience more success and less burnout when they learn to Go the Other Way.

Our BrainMinds evolved to protect us from danger. Seeking out capabilities in the midst of distress takes training and effort. It is like straining to see the animals hidden inside a 3D illustration. It takes concentration and looking and looking again until you suddenly see them! The good news is that when you finally learn to see your patient's underlying capabilities, you will always see them—remember the weevils in Chapter 3? When we are training these skills, we ask the participants to pause when the patient is anxious or in discomfort and ask themselves the question, "What is the capability at this moment underneath the anxiety and the sadness?" For example, Penny noted, "My stomach is so tight." She chuckled, and Beatriz immediately asked about that. Penny smiled, chuckled again, and discovered, "Because there is a little bit of this that is kind of . . .fun! And . . . playful!"

Even though our patients come for our help, some ultimately are afraid to give up their depression, anxiety reactions, dependencies, and so on. The Go the Other Way frame of mind will help you discern that reality sooner rather than after months of work. For example, after a few sessions with us, a young woman came to the surprising realization that although she had suffered with her depression for years, she was not ready to give up its comfort and familiarity. With this compassionate clarity, we could help her actually make a conscious choice about how she wanted to proceed rather than remain in her depression by default.

We believe that by approaching the patient and therapeutic process directly, we will always activate their highly evolved desires and needs to feel safe, cared for, and connected. We want to make those activations clear to help the patient become more open and vulnerable and orient them to their emotional competencies. Meeting those needs for safety, care, and connection will often trigger constraints such as fear, grief, and shame. For this reason and others, many therapists have been taught to adjust the distance and orientation of their chairs and body position to avoid activating their patients' fear, shame, or survival constraints. In Chapter 5 we explore the benefits of adjusting your chair and body position to purposefully engage the powerful nonconscious primary-level brain systems Safe, Care, and Connection, even though that engagement may trigger some of these constraints. We discuss how to develop a Therapeutic Attachment Relationship with your patients. This relationship can be the foundation on which you stand when you Go the Other Way in a proactive approach to the emotions of fear, shame, or survival constraints. In this way, you can change these patient factors directly to enhance the effectiveness of your therapy. When multiple brain systems operate in parallel (see Chapter 1), you can trust that other capabilities will arise to override the freeze or collapse reactions.

CHAPTER 5

The Therapeutic Attachment Relationship and Therapist Factors

....

The therapeutic relationship is the ground
on which the therapist stands.

BEATRIZ SHELDON AND ALBERT SHELDON

Relationship becomes medicine.

GEORGE THOMPSON,
"BRAIN-EMPOWERED COLLABORATORS"

In this chapter, we propose that you consider developing a Therapeutic Attachment Relationship to enhance all that you presently do and understand about the importance of the therapeutic relationship with your patients. We have found it helpful to develop a strong, intimate Therapeutic Attachment Relationship with our patients in the Transpiring Present Moment at the start of every session. We also encourage you to develop an enhanced therapeutic relationship with yourself to support your relationship with the patient. The opportunity to focus on the Therapeutic Attachment Relationship can start the instant you step into the office together with your patient. The quick-start description of how to operationalize the Therapeutic Attachment Relationship begins with the description of the mechanics listed below. The relationship with your patient is happening from that moment on. So it behooves us all to be mindful of its importance and challenges.

The Therapeutic Attachment Relationship goes beyond the therapeutic alliance by prioritizing the development of the attachment brain systems. In this intimate relationship, both the patient and the therapist are experiencing emotions, not just talking about their emotions. We achieve that goal by intentionally activating the primary-level brain systems of Safe, Care, and Connection constantly (Figure 5.1). Together these constitute the attachment brain systems— we have found that the Safe, Care, and Connection brain systems have played the biggest roles in the development of everyone's unique attachment patterns. These are the nonconscious brain systems that energize the infant's inborn patterns for attachment with the parent. The parent's tender facial expressions and inviting vocal intonation amplify feelings of interpersonal connection, mutual affirmation, and attachment. We have attempted to replicate these facial connections and inviting vocal tones to amplify activations of interpersonal connection, mutual affirmation, and attachment throughout each therapy session.

"Attachment is an inborn system in the brain that evolves in ways that influence and organize motivational, emotional and memory processes with respect to significant caregiving figures. For an infant, activation of the attachment system involves the seeking of proximity. Proximity seeking allows an infant to be protected from harm, starvation, unfavorable temperature changes, disasters, attacks from others and separation from the group" (Siegel 1999).

The Therapeutic Attachment Relationship can work like magnifying glass to address both patient factors and therapist factors precisely. A magnifying glass works in two ways: (1) It gives the viewer more precise and expanded information about the object being observed. The magnifying glass is a kind of microscope that brings details to light that are not visible to the naked eye. (2) It narrowly focuses the energy from one side of the glass on a specific point on the other side of the glass. A simple physical example of this is when you use a magnifying glass to focus the sun's energy to heat or burn something.

First, the sharp and enlarged focus of the Therapeutic Attachment Relationship can enable you to discover the nonconscious inner workings of your patient's BrainMind, the patient factors. You can observe and feel how their BrainMind is responding in the Transpiring Present Moment to the therapeutic process from the first minute of the session. For example, when you focus your eye gaze on the patient, you can discern psychophysiological evidence of their anxiety, quality

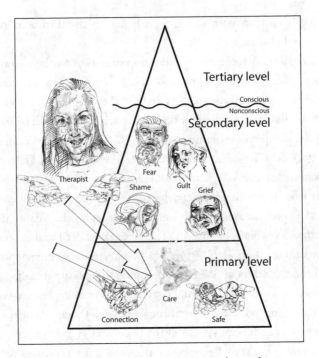

Figure 5.1: Therapeutic Attachment Relationship

of alertness, and level of safeness. You can see and feel their inner resources of Seeking, Play, and Motivation as well.

Second, the Therapeutic Attachment Relationship can help you embody and more precisely focus your energy at your patient's core self. This is a novel, unconditional direction of the energy from your Safe, Care, and Connection brain systems into your patient's primary and secondary-level brain systems. Your are utilizing some of your therapist factors by being an external generator to activate your patient's inner resources. This can be augmented by your proximity to your patient, and can enable them to have the psychophysiological experience of your care and attention. Your genuine care and availability for connection can be therapist factor–focused energy that will activate their attachment brain systems.

The interventions we use to develop the Therapeutic Attachment Relationship are primarily nonverbal, experiential, and embodied by the therapist. The nonverbal facial expressions and vocal tones contain embodied invitations to connect emotionally. There are a number of complementary elements through which you can communicate your desire to develop a Therapeutic Attachment Relationship: eye gaze, proximity of the chairs, chair orientation, sitting posture, body position (stance), hand and arm positions, depth of breathing, facial expressions, and tones of voice. All of those factors are always present in a therapy session. But it can make a significant difference if you employ these factors intentionally to establish the Therapeutic Attachment Relationship.

MECHANICS OF THE THERAPEUTIC ATTACHMENT RELATIONSHIP

Below we explore in-depth the underlying principles, benefits, and challenges of employing the Therapeutic Attachment Relationship in CIMBS. But first, we outline some of the practical aspects of how we implement this practice and give a simple case-study example.

Nonverbal Techniques
Eye Contact and Attachment Position
Imagine sitting in front of your patient with a constant, soft eye gaze that communicates your actual attention, connection, and safeness. A constant eye gaze can reveal your unconditional positive regard and care. You can feel the flow of energy between the therapist and patient when you observe this process. For some patients, a constant soft eye gaze might be too stimulating. You can help them learn to regulate their adaptive activations of Connection and Care brain systems, and to calm the fears or shame that might be stirred up by maintaining an intimate eye gaze. After all, if we want to help our patients to have connection in the outside world, connection starts with eye contact. So you can start with adjusting the eye gaze of connection, and whenever your patient makes a bid for connection with their eyes, your constant eye gaze communicates that you are right there, fully present and available for connection. When a person looks into the eyes of another, neural activation in the prefrontal cortex increases (Schore, 1994). When we sustain this connection, there's increased resonance and altered states of consciousness. All of this energy becomes available for synaptic growth.

Proximity between the therapist and patient also plays a role in developing the emotional resonance of a strong Therapeutic Attachment Relationship. We position two straight-back chairs directly opposite each other. We have found the best distance for enhancing the felt sense of care and connection is 26–32 inches between chairs. We personally sit forward in our chairs so the distance becomes 10–15 inches from knee to knee. Most therapists sit 70 (55–80) inches (135–210 cm) back from their patients. Their chairs are typically at a 45-degree angle from their patients' chairs, unless they are sitting behind the patient for psychoanalysis.

We refer to the therapist's body posture and proximity as the *attachment position* (Figures 5.2 and 5.3). It includes uncrossed legs, torso slightly inclined toward the patient, open arms, and erect body posture. This position can directly meet the patient's need for attachment in the session. The shared connection enables the therapist to more accurately read the inner workings of the patient's emotional states and respond precisely with that information. We recommend that you practice the attachment position with one of your colleagues before experimenting with your patients.

Figure 5.2: Therapist's Open Attachment Posture

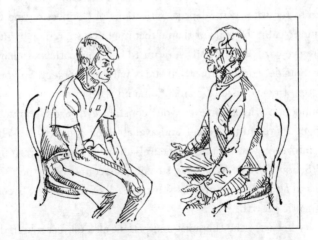

Figure 5.3: Building the Therapeutic Attachment Relationship

Embodiment of Safe, Care, and Connection

You can convey the qualities of safe, care, and connection to your patients in many ways. To start with, you can physically embody the activations of your own attachment primary-level brain systems. Below are some examples of how you can do this.

The following qualities embody the Safe brain system:

- Calm and collected
- Being patient and talking slowly
- Performing deep abdominal breathing
- Fully present and attentive

The following qualities embody the Care brain system:

- Having a tender facial expression
- Using inviting vocal intonations
- Feeling warmth inside
- Having shiny eyes

Shiny eyes occur when the therapist is experiencing simultaneous activations of several brain systems such as Care, Connection, Safe, Pleasure, Importance, Value, and Play. These activations will reveal themselves with psychophysiological phenomena which the patient sees in the therapist's eyes. We can observe shiny eyes as a result of increased light reflection in the therapist's eyes that comes from widening of the eyelids, midsized pupils, and typically some increase in tear production (with sufficient parasympathetic activation). The patient's experience of the therapist's care and shiny eyes can range from pleasure to terror.

The following qualities embody the Connection brain system:

- Having an open body posture
- Projecting an intimate and unconditional eye gaze
- Being fully focused on the relationship

Your patient's mirror neurons will pick up the presence of your nonverbal Safe, Care, and Connection brain system activations, and the same brain systems will become more activated in their BrainMind. These neurons mirror the behavior that is being observed as though the observer itself was acting. The repeated activations of each brain system will strengthen those capabilities in your patient. You can gather empirical evidence of the capabilities of your patient's Safe, Care, and Connection brain systems by observing the psychophysiological activations (Chapter 14) that occur. This process can serve your goal of developing a resilient Care, Connection, and/or Safe brain system in your patient's BrainMind. These activations will both energize your patient and calm some of the fear and vulnerability that are present as well. The simultaneous activations of primary-level Safe, Care, and Connection brain systems in both patient and therapist can become a kind of synergy. The two of you will become "brain-empowered collaborators" (Thompson, 2018).

Each of us is constantly reading the emotional states of people in our environment nonverbally and nonconsciously to determine whether they are safe (Porges, 2009). Porges refers to this process as neuroception. We are also determining whether these people are available for connection and social engagement with us. For example, your patient's BrainMind is always reading your eyes, eye gaze, facial expressions, and vocal tonality. When you embody Safe, Care, and Connection, your patients may feel your availability for attachment. However, your availability for attachment could also feel uncomfortable and even frightening to some patients, especially those who have suffered trauma.

Verbal Interventions

Explicit verbal assertions addressing the attachment brain systems seek to Activate, Facilitate, and reinforce each of these systems. Making these assertions again and again may feel repetitive and boring (to you) at first. The key here is that these assertions are activating nonconscious brain systems. The verbal content of the intervention can be short and easily understood cognitively. However, inside your patient's subcortical BrainMind, these assertions are activating both primary-level and secondary-level brain systems. They will activate in the context of the emotional arousal that comes with the Therapeutic Attachment Relationship. This arousal stimulates the release of dopamine from the amygdala (Medina, 2008) to facilitate learning and neuroplasticity.

For example, the repeated activation of the Safe brain system will recruit adjacent neurons to respond to this novel learning (see Chapter 2). With further reinforcement, each of these attachment brain systems may become increasing strong and ultimately resilient. When you work with a trainer at the gym to exercise your core muscles, your body is naturally developing increasing strength and coordination in those muscles and the nerves that control and modulate those muscles. This is one of the basic approaches to achieving our goal of developing resilient brain systems.

Verbal Activation of Safety: Patient Steve

The first step in any attachment relationship is activation of the Safe brain system. If the infant, child, or person is not safe, their BrainMind will be in survival mode and unable to attach. We have found that exploring safe explicitly right at the beginning of the session reveals valuable energy and information.

Safe, safety, and *safeness* have distinct meanings:

- *Safe* is the primary-level brain system that motivates the organism toward adaptive self-regulation and healthy environments. Safe is an expansive feeling inside ourselves, often radiating out from the chest. Feeling psychologically open and capable, patients often use the word *contentment* to describe their experience (see Chapter 11). This happens internally by ourselves. Patients often do not have access to an internal feeling of Safe. For example, they often say, "I do not feel safe to be safe."
- *Safety* is contextual and refers to the absence of dangers in the internal and external environment. For example, if my blood sugar is too low, it will set off a mix of reactions, and my cortisol level will go up to respond to that danger. If there is smoke, or gunfire, I will flee from the danger. I can be physically safe in this environment, and yet my body may remain unsafe with tension and high levels of adrenaline.
- *Safeness* (Gilbert, 2005) is a co-created relational experience. Since we are social animals, the psychophysiology of safeness affects all brain systems. There is a gradient to the quality of safeness in each relationship depending on the capabilities of each person. The face and the intonation of the voice convey our physiological state to each other (Porges, 2014).

The following transcript shows Albert working with safeness from the beginning of the first therapy session with a young man we will call Steve, who had suffered from depression and panic disorder for 10 years, since the beginning of his college years. A lot is happening at the start of the first session of therapy for every patient. We focus on the basic aspects of this vignette here, and then use other aspects to illustrate the principles and approaches of the Therapeutic Attachment Relationship throughout the rest of this chapter. After a couple of minutes inquiring about Steve's concerns, Albert starts with the Initial Directed Activation (Chapter 6) and sitting in the attachment position. He sits directly in front of Steve, with a constant gentle eye gaze and open body posture. Before he can probe Steve's nonconscious issues around safety, he must activate the conscious brain systems of Authority, Autonomy, and Awareness.

> **Albert:** Do you want to pay attention to yourself right now?
>
> **Steve [*Hesitation . . . then looks up*]:** I do. I want to better myself, but I sometimes I do tend to shut down, to move away and distract myself . So I am a little afraid of what might come up [*grimaces*].
>
> **Albert:** Okay, all three pieces are important. You do want to pay attention to yourself. You do want to be able to move forward. And you are afraid of what might come up if we do pay attention to you.
>
> **Steve:** Right, definitely [*nods*].
>
> **Albert:** What are you experiencing right at this moment?
>
> **Steve:** I am definitely feeling some elevated heart rate, some adrenaline, not anything overwhelming, like getting ready for a race.
>
> **Albert:** Right, some anticipation . . . ?
>
> **Steve** [*Nods.*]
>
> **Albert:** Some excitement . . . ?
>
> **Steve:** Maybe.
>
> **Albert:** About what we might learn today, what we might discover?
>
> **Steve:** It is true. Could be [*nods*].
>
> **Albert:** There is fear, and there is excitement. It is important that you can recognize the kind of energy that you have at the start of a race. That kind of anticipatory excitement, getting ready._
>
> **Steve:** Right, very easily it borders on the sense that there is something that I need to worry about. Some danger.
>
> **Albert:** That piece [of work] that you are doing right now is an important part of our work together: to differentiate the excitement and the potential of the anticipation, from the fear and danger. For this moment, to what extent do you feel safe?
>
> **Steve:** I feel safe about two-thirds of the way. I do not feel panic, but I also feel some lingering . . .

Albert: So part of you feels safe in here [*puts hands on torso*], and part of you feels unsafe [*moves hands off to the sides*].

Steve: Yeah [*nods*].

Albert: How safe do you know you are at this precise moment?

Steve: I know I am safe! But I don't feel safe.

Albert: How wonderful that you can see that. You know you are safe, and your body feels unsafe! These are two different feelings at the same time. I wonder which one is from the present moment?

Steve: I know I am safe.

Albert: How interesting, isn't it? You know you are safe, and your body feels unsafe. I wonder where this unsafe feeling comes from?

Steve: [*Nods, smiles*]: I guess it is from my past. I always feel unsafe.

Albert: How interesting, isn't it? We are differentiating these two feelings. One comes from your present and the other from the past. We are here together to help you feel safe in the present moment, even though there are all these other fears in your nervous system.

Steve: Right [*nods*], that is what I try to tell myself, that I am not in danger in here [*puts his hands on his chest*]. It is a hard lesson to ingrain.

Albert: That is right. It is hard when the fear is taking up so much space to put that aside and to encode and ingrain a deeper sense of safe.

Steve: I totally agree [*grimaces, shrugs, mixed*].

Albert: That is part of our work to help you tap into that capability [*hands on chest*] to feel and be safe even with all these internal alarms going off.

Steve: Right [*nods*].

The first verbal intervention, after the initial brief mediation and focus of attention (Initial Directed Activation, Chapter 6), is the invitation to the patient's authority and autonomy: "Do you want to pay attention to yourself right now?" This is a clear invitation to the patient's competence and his ability to choose to participate actively. Steve's response reveals mixed psychophysiological reactions: hesitation and then looking up. The verbal responses reveal a similar mix of wanting to better himself and being aware of habitual avoidances and psychophysiological shutdowns. This intervention is designed to test the patient's capacity for collaboration. The mixed responses teach the therapist that there are patient factors that are constraining the development of the Therapeutic Attachment Relationship. Basically the patient's BrainMind is constrained by fear. It behooves the therapist to address the fear and tap into Steve's capability of feeling safe in the present moment.

After acknowledging and affirming the patient's conflicted emotional state, the therapist explores the patient's capacity for self-awareness: "What are you experiencing right this moment?" Fortunately Steve is able to describe his psychophysiological activations: elevated heart rate, adrenaline, and anticipation. Some of those activations come from his present desire to connect with the therapist and some are from habitual reactions to various threats. Albert trusted the general principle that patients want to connect with their therapist, and so he could seek out the degree of competency of Steve's capability for connection underneath the more obvious fears and anxieties. He used the interventions "Some anticipation . . . Some excitement . . . about what we might discover . . ." to focus on the patient's capabilities for excitement about discovery. The focus on Steve's capabilities could experientially differentiate that proactive energy from the usual avoidant fears of exposure. When Steve began to be able to make the distinction between the fear and the excitement, Albert affirmed the importance of his capabilities for differentiation. This affirmation could play a role in helping Steve distinguish the transpiring excitement of starting therapy from the habitual fears that would normally inhibit him from being open or collaborative.

Once Steve's conscious capabilities were activated, Albert could begin to explore his nonconscious Safe brain system. For example, Albert asked, "For this moment, to what extent do you feel safe?" Steve's mixed responses provided further confirmation of the ambivalence about connecting with himself and with his therapist. He had both conscious and physiological fears about opening up and letting go of his usual avoidances. Albert affirmed the importance of safe and reinforced Steve's capability of feeling safe. Albert repeated the word *safe* to activate the nonconscious Safe brain system, strengthen it, and connect Safe with other capabilities such as Awareness. In this example, Albert helped Steve's capability of feeling safe even though part of him felt danger: "That is what I try to tell myself. I am not in danger in here."

Additional Verbal Assertions

Verbal assertions are useful for Activating the full range of brain systems. Below you will find examples of assertions to activate the Safe, Care, and Connection brain systems. These are assertions, not questions, and no verbal response is elicited. Each assertion is brief, often only four to eight words. The responses you are seeking are activations of the nonconscious attachment brain systems of Safe, Care, and Connection. The responses are often subtle, but you can trust that they are actually happening. We have tested these assertions thousands of times and observed the nonconscious psychophysiological responses (Chapter 14). In our outcome studies, our patients have been surprised to discover how differently, powerfully, and deeply in their bodies they feel these assertions. Our trainees often find that making these simple assertions is more difficult than they expected. It takes practice. Here are some examples addressing the Safe brain system. (The words in italics below are the words you might choose to emphasize.)

> Your *safeness* is *important.*
> *You* are *capable* of feeling *safe.*
> We can be *safe together.*

Repeating these kinds of assertions can show your patient that they have the capability of both feeling and being safe. There is a reality to safeness in the moment, and yet your patient may be feeling unsafe physically. This process of Differentiating the actual experience of the Safe brain system from the Fear brain system is a useful therapeutic approach, which we explore in depth in Chapters 8 and 11. These processes provide disconfirming emotional experiences, which can increase arousal and potential learning. The simple intervention, "To what extent do you feel safe?" can invite the patient into an exploration of safe explicitly. Steve's response, "I feel safe about two-thirds of the way. I do not feel panic, but I also feel some lingering [fear]." This disclosure shows how the patient is beginning to differentiate the Safe brain system from the Fear brain system.

Similar assertions can be applied to the Care brain system:

> We are paying *caring attention* to you.
> We *care* about what you *are experiencing.*
> You *are worthy* of our care.

And other assertions apply to Connection:

> We are here to *connect together* and *collaborate.*
> It is important that you *connect* with *yourself.*
> Our *connection* can be *safe* here.

By now you may have realized that we use *we* instead of *you* when we are talking with the patient. *We* is the first-person pronoun. We are in this and doing this together. We are two competent, capable persons working together. We can collaboratively deal with Steve's anxiety, his shame, and even his terror; he is not alone. *We* speaks to the empathy and emotional attunement, resonance, affect sharing, compassion, and affirmation of an emotionally engaged therapist (Fosha, 2000). One of our trainees has a pithy way of describing that value: "It's either two-way or no way!"

TESTIMONIAL FROM A TRAINEE:

If I may, I would say your work taught me that attachment is not simply about one human being to another but about a more generalized sense of attachment to oneself and the world, a sense of belonging here on the planet. So when you say, "You are welcome here," it is not just a sense of being welcomed by the mother/father, but also by a universal experience. The way the brain is rewired or integrated, as you say, feels to me like a process of reorganizing and connecting/attaching to one's own experience. It is an experience of coming home to oneself, or per-haps finding/making home in oneself. It's quite remarkable. :)

Verbal Activation of Care: Patient Lucy

Lucy was a 40-year-old woman who presented with depression and social anxiety. She also complained of low self-esteem, few friends, and difficulty dating. Those difficulties suggested that Lucy struggled to care for herself and to let others care for her. The Care and Connection brain systems are important patient factors to explore at the outset of therapy with patients such as Lucy.

In the following vignette, you will see how Beatriz worked to explicitly Activate and reinforce Lucy's Care and Connection brain systems. Beatriz used a mix of verbal and nonverbal interventions to sustain and reinforce the energy of Care and Connection. Verbal examples are the repetition of words such as *caring, importance, worthy, valuable*, and *lovable*. The repetition of these words was not tedious for Lucy. Her nervous system was dynamically aroused, and she experienced the same word differently each time. When we have experimented with this phenomenon, it appears as if the experience of Care goes deeper and deeper with each repetition (see Chapters 8 and 11). We also employed the nonverbal interventions described above, such as intimate eye gaze, attachment position, tender vocal inflections, open posture, silence, and making embracing movements (see embodying interventions in Chapter 6). For example, the therapist may put her hands on her chest to model a self-embrace, or hold out her hands and arms in an open gesture toward the patient.

Silence can be a powerful intervention. Silence conveys your trust in the process and in the underlying competencies of your patient. In the silence, you are making space for the release of nonconscious emotional learning.

This transcript begins 15 minutes into the session. Lucy is working with experiencing caring for herself. (The words that are said with emphasis are underlined.)

Beatriz: We are here to pay close, caring attention to you, and you are caring for you right now. You are paying attention to you right now. You are <u>being</u> important to you. You are <u>valuing</u> you, because what we pay attention to we value . . . [*silence, intimate eye gaze, hands on chest*]. I am also paying attention to you with all my might and my intelligence, and my capacity . . . [*sitting at the edge of the chair, hands and arms toward Lucy*]. I am <u>caring</u> for you too . . . [*long silence, intimate eye gaze*] and I am valuing you . . . [*long silence*]. You are worthy of our complete attention. What we pay attention to we value. We are valuing you. You are worthy of our attention. We are "worthing" you. <u>You are being</u> the most important person for us right now. How is that for you?

Lucy: That feels good [*hands on chest and smiles*], and it is not something I've grown up with. I did not get that kind of attention from my mother, you know. I am not used to that kind of attention. So it feels new.

Beatriz: You are being the most important person for us right now [*intimate eye contact, arms extended toward her*]. Are you being the most important person for you?

Lucy: Mmm [*hand on chest*], I don't know?

Beatriz: You are paying attention to you right now and nothing else. It is <u>happening</u> that you are <u>being</u> the most important person for you. And I am paying attention to you with all of me. You are <u>being</u> the most important person for me right now. We are both valuing you [*silence*].

Lucy: It is weird. I have a feeling right now. . . . You have a very motherly tone, and I feel a little grief [*starts crying softly*] almost like an infant. You know, like complete attention on the baby, and the baby just being [*hands on her torso*], just being and the mother giving the attention . . . [*cries some more*] not judging.

Beatriz: And here you are <u>being</u> enough. Nothing to do. Nothing to change. You are just being valuable and worthy. You just being is enough . . . [*prolonged silent, intimate eye gaze*].

Lucy: I feel some internal caring and compassion. I am worthy [*both hands on chest, and soft eyes*].

Beatriz: An internal caring, you say? What sensations tell you you are experiencing internal caring?

Lucy: It is like an internal soft warm blanket on my chest. This is new; I never felt that before! [*Crying softly.*]

Beatriz: It is <u>happening</u> that you are <u>being</u> lovable.

Lucy: That is another shift for me. I never felt lovable. A lovable person has qualities that I don't have [*quizzical look*].

Beatriz: And right now?

Lucy: Right now paying attention to myself in this way . . . [*quizzical look and smile at the same time*] is loving myself. I . . . I . . . am being lovable because I am loving myself [*surprised look*] . . . and you are too . . . ??

Beatriz: I am also paying attention to you with all of me. I am <u>loving</u> you [*silence*].

Lucy [*Crying softly*]: It feels new. It feels true that I could be lovable.

Beatriz: In the future? It is <u>happening</u> that we are <u>loving</u> you right now. You are loving you and I am loving you. We are both <u>loving</u> you.

Lucy: I am lovable!! [*Crying louder.*]

It is possible that working in this way, we are updating the relational learning that Lucy had when she was very young. Lucy's insecure attachment patterns are some of the most important patient factors to address in order to achieve successful therapeutic outcomes. We believe that by providing this unique Therapeutic Attachment Relationship in the Transpiring Present Moment, we can make changes to those patient factors. At the same time, we are harnessing the powerhouses of the Care and Connection brain systems (Panksepp & Biven, 2012).

In this segment, you can see how Beatriz is operating as an external generator, constantly adding her energy to the systems. She trusts that with sufficient energy and repetition, Lucy will be able to develop her own positive feedback loops (internal generators). In this way and others, Beatriz is helping Lucy develop resilient Care and Connection brain systems. All of these changes will help Lucy meet her needs for attachment, self-worth, pleasure, and release from distress (Grawe, 2007).

RESILIENT ATTACHMENT BRAIN SYSTEMS

You may recall that a distinct resilient brain system is capable of processing large amounts of emotional energy and information without shutting down or becoming depleted, even in states of stress and adversity (Chapter 2). It may be clear now that the Therapeutic Attachment Relationship is quite activating to a spectrum of conscious and nonconscious brain systems. If the BrainMind is highly activated by the Therapeutic Attachment Relationship, then there are many opportunities to direct that energy to develop specific brain systems.

You can utilize the Therapeutic Attachment Relationship to directly focus this energy with precise interventions to repeatedly mobilize one brain system at a time. Knowing that the Therapeutic Attachment Relationship is Activating will help you discover how your patient's BrainMind is responding to this arousal. You will see clues that can encourage you to explicitly explore one specific conscious brain system such as Awareness or one specific nonconscious brain system such as Safe.

When you repeatedly activate and reinforce one brain system, it will become increasingly resilient and capable. Your energy and interventions can promote positive feedback in your patient's specific brain system, helping to keep it active after the initial wave of emotional energy subsides. You can become an external generator (see Chapters 8, 11) to sustain the activation in order to further develop that brain system. Trusting the Therapeutic Attachment Relationship will help you persist with your precision and override your patient's nonconscious inhibitory feedback such as shame or fear. The Therapeutic Attachment Relationship will provide your patient with more ready access to your nervous system to share in affect regulation.

The Therapeutic Attachment Relationship helps therapists trust the process and their intentions in other ways as well. You can know that even when your patient's cognitions and complaints could throw you off course, genuine nonconscious activations are transpiring in the present moment as well. You will be able to keep developing a resilient brain system even when there are constraints and distractions. Let's look back again at the session with patient Steve:

> **Albert:** For this moment, to what extent do you feel safe?
>
> **Steve:** I feel safe about two-thirds of the way. I do not feel panic, but I also feel some lingering . . .
>
> **Albert:** So part of you feels safe in here [*puts hands on torso*], and part of you feels unsafe out there [*moves hands off to the sides*].
>
> **Steve:** Yeah, a little bit [*nods*].
>
> **Albert:** Again, it is important that we differentiate the safeness that comes from the present moment, versus the feelings of unsafe that you carry inside your body, that take up a lot of space.

In this vignette, Albert is working to develop the Safe brain system. The therapist invited Steve to pay attention to his own actual experience of safe. The patient was able to be aware of his mixed experience of safe and unsafe. With repeated explicit interventions to call out the Safe brain system, that system can become stronger. Orienting the patient to the present moment of safe will recruit other brain systems such as Attention, Awareness, and Authority to sustain the experience of safe in the present. This process of Facilitating the Safe brain systems will recruit the patient's own Secondaries (Pleasure, Importance, Value, and Motivation) to develop internal feedback to increase the resilience of the brain system. This process also provides the arousal, novelty, and emotional memory reconsolidation to tap into the BrainMind's neuroplastic potential (Chapter 15). With repeated attention to the Safe brain system in this and subsequent sessions, the patient will have the competency to be safe even when frightened. That is resilience.

The Therapeutic Attachment Relationship provides the arousal, repeated stimulation, and affect regulation necessary for new experiential learning that utilizes multiple forms of neuroplasticity. Neurons will fully develop only in the presence of adequate amounts of stimulation and under optimal levels of arousal (Schore, 1994). Thus the Therapeutic Attachment Relationship can be an ideal environment in which to develop resilient brain systems.

PRINCIPLES OF THE THERAPEUTIC ATTACHMENT RELATIONSHIP

Below we outline a series of Therapeutic Attachment Relationship principles that we have developed in our practice. These principles are neurobiological features of human evolution. They are what make the Therapeutic Attachment Relationship both an important and effective aspect of psychotherapy. Each principle has its own value and wisdom. Any one of them can provide you with guidance and inspiration in your relationships. We have tested these principles hundreds (thousands depending on the principle) of times and evaluated the results to give us empirical evidence to support each principle. These principles incorporate knowledge from physics, hydraulics, surgery, physiology, and psychotherapy outcome research. They all have straightforward practical applications that you can use in your own work. We will do our best to define each principle and illustrate how it operates.

We and our trainees have observed that when a therapist utilizes these principles, their treatment is surprisingly smooth, and even the most challenging patients appear easy. We believe that the efficiency and effectiveness of these principles is a result of the physiological activations, carefully focused energy, and activated power of the attachment (Safe, Care, and Connection) brain systems. As we describe each principle below, we also suggest some therapeutic approaches for putting these principles into practice.

1: Human Relationships Alter the Physiology of Both Persons

Mammalian nervous systems have a variety of mechanisms to take in information from the nervous systems of others and adjust their own physiology to that information. The mechanisms include reciprocal energy exchange, empathy, mirror neurons, and emotional contagion. These mechanisms evolved to help protect us from dangers and to facilitate collaborative efforts with others to promote survival. This knowledge can help guide you to step into physiological activations of the therapeutic connection that are unfolding in the session at any given moment. This principle is a corollary to principle 7 in Chapter 3: The therapist is an effective therapeutic instrument.

"The mind-body clash has disguised the truth that psychotherapy is physiology. When a person starts therapy, he isn't beginning a pale conversation; he is stepping into a somatic state of relatedness. Evolution has sculpted mammals into their present form: they become attuned to one another's evocative signals and alter the structure of one another's nervous systems. Psychotherapy's transformative power comes from engaging and directing these ancient mechanisms" (Lewis et al., 2000).

Approaches: When you sit in the attachment position (see above), you will more readily embody your interventions (see Chapter 6) and concentrate on your nonverbal communication. Remember that changes taking place in the present in response to your therapy will be more successful when you stay in the novelty of now and spend less time in the old patterns, trauma, and externalizations.

2: Need for Attachment Is Fundamental to All Mammals

Survival for all mammals depends on developing an attachment to care providers. Mammals are born too immature to survive without the safety, care, and connection of the parents, extended family, or group (herd, pack, clan). The patient's Safe, Care, and Connection brain systems seek a supportive and potentially healing attachment with their therapist. The Therapeutic Attachment Relationship meets patients' needs for attachment. Attachment is so important that the Fear, Grief, Shame, and Guilt brain systems evolved to protect these attachment relationships (see Chapters 2 and 14).

Approaches: Trust that your therapeutic process is activating the primary-level brain systems Safe, Care, and Connection. Your patient's mirror neurons are picking up your capabilities of Safe, Care, and Connection. Care for your patient out loud. "Yes! I care for you. I am caring for you."

3: Safe, Care, and Connection Brain Systems
Are Emotional Powerhouses

Nature evolved these distinct brain systems to facilitate attachment between the newborn and the care providers. All of these brain systems are distinct power generators. Harnessing these generators can help you and your patient override nonconscious emotional constraints and trauma. These brain systems often are not evident because they develop so early, and the individual has had years of practice to become adept with each of them. They have also been molded by the Fear, Grief, Shame, and Guilt brain systems.

Approaches: Energy works, no matter whether you can see it or not. Go the Other Way to orient the patient to the competency of the Safe, Care, and

Connection brain systems in the present moment. This reduces the energy loss that occurs when working with triggers and painful emotions. We invite you to focus on the attachment brain systems in addition to your capability to be comforters or analysts.

4: Focused Energy Can Do More Work

Therapeutic work requires focused energy (see Chapter 6). The second law of thermodynamics tells us that unfocused energy dissipates into heat. When we concentrate and focus energy, it becomes increasingly powerful. For example, if the water from a spring flows in all directions, it disappears quickly. However, if the water flow is narrowly focused into a turbine, it can generate electricity. The heart muscles focus energy to pump blood through narrow vessels against gravity. The Therapeutic Attachment Relationship can help the therapist focus more energy on the therapeutic process.

Approaches: When the therapist is more fully engaged, they can direct their energy precisely. The therapist's trust in their authentic care and interest helps them be bold. This engagement enables the therapist to more accurately attune to the patient.

5: Therapist Factors Play the Second Major Role in Successful Therapeutic Outcomes

There can be a tendency to believe that therapist factors are static and do not change. Indeed, research shows that the therapeutic outcomes for most therapists do not change over the years. But we know that therapist factors can and will change with intention, training, and practice. That is one of the motivations for writing this book. We know you can change, and the fact that you have read this far is evidence of sufficient interest and drive to become more fulfilled and expert in your work.

Approaches: There is a real relationship that transpires between you and your patient. Make that relationship one of your priorities, and it will narrow your focus to see what is actually happening in the inner workings of your patient's BrainMind. You will not need to spend so much of your energy trying to figure out what happened in childhood or yesterday. For example, in Baby Blues (Chapter 2), the main focus was on the mutual care that was being directed toward Ann, rather than trying to figure out what happened in the past to interfere with Ann's attachment with her baby, Dawn.

6: Sharper Instruments Cut Deeper With Less Effort

Sharp instruments have optimal effectiveness. A sharp instrument concentrates force in a smaller area so that less of the energy is dissipated into the periphery. This principle applies not only in surgery or dentistry but also in psychotherapy. This precision benefits the patient through specific activations and increased patient comfort (less pain). It also benefits the therapist by reducing fatigue, saving time, and improving the precision of interventions.

Approaches: The therapist is the therapeutic instrument. Hone that instrument and direct it to the patient's core. For example, "We are here together to help you feel safe in the present moment" is a sharply honed verbal scalpel. This sharpness is the most important benefit of the Therapeutic Attachment Relationship for some trainees.

ATTACHMENT WITH PATIENT AND SELF

Discerning a Patient's Attachment Patterns

A direct approach to the Therapeutic Attachment Relationship can help you discern how your patient's nonconscious emotional brain systems are processing this specific attachment relationship (Figure 5.4). Every patient's BrainMind has its own unique learned emotional biases in determining which connections are safe. The patient may overvalue some information and undervalue other nonverbal information. We all have a tendency to confirm our nonconscious emotional expectations. This process can also be referred to as transference or transference patterns of behavior.

Your patient will naturally be developing an attachment with you that is in some way familiar and comfortable to them. Some of those relational patterns will be adaptive to the therapeutic process and some of them may interfere with the goals of treatment. Your patient's previous attachment learning may compel them to respond to you in a distorted, adversarial, or defensive manner. For example, if early attempts at connection were met with repeated abandonment, the child will avoid connection. This might be the root of an avoidant attachment pattern. We could speculate that Steve's fear, verging on panic, at the outset of the session was a reaction to the attachment relationship that Albert was offering.

The strengths and limitations of your patient's attachment capabilities with you will also help you to discern their capability of being in relationship with

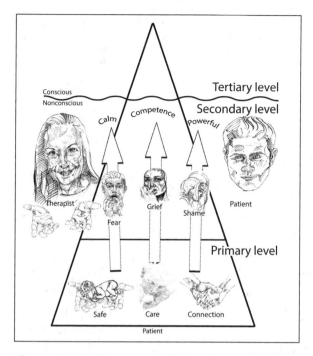

Figure 5.4: Collaboration With the Therapeutic
Attachment Relationship

themselves. What might have taken months to discover previously now is out in
the open immediately. It is interesting to observe how attachment patterns can
change within a session and between sessions.

Mindful Attachment With Ourselves

As we stated at the start of this chapter, a vital part of creating an effective Therapeutic Attachment Relationship is enhancing your relationship with yourself.
The Therapeutic Attachment Relationship is greatly enhanced by the extent to
which you can be mindfully present with yourself. Mindfulness can be described
as as an openhearted, moment-to-moment, nonjudgmental awareness (Kabat-
Zinn, 1990). When you direct mindfulness toward yourself, many simultaneous
experiences become activated and available to be noticed. The more you are
present to yourself, the more you will be present to the Therapeutic Attachment
Relationship. Your ability to have a therapeutic attachment with yourself evolves
over time and enhances your sense of well-being. "What we most need to give

the people we work with in medicine and psychotherapy is the full dimensionality of our presence" (Kabat-Zinn, 1990).

Many benefits arise from your effort to be mindfully present to your own internal attachment relationship throughout each therapy session. This effort helps us keep our own emotional balance and trust ourselves more completely. Mindfulness can open you up to more compassion toward yourselves and your patients. You can more readily tolerate the discomfort of your patients, and so be less tempted to rescue them from their (or your) distress. You can more readily feel your patient's presence, avoidance, or withdrawal. One of our trainees described his work as follows: "Since I view the work as primarily a direct nervous-system-to-nervous-system therapy, I can't help clients play, express care, assert themselves, or be autonomous, if I'm not simultaneously manifesting and expressing these qualities in myself."

Daniel Siegel emphasizes the importance of the therapist's ability to be mindful and fully present in the relationship to foster therapeutic success. He also focuses on how attunement between the patient and the therapist, as well as within the patient, are central to therapeutic healing. "The availability and empathy of the therapist that emerge with the therapist's own mindful presence may be a common source of healing in psychotherapy across the various 'schools' and specific orientations" (Siegel, 2007, p. 277). "Your steely determination and balance enables your patient to become confident that they can be competent" (Thompson, 2018). "You should belong first in your own interiority. If you belong there, and if you are in rhythm with yourself and connected to that deep, unique source within, you will be able to stand on your own ground, the ground of your soul" (O'Donohue, 1998).

BENEFITS AND CHALLENGES OF THE THERAPEUTIC ATTACHMENT RELATIONSHIP

Benefits for the Patient

The closeness that the therapist and the patient create as part of this attachment relationship promotes the activation of multiple brain systems, while at the same time it provides the emotional regulation that is necessary for emotional growth. The Therapeutic Attachment Relationship gives the therapist the ability to address patients' sense of safety (Porges, 2014), by which they are more open to connection and able to tap into more of their capabilities for neuroplasticity. This safe, intimate connection enables your patients to tolerate the high levels of emotional arousal that are necessary in order to build Fail-Safe Complex Networks.

One goal can be developing patients' direct experience of themselves within the relationship with the therapist. In this relationship, the priority is to bring patients into intimate contact with their innate competencies. They can come to rely on their own autonomy and authority rather than being dependent on any relationship, including with the therapist. It has been our experience that because of this therapeutic focus, patients end up having no need or desire to lean on the therapist. They come to know that they are much better equipped to make choices and manage their own emotions adaptively.

Daniel Siegel (1999, 2007, 2010a) has written extensively about how relationships are important in the makeup of our minds and the processes of neural integration. He coined the term *interpersonal neurobiology* to draw attention to the fact that the mind is both embodied and relational. Allan Schore's research has focused on the attachment relationship's importance in affect regulation and the neurobiology of emotional development. "By mediating and modulating environmental input, the primary caregiver supplies the 'experience' required for the experience-dependent maturation of the structural system responsible for the regulation of the individual's (affects)" (Schore, 1994). Much psychotherapy research points to the therapeutic alliance as the key to successful outcomes (Norcross et al., 2009).

We find that fostering the Therapeutic Attachment Relationship has numerous benefits, including the following:

1. It builds a greater sense of safety, and keeps increasing safeness even in the context of terror.
2. It helps enable the patient to be more present with their emotions and the process of therapy.
3. More of the brain systems are active when the attachment relationship is in focus.
4. It maximizes collaboration. It is easier to be attuned when working in the relationship.
5. It creates the best setting for affect regulation; there are shared data and fewer distortions.
6. It gives the therapy an energy and immediacy that moves the process along rapidly. The Therapeutic Attachment Relationship is an emotionally

charged event (Medina, 2008). It generates the arousal necessary for neuroplasticity and change.

7. It avoids all kinds of entanglements with details and externalizations that
   could otherwise preoccupy the therapy. There is generally less regression
   and less avoidance when the relationship is a central part of the focus in
   the work.

8. It avoids the need to figure out what is happening. We can trust the Therapeutic Attachment Relationship and our intentions, and the picture will
   develop when we keep paying attention.

Benefits and Challenges for the Therapist

The Therapeutic Attachment Relationship is a more powerful approach than
words can describe. This power presents both a benefit and a challenge. You
can more readily observe its significance when you see it demonstrated live, but
you can't fully appreciate it until you physically experience it directly. For this
reason, most of our Therapeutic Attachment Relationship teaching is accom-
plished with live demonstrations and experiential exercises. One of our trainees
described how working directly with the Therapeutic Attachment Relationship
changed her work after one weekend of training. "I used to have one transformative session a week. Now they happen every session." Another trainee said,
"My patient complained that I was like a fire hydrant with the intensity of my
attention." This approach is powerful, and so you will want to adjust this power
to each unique patient.

Benefit: A Wide Array of Therapeutic Options

The approaches to the Therapeutic Attachment Relationship we are proposing
can offer you a wide array of options to add to your therapeutic repertoire. We
invite you to consider focusing more of your attention and energy on activating and developing your patient's innate attachment capabilities. Prioritizing the
activation of the attachment brain systems can keep your process energized and
interesting, even when there are significant implicit emotional constraints. Our
work with the Therapeutic Attachment Relationship often approaches an 80:20
balance: 80% activating the attachment brain systems in contrast to 20% differentiating the constraints to those capabilities.

Certainly you will continue to be aware of your patient's symptoms, history, and conscious concerns, but this approach to the Therapeutic Attachment

Relationship can enhance the breadth and depth of your therapy. You may find that you do not need to spend so much effort to rework the emotional learning that resulted from developmental trauma and neglect. This approach will provide your patient a significant increase in novel experiential neuroplastic learning. This will happen on both primary and secondary levels of nonconscious emotional processing. There will still be energy and time for differentiating and treating the limitations of your patients' BrainMinds arising from the attachment patterns that they learned growing up.

The Therapeutic Attachment Relationship will dampen the patient's nonconscious reactivity and increase the perception (neuroception; Porges, 2014) that this relationship is safe. You will see that their face is becoming more animated and their voice has more prosody (rhythm and music). With this coregulation of the Safe brain system, the patient can have a felt sense that "I'm not alone. Someone out there is looking out for me." This connection can soothe, confirm, and validate the patient's experiences, and then stimulate, challenge, and encourage other activations that appear to be absolutely necessary for neural development (Schore, 1994). Trust occurs in therapy when the patient has meaningful nonconscious emotional experiences, not when the therapist says, "You can trust me" (Schore, 1994).

Our work with the Therapeutic Attachment Relationship has revealed many surprising discoveries. Often these discoveries are counterintuitive and at the same time transformative. For example, Albert was quite surprised by Patrick's experience of nausea (Chapter 3), which was released by a successful connection that developed in the initial therapy session. In Chapter 2 we saw how both Albert and Ann were surprised to discover Ann's nonconscious feelings of unworthiness that were obstructing her maternal drives to love her daughter. We encourage you to experiment with the activations that arise from precise and explicit attention to the attachment primary-level brain systems. Hang in there—you and your patient will provoke your own surprising transformative discoveries.

Challenges for the Therapist

The whole process of the Therapeutic Attachment Relationship can be surprisingly challenging for many of your patients and for many therapists. This novel attachment experience can be uncomfortable, disorienting, and even terrifying for your patient. The actual Therapeutic Attachment Relationship can be easily overshadowed by your patients' old relational patterns. A patient may become unsettled that you are not going along with their usual way of coping, but rather inviting them into a new experience. It can be difficult for some therapists to override the patient's usual way of coping and provide a new attachment experience. It takes more effort and patience to see your patient's subtle bids for connection when on the surface they are actively pushing you away with their avoidances, provocations, or ruminations.

The closeness that the therapist and the patient create as part of this attachment relationship is its own challenge. When we feel close to someone, it is harder to be the source of their discomfort, for example when we Go the Other Way. It takes intentional effort to stay in the Therapeutic Attachment Relationship so much of the time. We often hear that concern from our trainees. Much of psychotherapy tends to focus on symptoms, trauma history, developmental history, life problems, behaviors, and cognitions. It is challenging to stay in the Transpiring Present Moment, because it is unpredictable, intangible, and often uncomfortable for therapist and patient alike. Our BrainMinds prefer to save energy and keep doing what is more familiar, even when it does not meet our needs.

Concerns for the Therapist

Some trainees ask, "What if my patient is too fragile? She disregulates easily, and working with this level of closeness will be too difficult for her."

If you think your patient is too fragile to work with this level of closeness, that presents no problem. That observation can direct you to work toward developing your patient's conscious brain systems (the Aware, Attention, Authority, Autonomy, and Agency brain systems, Chapters 7–9). That treatment will help your patient regulate the anxiety and other emotions that are mobilized by the Therapeutic Attachment Relationship. You could also consider adjusting the exposure by sitting a little farther away. Patients are used to adjusting their ability to make eye contact. Your constant eye gaze can be a secure place for your anxious patients. In the debriefings during our weekend courses after our live exercises, we often hear that care and connection mobilize some mix of fear, shame, or guilt in the participants. Those reactions are typical consequences of working with this level of intimacy for all of us.

Trainees also may ask, "What is the risk of the patient becoming dependent on me with this explicit work on the Therapeutic Attachment Relationship?"

We have found that the risk of dependency is actually reduced by this process. The focus is on developing your patient's attachment to themselves. In addition, you are developing the patient's relationship with their innate competencies rather than making them dependent on any relationship, including with you. Patients will have no need or desire to lean on you when they know that they are much better equipped to make choices and manage their own emotions adaptively.

Chapter 6 describes an approach we call the Initial Directed Activation. We have developed this intervention to push a reset button in both the therapist and the patient to initiate the transition from ordinary life to the focused work of psychotherapy. The intervention seeks to direct each participant into a collaborative focused process. The phrases have been designed to both activate specific brain systems and test their functionality.

CHAPTER 6

Initial Directed Activation of Multiple Brain Systems

The Initial Directed Activation of multiple brain systems is a collection of interventions that carefully focuses the therapeutic process at the beginning of the session. This intervention contains two parts: first, a brief meditation, and second, a series of carefully worded assertions. The sequence of words gives you a structure and helps you direct your patient's attention to the work of therapy in the present moment. The intervention seeks to Activate many of your patient's conscious and nonconscious brain systems in a matter of a few minutes. Your patient's responses to these assertions can help you assess the functioning of distinct brain systems and help guide your focus when you finish the Activation. We utilize the Initial Directed Activation at the outset of every session with the vast majority of our patients.

This chapter describes the two steps of the Initial Directed Activation. We utilize a script for each part that gives explicit guidance to the therapist and patient alike. If you are looking for a quick start, try experimenting with one of the scripts with your patients, or look at the section at the end of the chapter on how to use the Initial Directed Activation. Successful psychotherapy requires work. For that reason, we explore the features of the Initial Directed Activation that focus the energy of the patient and therapist to be able to engage collaboratively in the work of therapy. A clinical transcript with commentary illustrates how the Initial Directed Activation brings the underlying strengths and constraints of the patient's brain systems to light at the beginning of the session. You may note that some of the assertions are intended to facilitate the development of the Therapeutic Attachment Relationship. We also discuss how to utilize this intervention and some of the challenges it presents.

The Initial Directed Activation is a carefully focused process rather than a technique. Our process emphasizes a series of dynamic emotional and relational interactions between the patient and the therapist. There are no questions and no effort to acquire any cognitive information. By contrast, a technique is a single intervention that seeks to discover some kind of cognitive content or to give the patient a specific outcome. Examples of techniques are deep breathing when we are anxious, or interrupting a negative thought in cognitive-behavioral therapy. The Initial Directed Activation process gives you an explicit opportunity to show your patient how directly you want to engage with them and narrow the focus of the therapeutic process (see Figure 6.1).

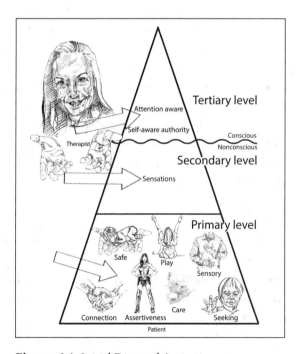

Figure 6.1: Initial Directed Activation

The intentions of the Initial Directed Activation are to:

1. slow the nervous system down with a brief guided meditation;
2. intercept distractions;
3. direct the therapeutic process clearly;
4. activate specific brain systems;
5. facilitate your patient's conscious awareness of present-moment inner experiences; and
6. tap into the patient's initial expectancy and hope.

THE TWO STEPS

Step One: The Directed Meditation Process

It has been our experience that when a patient first arrives in the office, their attention and energy are often dispersed and unfocused. They can be distracted by the difficulties in their life, preoccupied with problems from the past, and/or anxious about the future. More importantly, they are not aware of their competencies and resources that are available to help them focus their energy, desires, and drives to live fully in the present.

Even though the meditation is directed, it is also invited. We begin by saying, "I would like to invite both of us to close our eyes." The focus is on breathing, which is spelled out explicitly: "to take some deep breaths" and "to breathe in the stillness." The therapist also participates in and models the breathing repeatedly as well as using a soft voice, looking inward, and providing safeness in the moment. The patient's attention is then directed to become mindfully present to themselves and their body: "To become more present to ourselves [breathe] . . . to become more present to our bodies. . . ."

Why? The intention is to Activate the Safe brain system in both the patient and the therapist. For example, some patients arrive at a session with the fight/flight (sympathetic) part of their autonomic nervous system activated. The directed meditation can reduce this activation and open up the patient's capacities for social engagement (parasympathetic; Porges, 2011) and to participate more actively in the therapy.

Therapy is inherently destabilizing. The careful focus on the patient will typically mobilize an emotional disequilibrium. The initial meditation can help mitigate the discomfort of that imbalance. At the same time the therapist is directing both participants to become present to themselves, rather than focusing on problems or symptoms. In other words, the goal is to Facilitate mindful self-awareness rather than relaxation per se. For example, many patients note after the directed meditation that "therapy has felt destabilizing [*shifts in chair*]. The first process of getting quiet really helped."

Following is a sample transcript of the meditation instructions. This intervention is best said slowly and deliberately. The words in brackets and italics refer to directions for the therapist, such as to take a breath or to pause.

At the beginning of our session I would like to invite both of us to put aside our everyday concerns.

I would like to invite both of us to close our eyes for a few moments, and to take some deep breaths [*breathe*].

To breathe in the stillness [*breathe*]; to breathe in the silence [*breathe*].

If there are any distractions, to let them go [*breathe*].

To become more present to ourselves [*breathe*].

To become more present to our bodies [*breathe*].

To become more present to this moment [*breathe*].

[*Long pause. Open your eyes, and invite patient to open their eyes if they do not open them soon.*]

Our minds are often preoccupied by worries, ruminations, and endless chatter. The meditative step can push a reset button. For example, you may say, "Let's put aside our everyday concerns." "If there are any distractions, let them go." We want to do this collaboratively so that the patient recognizes that you are also putting away any of your own distractions so you can be more fully present with them. The interruption of distractions can reduce anxiety and avoid tangents.

Step Two: The Directed Activation of Multiple Brain Systems

This part of the intervention operates like an instrument. Like a surgeon's scalpel, it is sharp and focuses energy precisely, and like a neurologist's reflex hammer, it can activate specific neural circuits to reveal how they respond to the stimulation. Although this step includes a script, it is primarily a focused process designed to Activate and Facilitate distinct brain systems. At this point, we want to gather psychophysiological evidence of the inner workings of our patient's BrainMind. At the same time, it will mobilize energy to further the work of therapy.

Step Two of the Initial Directed Activation will Activate anyone's brain systems, so it can be best to see how it works first, without the intensity of a therapy session. You can read the intervention to your patient, but it works best after you have memorized it. Try practicing with a friend or colleague and see what you experience. It is not a long intervention, but it takes time for most therapists to become comfortable with it. The words in parentheses are the names of the specific brain systems that the Initial Directed Activation is designed to Activate.

> We are here together (Connection) to pay close and caring (Care) attention
> (Attention) to you . . . [pause].
> We (Connection) are here to help you feel (Awareness, Sensory) safer (Safe)
> inside yourself.
> We are interested (Value) and curious (Seeking) about whatever is happening (Sensory) inside of you and whatever you are experiencing (Awareness) without agenda (Guilt) or judgment (Shame) . . . [silence for 5 seconds, with direct eye contact].
> It is important (Importance) that you are present, attentive (Attention), and aware (Awareness) of yourself (Authority) and the sensations (Sensory) inside of you right now [pause].
> That energy and information will help guide us (Connection) today [pause].
> Being inside of you will help you direct (Autonomy, Agency) your mind and your life [pause, hands out toward the patient, with open palms, an intimate eye gaze, and sitting in an attachment position (see Chapter 5)].

At this point you can sit quietly and observe your patient's face, eyes, breathing, and body language.

PRINCIPLES OF THE TWO STEPS

The first step enables the therapist to bring themselves into a mindful state of consciousness. Mindfulness is an important foundation for a therapist (Chapter 5). It allows us to be in the best possible position to be open, balanced, resourced, and curious about what is unfolding within the patient, within ourselves, and within the process. In every session, our initial intervention is to direct ourselves and our patients through a couple of minutes of shared silent meditation. This sets the stage for both the patient and the therapist to be in a mindful state.

Several adjustments are very helpful to shifting our orientation: slowing down, speaking up, and embodying our interventions.

Slow Down and Speak Up

If you can slow down internally and externally, you will be able to be fully attentive to the diversity of phenomena that are unfolding from the first seconds of the therapy session. This means speaking slowly and pausing between sentences and interventions. At the same time, it is useful to speak up as you declare your interest and engagement. We have a common tendency to speak more softly when we slow down, which does not fully Activate the Seeking Brain System in the patient or the therapist.

One of our trainees made many new discoveries with her patients when she was able to slow down. Erica explained, "Going in slow motion lets something keep taking up space. When it comes out in the open, then we want to leave space for it to expand, as the waves of emotional activations increase and flow. And then I can say something to refresh it when the wave is over, to Activate it again, to enable it to take up even more space."

Embody the Interventions

We have found that it is very helpful when you are able to embody your interventions. What does that look like? We start in the opening moments, during the directed meditation. After we invite the patient to close their eyes if they are comfortable, we say, "Let's take a moment to focus on our breathing." As we do that, we take deep breaths ourselves, and even put our hands on our chests to bring our bodies into contact with our breathing. Not only are we calming our own anxiety, we are fully embodying the meditative breathing. After the brief meditation, we say, "We are here to pay close and careful attention to you together." As we say that, we reach out our hands toward the patient to communicate nonverbally our openness and interest in them and to nonverbally invite the patient to focus on themselves.

After a brief pause during which we observe their psychophysiological responses to that intervention, we say, "It is important that you are present and attentive to yourself." As we make that assertion, we put our hands on our torso to nonverbally communicate our intention that the patient be present emotionally and physically.

When we teach the concept of embodying interventions, we find it is unfamiliar to most therapists. You might be thinking, as our trainees have, "That is not the way I was taught," "That is not my personal style," or "I don't want to make my patient uncomfortable with my movements." However, we find that the patient feels a much stronger and more engaging response to the therapist who is using an embodied intervention. This is true even when the therapist practicing the intervention feels stilted, awkward, or inauthentic. Nonverbal embodied interventions have a power that is invisible on the surface and yet speaks to the nonconscious emotional brain systems in both therapist and patient.

Embodying the interventions is particularly important when the patient is having a new, foreign, or disorienting emotional experience. The patient accesses our nervous system all the time. It's part of human nature. We're always accessing other people's emotional systems, and we have been doing so from infancy on. There is this constant interaction between the nervous system of the infant and the mother, the infant and the father, and so forth over the course of time. We've all learned to be very aware of the other person, and that includes our patients with us. In this quiet setting, sitting close and face to face, our patients are hyperaware of us. It's so natural that they don't even think about it.

Therapists benefit from embodying their interventions as well. It helps us stay in our own bodies, with our own thoughts, and present to our own physiological activations. Being present in this way is very helpful for being able to read a patient's physiological activations. Outside of our awareness, our bodies are reading the nonconscious emotional activations in others all the time. This is a process of natural attunement, empathy, and mirror neurons. When we are not in our bodies, we do not read others' nonconscious emotional activations very well. Staying present to ourselves is especially important for a therapist who intends to provide the deepest level of healing for their patients.

No Expectations, No Judgment

Embodiment in this situation includes speaking the unspoken. For example, during poignant moments when patients are having a new experience, it's helpful to assert out loud, "We have no expectations." The patients weren't thinking about that consciously; they were just feeling uncomfortable, and because their nervous systems are so used to focusing on the other person, their orientation is to think, "What do I need to do to keep you comfortable?" (What do I need to do to keep my mother comfortable?) Interrupting that tendency can be very helpful: "We have no expectations." Part of them knows that cognitively, but when you embody it by saying it out loud, patients are able to calm down the part of their nervous system that is vigilant, trying to figure out, "What does my therapist want right now? What am I supposed to do? What's the expectation?"

The last part of our invitation to collaborate on the therapeutic task is to say, "Whatever you are experiencing right now is important and welcome. We will use that information to guide us in our process today." We embody that intervention by moving our hands up and down our torso to invite the patient to experience the physiology of their own activations. Please note how the invitations refer to *we*, rather than *you* or *I* (Chapter 5). We are co-investigators in this exploration and discovery. With this invitation, the therapist makes several things clear implicitly (embodied) and explicitly (verbally): that, collaboratively and unconditionally, we will observe the patient's nonconscious physiological emotional activations as they are unfolding in the Transpiring Present Moment.

Embodied interventions are more important and powerful than they first appear. There is a continuous resonant loop (Damasio, 2010) between the body and the primary-level brain systems at all times. That resonant loop is explored in depth in Chapters 10–12. When we conduct outcome evaluations with our trainees, they are usually very surprised by what a difference the embodied interventions make for both patient and therapist. So give it a try, and remember that it works even when you feel inauthentic, awkward, or ambivalent.

Activation and Observation

This two-step process can help you and your patient observe the many different phenomena that are unfolding from moment to moment. This observation process is a manner of gathering information about the actual activations transpiring in the patient's different brain systems. However, for some patients with obsessional tendencies, letting go of anxious distractions can be its own source of stress. This stress is one of the benefits of the Initial Directed Activation, because it brings your patient into an emotional disequilibrium (Panksepp & Biven, 2012). This disequilibrium will Activate multiple brain systems to enable the patient to learn from the novelty of this unique experience inside themselves and with their therapist.

At the end of the Initial Directed Activation, you will have both Activated several brain systems and gathered some valuable information about the nonconscious functioning of your patient's BrainMind. That information can direct your therapeutic process based on shared observable activations. For example, you may have noticed that your patient grimaced slightly when you expressed your intention: "We are here to help you feel safer inside yourself." Their grimace is a psychophysiological shift (Chapter 14) that can alert you to something happening in their Safe brain system. You could use that observation to focus your session on exploring and developing the Safe brain system. The clinical example in Chapter 5 illustrates how the therapeutic process worked to develop Patrick's Safe brain system.

PRIORITIES OF THE INITIAL DIRECTED ACTIVATION

There are two goals to keep in mind when performing the Initial Directed Activation. These goals can help you move forward in your task of building resilient brain systems and developing Fail-Safe Complex (integrated) Networks of brain systems.

First, Activate conscious brain systems to focus the patient's attention on a nonjudgmental self-awareness. Awareness, Attention, Authority, Autonomy, and Agency are the five conscious brain systems that we have found most useful in the therapeutic process. Each of them can enhance your patient's ability to participate actively in the therapeutic process and in practicing their competencies between therapy sessions. Their competencies are resources that we want to strengthen, Facilitate, and direct toward growth and adaptation. Your patient's Attention and Awareness, in particular, play major roles in helping you know exactly where your patient is and what they are capable of from minute to minute. In addition, it is important that this heightened awareness be nonjudgmental. "Assuming the stance of an impartial witness" (Kabat-Zinn, 1990) enables us to step back from our judgments and fearful reactions, while providing relief from stress as well (Thompson, 2018). Defining, Activating, Differentiating, and Integrating these five conscious brain systems are the focus of Chapters 7, 8, and 9.

Second, directly mobilize parts of the patient's nonconscious primary-level brain systems at the outset. Activating the nonconscious Primaries early in each session can provide both more energy for the work of therapy and flexibility to help us achieve our goal of developing Fail-Safe Complex Networks. You can see there is some overlap with the Therapeutic Attachment Relationship. Safe, Care, Connection, Seeking, Play, Assertive, and Sensory are the seven nonconscious Primaries. Each of them processes the unique activations that are transpiring in the session in its own way. When you Activate them intentionally, they can become increasingly resilient brain systems. These activations make the treatment of reducing the BrainMind's constraints and facilitating enhancers clearer and easier.

In addition, Activating these nonconscious primary-level brain systems at the outset could help you have more energy to work with. Work requires focused energy. Doing something different or new requires even more energy. It takes energy to move the person from sitting at home to arrive at your office; at that point, the work has already started. Therapeutic work requires much more energy. Each of the Primaries is a separate source of energy. Seize that energy at the start of the session. Patients come to therapy because they are stuck or constrained in their desires and capacity to experience pleasure and love in their lives. It will be like climbing up a mountain against the resistance of gravity, with pain and stiff joints. More energy, time, and patience are needed. Patients with serious symptoms such as chronic depression, panic disorder, PTSD, and so on require a great deal of precisely focused energy to change nonconscious internal contradictions and constraints.

GUIDELINES FOR THE INITIAL DIRECTED ACTIVATION

While pursuing the two therapeutic goals outlined above, there are several guidelines, intentions, and priorities to keep in mind that will maximize your success. We describe each of these below.

Be Specific and Explicit

A specific and explicit process can help you simplify and clarify exactly what kind of a journey you are embarking on together. "We are here together to pay close and caring attention to you." "We are here to help you feel safer inside yourself." When you make those assertions, you are showing your patient the paths you will be exploring together. If their nervous system is uncomfortable being the focus of close and caring attention, their body will usually reveal some evidence of that discomfort. If you had not made those explicit assertions, you would not know immediately of the patient's difficulty with being the focus of attention, or taking in caring attention, or feeling safer inside themselves. Please note that you are not asking questions to reveal this information. Questions would limit your patient to their conscious awareness. These specific and explicit assertions can reveal nonconscious psychophysiological evidence (Chapter 14) of important emotional information and processing.

The intentions of specific assertions are to prime the patient's mindful capacities and explicitly Activate and test different conscious and nonconscious brain systems. For example, the assertion "help you feel safer inside yourself" is directed at the patient's nonconscious Safe brain system and helps you tell them that you are prioritizing their experiences of safeness in your work together. "We are interested and curious about whatever is happening inside of you" activates the Seeking brain system in both you and your patient. The energy and drive of the Seeking system is insatiable, and the dopamine release that comes with the Seeking system greatly facilitates neuroplasticity and long-term learning.

Prioritize the Patient's Personal Experience

Patients' presence with themselves is a capacity that is important for well-being and mental health (Siegel, 1999). The Initial Directed Activation initiates and invites your patient's mindful and nonjudgmental self-awareness. "We are interested and curious about whatever is happening inside of you and whatever you are experiencing without agenda or judgment." Their capacity for self-awareness will naturally ebb and flow throughout the session. This priority can help them focus their attention on their transpiring connection to themselves in the moment. Therefore it can be useful to check in with their self-awareness frequently.

Your patients' presence with themselves will facilitate their ability to self-regulate their emotions. Your interest in their internal experiences will reveal that they are the focus of attention rather than anything or anyone else. This can enhance their capacity to authentically engage with you. Their direct experience will enhance their ability to feel safe inside and care for themselves. That is why we say to the patient, "It is important that you are present, attentive, and aware of yourself and the sensations inside of you right now."

The emotional activations that typically occur in the Therapeutic Attachment Relationship can often interfere with self-awareness. For example, feelings of shame, unworthiness, or fear may overtake your patient's conscious awareness. Invitations to their mindful self-awareness can help develop their Authority and Autonomy Brain Systems (Chapters 7–9). We all have tendencies to try to figure out what is expected of us. When you focus your patient's attention on their inner experience, you are implicitly showing them that you have no expectations of them. In this way, you are inviting their self-awareness and attention rather than searching for answers to your questions.

"In my own experience, a great transformation begins when we look at our minds with curiosity and respect rather than fear and avoidance. Inviting our thoughts and feelings into awareness allows us to learn from them rather than be driven by them" (Siegel, 2010a).

Start the Process of Gathering Empirical Evidence

In this context, empirical evidence refers to the observable activations and reactions that are unfolding in the therapeutic process in the Transpiring Present Moment. For example, you might observe how your patient becomes more animated when you make the brain systems of Care and Seeking explicit. Or you might observe that they shook their head slightly when you invited a shared interest and curiosity about their inner experiences. Whatever your patient is able to consciously observe is equally important information.

It can be useful to think of this process as the beginning of an empirical process in which you and your patient are collecting information of all sorts. The term *evidence* suggests that you will be approaching their experiences, self-awareness, and emotions in a mindful, nonjudgmental, or scientific fashion. This information can be observed and shared by both you and your patient from your respective vantage points. This evidence is unique insofar as it is transpiring in response to the Therapeutic Attachment Relationship and the Initial Directed Activation.

This empirical evidence can be useful in making assessments about the capabilities of several of your patient's brain systems. Your observations could also help you in your assessment of your patient's ability to engage in the therapeutic process. When you become more practiced with making empirical observations, you will be better equipped to assess your patient's nonconscious responses to your interventions.

A simple way to continue this process is with an invitation such as this: "Can you share with us what you are aware of experiencing right now?"

Keep the Focus on the Transpiring Present Moment

The present moment refers to that which is actually happening as time unfolds. These are moments of opportunity that are propitious for action (Stern, 2004).

The present is the moment when change can take place. We cannot change the past, and the future is out of reach. Antonio Damasio distinguishes between emotions that come from previous learned experiences stored in the BrainMind and emotions that arrive during present moment-interactions between the body and the central nervous system. It is much easier to access emotions from the past. Accessing emotions that arise from the body and the present moment is a slow and energy-consuming process (Damasio, 2003).

The Initial Directed Activation seeks to help the patient to be aware and attentive to their Transpiring Present Moment experiences. "It is important that you are present, attentive, and aware of yourself and the sensations inside of you right now." The present moment is a narrow focus, which can serve several purposes. There is a reduced tendency to become distracted by events and emotions that arise from outside the session. Awareness and Attention can be channeled carefully so that they are more energized and acute. This focus also helps in gathering and discovering novel information, evidence that is unfolding for both you and your patient. However, this process takes more energy and is slower than accessing cognitions, since the novel neural networks of the present moment are being created minute by minute.

COMMON QUESTIONS

Question: How do I start this process of Initial Directed Activation when my patient is used to telling me about their symptoms, their previous week, or the latest news about their relationship with their spouse?

Answer: There are several approaches that we have found helpful with our trainees making this same transition with their patients. "Would you be willing to try an experiment? Let's try a couple of minutes of meditation together. And see how that feels." Or, "Would you be willing to try an experiment? Let's try a few minutes where we focus exclusively on what you are experiencing right now." Or, "I would like to try a brief 5-minute exercise where we help regulate your anxiety together."

Question: I am used to following my patient's lead. Won't I be disrespecting their choice if I direct the therapeutic process with this Initial Directed Activation?

Answer: Your patients are leading you in several ways at any given time. For example, their longing for connection brings them into the session; their shame about connection causes them to avoid eye contact; their fear makes them freeze and their body gets tense; their increasing capacity to feel safe enables them to breathe more deeply; or they start talking about their annoyance with their boss. Which of those leads are you choosing to follow? When you start your therapeutic process with an Initial Directed Activation, you have narrowed the number of realistic paths that you and your patient could pursue. This initial intervention will help you more readily observe your patient's nonconscious and nonverbal leads. There are still many leads to explore.

CLINICAL ILLUSTRATION

The following is a transcript of the first therapy session conducted by Albert with a patient we will call Sandy. It illustrates how a session unfolds after the Initial Directed Activation of multiple brain systems. Words in brackets and italics contained in the dialogue describe physical movements. Albert's internal thoughts discerning brain system activations and trying on different responses are indented.

Prioritize the Patient's Personal Experience

Albert: Can you share with us what you are aware of experiencing right now?

Sandy: I am feeling tension in my chest.

[Albert's internal thoughts]: Good, let's reinforce and expand her self-awareness.

Albert: The fact that you are aware of the physical tension in your chest is very helpful [*hands over chest*].

Sandy: Okay [*nods*].

Albert: What else are you aware of feeling? What else are you noticing?

Sandy: I feel tension in my shoulders and neck. Like there is something pressing down on my chest [*hands on her shoulders*]. I can breathe, but I cannot take a deep breath. I can try really hard and it does not work.

Albert: Are there any other physical manifestations of this anxiety besides the tension in your chest, neck, and shoulders?

Sandy: I have to keep my thinking on track [*hands to her head*]. I get distracted.

[Albert's internal thoughts]: Good self-awareness. She is clearly very anxious, so let's check in with other parts of her body to further down-regulate her anxiety.

Albert: It is difficult to focus. Does it affect your vision or your hearing?

Sandy: No.

Albert: Your throat?

Sandy: My jaw is really tight [*hands on her jaws*]. That would be another manifestation.

[Albert's internal thoughts]: Even though she is describing pervasive physical anxiety, she is not fully immobilized or shut down. Let's keep regulating her anxiety together.

Albert: Does it affect your heart at all? Such as heart racing or palpitations?

Sandy: No, it is slow.

Albert: How about in your abdomen?

Sandy: I am a little hungry. I feel like eating, but I am not really hungry. That would be a symptom too. Like, stuff it down, get rid of the anxiety [*pushes her hands down her torso, sighs*].

In these two minutes of the session, the patient's personal experience of herself has been the only focus of attention. The process here is intended to expand her capacity for self-awareness and reinforce it. We are also showing her that prioritizing and acknowledging her experiences are important parts of our therapeutic process. The focus on developing her self-awareness is actually reducing her anxiety at the same time. She is describing her body's activations that are transpiring at this moment in the session. She is also self-aware of her own emotional constraints and the impulse to "get rid of the anxiety."

Focus Conscious Attention on Nonjudgmental Awareness

[Albert's internal thoughts]: This is an important transition point. She is describing her reluctance and/or resistance to her own emotional experiences. This is important information that we want to help her welcome and explore collaboratively. We can start the process of gathering and differentiating emotional information.

Albert: We want to bring the anxiety out into the open [*hands open to the sides*].

Sandy [*Appears emotionally moved, eyes start to water, nods*].

Albert: The anxiety is really welcome, to keep paying attention to the physical aspects of it, the emotional aspects of it, and the mental dimensions. We want to take the anxiety and put it through a prism. . . .

Sandy [*Nods strongly*].

Albert: . . .To discover all the different colors, all the different energies packed into the anxiety.

Sandy: Yeah, I feel like now I am going to cry, and I am trying not to [*cries softly*]. It makes me feel better if I cry, but I do not think it is a good thing [*sighs*].

[Albert's internal thoughts]: Another important transition. We want to welcome her authentic emotional experiences that are transpiring now. The psychophysiological phenomenon of her tears reveals valuable information about the inner workings of distinct brain systems. We also want to help her observe the difference between the activations of tears in the present and previous thoughts that her tears are not good.

Albert: I want to welcome your tears [*hands open*]. And that they are another physical phenomenon that is welcome. I can see that there are several different emotional dimensions of you that are bringing the tears.

Sandy [*Nods, looks up, more tears, sighs*].

Albert: The tears are something we can notice—what is generating the tears, and listen to the wisdom of your tears.

Sandy [***More animated, takes off jacket***]: I am getting a little warm.

Albert: Any sense of what has shifted inside you that has brought the tears?

Sandy: A release [*opens her arms a little*]. It is not crying for any reason, a way to release some of the anxiety. Also taking the time for myself to be back in therapy [*more tears, sighs*]. And I am scared and I am happy.

Albert: You are both scared to be back in therapy and happy to be doing something for yourself.

Sandy: I am proud of myself.

[Albert's internal thoughts]: This is an important development in her evolving self-awareness. She is differentiating her transpiring emotional activations quite spontaneously. We want to reinforce her competencies.

Albert: And you are proud of yourself [*hands on chest*]. That is another feeling. You are happy, proud, and scared.

Sandy: And I am anxious.

Albert: So we can keep taking the anxiety through a prism. We can help you get your emotions out in the open, and release them, so you can feel proud. What happens when we draw attention to your being proud of yourself?

Sandy: I do not focus on it very often.

Albert: So what happens when we focus on it right now?

Sandy: I want to focus on something else.

[Albert's internal thoughts]: This is an important discovery we are making. She is feeling proud, and it is triggering discomfort and avoidance. This is an important therapeutic opportunity. How interesting!

Albert: Interesting [*more animated voice*].

Sandy: It makes me . . . yeah, yeah, proud, whatever . . . [*dismissive gesture*].

Albert: Isn't that interesting?

Sandy [*Nods*].

Together Sandy and Albert have been gathering information about her internal activations. She is doing very well being present and aware of her inner experiences. The process keeps repeating, sustaining, and reinforcing her awareness in order to further develop her awareness competency and to gather more information about the mix of activations that is unfolding. This directed process can help exercise and train her Awareness brain system in order to help her stay present and regulate her anxiety. This repeated activation of her Awareness brain system can increase the resilience (Chapter 1) of this distinct brain system.

The focus remains on the patient's multiple manifestations of her anxiety, which will provide both therapist and patient more valuable information about how anxiety is manifest in different parts of her body and nervous system. It especially important to note that as a result of the Initial Directed Activation, Sandy is exploring her actual transpiring experiences of anxiety, rather than talking about her anxiety. By prioritizing the patient's ongoing emotional experiences, the energy of those emotions is visible, palpable, and available for treatment. The actual energy of her anxiety can be viewed as a ray of light that the therapeutic process can now direct through a prism (Figure 6.2). The different colors represent the different waves of emotional energy that are present under the surface. In this example, her pride, her happiness, tears, and warmth are being revealed both consciously and physiologically.

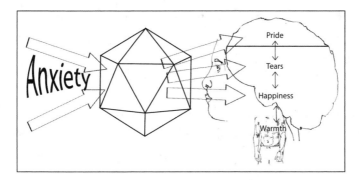

Figure 6.2: Sending Anxiety Through a Prism

Surprising Discoveries and the Present Moment

The carefully focused energy of the Initial Directed Activation can sometimes lead to surprising discoveries that are often counterintuitive, confusing, irrational, and unanticipated. Discoveries are novel and exciting. Discoveries mobilize our curiosity even when they come from the release of painful constraints.

In this example, when Sandy feels "yeah, proud, whatever," notice how with the increased intimacy and the experience of positive feelings toward herself, she moves out of the present moment into some kind of avoidance. We could speculate that she is afraid of intimacy with herself or with her therapist. Perhaps the experience of her self-worth and feeling proud of herself might have stirred up the secondary-level brain systems of Shame or Guilt.

In the next several minutes of the session, Albert keeps the process in the Transpiring Present Moment. You never know what will arise when you keep the process in the uniqueness of now.

[Albert's internal thoughts]: There is a mix of brain system activations happening right now. This is an opportunity to stay in the novelty, make new discoveries, facilitate new learning, and support her in her emotional disequilibrium.

Albert: There must be something else going on that makes you want to fast forward through "proud" [*moves hands up his torso*].

Sandy [*Sighs, nods, squirms*]: Yeah . . .

Albert: That is the kind of thing we want to observe. Proud, that is a reasonably good feeling, and yet part of you wants to go fast through that.

Sandy: Let's get through it.

Albert: We are focusing on your feeling proud, and then what happens? [*Arms and hands open up.*]

Sandy: It goes back to anxiety [*sighs*].

[Albert's internal thoughts]: This is a good place to hang out. There are changes happening under the surface. I wonder what will become conscious.

Albert: So there is some discomfort. Is it the focus on proud or is it the focus on this other part of you that is uncomfortable?

Sandy: I do not know [*deep breath*]. . . . It is just the focus on me in general! [*Squirms more.*]

[Albert's internal thoughts]: Great. This is a huge shift of awareness. She has discovered something very valuable in herself and the potential of therapy. Let's keep building her increasing resilient and complex self-awareness.

Albert: That is helpful. I was wondering that too. What is it like when we focus all of our attention together, and pay very careful attention to you? [*Hands reaching out toward Sandy.*]

Sandy: It is not something I have been used to [*her voice is trembling, on verge of tears*]. It feels strange.

[Albert's internal thoughts]: She is having an adaptive novel emotional disequilibrium that we want to facilitate and sustain.

Albert: It feels strange.

Sandy [*Nods*].

Albert: Okay, all right.

Sandy: Yeah . . .

[Albert's internal thoughts]: She sounds tentative. Let's invite her authority and choice to receive our attention and see what transpires.

Albert: Do you want our attention?

Sandy: Yeah, and I want to get to the point where it does not feel strange [*holds her head up more, and her voice is stronger*].

The outcome of the Initial Directed Activation has helped Sandy accomplish a great deal in a short time, roughly 10 minutes into the session at this point. This directed process has been facilitating Sandy's awareness of her authentic experiences that are transpiring minute by minute. Her self-awareness is not being overshadowed by her intense anxiety. In fact, her mindful and curious presence has helped interrupt some of her fear circuits from the amygdala (Grawe, 2007; see Chapters 1, 13) and keep her open in the therapeutic process.

In this section, you can see how Albert keeps bringing her back to the present-moment experiences that her nervous system is trying to avoid. When Albert was keeping her in the present moment, he was opening her up to the dynamic activations of different brain systems and new learning that was unfolding. At the same time, he was interrupting her defenses, resistances, and avoidances by keeping the focus on her adaptive capacities. Her competencies at this moment include her conscious self-awareness, her careful attention to her inner experiences, and her authority to choose to be the focus of attention.

You may ask, why not ask about her discomfort or avoidance? The avoidance is a familiar phenomenon in Sandy's BrainMind, and we believe it is more helpful to focus on what adaptive activations are being avoided. Some of her discomfort is a result of inviting her to put aside her anxiety and focus on feeling proud. She is out of her comfort zone, and that is where new learning and neuroplasticity develop. Asking about her discomfort is likely to get her into her head and out of her bodily experience that is transpiring now. And it could be more useful to discover the nonconscious sources of her discomfort and avoidance that will be revealed in the process.

Discovering Competencies

[**Albert's internal thoughts**]: She has asserted herself with her Authority for the first time in the session. Let's reinforce her assertion.

Albert: Great. Is it important to you that we pay attention to you? [*Reaching out toward her.*]

Sandy: Yeah. I ignore myself too much [*puts hand to face*]. I mean, that is where a lot of the anxiety comes from. Not listening or being true to myself. Or ignoring things that I know are true.

Albert: All right. We want to hear what is true and notice whatever gets in the way of holding onto your truth. What gets in the way of you acknowledging your truth. In which ways you dismiss yourself. It is a reaction.

Sandy: I can finally breathe [*sighs, wipes tears away, nods, starts to sit up, holds her head higher*].

[Albert's internal thoughts]: She can breathe! We want to facilitate this adaptive awareness and experience.

Albert: What are you noticing right now? [*Reaches hands to patient*].

Sandy: Trying to sit up straight [*sits up more*].

Albert: What is inspiring you to sit up straight right now? What is happening that you want to sit up straight?

Sandy: I do not want to waste therapy. I spent lots of months fighting with my previous therapist. It was not useful. There is a large part of me that would like to self-sabotage, and I do not want that to happen.

[Albert's internal thoughts]: She is both identifying and experiencing her self-sabotaging habit pattern. Let's explore this new differentiation of her self from her habit patterns.

Albert: Some aspects of you that are ambivalent.

Sandy [*Nods.*]

Albert: That are maybe self-defeating or self-sabotaging. If you are aware of them, let's get them out in the open. Let's be aware of them [*opens arms and hands*].

Sandy [*Nods*]: Okay . . .

[Albert's internal thoughts]: It is important that all of her dimensions feel welcomed, especially those parts that she dislikes or is afraid of.

Albert: Do you sense any part of you that is wanting to fight right now?

Sandy: Part of me just wants to be anxious: "You can't breathe, you can't breathe!" The loop [*moves hand in a circular motion*]. It is tempting to feel, "I can't breathe, I can't breathe!" [*Speaking louder.*] And go crazy and not think about anything else. I know it is not true. I can breathe, and I have not passed out yet [*sighs, shifts in her chair.*]

[Albert's internal thoughts]: She has made an important discovery. What she has referred to as self-sabotage is actually discomfort with being present with herself, her emotions, her body, and her competencies.

Albert: It is important to notice that mechanism. That part of you is more comfortable being anxious.

Sandy [*Nods*]: Yeah.

Albert: There is an old feedback loop there. It is like holding onto a familiar railing: "I can't breathe."

Sandy [*Nods*]: Yeah.

Albert [*Reaching hands to patient*]: We are focusing on you, and this is weird.

Sandy: Yeah.

Albert: We are focusing on you, and your anxiety, and your pride.

Sandy [*Sighs*]: Yeah.

Albert: And you're sitting up [*sits up*].

Sandy [*Sits up more and voice louder*]: Yes!

Albert: When I said we are here to pay careful attention to you, what did you notice?

Sandy: It made me happy. It made me cry.

Albert: That is part of what is packed into your anxiety; happy, touched, and scared. What is happy about our paying attention to you?

Sandy: It means that I will get to know who I am [*cries gentle tears*]. Hopefully to get to know what I enjoy.

Albert: So we are helping you meet those needs of getting to know yourself.

Sandy [*More tears, nods*]: Yeah.

Albert: To meet your needs and take care of yourself in a new way. Is that important to you?

Sandy: Yeah! I do not want to look for that in someone else, or ignore it in myself [*wipes tears away*].

The results of the Initial Directed Activation of multiple brain systems are further revealed in this segment. There is good clarity about what the patient has struggled with for years. Sandy was not aware, until this moment, of how she was more comfortable holding onto her anxiety—"I can't breathe"—than letting it go. She is discovering from the internal activations of her own Authority, Autonomy, and Assertiveness brain systems that she wants to get to know herself deeply. She no longer wants to look for that knowledge in someone else, such as a partner, a friend, or her therapist. Seeking that insight from others may explain why she has had a series of unsuccessful relationships.

She is discovering a new competency to pay attention to herself and her intimate emotional experiences inside. She is experiencing a new competency to meet her needs to be acknowledged at this moment. She has been able to stay present to her internal emotional experiences of pride, happiness, and feeling moved. She kept opening herself up to the discomfort that was surfacing in the

Transpiring Present Moment. She kept making observations about her anxiety rather than holding onto her anxiety.

In what ways does the Therapeutic Attachment Relationship play a role in this vignette? The therapist is totally focused on and connected to the patient rather than her anxiety. The therapist's interest and welcoming acceptance of her anxiety communicate Safe and Care. The therapist is affirming and caring about the patient's experiences and observations rather than asking for explanations. The therapist is revealing that he is comfortable to stay in the closeness of the complex mix of emotions that are arising without having to figure them out or take them away.

BENEFITS OF INITIAL DIRECTED ACTIVATION (OF MULTIPLE BRAIN SYSTEMS)

Klaus Grawe (2007) wrote about the inherent psychological needs that we all have: increased pleasure, reduced distress, orientation, mastery, coherence, attachment. There is neuroscientific evidence for inherent neural circuits that evolved to help us meet those needs. When we meet those needs in therapy, the patient can have a reduction of anxiety (stressor hormones such as cortisol) and an increase in motivation (dopamine; see Chapter 15) and ability to connect with others (oxytocin).

Orientation and Clarification

The Initial Directed Activation can meet your patient's needs for orientation. Orientation refers to where we are and what are we here to do together. "We are here to get to know you better and help you get to know yourself better." With this intervention, you are making clear that your intention is to develop multi-dimensional connections with her person, rather than her problems, symptoms, or behaviors. This narrow focus will bring up your patient's intrinsic motivation, ability to concentrate, determination, and willpower (Grawe, 2007).

Clarity about the process can make it easier for your patient to discover their innate competencies. The Initial Directed Activation helps the therapist to have clarity and Trust the Process (Chapter 3), and to stay focused to the full spectrum of the patient's nonconscious activations. This focus will also help your patient meet their need for mastery. When one of their competencies comes to the surface, you can validate it and strengthen it repeatedly. For example, after Sandy said, "I am feeling proud," notice how Albert repeated the word "proud" eight times to validate and facilitate that specific internal competency. Her sense of pride in herself will help her develop internal positive feedback mechanisms within the Value and Important secondary-level brain systems in order to enhance her own strengths. In this way and others, she is participating in developing her own resilient brain systems such as Awareness, Authority, and Assertiveness.

Reduced Distress

The narrow focus of Initial Directed Activation can uncover the various aspects of your patient's anxiety immediately. This focus can help you anticipate the presence of anxiety and be curious about what form it is taking. You can feel safe and be more comfortable stepping right into the anxiety with confidence, rather than trying to figure out the causes or trying to reduce the anxiety. Providing a sense of safeness will help your patient be more open to their own fear. Now the anxiety becomes a source of energy and information, no longer a symptom to fear. The image of sending the anxiety through a prism (Figure 6.2) can help you and your patient normalize the anxiety that is always an important element of therapy.

Psychophysiological research has shown that breath awareness and training have the effect of stimulating the parasympathetic part of the autonomic nervous system (Porges, 2011). The autonomic nervous system is a nonconscious control system that regulates bodily functions such as heart rate, digestion, and respiratory rate. Relaxed breathing is capable of reducing pain, anxiety, and depression. Relaxed breathing also enhances both normal absorption and engagement in everyday and therapeutic activities. Your patients can discover that their inner experiences are reliable information with which to learn and to make choices (Fogel, 2009).

Potential for Change and Learning

This initial intervention can set the stage to help you and your patient be fully present to yourselves, each other, and the therapeutic process. "To create new memory content, which can then change subsequent experience and behavior, the person needs to take in new sensory experiences that can change old memory content" (Grawe, 2007). The Initial Directed Activation can increase the number of elements that enable new learning and neuroplasticity to occur. Novelty and change can happen now.

We arrived at the elements of this intervention along several different paths over the course of 25 years. There is a special energy, a kind of expectancy, that is available at the very start of each therapy session. We have found this to be true even with patients we have seen for longer periods of time. We wanted to develop an intervention to harness that optimistic anticipation. That expectancy is often hidden, so we sought to bring it out into the open. The energy of both the therapist and patient can easily be diffused or become dissipated without some careful focus and direction.

It is important that we get out of our heads and into our novel embodied emotional experiences if we are to have the necessary arousal for neuroplasticity and long-term changes. We determined to be intentional and to explicitly call on many of the brain systems to both Activate them and welcome them into the session. There could be a hundred different paths to take in any given session, but we preferred to make thoughtful selections rather than leave that choice to fate. It has been useful to communicate our trust in ourselves, the patient and the process at the beginning of every session. This intervention declares that we are ready to step into a deeper therapeutic process immediately.

How to Use the Initial Directed Activation

You can use the intervention process we have described in this chapter to start a session, or you can use it at any point in a session when you choose to shift the session into a more experiential, nonverbal, and nonconscious therapeutic process. You can use the Initial Directed Activation with or without the components of the Therapeutic Attachment Relationship. They can work independently. However, they work best when you use them together.

If you would like to experiment with this series of interventions, we suggest that you might practice it with one of your colleagues, friends, or family members. As mentioned above, it will Activate anyone's brain systems, so it can be best to first see how it works without the intensity of a therapy session. It works best after you have memorized it. It is not a long process, but it takes time for most therapists to become comfortable with it. Don't forget to embody the assertions and sit in an attachment position (Chapter 5). For example, gently reach out your hands toward your patient when you assert, "We are here to pay close and caring attention to you. . . ." When you are more comfortable with it, you will be able to say it slowly and meaningfully. Your patient will be able to feel your sincere intentions to connect with them and help them connect with themselves.

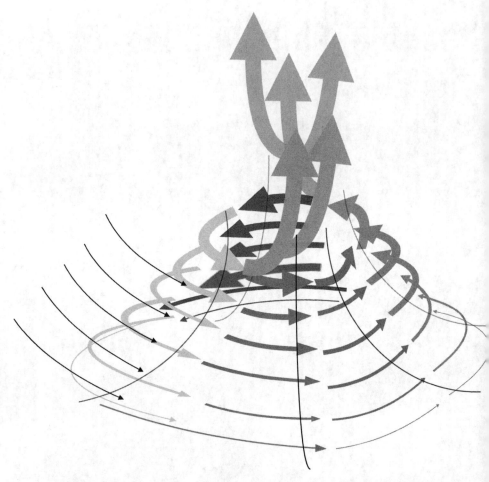

Spiral of Activating, Facilitating, Differentiating, Training, and
Integrating Tertiary Brain Systems

Deeper Dive Into Multiple Brain Systems

In Part I of this book, we introduced you to the origin, terminology, and basic neurobiological principles of CIMBS. We presented some case studies to give readers examples and demonstrations of how CIMBS therapy sessions are actually conducted. And we highlighted three fundamental therapeutic strategies we employ in ways that are distinct from more conventional psychotherapy: Go the Other Way, the Therapeutic Attachment Relationship, and the Initial Directed Activation.

In Part II, we take a deeper and more detailed look into the fundamentals of CIMBS theory and the methodology of how to practically apply this paradigm in psychotherapy. Part II includes four sections: on the tertiary-level (conscious) brain systems (Tertiaries), the nonconscious primary-level brain systems (Primaries), nonconscious secondary-level brain systems (Secondaries), and finally psychophysiological phenomena and neuroplasticity. The following chapters are intended to help you better get to know the 20 emotional brain systems that we have found most effective in our teaching and practice as psychotherapists. The first chapter of each section goes into depth about the brain systems at that level. The second chapter illustrates a variety of therapeutic processes Activating, Facilitating, and Differentiating brain systems at that specific level. The third chapter provides a broader perspective where processes of Training and Integrating distinct brain systems are illustrated.

CONSCIOUS BRAIN SYSTEMS: A DEEPER DIVE

In this introduction, we begin by providing a basic overview of the therapeutic steps involved in conducting a series of sessions with a patient: Activating, Facilitating, Differentiating,Training, and Integrating. In Chapter 7, we describe the importance of assessing and obtaining clinical collaboration when beginning with a new patient. We have found that the ability to collaborate is often an important patient factor that plays a major role in the progress of successful therapy. Addressing the ability to collaborate at the beginning of therapy can bring unexpected challenges out into the open right away. At the same time, focusing on the patient's ability to collaborate greatly enhances the explicit work with the conscious brain systems.

We follow by introducing our concepts of the conscious and nonconscious self. We conceive of the self as the dynamic process by which all of the levels of the nervous system are involved with each other and are engaged by the therapeutic process. Then we focus on the conscious brain systems, the Tertiaries—the A-Team (Figure 1.3) of Awareness, Attention, Authority, Autonomy, and Agency—expanding on the definitions we introduced in Chapter 1. Later in the chapter we utilize clinical examples to illustrate and highlight the resilient development of each of the Tertiaries. We finish this chapter by describing the main types of brain system dysfunctions that we encounter, which involve all levels of brain systems.

Chapters 8 and 9 explore and illustrate what we have learned about in the inner workings of the BrainMind's capacities to experience personal power, autonomous authority, and agency. In Chapter 8 we explore in greater depth Facilitating, Differentiating, and Training, and in Chapter 9 Integrating, of conscious brain systems. Each of those chapters includes one or two case studies that illustrate those processes.

In Chapters 10–12, we similarly examine how we apply the same therapeutic steps to nonconscious primary-level brain systems, the Primaries. We devote the most attention to the conscious (Tertiary) and bottom (Primary) levels because our most productive therapeutic access to brain systems is through these levels, which constitute the top and bottom of the iceberg. Anger is a special emotion, explored in depth in Chapter 10. The enhancing and inhibiting secondary-level brain systems (Secondaries), however, are always playing a significant role no matter whether you are working with conscious or nonconscious brain systems. They will be operationally woven into all of the following chapters.

We devote Chapter 13 to defining and illustrating the enhancing and inhibiting roles of Secondaries in depth. For example, the Enhancing Value and Importance brain systems are utilized for Facilitating the Awareness, Attention, or Authority brain systems. In cases where the Secondaries are maladaptive because they have become closed, hyperactive, and entrenched—for example, if the Fear brain system has developed a Static Contradiction with the Connection brain system—the therapeutic alliance will be constrained. Such a fearful inhibition could be best dealt with directly by Facilitating several brain systems at other levels, which will develop new adaptive learning to override the fear reactions. Facilitating the Tertiaries or Primaries will naturally inhibit the constraints arising from the Secondaries, and it often prompts the secondary-level conflicts to resolve through spontaneous self-organization (Chapter 9).

What are the important concepts here? There are many brain systems that can inform you about the actual functionality of your patient's emotional brain systems and help you be more effective and engaged in your therapy. The conscious brain systems—via the spoken word—are our main portal to working with the patient, and so they are a necessary starting point for the therapist. But we have already pointed out the importance of nonverbal communication that you also use, both with your own body and with your power of observation of the patient's psychophysiology.

You may recall that we went to some lengths to distinguish the terms *emotion*, *nonconscious emotional learning*, and *emotional brain systems*. These differences may be more challenging to grasp in the next chapters. Many of the names of the nonconscious brain systems are the same as those of emotions we are all familiar with: Care, Safe, Connection, Play, Seeking, Fear, Shame, Grief, Pleasure. The conscious brain systems, the A-Team, are not immediately identified with emotions, but those brain systems are intimately involved with our conscious experience of emotions.

It can be helpful to keep in mind that all human beings are born with the same emotional brain systems. They are hardwired. These systems operate as generators of energy, processors of information, and sources of highly evolved neurobiological wisdom. They are always active, idling in the background, although we do not usually feel the emotions that can arise from those systems. For example, your patient's Safe brain system is operating in some limited way even when they are consciously feeling only fear or panic. That can be important to keep in mind when you are trying to update the nonconscious emotional learning (Go the Other Way) of a patient with an anxiety disorder or panic attacks. Even when your patient is fearful or shamed, there will be glimmers of safety, caring, and connection that are transpiring in the Therapeutic Attachment Relationship.

MULTIPLE APPROACHES

As we have described in earlier chapters, there are five broad approaches to working with multiple brain systems: Activating, Facilitating, Differentiating, Training, and Integrating.

Activating refers to the specific and precise use of verbal and nonverbal (embodied) interventions to arouse one or more neural circuits or brain systems. Activating mobilizes a brain system to utilize its wisdom, energy, and processing capabilities. Activating also tests the functioning of a distinct circuit or system to determine whether its responses are hyperactive, moderate, or hypoactive (Chapter 7). At the start of each session, we use the Initial Directed Activation (Chapter 6) to Activate a range of brain systems, with the assistance of the Therapeutic Attachment Relationship (Chapter 5).

Next we move on to selectively Facilitating specific brain systems in order to harness their energy and resources. We use the term *Facilitating* to refer to several specific psychotherapeutic interventions intended to ease, speed, and enhance treatment. Facilitating involves sustaining and reinforcing the Activation of adaptive neural circuits and brain systems. Activating is like pressing the ignition to start your car engine, and Facilitating is like pumping the gas pedal to get the engine warmed up and ready to perform. Therapists are Facilitating when they focus their energy and interest on specific observable competencies of the patient as we seek to Go the Other Way in this Transpiring Present Moment. The therapist is operating as an external generator when they add their energy to the patient's competencies.

Reflecting is another category of interventions for Facilitating the patient's competencies. *Reflecting* refers to selectively noting adaptive, distinct brain system activations that arise spontaneously in the process and then turning that energy back toward the patient with greater focus and precision. In this manner, you are intervening like a parabolic reflector in which the patient's competence or capability is reflected back in a more precise and intense way so that they can reexperience their competence on a deeper level. A parabolic reflector has one trick that makes it useful: the vast majority of energy that hits the reflector is focused on a single point. Reflecting is therefore a more potent intervention than mirroring or matching your patient's experiences.

At times, Facilitating can change the trajectory of treatment and accomplish changes that would otherwise be impossible. In the CIMBS paradigm, we have chosen to Facilitate the resources and motivational energy of each distinct brain system. Facilitating can become one of your most important instruments, even more crucial than problem-specific intervention strategies (Grawe, 2007). Facilitating new adaptive neural circuits and brain systems is a key and unique treatment approach of CIMBS.

Facilitating intends to mobilize positive energy and resources. This positive energy can enhance engagement and shift the nervous system's orientation from avoidance to approach. These interventions can help you trust in and harness the power of motivational circuits that are part of the Primaries, Secondaries, and Tertiaries. Many forms of therapy focus on the patient's problematic symptoms. This multiple brain system paradigm can shift the focus, Facilitating the capabilities of multiple systems to replace or override the problematic nonconscious emotional learning. Facilitating competencies will simultaneously inhibit maladaptive neural circuits.

Facilitating invites the therapist to take the initiative and responsibility for the treatment process. Chapters 4–6—on Go the Other Way, the Therapeutic Attachment Relationship, and the Initial Directed Activation—all describe specific approaches to Facilitating. For example, in Chapter 4, the therapist is invited to pay attention to the adaptive emotional competencies that the patient is revealing in the moment rather than to the more obvious problematic symptoms, behaviors, or thought patterns that seem to overwhelm them. Focusing energy on one of your patient's resources (brain systems) can take the patient out of their baseline equilibrium into a higher level of functioning. Facilitating interventions will mobilize brain systems on all four levels (body, brainstem, basal ganglia, and neocortex) of the nervous system.

Knowing the challenges of Facilitating can help you persevere if you become discouraged. The creation of new and restrengthening of already present neural circuits takes time. "Activating impoverished neurons is not easy because they tend to resist such effort" (Grawe, 2007). Facilitating multiple brain systems will often uncover conflicted, inconsistent, and incongruent emotional goals. For example, the motivation to connect in order to meet the need for attachment may conflict with the goal to avoid connection because it is unsafe.

Facilitating continues and flows into the Differentiating and Training process. *Differentiating* refers to dynamic therapeutic processes that enable the therapist and patient to distinguish and experience the distinct nature of one or more neural circuits and/or brain systems. Differentiating can mean paying attention to multiple systems with equal interest or singling out one or two for special interest. Differentiating also means disentangling and interrupting rigid, maladaptive emotional habit patterns that interfere with the capabilities of other systems. Differentiating strengthens both active and hypoactive systems, modulates overactive systems, and disentangles systems that are in conflict.

Training refers to intentionally and actively exercising and modifying specific neural circuits and brain systems. Training is a form of contextual learning, which has been found to be important for long-term change (Langer, 2016). In the session, the therapist exercises, reinforces, and enhances a neural circuit repeatedly to improve its functionality. Training also refers to the work that the patient takes home between sessions. The BrainMind has a five-hour window of increased flexibility and neuroplasticity at the end of each session. We recommend refreshing the learning of the session to take advantage of that window of opportunity (see Chapter 15). The therapist and patient decide on precise exercises that can be practiced between sessions to maintain and increase the experiential learning of specific neural circuits and brain systems.

What is the benefit of training? The training of these adaptive neural circuits will help make them conscious. This often enables the patient to access them autonomously and spontaneously. These new neural circuits will recruit more neurons as the BrainMind adapts to these novel experiences. With further repetition, the circuits may become myelinated and thus 10 to 100 times faster. It takes time for the brain to adjust to these new neural circuits. The BrainMind will delete neural circuits that are incongruent or not readily valuable. Training will help the patient's BrainMind learn the salience, pleasure, and power of these new neural circuits. The coordination between these distinctive brain systems requires further repetition and practice.

Finally, when individual brain systems are functioning well independently, we Activate and Facilitate them simultaneously to work together. Sustaining these activations is how you enable Integrating to unfold. *Integrating* refers to the simultaneous and cooperative parallel processing of energy and information by multiple distinct brain systems. Integrating is a process that takes place naturally in the nervous system. The therapist can intervene to direct the Integrating process as a treatment that keeps multiple systems active even when such constraints as fear, shame, or fatigue get in the way. This treatment can lead to the opening of closed systems and the releasing of spontaneous self-organizing capacities of the BrainMind. The goals are to develop multiple brain systems that are strong and interacting alongside each other, in parallel processing, so that they provide each other resiliency and form, dare we say, a Fail-Safe Complex Network.

Each of these therapeutic steps, Activating, Facilitating, Differentiating, Training, and Integrating, can take place on a horizontal and/or vertical plane. For example, horizontal Facilitating and Differentiating means the process is directed primarily at one level of mental processing such as the Tertiaries. This means that the therapist's attention is directed at Facilitating and Differentiating the Awareness, Attention, and Authority brain systems. This is the focus of Chapter 8. Alternatively, with vertical Facilitating and Differentiating, the therapist might choose to focus on multiple levels of mental processing with the Safe and Assertive brain systems. This is the focus of Chapter 12. In the real world of therapy, horizontal and vertical Activating, Facilitating, Differentiating, Training, and Integrating are happening to some extent at the same time, even when you are narrowing your focus on one brain system or one mental level of processing.

Each of the words we use to label our therapeutic steps describes a transpiring dynamic treatment process: Activating slides into Facilitating, which morphs into Differentiating and Training, opening the doors to the processes of Integrating. Treatment occurs in all phases of this therapeutic paradigm. For example, when working with conscious brain systems, the focus of Chapters 7–9, Activating the Awareness brain system will naturally bring patients into an increased state of mindfulness. They will be less burdened by their anxiety or depression, and then it becomes an easy transition to shift the focus from Activating the Attention and Awareness brain systems to Facilitating those brain systems by harnessing the energy of the enhancing Secondaries such as Motivation or Value. A simple intervention, sincerely applied, moves the process forward, evoking "Great Awareness." The increased mobilization of the Awareness brain system will inhibit any constraints, such as Fear circuits, that generate the patient's anxiety or other symptoms.

When you choose to utilize a multiple brain systems perspective in your therapy, Differentiating the patient's Awareness, Attention, and Authority brain systems provides further treatment. Even at the most basic level of therapy, working with brain systems potentiates Integrating of multiple systems, providing the mental flexibility we all could use. There is so much more you have to offer when you go on to harness the energy and wisdom of distinct brain systems.

EXPLORING THE UNKNOWN TOGETHER

As we outlined earlier in the book, CIMBS is a different paradigm from what you may be accustomed to. Other therapies make decisions and choose interventions to address the patient's dysfunctions. We are proposing that you make decisions and choose interventions for Activating, Facilitating, Differentiating, Training, and Integrating the adaptive capacities of the emotional brain systems. In the following chapters, you will observe that about 80% of the therapeutic energy is directed to developing the innate resources and only about 20% of the energy is addressing the patient's dysfunctions in order to develop resilient brain systems.

You might anticipate that our treatment process would take each of these steps one at a time, completing each before moving on to the next: Activating, Facilitating, Differentiating, Training, and Integrating. Our minds prefer simple linear sequences that we can follow—well-defined protocols that can be documented step-by-step in treatment manuals. But the CIMBS paradigm mostly does not lend itself to straightforward roadmaps or protocols.

The foundational approaches and interventions described in the previous chapters—Go the Other Way, the Therapeutic Attachment Relationship, and the Initial Directed Activation—provide relatively simple and well-defined cookbook procedures that you can follow with your patients to get the therapeutic process started. But as your sessions proceed, you enter a domain where you can't rely on an established sequence of procedures. In this book, we do not offer a roadmap to help you find the shortest and fastest route to relief for your patients. CIMBS therapy does not follow a direct road from a starting point to an end point.

Activating, Facilitating, Differentiating, Training, and Integrating are neither sequential boxes to be checked nor mileposts on the direct path from dysfunction to health. In fact, you will typically employ them out of sequence or even simultaneously, with repeated steps forward, backward, and to the side. They are a set of powerful instruments at your disposal, and you will need to use each of them many times over as you treat your patient.

THREE METAPHORS OF TREATMENT: PUZZLES, MAZES, AND TEAMWORK

The structure and patterns of the therapeutic processes, interventions, and treatments we illustrate in the next chapters are improvisational. Remember that the Complex Integration of Multiple Brain Systems is primarily a neurobiological paradigm rather than a modality or treatment model. These chapters provide you with the instruments and knowledge that can potentiate limitless treatment possibilities and show how you can personally operationalize this wisdom for (with) your patients. The processes, interventions, and treatments are hard to describe and put into words. We will try, using several metaphors that each provide distinct perspectives, wisdom, and discoveries.

These treatments have evolved to direct energy and neurobiological information. Your focused energy and attention will change whatever system you engage with. When you pay unconditional caring attention to your patient, you change them. The advantages of the Therapeutic Attachment Relationship, Initial Directed Activation, and Go the Other Way are that the energy and intention are precisely and carefully focused. The energy and intention are focused on capabilities and competencies of multiple brain systems at all four levels of the nervous system. The more precise the focus, the more change is possible. When you know these facts, you can more readily trust the processes, interventions, and treatments. In this paradigm your energy can operate as a laser. Focused energy can do work, whereas unfocused energy is easily dissipated (second law of thermodynamics) and therefore less effective.

Puzzle

Imagine treating your patient and their condition as if you were working on a jigsaw puzzle. Some of the puzzle pieces are the neural circuits that make up brain systems. You start noticing the pieces and looking for pieces that alert you to their underlying capabilities. (That is the Initial Directed Activation.) Another puzzle piece is the dynamic manner in which the neural circuits interact with each other. You seek to discern what their arrangement is at this moment today.

Then you pick up a piece (Activate) and examine it (Facilitate). Next you compare it to other pieces to see where they seem to intersect (Differentiate). Eventually you can interact with multiple pieces together (Integrate).

There are many pieces on the table, and you choose to start with one or two that catch your eye. In this process, you do not expect to start at one side of the puzzle and proceed in an orderly fashion directly to the opposite side. Instead, you work on a piece here and a few pieces there in different clusters over different parts of the puzzle. You work with the pieces of the puzzle that are able to be connected at this point (competencies), rather than getting stuck pondering the pieces (problems) that do not seem to fit anywhere. Gradually, with repeated steps, the bigger picture begins to emerge, and the task of assembling the puzzle becomes easier and more rewarding. But your patient has had many small, satisfying, and self-reinforcing successes along the way that kept the process moving forward. The next week we pick up the puzzle again, but not the part we were working on last time, because the dynamic puzzle has changed. Start where the patient is each time. We notice these new clues and puzzle pieces and follow their threads to the capacity, capability, and competence hidden in each puzzle piece. Each session is a mystery for both you and the patient.

Maze

Or imagine treating your patient and their condition as if you were finding your way through a maze. In a conventional maze, you seek the one best path from start to finish. You may take numerous wrong paths before you find the correct route. But in this paradigm, your mission is to explore and improve the maze. There is no wrong way. Any path you take will engage changes in the patient's brain systems, which will open new paths to explore. The pathways of the maze are the connections between brain systems. You strive to work with your patient to find the dead ends (closed systems) and open them up in order to reconnect them with the rest of the pathways. You work toward developing new pathways rather than talking about the problems or the past. You wish to expand any constricted pathways to make them easier to traverse. In the process, you will Activate, Facilitate, Differentiate, Train, and Integrate many different times— perhaps in the course of just a few moments within a session, and perhaps several times a session—as you and the patient together learn your way around and become more adept at traversing all the pathways.

Athletic Team

In one important respect, both the puzzle and maze metaphors fall short, however. Neither of them exhibits the equivalent of neuroplasticity. Suppose that as you pick up each puzzle piece, it responds to your touch. The picture on it becomes sharper, and it begins to change its shape so it fits more closely with its neighbors. Or suppose that as you walk through a maze, the pathways widen beneath your feet and make your way clearer and easier to follow. These imagined puzzles and mazes are organic, living entities, and your presence will influence them to grow and change. You are like the coach of an athletic team, and you Activate, Facilitate, Differentiate, and Train the various skills of each athlete playing each position on the team to improve their individual skills. Then you experiment with various combinations of players to Integrate their enhanced talents and foster a strong, unified, and resilient team effort.

The path you follow with your patient will likely be circuitous and repetitious, but not random or arbitrary. In each session, it will be guided by your ability to seek out the patient's awareness of their psychophysiology and emotions in the Transpiring Present Moment. These are essential clues to the condition of the patient's brain systems. Your job as the therapist is to use these clues to perceive the brain systems that need treatment and to steer the patient to attend to them. As together you repeatedly revisit, Differentiate, and Train these brain systems, individually and in parallel, you both will witness how small stimuli that the therapist provides can trigger large shifts in the patient's condition. When brain systems are ready to begin Integrating, the natural forces of spontaneous self-organization kick in, the puzzle rapidly becomes simpler and more rewarding to assemble, and the maze becomes easier to traverse. At this stage, you both will feel the enhanced abilities of the individual systems and the intensified energy that comes from multiple systems functioning synergistically.

Let us add one more level of complexity: consider that the metaphorical puzzle, maze, or athletic field is actually four-dimensional. You are fitting puzzle pieces, exploring paths, or deploying players at all four levels of the nervous system: peripheral, primary, secondary, and tertiary. This dimensionality makes the therapeutic process both more challenging and more powerful. Your ultimate goal is for brain systems to Integrate in two ways. There is horizontal integration, by which brain systems Integrate at the same level with each other, such as Attention with Awareness, both conscious brain systems. There is also vertical integration, which is brain systems Integrating between different levels. Both are necessary, but the latter is the key to effective therapy. Even as we focus on working with conscious brain systems in the next three chapters, we will show that the peripheral nervous system and the nonconscious brain systems will always be intimately involved.

The steps of Activating, Facilitating, Differentiating, Training, and Integrating are repeated over and over again in a cyclical treatment process. This is an iterative process, a term borrowed from computer programming. It refers to a process in which the same sequence of steps is repeatedly applied to a problem, coming closer to the desired outcome with each reiteration of the sequence.

The upward spiral in the figure begins with the simple Initial Directed Activation of a range of brain systems, followed by a choice to begin Activating, Facilitating, Differentiating, and Training a selected brain system to work on first. At each cycle or iteration in the figure, notice that additional brain systems are recruited to the therapeutic effort, and they begin Integrating with the system(s) Activated earlier. The farther the process develops, the greater the amount of energy and information that these Integrated brain systems can assimilate and channel. You and your patient can observe and physically experience this energetic spiral. It will feel as if you are circumscribing tighter and tighter circles, stoking your shared energy and containing it in a more and more concentrated emotional space. Your ultimate goal is the Fail-Safe Complex Network, in which the patient's brain systems are all active and reinforcing each other's smooth functioning.

CASE STUDIES

We have spent the last several chapters demonstrating to you, in theory and in case study examples, how we assess the conditions and interactions of our patients' various brain systems in sessions, and how we choose to Activate them, and so on, accordingly. Those examples all provide very important instruction in the basic workings of CIMBS. But now we move on from the novice phase to the advanced phase of instruction, and we are going to pull that rug out from under you.

In this phase, you will see that, as we work with a patient, we do not necessarily think directly about identifying which brain systems to target and exactly which interventions to employ at what stage. The therapeutic mechanisms become intrinsic within us. We operate based on knowledge and intuition, and in the session we experience a flow that involves all levels of our nervous systems as well as the patient's. Returning to the analogy of the jazz musician, we are like the pianist who no longer needs to look at the keys, or the singer who no longer needs to read the sheet music, and can improvise from a deeper level of skill.

The therapeutic process we present below is primarily experiential rather than verbal or cognitive, so the transcripts metaphorically contain the music, score, and lyrics of the session. The lyrics are the unedited words that were spoken in the session. The music (in italics) refers to the descriptions of the non-verbal body movements, facial expressions, voice tones, and other psychophysiological phenomena that reveal the emotional activations of both participants. The score refers to the therapist's inner thoughts and moment-to-moment decision points to promote the ebb and flow of Activating the brain system and therapeutic intentions. Although the focus is on the conscious brain systems in Chapters 7–9, naturally the Primaries and Secondaries are in evidence as well. The therapist's inner observations will help you see through the eyes of the therapist the distinct psychophysiological phenomena that are providing evidence of the functioning of the primary and secondary-level brain systems. Please remember these suggestions for all of the transcripts in Part II of the book.

Often it is only in retrospect, as we view and analyze a video recording together, that we dissect the process to determine which brain systems were engaged, how they were behaving, and why our interventions had the effects that they did. As you read the case studies in the chapters that follow, please interrupt any effort your brain is making to figure out what is happening in the session. Rather than figuring out what the therapist is doing or what the patient is saying and experiencing, trust your capacities for observing with different lenses and from different vantage points. Let yourself be moved in our own unique way by this and subsequent therapy sessions.

CHALLENGES: ALL THERAPISTS ARE ANXIOUS

Our trainees sometimes ask if we are anxious at the beginning of a session. We both acknowledge that we are anxious at the start of every session. We don't know what to expect. We are grateful that with this paradigm, we can let go of our need for control and understanding, and approach each session with curiosity and compassion. We can channel our anxiety into expectancy (Seeking) and let go of our own and our patient's expectations. It makes it so much easier to approach each session as an exploration and experiment.

Therapists are often afraid:

1. They will fail: "I won't know what to do. My treatment will not be successful."
2. "My patient is not ready for this much . . . (fill in the blank: emotion, intimacy, immediacy, unpredictability, lack of control)."
3. "I am going to cause a reaction" or "My patient will have a (grief, shame, anger, panic, rage) reaction." Yes, there will be a reaction because you are being a therapist, rather than a friend, parent, sibling, partner, spouse, adversary, boss, and so on. When there is a reaction, Go the Other Way—and be curious. What was happening before the reaction? The shame does not come from the present but from the past. What was happening in the session the moment before the shame reaction occurred? For example, was the patient being assertive, feeling playful, or opening to the connection?
4. Not to know what is going on. "I can't figure it out." "I can't help my patient figure it out." "They will discover that I don't know what I am doing."

What does it take to explore, experiment with, and practice this process? Try a little curiosity and muster a little courage. In one sense it can be simple and direct. The Therapeutic Attachment Relationship and Initial Directed Activation are fairly simple. However, persisting in the Facilitation process takes a commitment to learn a different way of operating. You will learn to install a new operating system to add to the ones you are already familiar with. You will need to access your assertive drive and try something different to treat your patients more efficiently and effectively. It may take a leap of faith when there is no treatment manual, no protocol, no specific sequence of interventions or tasks.

TRUST THE PROCESS

In Chapter 3, we introduced you to Trust the Process. In the next nine chapters, we give you many illustrations of how and why you can come to Trust the Process for yourself and others. On a conceptual level, Trust the Process can become a foundational therapeutic principle, and on a practical level, it is many different therapeutic instruments, guidelines, approaches, and treatments. When you Trust the Process, you will be effectively operating at multiple levels of your patient's nervous system. You will be able to help your patients change

IT IS EFFECTIVE TO TRUST THE PROCESS BECAUSE CIMBS MOBILIZES 10 DISTINCT, WELL-DOCUMENTED TYPES OF NEUROPLASTICITY:

1. Novelty (LeDoux, Medina, Siegel, Grawe)
2. Self-efficacy (Schwartz, Siegel, Grawe)
3. High levels of arousal (Medina)
4. Focused process, effort, mental force, and attention (Schwartz, Grawe)
5. Constraint-induced neuroplasticity (Davidson, Doidge 2015)
6. Emotional memory reconsolidation (Ekman, Panksepp & Biven, 2012)
7. Change occurs only in the present; experiential learning (LeDoux)
8. Reinforcing adaptive neural circuits: "Neurons that fire together wire together" (Hebb, Grawe)
9. Neural synchrony (Davidson, LeDoux)
10. Neuroplastic competition (Doidge, 2015)

Trust the Process offers an umbrella of dynamic phenomena that can give your therapy focus, energy, and precision. The Process refers to:

1. The therapist's attention to the Therapeutic Attachment Relationship, Transpiring Present Moment, psychophysiological phenomena, and Initial Directed Activation
2. Activating, observing, Facilitating, and Differentiating the primary-level, secondary-level, and tertiary-level brain systems
3. Sustaining, Training, and Integrating multiple distinct brain systems

the structure of their BrainMind and the manner in which their brain systems process energy and information. Trusting the Process can help you more readily let go of expectations, let go of needs for positive feedback, and welcome discomfort and feelings of being off-balance.

It may seem that we are simply asking you to trust us—that we are offering you psychotherapeutic techniques validated by our many years of experience. But there is more to trust in this paradigm we are presenting. This process is solidly based on proven neurobiological knowledge of brain systems, psychophysiology, neuroplasticity, neurotransmitters, and different neuroanatomical levels of the nervous system. You can trust the foundational neuroscience of CIMBS as you trust your intuitive and learned belief in the reliability, truth, and strength of such natural phenomena as gravity, biochemistry, and biology.

When you read the case studies in these next seven chapters, you will observe how we choose to intervene in patients' responses. You may wonder what prompted the therapist to do this or that. It is a combination of intuition, experience, curiosity, scientific experimentation, treatment priorities, patient factors, and therapist factors. We choose a brain system to explore because in some way it has called to us, and we are curious and interested, not because we are smart, knowledgeable, or experienced.

As we mentioned in the introduction at the beginning of the book, some of the case studies are long and repetitive. They are intended to give a more in-depth experience of the process from the perspective of both therapist and patient. As you will see, in order to successfully Facilitate, Differentiate, and Integrate multiple brain systems, lots of repetition is required. If you are not ready to immerse yourself in that experience, you could skip over it and check it out later if you have developed a deeper interest in learning more.

The improvisational nature of this paradigm, with its therapeutic processes, interventions, and treatments, may seem daunting at first. You may wonder how you can know which brain system to target or which therapeutic instrument to use to help your patient. We suggest you keep a beginner's mind in which there are endless possibilities. Put aside the limitations of your expertise for now. This becomes a process of discovery rather than explanations. You could choose to intervene in a different way and provide excellent treatment.

When you Trust the Process, you can have confidence in stepping through any of the numerous entry points into this psychotherapeutic approach. Once you have embraced the intimacy of working with brain systems, there will be new crossroads at every minute and every turn. It can be a relief to no longer have to rely on nor be constrained by any therapeutic modality. Any path could be useful when your orientation is to Facilitate distinct brain systems. It does not matter which one you choose, as all will focus the treatment energy for more effective therapeutic results. You can look at the empirical evidence after each intervention, make a hypothesis, and then choose one of numerous possible next steps. Because the process is not linear, there are no dead ends. You can be a complete novice and the process will still work, no matter how you fear you are bumbling. But rest assured that these instruments are highly effective no matter how you use them.

Trusting the Process, rather than the intervention or the choice of which path to take, makes it all work. Your patient may not be able to tell you that it is working, and you may be tempted to give up before the results are visible. You may worry that the process and your patient's responses to it are out of your control. It's awkward at first. When you miss an opportunity because you took a different path, the source of the missed opportunity is not gone—it will keep presenting itself if it is important or needed. You could choose to focus on Awareness and this could happen, or you could focus on Care and that might happen. Any path would have added growth for the patient, as they learn something new and you do too. Underlying constraints will either reveal themselves again or will melt away because of the new adaptive learning that is being developed and installed. The nature of this treatment paradigm fully engages the patient factors and therapist factors, and for those reasons it is the most effective paradigm we have seen demonstrated.

CHAPTER 7

Conscious Brain Systems: The A-Team

···

DEVELOPING PSYCHOPHYSIOLOGICAL COLLABORATION

Several years ago Albert did an initial intake with a patient we will call Carol, a depressed woman, who agreed to start psychotherapy two weeks later. When Carol came back for her first session, she brought her husband. She wanted to ask a few more questions and see if her husband had any concerns of his own. After they explored all of her questions, she said she was satisfied. At that point, Albert wanted an explicit commitment from Carol to start the process, so he invited her by saying, "Do you want to do therapy?" She immediately looked to her husband and asked him, "Do you think this is a good idea?" He said it was completely up to her. Albert invited her again: "Do you want to do therapy?" She asked him for his advice, and he turned it back to her. Albert invited her again: "Do you want to do therapy?" This time Carol admitted, with a slight shake of her head, "I am really afraid. I do not know if it will help me." Together they acknowledged and welcomed her fear of the unknown. So Albert invited her a fourth time: "Do you want to do therapy?" This time Carol was able to emphatically say "Yes." She sat up and spoke with a deeper voice as she observed, "I know that this is what I want to do to better myself. I feel more physically solid." Together they reinforced her experience of trust in herself. This example highlights the importance of both inviting collaboration explicitly and carefully Activating the patient's Authority, Autonomy, Agency, and Assertive brain

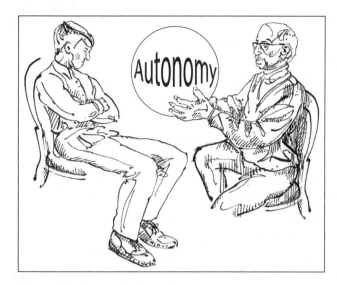

Figure 7.1: Giving the Patient Autonomy

systems. This process may seem repetitive at first. However, we hope you can see how the invitations are intended to harness the power of each of these brain systems to enable the therapy to be more effective on multiple levels of the patient's BrainMind. Figure 7.1 is intended to illustrate how the therapist can help the patient harness their own power, authority and autonomy.

We chose to start this chapter with a story about collaboration and Activating the Authority, Autonomy, and Agency brain systems. We sometimes tell this story in our training courses in order to bring home the importance of collaboration and to show how quickly and simply you can Activate several of the conscious brain systems. We defined Activating in Chapter 1, illustrated it in Chapter 6 with Initial Directed Activation, and this chapter will give you other perspectives and approaches to Activating with an emphasis on the Tertiaries. If you choose to utilize the Therapeutic Attachment Relationship or Initial Directed Activation, or focus your shared awareness on the Transpiring Present Moment, you will be simply and skillfully Activating multiple conscious and nonconscious brain systems. There is nothing complicated about Activating, but when you keep that as one of your deliberate intentions, your therapeutic process will harness the power of many brain systems. That is where the magic comes from. The following chapters examine other tools in the CIMBS therapeutic toolbox: Facilitating, Differentiating, Training, and Integrating. As we just described when introducing this second part of the book, these actions can be applied in unpredictable sequences, and even all at once.

There are several simple paths to Activating the Tertiaries at the start of any session. You could focus on Awareness by starting with "How is your *presence with yourself* right now?" or Attention with "What are you experiencing *right now?*" or Authority with "Do *you want to* pay attention to yourself right now?" You can utilize the Initial Directed Activation and observe the psychophysiological phenomena of specific brain systems in response to your intervention (Activation). We have chosen to start exploring Activating the Tertiaries from the perspective of collaboration because of its importance in therapy and the Therapeutic Attachment Relationship. We recommend starting with the Initial Directed Activation because of how well it brings the therapist and patient into the Transpiring Present Moment and Activates a broad range of brain systems. However, sometimes there is some system or psychophysiology that is calling for our attention, as in the case story above.

You have already seen lots of examples of Activating in the case studies from the earlier chapters. This chapter adds some key details about Activating the Tertiaries such as collaboration. The succeeding chapters devote more attention to the therapeutic processes of Facilitating, Differentiating, Training, and Integrating.

EXPLICIT (CONSCIOUS) COLLABORATION

All patients approach therapy with some level of ambivalence. Each patient has their own distinct background that contributes to their ambivalence. Unless we address it explicitly, this ambivalence will usually stay under the radar, and you will be working in frustration around the ambivalence without realizing it. Many therapists have a tendency to presume that their patient's presence in the session is evidence of their desire and ability to collaborate. We have found that if you do not explicitly test their capability for collaborating, you will not discover either their actual competence at collaborating—which may be hidden and therefore implicit—or some of the constraints that are holding back your progress.

"Do you want to do therapy?" is a simple invitation that is often overlooked. This intervention is actually an explicit invitation to collaborate. Carol was not yet ready or able to collaborate at the beginning. She projected her power onto her husband and then onto Albert. The repetition of the invitation helped drill down underneath her baseline powerlessness to uncover the deeper constraint of her Fear brain system: "I am really afraid." The next invitation further activated her Authority and Autonomy brain systems, and this shifted her internal emotional balance. This time her psychophysiology changed significantly. Carol's body claimed her full posture. The psychophysiology of Carol's voice revealed a reduction in fear and an increase in her ability for social connection (Porges, 2011). Her words were congruent with this internal shift in her BrainMind. This evidence also showed us that her "Yes" was not a compliant agreement (with the therapist). Carol's spontaneous assertions, "I feel more physically solid," and "I know that this is what I want to do to better myself," revealed evidence of her new competence in collaborating with her therapist in the frightening work of therapy. Each of these four invitations helped Carol learn that Albert trusted her authority and autonomy and that he wanted her to come to trust her own authority and autonomy as well.

We started experimenting 20 years ago with enhancing our patients' will and drive in order to help them participate more actively in their therapy. As we were experimenting with the Therapeutic Attachment Relationship, the Initial Directed Activation, and explicit collaboration, we sometimes tried this intervention: "Do you want to pay attention to your self?" When we explicitly invited their choice to exercise their will or drive, we discovered that many patients were unable to respond. We received responses such as, "I am afraid of what I will find." "I am caught up in my obsessive worries." "I freeze when you ask that question." "I don't feel worthy." Patients might change the subject, talk on as though they did not hear the invitation, or give a compliant answer such as, "That's why I am here." What do you make of those responses? Initially they were puzzling to us as well. None of those responses actually answered the invitation.

In ordinary conversation, one might respond to the content of their responses. For example, "I am afraid of what I will find" might cause you to try to reassure them. Or "I am caught up in my obsessive worries" might cause you to inquire about their worries. But we wondered what was happening in their conscious minds that made them unable to answer the invitation. We realized that the patient's inability to answer that invitation could provide us with information about constraints on their conscious brain systems.

Clearly these patients were not capable of claiming their authority. On the surface, it seemed like they could express their wants, emotions, and fears.

When we tested their ability to actually exercise their autonomous desire to get help for themselves, however, they could not respond to the invitations. Carol is an example of this. Even though she came to the session to start the process of psychotherapy, she could not seize her autonomous authority and personal power to collaborate in the process.

The invitation to collaborate in therapy seems like such a respectful, benign intervention. What seemed so simple turned out to be much more complicated. These invitations to patients' authority were activating nonconscious psycho-physiological reactions such as fear, shame, or guilt. That was surprising to us. What was happening inside our patients' BrainMinds when invitations to their authority triggered such reactions? These counterintuitive emotional reactions told us that much more was going on underneath the surface.

Our patients were equally surprised to discover that they could not respond to invitations to their autonomous authority. "I don't know why I can't answer that invitation." Our respect for their autonomous authority was unfamiliar, dis-orienting, and uncomfortable for them. Often we discovered that no one had ever invited them to collaborate on an empowered level. They did not have an internal search pattern or a felt sense of their own autonomous will, choice, or authority. We welcomed these discoveries, because they provided us with empirical evidence of transpiring psychophysiological phenomena that we could not explain at the time. This insight opened up some new avenues of exploration and further discoveries.

We began to experiment with discerning the underlying brain-system roots of those reactions. What we discovered was that some patients were unable to answer that question because they had little or no self-awareness. Some were unable to direct their attention to the invitation. Some had little sense of their own authority. Some were frightened to express their autonomy. And some had no sense of their own self-agency. We tested our hypotheses that awareness, attention, authority, autonomy, and agency are actually distinct conscious brain systems. Our research confirmed our hypotheses and guided us in developing treatments for Differentiating, Facilitating, and Integrating these conscious brain systems. There are probably other important conscious brain systems, but these five A-Team systems are the ones that we have found most useful in psy-chotherapy. Each one can be a teammate for you and for your patient. Team-mates potentiate collaboration. We explore that relationship further in this and the next two chapters.

Figure 7.1 is intended to show you what it looks and feels like figuratively when the patient is unable to take the ball of their own autonomous power. Figure 7.2 attempts to show you what it looks and feels like when the patient is able to seize their autonomous power and run with it. The energy in the room changes greatly when the patient is able to override their fear, grief, shame, or guilt and experience the sense of power and freedom of movement. There are significant psychophysiological shifts that provide you with empirical evidence that they now have access to their autonomous power. The voice, body language, facial expressions, eye contact, and posture changes provide empirical evidence that there has been a liberation from previous constraints and implicit emotional learning.

7.1. Therapist handing the power ball of authority to patient who cannot take it. He keeps his arms crossed and turns aside.

7.2. The patient stands up with the power ball of his autonomous authority firmly in his grasp. Now he can fully collaborate—but not until then!

Figure 7.2: The Patient Owning Autonomy

IMPLICIT (NONCONSCIOUS) COLLABORATION: DISCOVERING THE SELF

This process of inviting explicit collaboration revealed that many different patients do not possess ready access to a strong sense of Self. What is the Self? Each conscious brain system has highly evolved self-functions (Damasio, 2010; Panksepp & Biven, 2012). The self-function of each brain system evolved as a result of the saliency of the activations that further the needs of that system. There is no simple definition of the Self, but for our purposes, Self is not a thing but a dynamic process (Damasio, 2010). We have studied several different neurobiological perspectives on how the BrainMind creates the Self by integrating the functioning of the different levels of the nervous system (please see the sidebar on Self on page 186).

Please recall (Chapter 1) how our nervous system processes energy and information primarily from the bottom up. The lowest level is the peripheral nervous system and the body, next the brainstem, then the basal ganglia, and finally the neocortex. The lowest three levels are all nonconscious, and only the top level is conscious. Each level has different capabilities that contribute to forming the Self. Being conscious, having a mind, and having a Self are different brain processes produced by the operation of different brain components. Ideally, they merge seamlessly on any given day. With practice, you can learn how to readily detect these different levels of Self in your patients.

As we researched Activating conscious brain systems in explicit conscious collaboration, we found that the source of many of patients' difficulties came from lower levels of the nervous system. Activating conscious-level systems was also Activating nonconscious brain systems. It became clear that, in order to work with the conscious brain systems effectively, we also needed implicit collaboration from the nonconscious brain systems. That is, we needed to engage the entire Self, including the nonconscious brain systems that might be entangled with or constraining the conscious brain systems.

Our description of the Self may seem foreign to you, since it refers to nonconscious dimensions of Self. This definition may conflict with your own felt sense of self. Think of the iceberg again. The Self you are aware of is the tip of the iceberg in yourself or in others. Although in this chapter we focus on the conscious brain systems, we must also look at their inseparable relationship to the hidden mass of iceberg, the nonconscious brain systems, to understand the Self.

In the example of Carol above, not all of her responses came from her conscious brain systems. We saw that fear was limiting her sense of personal power. Her psychophysiology provided empirical evidence that her shift to conscious assertions of increased authority had roots in a deeper place in her nonconscious nervous system, the Motivation and Assertive brain systems. You cannot readily know the capabilities of the nonconscious levels of the Self unless you explicitly test those neural circuits.

We as therapists tend to take our Self for granted. So we often take our patient's Self for granted as well, and they also do not know their own quality of Self. For example, what kind of a Self does the person have who can only vigilantly scan for danger? They are constantly in survival mode, and so they cannot take in the safeness, care, or connection of the therapist or other relationships.

Understanding the multidimensionality of the Self and early evolutionary development of self-processes has helped us understand Carol and many others like her. If the patient's nervous system was constantly in survival mode during early childhood, the capabilities of the Self will be quite different from those of someone whose survival was not threatened. The BrainMind of an unthreatened child will be able to develop a more flexible, integrated, and resilient Self especially at the deepest nonconscious level.

When you fully Activate and test your patient's Self capabilities, you can discover the inner workings of their nonconscious mind. Focusing your relational energy and directing the process will reveal patient factors that would otherwise remain invisible. This knowledge can be a two-edged sword. The benefit is discovering hidden capabilities that will enable the patient to more fully participate in their therapy. It can go straight to the heart of the nonconscious constraints, and at the same time activate the patient's capabilities for seizing their autonomous authority to fully collaborate in the therapeutic process. However, these functions can be underdeveloped or shut down by nonconscious pain, shame, and/or fear.

The accompanying sidebar summarizes some research findings on levels of the Self. In the coming chapters, we refer in particular to the Reflective Self, which is consciously aware of its separateness from others. This conscious level of the Self participates in such brain systems as Autonomy and Awareness.

MULTIPLE LEVELS OF SELF

The following discussion detailing some of the different aspects of the Self may be academic but has had practical benefits for us (Figure 7.3; see the four levels of self). These academic underpinnings have helped us make sense of counterintuitive and anomalous phenomena found in our clinical research. This knowledge has helped us trust the therapeutic processes of Activating, Differentiating, and Integrating multiple brain systems. This knowledge has also reinforced our trust in the highly evolved and powerful nonconscious emotional brain systems.

Nonconscious Levels

Body Self: Resonant interface (body-loop; Damasio, 2010) between activations in the body, peripheral nervous systems, and spinal cord. For example, the heart relays information about rate and pressure to the vagal nerve, facilitating a heathy blood flow homeostasis.

Brainstem Self

1. Each primary-level brain system has its own ability to sustain its activation (Self-function; Damasio, 2010) through some mix of internal feedback. Biological value has influenced the evolution of these brain structures.
2. Some mix of primary-level brain systems operating simultaneously with their own sustainability produces the Core Self (Damasio, 2010).

Basal Ganglia Self: The interface between secondary-level and primary-level brain systems produces our personalities and emotional and behavioral patterns that are familiar to us and to those who know us. This dynamic Self is more complex and nuanced and modulates the activations of the Body Self and Brainstem Self. You can observe the adaptive and maladaptive aspects of the Basal Ganglia Self. Recall that this level of the BrainMind is where nonconscious implicit emotional learning takes place.

1. Adaptive: self-possessed, self-soothing, self-assured, self-confident, self-worth, self-esteem
2. Maladaptive: self-effacing, self-conscious, selfish, self-defeating, reactive self, dissociative, depersonalized

Conscious Level

Cortical Self: At this level there is a range of subjective experiences and observations. These experiences may or may not be under the conscious direction of the patient.

1. Autopilot Self (without thought), Compliant Self, Defiant Self, Mindless Self, Subordinate Self, Ruminative Self
2. Reflective Self (thought-full), Autonomous Self, Self-efficacy, self-aware, self-affirming

Reflective Self is consciously aware of its separateness from others. Damasio uses the expression *autobiographical* self and Panksepp uses *idiographic* self to describe this quality of self.

Your patient's Body Self is revealed by the variety, spontaneity, and complexity of their physical movements. The Brainstem Self is revealed by the range and activations of the primary-level emotions such as Care, Connection, or Play. You can observe your patient's Basal Ganglia Self by noting the fluidity and flexibility of their range of emotional activations. The Cortical Self manifests with the patient's

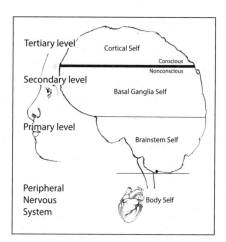

Figure 7.3: Levels of Self in the BrainMind

conscious presence and awareness of their thoughts and ability to choose the focus of their attention. The rest of the chapter explores in greater depth the BrainMind's conscious brain systems that arise from your patient's Cortical Self.

Activating Levels of Self

The Therapeutic Attachment Relationship will naturally activate the Body Self and the Brainstem Self. The patient's body is reading your body and energy at all times (Porges, 2011). Your intimate presence will mobilize your patient's Safe, Care, and Connection brain systems. You can observe how their psychophysiology responds to those activations. Your Initial Directed Activation will further activate the Body Self and the Brainstem Self. You can come to trust that your energy will activate those systems. Then you can observe the Conscious Self and explore their Self-Awareness with an invitation such as, "What are you aware of right now?" They could have 1,000 different responses and then you can follow one or more of those transpiring leads.

CONSCIOUS BRAIN SYSTEMS IN DEPTH

When you read Carol's story about collaboration above, or Ann's transcript (Baby Blues in Chapter 2), what were you aware of feeling inside yourself? What did you experience as you read about each of those interactions? We ask those questions to bring you in touch with your own Awareness, Attention, and Authority brain systems. We have found that the more we are present to ourselves, the more attuned we are to our patients. We all tend to take our conscious mental capabilities for granted because they seem to be ever-present when we are awake. We rarely take a closer look to discern the quality of our Authority or Agency brain systems at any given time. The capabilities of the conscious brain systems tend to remain constant from year to year. They are part of our personality and habit patterns.

Looking at your patient through the lenses of the conscious brain systems can help you see patient factors in a different light, literally. The metaphor we have found useful with our trainees is to imagine looking at the patient through a multifaceted prism. When you send light through such a prism, the energy is refracted into many distinct beams with a rainbow spectrum of colors. Each beam could represent a brain system, and the colors reveal the continuum of activity within that brain system. Each capability has its own value. They are not sequential but simultaneous; they operate in parallel, as we described in

Chapter 2 (Figure 2.2). Below we expand on the definitions of the conscious brain systems that we first presented in Chapter 1.

Awareness

Our Awareness brain system detects and observes the presence of bodily sensations and activations of other parts of the nervous system. Our Awareness brain system is on a conscious-nonconscious continuum. For example, our bodies are sending information about sensations to our BrainMinds at all times. We are not conscious of most of that information or energy. We only become conscious and aware of those activations when they cross some threshold in the secondary-level brain systems and activate the conscious capabilities of the tertiary-level Awareness brain system. That threshold is not fixed; it varies from person to person, and depends on many internal factors as well. Have you ever noticed that your awareness of fear is not afraid even when you are terrified (Kabat-Zinn, 1990)?

The Awareness brain system can be observed when your patients are able to carefully reflect on and describe their authentic internal experiences that are congruent with your observations. For example, the patient might spontaneously say, "I am feeling quite anxious right now," or "I am feeling surprisingly calm." Sometimes the Awareness brain system is active yet underdeveloped, and so there are few if any words to reveal the awareness of different emotions or bodily sensations. For example, a patient we will call Daniel was feeling touched by the care he was receiving, and had tears running down his cheeks, and yet, when asked, he was not aware of what he was feeling or the presence of his tears. The Initial Directed Activation contains several activations and invitations that are directed toward the Awareness brain system: "It is important that you are present, and aware and attentive to yourself. What are you aware of right now?"

Figure 7.4: Awareness Brain System

The Awareness basketball player (Figure 7.4) illustrates an open body posture, open eyes, and open face. This player can be aware of whatever is happening inside his body and around his person.

Attention

Our Attention brain system is also on a conscious-nonconscious continuum. Our nonconscious BrainMind is paying attention to many things at all times. The brainstem is paying attention to our blood pressure, heart rate, body temperature, and nonconscious emotional activations as well. For example, if there is a loud noise, our conscious attention will be hijacked by the Fear and Safe brain systems, which will initiate innate survival strategies. We have no choice in the matter, and often we are not even aware of what took over our attention. Conscious-level attention can have a range of qualities. We could be daydreaming, ruminating, or intensely focused on something important to us. When the Attention brain system is activated, you can observe that your patient is able to mindfully direct their conscious focus toward their internal experiences or any topic.

The Attention basketball player (Figure 7.5) is concentrating carefully on dribbling the basketball while also paying attention to his teammates. You can see and feel the intensity of his attentional focus. You can observe your patient's ability to focus attention by noting the nature and quality of the eye gaze. For example, are they focused off to the side to concentrate more clearly internally, or is their gaze random and unfocused?

Figure 7.5: Attention Brain System

Authority

The Authority brain system enables us to discern and be open to our own unique wants, desires, preferences, and choices. This system is the author of those longings, wants, and desires, and probably has its roots in the self-functions of the nonconscious Primaries such as Care, Seeking, and Play. Patients have varying capabilities to know and express their wants and desires. The example of Carol revealed how Activating the Authority brain system can play a major role in therapeutic collaboration. You could observe how those Activations helped Carol "show up" inside herself and exercise her ability to make choices and take a more active role in her life.

When our Authority brain system is well engaged, we are consciously clear about our wants and desires. We have the ability to make basic choices that reflect our preferences and feelings. The Authority brain system enables your patient's ability to experience subjectivity (Panksepp & Biven, 2012) and have access to experiential memories (Damasio, 2010). You can observe psychophysiological activations of the Authority brain system when your patient speaks with a deeper and more resonant voice. Their body language is more fluid and spontaneous. They look more comfortable in their own skin.

The Authority basketball player (Figure 7.6) is exercising her authority to choose to pass the ball to one of her teammates.

Figure 7.6: Authority Brain System

Autonomy

The Autonomy brain system knows we have the freedom to be independent and self-governing. It enables us to be comfortable being separate from the judgments and expectations of others. With this capability we can make informed, unco-erced choices and decisions. The ability to make choices that go against the expec-tations and desires of important people in our lives is a unique capability of this brain system. For example, many patients grew up in environments where mak-ing autonomous choices was threatening to their relationships with their parents. They learned to shut down their desire for autonomy because it felt unsafe.

Many people have trouble distinguishing between the capabilities of the Authority and Autonomy brain systems. Some patients can experience their own wants and desires, yet they do not feel safe to exercise their autonomy and speak up for their ability to be separate from the needs and wants of others. For some, bringing the patient into direct contact with Autonomy can be "anxiety-provoking like crazy." They do not comprehend or experience themselves as having a choice. Albert kept asking about Carol about her choice; she later remarked, "It felt foreign to me, and that was surprising to know that. It piqued my interest and curiosity. At the same time I felt that my authority was being valued, and so I was feeling safer. I had a sense that the therapist was not going to charge ahead without respecting my autonomy."

Your patient's Autonomy brain system will enable them to readily make decisions that override the innate tendency to please others. Patients with a resilient Autonomy brain system can both collaborate and say "no" independently. This brain system can give our patients a sense of their own esteem. For example, Carol did not have access to her Autonomy brain system at first. She deferred her choice to get help for herself to her husband, to her therapist, and then to her Fear brain system. Later, her Assertive and Motivation brain systems were able to provide enough energy to override her Fear and people-pleasing patterns.

The Autonomy basketball player (Figure 7.7) is operating independently and collaborating with the others. That player is not limited to playing a supportive role.

Figure 7.7: Autonomy Brain System

Agency

The Agency brain system refers to our capability to direct our power and trust, enabling us to make things happen in our life. When we have access to our Agency, we can let go of control and our expectations. We come to trust our Self, wants, and intentions, and we no longer need to manipulate or control a particular outcome. This brain system plays an important role in our self-efficacy (Chapter 15). To help you understand the difference between Agency and Authority, let's use an automobile as a metaphor. Authority is the driver making choices, Autonomy the engine generating the power to take us where we want to go, and Agency the transmission delivering the energy to where it can be put to productive use. Helping your patient have access to their Agency brain system can transform your therapy and help them take charge of their lives.

Your patient becomes more animated as they express and embody their desires. The Agency brain system is revealed in the patient's present-moment spontaneity of voice, facial expressions, and animated posture and body language. The more the patient can be emotionally (passionately) invested in their wants, the more power and effort will be available to exercise their Agency. For example, Carol started to engage some of her Agency when she said "yes" emphatically. Her voice was deeper, and her body posture became more erect. You might observe other psychophysiological phenomena such as spontaneous animated gestures or hand and arm movements to show determination.

The Agency brain system is naturally connected to the nonconscious primary-level Assertive brain system at the level of the brainstem. No matter how much your patient struggles with procrastination, passivity, or defiance, their Agency brain system brought them to seek help. Each of the conscious brain systems operates independently, but the ability to work with Agency often depends on access to the Authority and Autonomy brain systems. Working with your patient's agency can meet their needs for mastery and self-esteem.

The Agency basketball player (Figure 7.8) is shooting the basketball. He is exercising his self-determination and self-efficacy. He is actually making things happen in his life.

Figure 7.8: Agency Brain System

BRAIN SYSTEM DYSFUNCTIONS

In the next two chapters, we go into depth about Activating, Facilitating, Differentiating, Training, and Integrating conscious brain systems. But before we can go into detail about the methodology of working with conscious brain systems, we want to elaborate on the types of brain system problems that we need to treat. After years of experimentation, we have discerned that there are at least three common types of brain system dysfunctions that can cause constraints in the BrainMind and may be the source of symptoms: hyperactive, hypoactive or underdeveloped, and hyperconnected or entangled brain systems. Observing psychophysiological phenomena (Chapters 2, 14) can give you clues that reveal which brain systems may be hyperactive, hypoactive, or hyperconnected.

The following descriptions include examples from previous case studies and one new case study to highlight psychophysiological phenomena that give the therapist evidence of dysfunctional distinct brain systems. These dysfunctions illustrate what we stated above, that we cannot treat the conscious brain systems in isolation from the secondary- and primary-level brain systems, where the ultimate source of the problems may lie.

Hyperactive

Hyperactive systems are automatized, conditioned sets of neural circuits that have been activated so frequently that they have become rigid and closed to new learning. They have the highest probability of being activated by certain stimuli that are sometimes called triggers. These automatized neural circuits create habitual behaviors that can become reactions, defenses, resistances, and personality phenomena. For example, a hyperactive Fear brain system can shut down all the other brain systems (survival trumps anything else; Figure 2.4), and therefore can prevent even the awareness of the other brain systems.

When one or more brain systems are hyperactive, the psychophysiological activations of those brain systems are out of proportion to the transpiring situation in the session.

You may be familiar with examples of PTSD. Even though the trauma occurred years ago, the hyperactive Fear brain system has been unable to progress or heal. Even minor stresses such as a loud noise or sudden movement might trigger a hyperactive Fear brain system and push the person into survival mode. This overreaction might prevent the Awareness, Safe, or Connection brain systems from moderating the terror reaction.

For example, in Chapter 5, Steve's attention brain system appears to be on high alert. His vigilant attention is causing psychophysiological changes including an increased heart rate and shallow breathing. He is looking out for dangers around or inside himself. He tries to reassure himself that he is okay, but continues to feel unsafe. Albert is able to activate Steve's Awareness and Authority brain systems to override his near-panic anxiety.

Hypoactive

Hypoactive brain systems have been activated so rarely that they are weak, underdeveloped, and unlikely to be activated. Even when activated, they are unable to handle large amounts of energy and information without shutting down. There is little or no psychophysiological response when the therapist intentionally Activates a distinct hypoactive brain system. We do not need to understand or figure out what caused the brain system to become hypoactive in order for our interventions and treatment to be effective.

For example, consider the case story of Barbara. Beatriz began the Initial Directed Activation and immediately encountered a hypoactive conscious Attention brain system. She quickly discerned that the Care and Connection brain systems were also hypoactive.

> **Beatriz:** We are here to pay close caring attention to you [*shiny eyes, intimate eye gaze, warm smile, and moving her arms toward Barbara*]. What happens when I say, "We are here to pay close caring attention to you?"
>
> **Barbara:** I don't know how to pay caring attention to me. It is as if it is blank inside of me. As if I don't have any knowledge of ever doing it. Paying loving attention to me is blank inside of me. It is like I am in front of a blank wall.

By Activating the conscious Attention brain system and using it as a portal to the nonconscious, Beatriz was able to access and Activate the deeper level brain systems. Every time Beatriz Activated Barbara's Care brain system, Barbara's face and body remained perfectly flat and unresponsive. After Beatriz repeatedly Facilitated Barbara's Care brain system, she began to experience a sense of warmth in her chest for a second, and then it would disappear. Recognizing that the Care and Connection brain systems were underdeveloped, Beatriz focused the therapy on Activating and Facilitating those brain systems. She activated and reinforced Barbara's feeling of warmth toward herself inside her chest again and again until Barbara was able to sustain the feeling of caring attention toward herself without shutting down.

We learned later (on her one-year follow-up) that Barbara's mother had been depressed when she was growing up, and that whenever Barbara sought care and embracing, her mother would push her away, saying, "Don't bother me right now. Go away. I don't like being touched." Barbara learned to repress her innate Care and Connection brain systems to survive and keep herself in her mother's good graces. And so these brain systems became underdeveloped and weak. But it is a demonstration of the unique nature of CIMBS that Beatriz was able to treat Barbara effectively while staying in the Transpiring Present Moment and without ever delving into that family history.

Hyperconnected

There is an old saying in neuroscience that "neurons that fire together wire together" (LeDoux, 1996). Because of trauma or neglect, some brain systems have fired together repeatedly and persistently for such long periods of time that they have come to operate as a single functional unit. These hyperconnected or entangled brain systems are undifferentiated and are in need of Training and treatment. The psychophysiological responses are constrained, conflicted, or even contradictory when brain systems are entangled. Differentiating hyperconnected brain systems requires persistence, patience, and trust.

Hyperconnected brain systems often involve primary-level brain systems being entangled and constrained by secondary-level brain systems (Figure 3.1).

In Chapter 4, we presented patient Penny, who began therapy in a nearly frozen state. Beginning with her conscious Awareness brain system, Beatriz gained access to Penny's Primaries and Secondaries to discover how her Play brain system was hyperconnected with the Fear brain system:

> **Penny:** It feels like fun! . . . [*scrunches her face and turns her face sideways*]. And now my palms are clammy and my mouth is dry. My throat hurts. I need to go and hide! I know I am safe in my head but my body tells me that I need to run and hide!

One source of Penny's sensory information—"It feels like fun!"—was coming from her body at this transpiring moment in time. The other source—"my palms are clammy and my mouth is dry. My throat hurts. I need to go and hide!"—was likely emotional entanglement from previous learning or trauma.

We learned later (in her one-year follow-up) that Penny was born with a congenital heart condition and needed to have three open-heart operations before the age of one. Her mother would become very agitated when Penny followed her innate instinct to play. She shamed her daughter's play, calling it dangerous and unsafe. Therefore Penny's Play brain system became entangled with her Fear and Shame brain systems. Those brain systems were not able to develop their own unique potential to generate energy, process information, or have access to their own independent evolved wisdom. Again, this history was interesting, but was not necessary for her treatment to succeed.

TABLE 7.1 : **Key Characteristics of Brain System Dysfunctions and Their Psychophysiological Symptoms**

Brain System Dysfunction	Nature of Dysfunction	Psychophysiological Phenomena
Hyperactive	Activated too frequently, highest probability of firing	Psychophysiological activation out of proportion to the situation
Hypoactive	Fired too little, weak, underdeveloped, unlikely to be activated	Little or no psychophysiological response when activated
Hyperconnected	Brain systems fused or entangled with each other	Psychophysiological responses constrained, conflicted, or contradictory

ACTIVATING CONSCIOUS BRAIN SYSTEMS

The Therapeutic Attachment Relationship and the Initial Directed Activation will mobilize the conscious brain systems. Your focused and directed energy toward the patient's Attention and Awareness brain systems, for example, will energize their BrainMind and awaken their sense of themselves and their present-moment experience. You may be able to detect to what extent Activating these systems is coming from within the patient and/or from your interest and care. The therapist can both mobilize the power-generating capacity of these systems and also provide external processing capacity. Change requires energy, and the therapist can be an instrument of change.

Repeatedly Activating and Facilitating the conscious brain systems will make them stronger and increasingly resilient. These resilient differentiated brain systems will become your patient's teammates. Resilient brain systems will generate their own energy, tap into their own wisdom, and process the energy and information effectively and efficiently.

For example, in Chapter 5, we used the intervention "Do you want to pay attention to yourself right now?" to activate patient Steve's Attention and Authority brain systems and test how they functioned. That intervention contained an implicit respect for Steve's autonomy, as well as trust that his Authority brain system would be activated by our intervention.

Assessing Conscious Brain Systems

Let's assess the results of the question, "Do you want to pay attention to yourself right now?" The patient might immediately say, "That's why I am here [*slight head shake*]." What do you make of that reaction? Are they shaking their head in disbelief (that you would ask such a senseless question)? Is there a nonconscious reaction of "no"? Was their response immediate, without a pause to ponder the invitation? Did they not actually answer the question? Was there no assertion of authority, such as "I want . . ."? Such answers reveal compliance. In a sense they are saying, "I am here to do what I expect or what is expected of me."

As we described earlier in this chapter, in ordinary conversation you might go along with their statement, "That's why I am here," and assume that they do want to pay attention to themselves. However, as therapists we can also pay attention to other important information. For example, this answer was not collaborative. The patient shook their head, seemingly unknowingly. What are the issues that come to mind that you could explore? There are lots of options. You could accept the nonconscious compliance for now and move on. You could ask them about their head shake: "What are you experiencing to make you shake your head just now?" You could check in with their authority once again by asking, "Do you want to pay attention to yourself right now?"

When you are assessing the conscious brain systems, the verbal content of the patient's response is not as important as the extent to which their Authority brain system showed evidence of being Activated and able to respond to the invitation. Other questions you could consider: Are they responding to the content of your question or to the intention? Are they responding to you, the person in authority, or to their own inner authority? How did they physically respond to your explicit respect for their authority with this intervention?

You can think of these Activating interventions as instruments with which you can directly test the functioning of your patient's conscious brain systems at this moment. You can gather empirical evidence of how each system is functioning by directly observing their psychophysiological responses to each intervention. In this way you can make your own nonverbal assessment of the A-Team, rather than being limited by your patient's conscious description. These assessments will reveal your patient's competencies, but will also provide you immediate feedback on the results of your tests. You will have valuable information with which to guide your subsequent interventions. For example, they might grimace when you ask them, "What are you aware of right now?" Or they might nod in acknowledgment when you assert, "It is important that you are present, aware, and attentive to yourself."

How Do You Do It?

It takes some practice to change your mindset to direct your attention to conscious brain systems rather than the patient's story, history, symptoms, trauma, or crisis. The Initial Directed Activation includes a brief meditation and focus on mindful breathing. Psychophysiological research has shown that breath awareness can activate the parasympathetic nervous system, replacing effortful with relaxed breathing, reducing pain, anxiety, and depression, and enhancing both absorption and engagement (Fogel, 2009). The Initial Directed Activation has specific interventions that invite activations of the Awareness, Attention, and Authority brain systems. The therapist's role is to be an auxiliary self, to augment the patient's Reflective Self. We want our patient to be awake and attentive in order to self-observe and intervene on their own behalf.

SUMMARY

Discovering the patient's ability to be a full partner in the therapeutic process can change the trajectory of the treatment process. Collaboration adds to the efficiency and effectiveness of therapy. When you develop explicit collaboration, you will also uncover the qualities and layers of your patient's Self capabilities. Activating and assessing the functioning of each of the conscious brain systems provides immediate benefit to the patient and can change patient factors in the first minutes of each and any session.

CHAPTER 8

Facilitating and Differentiating Tertiary-Level Brain Systems

As we described in Chapter 7, CIMBS therapy proceeds through the broad processes of Activating, Facilitating, Differentiating, and Training the conscious emotional brain systems: Awareness, Attention, Authority, Autonomy, and Agency. In this chapter we use a case study to illustrate and operationalize how to do these steps more in depth. In Part I, we offered patient case studies of how we conduct our therapy sessions as detailed lessons in the basic techniques of CIMBS. Now, as we suggested in the introduction to Part II, we want to move to a higher level. Please interrupt any effort your brain is making to figure out what is happening in the session. Rather than figuring out what the therapist is doing or what the patient is saying and experiencing, trust your capacities for observing with different lenses and from different vantage points. Let yourself be moved in our own unique way by this and subsequent therapy sessions.

Below we present a patient named Claire. In the case study, our interventions give examples of how to Facilitate the conscious brain systems by using the therapist's attention, narrow focus, repetition, and reinforcement. It may be helpful to remember that whenever we "touch" (direct our attention toward) a brain system or psychophysiological phenomenon, that system will be altered. We trust the benefit of our attention and our interventions for Facilitating the patient's emotional brain systems. We believe that Activating and Facilitating neural circuits in a very targeted, structured, intensive, and enduring manner will promote the formation of new neural circuits and enhance the neural assemblies that make up each brain system. You will be able to see how focusing on the patient's innate emotional resources is effective in inhibiting their emotional dysfunctions without needing to explore them directly.

After the Initial Directed Activation, we usually follow with the sentence, "What are you aware of?" to specifically Activate the Awareness and Attention brain systems. These brain systems can go straight to the core of any conscious constraints that may be present, and at the same time prompt the patient to fully collaborate in the therapeutic process. After activating the Awareness and Attention brain systems, we continue Activating other conscious brain systems one by one, assessing the functionality of each conscious system. The other brain systems are recruited to add more energy, processing power, and evolved wisdom. The simultaneous Activation of multiple conscious brain systems will bring the therapeutic process to life, and it also helps in stimulating neuroplasticity for the long term and changing the structure of the BrainMind. It is important to emphasize that although we are Activating the brain systems one by one, we are also Facilitating, Differentiating, and Training at the same time in a circular or spiral fashion. The interventions are not sequential.

CASE STUDY: CLAIRE

The following is the actual transcript of the first session of a 35-year-old woman we will call Claire. This transcript will help us illustrate Activating, Facilitating, Differentiating, and Training of the conscious brain systems. We use *italics* to point out the psychophysiological phenomena and body movements and underscoring for words Beatriz emphasized. Interspersed through the transcript are Albert's commentaries.

Claire arrived at her first therapy session with Beatriz saying, "I am so depressed that I am almost catatonic."

The transcript starts after the Initial Directed Activation:

Beatriz: What are you <u>aware</u> of?
Claire: I don't know [*facial grimace*].
Beatriz: That is okay. "I don't know" is the perfect answer.
Claire: I am <u>aware</u> of what I see, what I hear [*mouth tense*].
Beatriz: Mm hmm.

Claire: I am <u>aware</u> of my breath [*breathes deeper*].

Beatriz: Good <u>awareness!</u> Tell me about your breath.

Claire: I sort of have to remind myself to deep breathe because I am very tense.

Beatriz: Mm hmm. So right now you are feeling tense?

Claire: Yes.

Beatriz: Where [*hands over torso*]?

Claire: In my chest [*verging on tears*].

Beatriz: Good <u>awareness.</u> You are being aware of the tension in your chest. You are being <u>aware</u> of yourself, experiencing you. You are being capable of being <u>aware</u> of you, which is very important [*hands over her torso*]. It is already <u>success.</u> You are being <u>capable</u> of being <u>aware.</u> This is very good!

Claire: That feels good. I am usually not that <u>aware</u> of me. I live outside of me.

Beatriz: And right now you are experiencing you, as you are being aware. How is it for you, that you are being capable of being <u>aware</u>?

Claire: My tension is less [*voice deeper*].

Albert's commentary: When Beatriz asks Claire about her tension, she does not want to pay attention to the anxiety that produces the tension. She wants to show Claire her own capacity for being aware. Beatriz is directly Activating Claire's Awareness brain system with the initial open-ended invitation to her awareness. Then she proceeds by Facilitating the same brain system. We can count nine times that Beatriz calls out awareness. Beatriz continues to Facilitate a mindful awareness when she accepts that Claire does not know what she is feeling. Beatriz is also Facilitating the Awareness brain system by pointing out her competence: "You are being capable of being aware." She also values Claire's effort: "This is success." The interventions may feel repetitive, but every time we Activate and Facilitate the brain systems, we are actively modifying specific neural circuits, and the patient is in a different place inside themselves with each repetition. As we can see, Claire's awareness gradually goes from the concrete, such as sight and sound, to breath awareness. We have asked many patients directly whether it feels repetitive, and invariably their answer is, "No, I needed the repetition." We can see evidence of that phenomenon when Claire replies, "That feels good. I am usually not that <u>aware</u> of me. I live outside of me." Focusing on the patient's innate emotional resources is effective in inhibiting the emotional dysfunctions without needing to explore them directly. Activating and Facilitating her Awareness brain system provides immediate benefit to Claire's psychophysiology: "My tension is less."

> **Beatriz:** You are paying <u>attention</u> to you and the changes inside of you. You are being capable of being aware right now. You are also paying <u>attention</u> to you. What happens when I say that you are being capable?
>
> **Claire:** I feel strong [*nods, surprised, stronger voice*].
>
> **Beatriz:** Oh, tell me about strong! How are you experiencing strong?
>
> **Claire [*Smiles, brightens up*]:** I feel a little happy to hear that. I feel a little strong.
>
> **Beatriz:** Those are beautiful words [*animated gestures*]. What are the sensations in your body that are telling you that you are experiencing strong or happy?
>
> **Claire:** My pulse is accelerating a little bit [*hand over heart*]. Like a little bit of push up. I am feeling a little happy [*smiles, deep breath, nods*].
>
> **Beatriz:** Good <u>awareness</u>. You are paying <u>attention</u> to the changes inside of you.
>
> **Claire:** I don't feel the overwhelming feeling of fear and sadness that I came in here with [*suddenly her demeanor changes and she starts crying*].
>
> **Beatriz:** What just happened?
>
> **Claire:** I don't know [*shrugs*]. Those feelings of happy got stomped down.
>
> **Beatriz:** Good <u>awareness</u>! You are paying <u>attention</u> to the changes inside of you.
>
> **Claire:** Mmm. I released a little sadness. I am feeling warm now [*takes off her jacket*].
>
> **Beatriz:** Interesting, these feelings of happiness and strong get stomped down.
>
> **Claire:** What does it mean?
>
> **Beatriz:** I don't know.
>
> **[Both laugh.]**

Albert's commentary: Beatriz is Activating and Facilitating Claire's conscious brain systems further by adding the Attention brain system. One of the ways we Differentiate one brain system from another is by calling it out by its name. Beatriz is also shifting the nervous system's orientation from avoidance (fear) to approach (warmth). Even when Claire's happy feelings get stomped down, Beatriz keeps Activating and Facilitating the adaptive circuits of her Awareness and Attention brain systems. These continuous circular interventions of Activating and Facilitating will enhance those systems and build more resiliency.

Beatriz: Tell me about the laugh.

Claire: I don't know what is going on, but I am embracing it.

Beatriz: Great! [*Excited voice.*] What is happening?

Claire [*Continues to laugh*]: I don't know [*moves head sideways and smiles*].

Beatriz: There is this happy feeling. How are you experiencing that?

Claire: I feel this lightness. My jaw is lighter [*hand holds jaw*]. My mouth, my face, and my chest also are lighter.

Beatriz [*Puts her arms out*]: And tell me, what do you <u>want</u> with this lightness at this tiny little moment?

Claire [*Rolling her eyes and making a quizzical face*]: Ahahah . . . what do I <u>want</u>? [*Grimaces and rolls her eyes again, whispers*] I don't know what I want.

Beatriz: Just at this tiny little moment. Not forever, just this little second.

Claire: I <u>want</u> to get better! [*Grimaces.*]

Beatriz: Do you <u>want</u> to keep the lightness, just for this little moment?

Claire: Yes, yes [*nods*].

Beatriz: How do you know that that is what <u>you want</u>?

Claire: I don't know. I don't know. I know I don't want to feel sad.

Beatriz: So you know what you don't want. That is very good, and what do <u>you want</u> just at this little moment?

Claire: I wish I had answers for what happened.

Beatriz: Yes, I know [*hurt showing in her face*]. That is a wish. And if we come back to this little moment, just right now? What do you <u>want</u>?

Claire: I think I want the lightness [*nods, smiles, brightens*].

Beatriz: Is that a <u>want</u>?

Claire: Yes, yes.

Beatriz: How do you know that is a <u>want</u>?

Claire: Because I don't want to feel bad.

Beatriz: That is what you don't want. How do you know that that is what <u>you want</u>?

Claire: I don't know. I never know what I want.

Beatriz: That is great that we know that. It is very interesting, isn't it? There is a bit of a difficulty experiencing the "I want," experiencing your authority. You know what you don't want, but you don't know the "I want." That is very interesting. Are you curious about that?

Claire: Yes, I've always had that problem. I am never clear, so I end up doing what other people want.

Beatriz: And right now, just at this little moment, what do <u>you</u> <u>want</u>?

Claire: To be clear.

Beatriz: Can you put "I want" in the sentence?

Claire: I want to be clear . . . [*rolling her eyes, pondering*]. I want to be clear. . . . I want to be clear [*voice becomes stronger*].

Albert's commentary: Beatriz is directing Claire's attention to her laughter, which is empirical evidence of a significant psychophysiological shift inside of her nervous system. After Facilitating and enhancing Claire's awareness of the lightness in her face and chest, she chooses this moment to activate the Authority brain system by inviting Claire to focus on her wants. This intervention helps Beatriz assess Claire's Authority brain system, and they both learn that she has limited access to the competence of that system. So the decision to Activate, Facilitate, Differentiate, and Train that brain system is in order. Beatriz seizes this opportunity to continue the constant circular process of Facilitating by becoming an external generator, repeatedly Activating, Facilitating, and Training Claire's Authority brain system.

Beatriz: What happens when you say "I want"?

Claire: I want . . . want. . . . It sounds funny [*nods*].

Beatriz: Tell me more.

Claire: It feels as if I am demanding or something.

Beatriz: How fascinating, isn't it? You saying your <u>authority</u> out loud, feels . . .

Claire [*Interrupting*]: Wrong! As if I am saying something bad.

Beatriz: How fascinating. Saying your own <u>authority</u> out loud feels wrong. Feels as if you are demanding.

Claire: That is bad [*scrunches her face*].

Beatriz: We are not here to judge. We are just here to be curious, and interested about what comes out. Do you <u>want</u> to have your own <u>author-ity</u>? And differentiate it from the feelings of it is "wrong" or "demanding" to say your <u>want</u>?

Claire: Yes, yes. That is strange [*emphatically moving her body backward and forward*].

Beatriz: How do you know that is what you <u>want</u>?

Claire: It makes sense. Because I feel the truth in that. The importance of that. I can't ignore that [*nods*].

Beatriz: Yes. What are the sensations of "this is true, this is important"?

Claire: It makes me feel stronger. I feel very calm, tuned in with myself. . . . I <u>want</u> feels rude, feels bad. Wow! So weird. Now, I feel dizzy. I do not know what it means.

Beatriz: Yes, dizzy is the perfect place to be! It seems to me that when you feel dizzy, you are outside of the usual emotional patterns in your brain. Our task is to do and redo what makes you feel dizzy, because this is new. What made you feel dizzy?

Claire: <u>I want</u> [*one hand makes a fist*]. Wow, that is weird. Every time I say "I want," I feel dizzy. It feels bad saying it. Like it is rude to say it.

Beatriz: Great, now we know what to work on. To differentiate your <u>want</u> and your <u>authority</u> from the feeling of "it is wrong to say my want out loud," and to differentiate it from "it is rude to have my authority."

Claire [*Nodding emphatically*]: Yes, it is weird because I consider myself an independent woman. But I was afraid to tell my fiancé what I wanted. Afraid that he will not like me or that I will let him down or something like that. That is so weird.

Beatriz: So we need to strengthen the "I want" so you can have your own <u>authority</u> and not sacrifice your <u>wants</u>. And what is the purest form of "I want"? "I <u>want</u> my <u>want</u>. I <u>want</u> to have my <u>want</u>. I <u>want</u> to have my authority."

Claire: Okay? [*Puzzled face.*]

Beatriz: Do you want to have your <u>want</u>? Do you <u>want</u> to own your <u>want</u>?

Claire: Yyyyes? . . .[*Grimaces*] I do [*small movement of assertion of the hand*].

Beatriz: Tell me what is happening. You just moved your hand! [*Mimics assertion of the hand.*]

Albert's commentary: Beatriz has found a hyperconnection between Claire's Authority and Guilt and/or Shame brain systems. The action of the Shame brain system is apparent because Claire says that expressing her wants feels bad, wrong, and rude. Beatriz starts the Differentiating process, first by bringing in states of curiosity and self-awareness, followed by continuing to Facilitate Claire's Authority brain system. She then welcomes Claire's awareness that expressing her want feels bad, wrong, and rude, and she redirects their energy (Go the Other Way) toward Claire's competency. Third, Beatriz triggers the spontaneous activation of Claire's Value brain system, directing the attention to the value of having her want. Beatriz continues the process of Differentiating by constantly circling through Activating and Facilitating, as well as being an external generator to energize the process further. This process helps Claire sustain the novelty and value of her Authority brain system. Claire is in an emotional disequilibrium, as evidenced by her feeling weird and physically dizzy. Notice that there is no exploration of her backstory as to why she feels that it is wrong or rude to have her authority. The Differentiation happens when we give preference to the adaptive brain systems of Awareness, Attention, Authority, and Autonomy (Tertiaries) and the enhancing brain systems of Value and Importance (Secondaries).

Claire: I do. I <u>want</u> my authority [*moves her hands with assertion again*].

Beatriz: Can you feel the movement of assertion of your hand? Right there! [*Mirrors her hand movement.*]

Claire: Yes, but it is new [*smiles, laughs out loud*].

Beatriz: It is weird. Great awareness! What do you <u>want</u> at this little moment? Do you want to bring "I <u>want</u> my <u>want</u>" and the movement of your hands together with muscle memory?

Claire: Yes, I <u>want</u> my <u>want</u> [*open hands moving forward with strength*]. I <u>want</u> my authority. It comes for a split of a second and then it is like I am afraid to show it. I'm scared to say it [*apprehensive, puzzled look*]. And then I lose it!

Beatriz: How interesting. Having your own authority and saying your authority out loud and bringing your assertive hand out is entangled with unsafe and wrong. How fascinating. Two inhibitors, unsafe and wrong. No wonder it is so difficult to have your <u>want</u>. How safe do you feel right now?

Claire: I feel safe [*nods*].

Beatriz: How safe are you in this relationship with us?

Claire: Safe [*ponders, smiles*].

Beatriz: How safe are you inside of you?

Claire [*Shakes head*]: Not that safe, because I have all these hurt feelings.

Beatriz: Right now?

Claire: Now, I am safe.

Beatriz: Are you safe with your <u>authority</u>? Is that what you <u>want</u>?

Claire: Yes! That is what I <u>want</u>! [*Emphatically, body moving forward.*]

Beatriz [*Smiles*]: How do you know that is what you want?

Claire: My want is very important to me [*voice stronger*].

Beatriz: What you want is important. What you want matters. Your want is valuable.

Claire: I get overwhelmed. That made me feel dizzy! Warm and heavy in my head.

Beatriz: Great, we need to do and redo what is making you feel warm, dizzy, and heavy. It seems to me that your brain is learning this newness.

Claire: Oh wow. It feels good.

Beatriz: Learning that your want matters. . . .

Claire: It feels good [*nods, surprised*].

Beatriz: What is making you heavy and dizzy?

Claire: My wants! [*Laughs.*] I feel my authority, and it is overwhelming. I don't know why or how, but it feels overwhelming.

Beatriz: How curious. Great that it is out in the open, so we can work with it.

Claire: I feel stronger, calm and in tune with myself. More energy inside of me and yet I still feel apprehensive.

Beatriz: Great. Good work! You are feeling both energies at the same time. The strength of your authority and showing your hands with assertion [*moves her hands with assertion*] and the apprehension, unsafe to be in your <u>authority</u>. Wonderful. Let's stay here experiencing both energies at the same time. Your <u>wants</u> are important for us. Your <u>authority</u> matters to us [*moves her hands with assertion again*]. Does your <u>authority</u> matter to you?

Claire: Very much. My <u>want</u> is important to me. My <u>want</u> matters [*moves her hands with assertion*]. I feel dizzy again.

Beatriz: Wonderful awareness!

Claire: I feel warm, heavy in my head, calm, and as if I am on drugs or something.

Albert's commentary: Beatriz picks up the spontaneous psychophysiological activation of the Assertive brain system when Claire assertively moves her hands. It is interesting how Beatriz directs Claire's attention to her awareness of being and feeling safe. It is important that Beatriz helps Claire exercise her Attention, Awareness, and Authority brain systems to reorient her to the present-moment experience of safeness. This Training helps Differentiate her present feelings from the learned experience of the past, when it was "not safe to have [her] wants." This repetition will also enhance the resilience of each of those brain systems and help her override the inhibitions of her Fear ("scared"), Shame ("rude"), and Guilt ("wrong") brain systems. Claire discovers that experiencing her authority and saying her wants out loud makes her feel both good and apprehensive. That discovery can change the constraints of those implicit memories about her authority and wants. There is evidence that Claire's Authority brain system is Differentiated enough that it is beginning to develop a positive feedback loop (internal generator), judging by Claire's declaration that "I feel stronger, calm and in tune with myself. More energy inside of me." The phenomenon of dizziness and disequilibrium that she describes happens often in our therapies. We explore it in Chapter 15.

Claire: Mmm . . . [*scrunching her face, head, and body to the side*].

Beatriz: Is this really what you <u>want</u>? Or are you just being a good student for me?

Claire [*Giggling*]: No, I need to want my want. I need to want my want [*making faces*].

Beatriz: Is that your <u>autonomy</u> though? Are you honoring yourself, as different from doing what you think I want?

Claire: I am not sure what is going on exactly, but I feel uncomfortable when I say I want my want.

Beatriz: Yes, of course. It will be uncomfortable. Newness is always uncomfortable. And in uncomfortability we grow. Great, you are growing right now. And I still don't know if that is what you <u>want in</u> your own <u>autonomy</u>, honoring your wants even if they are different from what I want.

Claire: I can feel it, that I am not giving myself the authority. It is very strange. I wasn't aware that that was so . . . [*opens her arms and struggles with the words*] present or so powerful in me.

Beatriz: Interesting, isn't it? And also are you following me, or are you following you?

Claire: What?? I don't follow.

Beatriz: I want to know, what is your <u>autonomy</u> right now? Have you asked yourself, Is this what I <u>want</u>? [*Emphasis on "I" and pointing at her chest.*] Are you honoring yourself as different from what I, myself, want for you? Ask yourself: Am I honoring myself right now or am I just following her? [*Points at herself.*]

Claire: Oh, I see what you mean. No, I <u>want</u> to have my authority even if you don't <u>want</u> it. I am honoring me, and I don't care if you like it or not. It is amazing what I have deprived myself of. . . . I did not know I was not honoring me and giving my want to somebody else. I disappeared in the relationship. I don't <u>want</u> to do that any more.

Beatriz: Wonderful! So we are going to have to finish soon. What do you want to take home with you?

Claire: My <u>wants</u>.

Beatriz: So do you remember your internal sensations when you said, "I <u>want</u> my <u>want</u>"?

Claire: Yes! Warm inside, strong hands, strong stomach, like standing up inside of me, and a column up my front!

Beatriz: Great, so those are the sensations of you experiencing your own authority. And you need to repeat those sensations in your body again with strong hands and saying, "I . . ."

Claire: I want my want, my authority [*strong movements of hands*].

Beatriz: Wonderful! Is there a drive for that? Is there an <u>agent</u> inside of you, to make your wants happen, to be the <u>agent</u> of your wants?

Claire: My body is moving forward, like, to go and do it! [*Body moving forward, open hands in up-and-down motion.*]

Beatriz: Now you can be the <u>agent</u> of your own wants and be in charge of your life. So now you are the inside generator of connecting with your authority, and it will be important that you do this bodily connection again and again for the next five hours and during the week, like every hour, especially when you are doing exercise and before you fall asleep. So it becomes integrated into you. This is for you [*extending her arms toward her*].

Subsequent sessions were dedicated to continue Differentiating Claire's Autonomy and Authority from her fear and shame.

Albert's commentary: After Beatriz's realization that there was a budding positive feedback loop in the Authority brain system, she chose that moment to Activate and assess the Autonomy brain system by inviting Claire to focus on her wants, as different from Beatriz's wants and desires. They both discovered that her Autonomy brain system was also hyperconnected, but that the process of Differentiating her Authority brain system was also Differentiating the Autonomy brain system enough so she could begin to honor her own wants and desires. The session finished with a Training exercise, an invitation to practice at home by exercising the physical sensations from the differentiated neural circuits in session. The goal here is to expand the conscious felt sense of the Authority, Autonomy, and Agency brain systems and hopefully develop resilient brain systems in between sessions.

FACILITATING

We further defined Facilitating in the introduction to Part II. It involves repeatedly returning to an Activated brain system to bring it to a state of full operation, the way we warm up and loosen up a muscle when we are working out. Sending focused energy toward the capacities of the brain systems can take our patients out of their baseline equilibrium into a higher level of functioning. Facilitating is done in a circular and repetitive fashion. Facilitating multiple brain systems will often uncover brain system dysfunctions. Here are several examples:

- Being aware of anxiety reveals the patient's capacity for being aware and not just overwhelmed by the anxiety.
- A small smile reveals play activation in the middle of feeling uncomfortable and anxious.
- A sudden change of position from a slouched position to sitting up reveals possible Activation of the Assertive brain system.

Methodology of Facilitating
The next section of this chapter is more of a how-to manual. We suggest that you read the interventions slowly and maybe copy them into a cheat sheet so

you can remember them when you are in the trenches. You may also want to memorize some of the interventions so the therapy goes smoothly. A valuable tool when seeking to Facilitate is the ability to act as an external generator. As we said in Chapter 2, an external generator is a therapist who Activates and Facilitates, again and again, a brain system that would otherwise come to rest and lose its power. An external generator both Activates and has the potential to be a positive feedback loop to the brain system that is being Activated. A positive feedback loop is when one Activation enhances another one, which reinforces the first one.

We have developed four ways of Facilitating:

- Focus on the adaptive emotional competencies that the patient is revealing in the moment, rather than on the more obvious problematic symptoms, behaviors, or thought patterns that seem to overwhelm them. This is an example of Go the Other Way.
- Break old habits. Inviting the patient repetitively to override their natural tendency to behave in familiar ways will Facilitate new and uncomfortable, but adaptive, behaviors. For example, with Claire, Beatriz said, "Do you want to bring 'I <u>want</u> my <u>want</u>' and the movement of your strong hands, one more time even if it feels wrong, and unsafe?"
- Be the external generator. Directing focused energy onto one specific brain system, and naming the feeling or behavior associated with it, will keep stimulating it again and again. The therapist keeps on sending energy to a brain system in order to keep it Activated, to keep the power circulating for one more round, and one more round. In addition, you can recruit and direct the energy of the Primaries—for example, curiosity (Seeking), delight (Play), and Care—to keep Facilitating conscious brain systems such as Awareness. "Good <u>awareness</u>. You are being <u>aware</u> of your tension in the chest!" "This is success already!" (Delight.) "You are being <u>aware</u> of yourself, experiencing you." "This is very <u>interesting</u>!" (Seeking.) "And right now, we are caring for you as you are being aware of yourself" (Care).
- Activate the enhancing brain systems. The enhancing Secondaries also have great power to augment the conscious brain system that you are Facilitating as an external generator. We elaborate on this process when we discuss secondary brain systems (Chapter 13). For now, Table 8.1

shows some examples of assertions that could harness the power of the enhancing brain systems, along with the neurotransmitters that these Activations can release. Notice that these interventions are assertions and not questions, even if posed as questions.

TABLE 8.1: Facilitating Enhancing Brain Systems

Enhancing Brain System	Neurotransmitter Possibly Released	Verbal Activation
Value	Acetylcholine	This is success. Your awareness is valuable. We are valuing you. You are worthy of our total attention. Is there a small feeling of satisfaction right now? You are feeling a sense of accomplishment in your progress.
Important	Dopamine	How do you know this matters to you? What you want matters! You are important to us. It is important that you stay in the awareness of you. Your awareness matters.
Pleasure	Opioids	There is a small smile right now. Is there a light feeling inside of you? Small satisfaction? What are you experiencing that tells you it feels good to be in charge right now? It feels good to be in your authority.
Motivation	Dopamine	You are being capable. Can you feel your determination to go for what you want? Your body is moving forward a little bit; can you feel the drive inside of you right now? Your determination.

When Do We Facilitate?

- When we feel stuck and are running out of energy. Facilitating is particularly useful when you feel discouraged that nothing is happening and your patient is stuck. Mobilizing the enhancing brain systems in a repetitive circular way (as an external generator) will get you out of the stuck place, because you are mobilizing positive energy and resources. This positive energy can enhance engagement and shift the nervous system's orientation from avoidance to approach.

- When we are working with hypoactive brain systems. The Facilitating process will strengthen the neural circuits that are present. "Activating impoverished neurons is not easy because they tend to resist such effort" (Grawe, 2007). Focus energy on the hypoactive brain system, calling it by name in order to keep stimulating it again and again. In addition, harness the energy of the enhancing brain systems simultaneously with the hypoactive brain system that you want to develop, and keep on being the external generator. Here are examples from Claire's case study:

Importance brain system: "How important is this for you, to continue to experience your authority inside of you?" "Your taking charge is very important for us."

Value brain system: "Well done! Are you feeling some satisfaction inside of you? You are being capable of being aware." "We are valuing you as you as you are being aware of yourself."

Motivation brain system: "Can you feel the determination inside of you to pursue your own authority?"

Pleasure brain system: "It feels good to be in charge of you right now." "Playing together feels good inside." "What are you experiencing that tells you that it feels good to love yourself?"

- When you need to Differentiate a hyperconnection. Facilitating enhancing brain systems can stimulate adaptive neural circuits, and will simultaneously inhibit maladaptive neural circuits. For example, Beatriz found a hyperconnection between Claire's Authority brain system and her Shame and Fear brain systems. Beatriz became the external generator, stimulating the Authority brain system again and again, inviting Claire to continue experiencing her authority, and not paying too much attention to the feelings of being unsafe and wrong. At the same time, Beatriz was Activating the enhancing brain systems in relationship with Claire's Authority.

Facilitating can be especially useful when the patient has been triggered, which may happen to patients with PTSD. Activation and Facilitation will open up what we call the closed loop of hyperconnectivity. A closed loop refers to neural circuits that have fired repeatedly and persistently for such long periods of time that they have become rigid and closed to new learning. In order to open up this closed loop, we need to Activate and Facilitate other brain systems. For example, consider a mother who lost her son 10 years ago and has been unable to move through her grief. She reports crying every day, various times a day, and she is not moving forward in her life. We could say that her Grief brain system is hyperactive and has become a closed loop. She is suffering from a syndrome called pathological mourning. In therapy, we could Activate and Facilitate other brain systems like Safe, Care, Play, and Connection in order to open up the closed loop (see Differentiating below).

DIFFERENTIATING

This chapter focuses primarily on Differentiating the conscious (A-Team) brain systems, but you will see that Differentiating often involves all levels of the nervous system. Differentiating enables the patient and therapist to harness the energy and wisdom of multiple brain systems in novel ways. The processes of Differentiating are particularly important for enabling structural changes (neuroplasticity) of the BrainMind. Differentiated brain systems operating in parallel are flexible and open to new learning. Small changes in Differentiated systems can lead to large changes in a complex integrated system (Siegel, 1999). Differentiating requires the energy and collaboration of both the patient and therapist to override the familiar maladaptive equilibrium and the frequent discomfort or pain that are a natural outcome of Differentiating.

Differentiation is in general a mix of isolating specific brain systems and repeatedly Activating and Facilitating them. Differentiating is especially important when one brain system is entangled or hyperconnected with another. Differentiating is effective because it utilizes the neurobiological wisdom of the body. Some of the neurobiological principles that were introduced in Chapter 3 are especially relevant here:

1. Differentiated brain systems process energy and information in parallel.
2. Change requires energy.
3. Sustained experiential learning changes the structure of the brain.

Methodology of Differentiating

Once we have Activated and assessed the initial Tertiaries, spotted possible dysfunctional systems, and perhaps Facilitated key primary and enhancing secondary brain systems, we are in position to begin the process of Differentiating.

An important part of Differentiating any dysfunctional brain system is our ability to foster parallel processing. This phenomenon, described in Chapter 2, refers to concurrently Activating other previously Differentiated brain systems simultaneously with the specific brain system that is presently being Differentiated. With parallel processing, the patient can feel safeness and fear at the same time. Often the increased energy and processing capacities that result from Activating and Facilitating other brain systems will release hyperactivations and constraints that originated from developmental learning.

Keep in mind that Differentiating is also circular in a spiral process (Figure 8.1). The interventions are not sequential. Differentiating is most successful

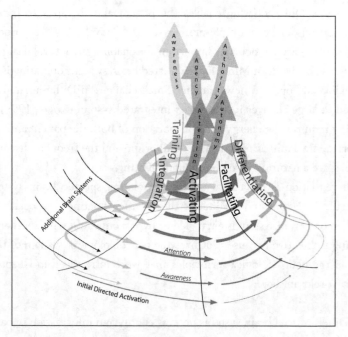

Figure 8.1: Spiral of Activating, Facilitating, Differentiating, Training, and Integrating Tertiary Brain Systems

when it takes place in the Transpiring Present Moment, in which you and your patient can both observe and experience the hyperactive, hypoactive, or entangled brain systems in real time. Below we describe practical therapeutic steps for Differentiating each of those three types of brain system dysfunction.

Differentiating Hyperactive Brain Systems

In our research, we have found that the brain systems that most commonly become hyperactive are the Secondaries: Fear, Grief, Shame, and Guilt. When these brain systems become hyperactive because of trauma and/or neglect, they lose their positive capacity to modulate other brain systems (Chapter 13). Instead, they become part of closed loops. We need to open up these closed loops so that the neural circuits will be open to new learning.

For example: A 35-year-old man who is unable to learn new things because he does not want to "do it wrong," as he puts it, said, "I don't want to take golf lessons because I don't know how to play golf." Every time he tries new things, he is disappointed in himself because he cannot do it perfectly and feels like vomiting. We could say that his Shame brain system is hyperactive.

We offer two steps to Differentiate hyperactive brain systems. First, bring the patient into the Transpiring Present Moment and direct their attention to the awareness that they are Safe. Developmental learning from the past, not the present moment, is causing whatever terror they feel. Repetition is important. For example: The following intervention has seven repetitions as we work with safeness. Let's remember that every time we activate and "touch" a brain system, we are actively modifying specific neural circuits, and the patient is in a different place inside themselves with each repetition.

How safe do you know you are at this moment in time?

Just in your head, not in your body. How safe do you *know* you are?

Look around you. How safe do you *know* you are? (Ask patient to literally look around).

You are aware of being safe in the adult present of you, right now.

How interesting—you know you are safe, and your body feels unsafe, at the same time. Are you curious about that?

You are safe even if your body tells you that you are unsafe.

It is safe to be safe.

We help the patient discover the distinction between the bodily feelings of being unsafe and the present-moment safeness. This is a disconfirming emotional experience; note that it needs to be repeated numerous times to become effective. But with that reinforcement, it will provide new learning and possibly open up the closed loop. At the same time, we are promoting the development of the Awareness brain system.

Second, foster parallel processing. Parallel processing is a step used in every type of differentiation (see Chapter 2), referring to the concurrent activation of other differentiated brain systems and Integrating them with the specific brain system that is being differentiated. With parallel processing, you can feel safeness and fear at the same time. Often the increased energy and processing capacities that result from Activating and Facilitating other brain systems will release the hyperactivations and constraints that originated from developmental learning. Activating the hyperactive system in unfamiliar ways could interrupt the feedback loop that keeps the system closed. For example, being in the Therapeutic Attachment Relationship will Activate and Facilitate the Safe, Care, and Connection systems (Primaries), which could interrupt the hyperactive brain system. Activating the enhancing brain systems to modulate the hyperactive brain system could also facilitate the flow of energy and information that has been blocked by a hyperactive system such as Fear, Shame, Guilt, or Grief.

ACTIVATING AND FACILITATING HYPOACTIVE BRAIN SYSTEMS

We have developed three steps that can promote the development of a hypoactive brain system.

1. Activate the hypoactive brain system by naming the feeling or behavior that accompanies it. When you name the system out loud, you will inevitably reinforce the capacity of the brain system, and it can make the brain system stronger and increasingly resilient. For example, to Facilitate the Awareness brain system, you could say, "Good awareness. You are being aware of your tension." Or to Facilitate the Play brain system, say, "We are aware that we are playing right now! We are having fun right now."

2. Harness the energy of the enhancing brain systems simultaneously with the activation of the hypoactive brain system that you want to develop. This intervention is another example of fostering parallel processing.

3. Operate as an external generator. Acting as an external generator can prove very useful for Activating as well as for Facilitating the hypoactive brain system. For example, when the patient is suddenly aware of themselves and you say, "Good awareness!," you are providing an external positive feedback of appreciation and esteem for their competence of awareness. As an external generator, you keep on Activating and Facilitating that Awareness system. When the patient becomes aware of something else, then you add the positive feedback of your esteem and your appreciation for their awareness.

The therapist also asks about the sensations caused by the brain system that is being Activated, and then asks the patient to keep those sensations afloat and remember the sensations in the body one more time, again and again. For example, Beatriz asked Claire to bring back the body sensations of her Authority brain system: "Do you want to bring back the sensation of your authority one more round, just one more round? Remember the sensations with muscle memory?" With time and practice, that system will become stronger, becoming its own internal generator and developing self-sustaining positive feedback loops capable of becoming a resilient brain system.

DIFFERENTIATING HYPERCONNECTED OR ENTANGLED BRAIN SYSTEMS

Disentangling is the term many patients use spontaneously to describe their felt sense or visceral experience of letting go of constraining emotional learning from the past. Above, we discussed Differentiating hyperactive brain systems, and in many ways working with hyperconnected systems is similar, because the hyperconnection may result from hyperactive Secondaries such as Fear or Shame. We have developed three steps in the process of Differentiating hyperconnected brain systems:

1. Help the patient to stay aware of the different energies of the several brain systems that we are Activating at the same time, what we call the three-ring circus. In the example of Claire, she feels her authority for one second, then immediately the fear and the feeling that it is wrong come in, taking away her feeling of authority. Beatriz invites her to keep feeling her authority as she also feels the fear, guilt, and shame: "How are you physically experiencing this feeling of your own authority? How are you physically experiencing these feelings of being unsafe and wrong? We are staying here experiencing your authority as the feeling of standing up inside of yourself, as you feel the sensation of your throat closing up and the tension in the chest. We are staying in the middle of the three-ring circus." Maintaining this simultaneous felt sense enables Claire to disentangle and Differentiate the conflicting feelings of fear, guilt, and shame as she struggles to hold onto her desires.

2. After staying in the felt sense of the three-ring circus, the next step is to begin to Go the Other Way. You can further Differentiate the entanglement by paying greater attention to the adaptive capacities of the brain system that is being Differentiated than to the sensations arising from any entangled brain systems. This preferential focus will tend to override the inhibitory effects of the maladaptive learning. For example, Beatriz targeted Claire's Authority over the entanglements from Fear, Guilt, and Shame: "And we are here paying attention to the experience of your sensations of your authority; standing up inside of you, experiencing the strength in your hand and fist, and we are not paying too much attention to the other energies of unsafe and wrong. Those sensations are already very strong. We don't need to strengthen them further by paying attention to them."

3. Next, continue to Go the Other Way by Activating the enhancing brain systems to support the brain system that you are Activating, Facilitating, and Differentiating. In the case of Claire, Beatriz Activated her Value, Pleasure, and Importance brain systems: "It is valuable that we are together paying attention to your sensations of standing up inside of yourself. The sensations of your authority. It feels good inside experiencing the sensations of strength and power inside of you. These feelings

are very important for you. You experiencing your authority matters to you."

As you can see, through this series of steps, we are encouraging parallel processing by Activating and Facilitating the Primaries, Secondaries, and Tertiaries in connection with the brain system that we want to Differentiate. Parallel processing can promote and strengthen your ability to Differentiate hyperconnected brain systems, and in that way strengthen the development of a brain system that could have been atrophied or inhibited by the hyperconnections. Here are some examples of verbal interventions that can foster parallel processing with the Authority brain system:

Safe brain system: "It is safe to experience your authority in our relationship."

Care and Connection brain systems: "You can have the three experiences together: being loved as you are experiencing connection and standing up in your authority."

Seeking brain system: "It is curious and interesting to see you experiencing your authority in front of us."

Play brain system: "And it is fun to see you experiencing your authority in front of us."

In these examples, the therapist is activating multiple brain systems simultaneously and connecting them with the activation of the Authority brain system. We believe that when we Activate, Facilitate, Train, and Integrate this newly redeveloped brain system that has been stunted by the entanglement with inhibitory brain systems, we build resilient and Fail-Safe Complex Networks.

Table 8.2 gives a comprehensive summary of what we have presented on defining, identifying, and Differentiating conscious brain system dysfunctions.

TABLE 8.2: Differentiating Brain System Dysfunctions

Brain System Dysfunction	Psycho-physiological Phenomena	Differentiation	Steps to Differentiation	Examples of Interventions
Hyperactive: automatized, conditioned sets of neural circuits that have been activated so frequently that they have become rigid and closed to new learning. They have the highest probability of being activated, sometimes called triggers.	Psychophysiological activations of one or more brain systems are out of proportion to the transpiring situation in the session.	Simultaneous activation of other brain systems will differentiate the hyperactive brain system.	1. Bring patient into Transpiring Present Moment of Safeness. 2. Parallel processing: concurrent activation of other brain systems, integrating them with the specific brain system that is being differentiated.	1. "How safe do you know you are at this present moment?" 2. "How interesting. You know you are safe and your body feels unsafe at same time." 3. "You can have three experiences together: being loved, having your authority, and feeling wrong at same time."
Hypoactive: rarely activated systems. They are weak, under-developed, and unlikely to be activated.	Little or no psychophysiological response when therapist activates that specific brain system.	Continuous activation of the hypoactive brain system.	1. Activate hypoactive brain systems by name. 2. Activate enhancing brain systems simultaneously with the hypoactive brain system (parallel processing). 3. Therapist operates as an external generator.	1. "This is your authority coming through." 2. "It is important to continue experiencing your authority." 3. "Bring back with muscle memory your feeling of authority and keep it going one round more."

TABLE 8.2: Differentiating Brain System Dysfunctions				
Brain System Dysfunction	Psycho-physiological Phenomena	Differentiation	Steps to Differentiation	Examples of Interventions
Hyperconnected: brain systems that have fired together so persistently that they have become a single functional unit.	Psychophysio-logical responses are constrained, contradictory, or conflicted.	Helping the patient to stay in the psychophysio-logical sensations of the different energies that are being activated.	1. "Three-ring circus: experiencing felt sense of the different brain systems. 2, Give preference to sensations of capacities of the system that is being differentiated. 3. Activating enhancing brain systems around the adaptive component of the brain system being activated (parallel processing).	1. "How are you experiencing physically these three energies: your authority, and the feelings of unsafe and wrong? 2. "Paying attention to the sensation of your authority over other sensations." 3. "Your authority matters to us. It is worthy and valuable. It feels good." 4. "We are Caring and Connecting with you as you are experiencing and being aware of your authority."

TRAINING

We use the term Training to refer to the process of exercising the adaptive neural circuits that we are Activating, Facilitating, and Differentiating during the therapy session. As described above, this is similar to working out at the gym with your trainer, who gives you specific exercises to strengthen and enhance specific muscles with multiple repetitions. Training develops and enhances the inherent strengths of specific brain systems. This explicit repetition helps the patient isolate distinct adaptive brain systems and neural circuits. The Training process includes the constant activation of neural circuits in a very targeted, intensive, and enduring manner to facilitate the malleability of the brain (neuroplasticity). The training process is experiential and is not limited by cognitive understanding.

We have developed three different goals for Training patients: to help them become their own internal generator, to develop parallel processing, and to instruct them how to continue training in between sessions and at home.

Developing an Internal Generator

"One can change the brain via sufficiently intensive influences in such a manner that self-sustaining new structures emerge, which then become the foundation for enduring changes in experience and behavior" (Grawe, 2007).

Internal generator refers to our BrainMind's ability to develop nonconscious enhanced adaptive emotions and behaviors. Developing an internal generator will enable the patient to develop self-sustaining positive feedback loops that with time and practice could become a resilient brain system. Training can take place constantly throughout the session by simultaneously exercising distinct brain systems. We believe that by improving the performance of each brain system, we also improve the inherent capabilities of the BrainMind. Training also must take place in between sessions. Fifty minutes a week in a therapy session does not do the trick. We believe that the patient will need to develop self-sustaining new neural circuits, and for that to happen they will need to exercise the distinct neural circuits in between sessions.

You can access the internal generator by:

- Paying attention to the enhancing brain systems. These systems strengthen adaptive motivations, behaviors, or emotions. Evolution has installed innate feelings of pleasure or importance to provide nonconscious positive feedback (enhancement) to our adaptive behaviors. You can help your patient bring awareness and attention to the enhancing psychophysiological sensations that are happening under the surface coming from the Pleasure, Value, Importance, and/or Motivation brain systems.
- Inviting the patient to repeat and sustain the awareness of the sensations (Sensory brain system), "one more round" or "one more time." For example, we might say, "Try bringing up the sensations with 'muscle memory' for one more round." This very targeted, intensive, and enduring experience strengthens that neural circuit. In contrast, we avoid giving attention to inhibiting brain systems, because we would not want to inhibit adaptive circuits.

Parallel Processing Training

Once your patient can sustain awareness of the sensations as the enhancing brain systems are Activated, then you can begin training the patient in parallel processing. In the following example of parallel processing Training, the therapist activates eight differentiated neural circuits or brain systems and Integrates them with the specific Authority brain system.

Patient: I can sustain the sensations of standing up inside of me, as I feel the strength of my muscles in my solar plexus and experience my strong hand and my authority in front of you.

Therapist: As you are standing up inside of you, and experiencing your strength, demonstrating the strong hand of your own authority here in front of us, we are caring (1, Care brain system) for you, and we are connected (2, Connection brain system) together as we see you in your authority standing up inside of you. And you can have the three energies together: you in your own authority, being cared for, and in connection with us.

It is safe (3, Safe brain system) to show your authority in front of us, in our relationship, and we are caring for you as you are in your authority. It is curious and interesting (4, Seeking brain system) to see you in your authority! And it is fun to see you strong in your authority in front of us, aware (5, Aware brain system) and paying attention (6, Attention brain system) to your sensations (7, Sensory brain system) and in your own autonomy (8, Autonomy brain system)!"

Exercise and Practice at Home

Your trainer or physical therapist will typically give you relevant exercises to practice at home to further develop what you learned during your session. These exercises serve several purposes; they strengthen the muscles and nerves that underly each movement, increase the speed of the neural circuits so that your movements are more precise, and develop further coordination so that awkward, weird, foreign movements can become increasingly graceful and second nature. Similarly, with time and practice, each differentiated brain system can become stronger and self-sustaining as it develops positive feedback circuits. The process of doing practice exercises at home (homework) in between sessions will help to develop resilient brain systems.

We suggest that you ask your patients to do four exercises to expand their conscious felt sense of the brain systems that you are trying to strengthen:

1. Ask the patient to set aside an additional 15 free minutes after each session to reinforce the physical sensations from the neural circuits that were Differentiated in the session. Have the patient write down the physical sensations they felt as the neural circuits were Differentiated, such as "warmth in my chest," "strength in my core muscles," or "a rod up my back." Then they should go for a walk for 15 minutes, repeating the physical experience of those sensations. For example, we asked Claire to walk around the block, repeating the physical sensations that she feels when she thinks, "I am experiencing my own authority," "Standing up inside of me," or "I am feeling the strength in my solar plexus, shoulders back and open chest, neck high." As she held her hand in a fist with strength, in the same way that happened spontaneously in the therapeutic session, she would repeat out loud, "I want my want. I want my own authority."

2. Have the patient repeat this process again and again during the week between sessions. The experience of the sensation will take no more than a few seconds.

3. Also have the patient repeat evoking the sensations when they do any kind of physical exercise during the following week.

4. Have the patient repeat the sensation process as they fall asleep. These new neural circuits need repetition and reinforcement or they will be deleted (pruned) by the brain during sleep when it does its usual housekeeping.

Repetition can keep Activating and Facilitating the specific brain system that has been Differentiated. These brain systems can keep evolving throughout the patient's life span, developing even greater competency. Neuroscience tells us that synapses strengthen or weaken with use or disuse (LeDoux, 1996). We have witnessed this phenomenon every time we see our patients for 1-, 5-, or 10-year follow-up sessions. Invariably our patients continue growing, even after the therapy has finished, because they have developed self-sustaining resilient brain systems.

Figure 8.1 is our attempt to illustrate the experiential feeling of these therapeutic processes. This figure is designed to evoke the circular, upward spiral approaches and interventions as we work with the conscious brain systems, starting with the Initial Directed Activation, then Facilitating the Awareness and Attention, and Activating other brain systems in parallel processing. This continuous process of Activating, Facilitating, Differentiating, and Training could culminate in building a resilient and Fail-Safe Complex Network of conscious brain systems.

SUMMARY

It is our hope that this chapter has been successful in illustrating the processes of Facilitating, Differentiating, and Training the Tertiaries. Each of these processes contributes to the treatment process and the development of resilient brain systems. As we mentioned in the introduction to Part II, you can Trust these Processes because they utilize multiple forms of neuroplasticity. The circularity and repetition are necessary to change the structure of the BrainMind. Chapter 9 illustrates the processes of Integrating multiple conscious brain systems, leading to the development of Fail-Safe Complex Networks.

CHAPTER 9

Integrating Resilient Conscious Brain Systems

....

Having looked at the steps of Activating, Facilitating, Differentiating, and Training, we now turn to examining the Integrating phase of the CIMBS therapeutic process. As you recall, Integrating is a treatment process directed by the therapist who Facilitates keeping multiple systems active even when fear, shame, or fatigue get in the way. Integrating involves a shift toward cooperative and synergistic brain system functioning that sustains and is the result of the simultaneous parallel processing of energy and information by multiple distinct brain systems. Integrating is a natural process that can lead to releasing the spontaneous self-organizing capacities of the BrainMind and the opening of closed systems.

As we described in the preceding chapters, Activating and Facilitating each of the conscious brain systems enhances the patient's capacities to be present to their whole experience, maintain their emotional balance, and take charge of their lives. Next, Differentiating these distinct brain systems enables the patient to have more flexibility and emotional competence. The therapist's interventions can keep Activating, Facilitating, and Differentiating these conscious brain systems, enabling them to become increasingly resilient. This circular process can Integrate these brain systems by sustaining and enhancing each system simultaneously. Integrating resilient brain systems gives rise to a Fail-Safe Network of brain systems. We use the present participle of the verb *to integrate* in order to highlight that the processes of Integrating can be continuous. Within our multiple-brain-system therapeutic processes, Integrating is constantly active, dynamic, and naturally evolving. Integrating is an ongoing set of processes that needs to be sustained in order for new learning to be long-lasting.

INTEGRATING, SELF-ORGANIZING, AND COMPLEXITY

Your careful attention to the conscious brain systems will support your patient's (BrainMind's) capabilities for Integrating those systems. However, Integrating is a whole series of processes that unfold on all four levels of the nervous system. Most Integrating takes place in the nonconscious brain systems and therefore will be mostly invisible and nonverbal.

Your interventions can create brain system networks that naturally and spontaneously self-organize to increase complexity. *Self-organization* is a term that was initially introduced to science in 1947 by W. Ross Ashby, an English psychiatrist. Self-organizing is a process by which some form of overall order arises from interactions between differentiated parts of an initially disordered system. Self-organizing phenomena are observed in nature, physics, chemistry, and biology. Self-organizing is called *spontaneous order* when it is observed in the social sciences. For further explanation, we would need to step into complex systems and chaos theory, where it is easy to get lost.

Since Integrating is naturally spontaneous, and mostly nonconscious, how it plays out is necessarily out of your control. You and your patient focus your energy and attention, and what unfolds depends on variables you cannot anticipate. This experience can be scary for patient and therapist alike. Because Integrating is often uncomfortable, novel, and scary, opportunities for Integrating can be missed, neglected, or unintentionally avoided. As the patient's emotional development evolves, they will discover new competencies and at times previously unknown nonconscious emotional constraints or contradictions. These shifts in energy and information flow in the BrainMind can release other emotions such as grief, pain, terror, or shame. Some of these discoveries are hard won, and others can be quite surprising and unanticipated. Often the new competencies bring higher levels of complexity, which can enhance the spontaneous self-organizing capacities of the BrainMind.

Daniel Siegel makes the concepts of spontaneous self-organizing and complexity more approachable with these ideas: Self-organization is one of the fundamental emergent properties of complex systems, and it determines the way that any developing complex system evolves or unfolds. This unfolding can be optimized or constrained. When it's not optimized, it moves toward chaos or toward rigidity. When it is optimized, it moves toward harmony and is flexible, adaptive, coherent, energized, and stable (Siegel, 2018).

WEAVING OPEN SYSTEMS

Integrating is the weaving together of multiple active systems in the present moment. The systems need to be active and open to be able to receive the influence of other systems in order for Integrating to unfold. In contrast, a closed system is not receptive to the influence of other systems. We will try our best to tease these layers apart in the context of psychotherapeutic processes that focus on Integrating multiple brain systems.

Integrating also refers to the continuous parallel processing of energy and information that can operate when multiple distinct brain systems are interconnected rather than constrained. It can be difficult to get one's mind around the concepts of parallel processing and Integrating, because linear processing and causality require less effort and fewer brain systems. The most straightforward approach to understanding Integrating is to focus on the simultaneous parallel processing capacities of your own BrainMind. Imagine eating an apple. The visual brain system sees the shape and color. The taste brain system has one experience, and the smell (olfactory) system has a different one. You can imagine hearing the crunch as you bite into the apple even as you imagine the taste of the apple. All of that information is Integrating seamlessly and with no conscious effort. Our BrainMind is naturally integrating information about our inner experiences whether they reach a conscious threshold of importance or not.

Integrating happens naturally all the time in children. Their nervous systems are primed for learning and experiencing, and they approach each moment with a beginner's mind. We accumulate vast amounts of emotional learning in childhood that become part of our personalities, our adaptations to our families and communities, and our worldview.

The processes of Activating, Facilitating, Differentiating, Training, and Integrating develop new levels of resilience and flexibility that we call the Complex Integration of Multiple Brain Systems. Integrating Differentiated systems creates the synergy of the whole being greater than the sum of its parts. This synergy means that the many aspects of our lives can each be honored for their differences when brought together in harmony. Integrating allows brain circuits to fire together that perhaps have never fired in a coordinated way before, giving people a sensation of inner awareness that they may never have had (Siegel, 2018).

NOVEL DISCOVERIES: JOHN

As an example of Integration, we will look at the case of a patient we will call John. John suffered irrational and obsessional self-punishing worries, which became disabling for him in childhood. He received therapy and medication for years to be able to function in his life. After he finished his education and was working in a challenging job, his symptoms became more problematic. He sought us out to see whether a different therapy could manage his symptoms more successfully. In the first several sessions, Albert worked with John's limited self-awareness and his very high level of anxiety. Albert and John were successful in helping him get beyond some of his fear of actually engaging with his symptoms rather than suppressing or avoiding them. The following are some brief excerpts from his fifth therapy session to illustrate how simultaneously Activating and Facilitating John's multiple brain systems enabled them to Integrate and achieve a new level of complexity. As an additional benefit, he made new discoveries about his competencies and some nonconscious emotional constraints. The session starts after the Initial Directed Activation.

Albert: Do you want to do therapy today?

John: Yes I do. It is very important [*voice becomes deeper and stronger*]. I feel like I have some emotions that I would like to be in touch with.

Albert: What do you experience with that invitation?

John: It is different each time. I never know what is going to come out of it—which is very different from every therapy that I have experienced in the past. Just now I felt very mindful. There was a flutter of excitement and an energy that came straight up [*moves hands from pelvis up to chest*], almost like a spotlight, comes up from the bottom of my torso straight up my body. I felt some trepidation with those invitations, but also, stronger. I also felt a little sad [*tearful*]. I do not know why.

Albert [*Hands over his torso*]: To what extent do you feel safe right now?

John [*Voice deeper*]: I think I do feel pretty safe actually. I feel pretty physically safe. And right now I feel [*smiles*] almost like there is a glass wall in my head that is separating my active thoughts from all these anxieties on the other side [*hands demonstrate the wall*] that I can see and want to get rid of.

They moved on to Facilitate John's awareness and attention to his mix of feeling strong and needing to defend himself from his anxieties. This combination of feelings is an example of the engagement of Secondaries as we work with conscious brain systems. John started to discover how he was actually experiencing being physically threatened and attacked by his anxieties. He was able to be present to how his lower abdomen literally tensed up to protect itself from his anxieties. This was the beginning of the Integrating process, which included simultaneously focusing the energy of his attention and authority, observing his physical anxieties, maintaining his mindful state of awareness, and feeling his assertive drive and motivation to override his fearful reactions from the past. Seven different brain systems were operating in harmony together. He had a sudden understanding of why he had trouble at work: "I think that I always feel under attack on the inside. That is why, when I feel attacked externally, I collapse. I feel great shame. So I get really tired."

This process of Activating, Facilitating, and Differentiating his Attention, Awareness, and Authority brain systems enabled the new competencies of John's Reflective Self, which is consciously aware of its separateness from others (see sidebar, Chapter 7). Together they were experientially Differentiating his habitual internal self-attack from his competence at interrupting that pattern. John had feelings of pleasure at bringing this pattern out into the open. He had a new understanding of how this pattern had cost him a great deal in his life. Within the processes of Activating, Facilitating, and Differentiating multiple brain systems, many opportunities for Integrating will unfold. Often there are opportunities for Integrating that the therapist does not notice. The key is to be able to trust that they are happening and to help the patient sustain the Integrating in spite of the feelings of disorientation, discomfort, and release of pain or shame.

John: I am impressed with myself when I think about it from this perspective.

Albert: Good. What is it like to feel impressed [*hands over torso*], to be proud of yourself?

John: It feels really good, and it feels like I have won something [*face brightens*]. Like I have been praised wholeheartedly.

Albert: By whom?

John: By myself [*surprised*].

Albert: By yourself—that is a great counterbalance to this internal attack. It feels good to get it out in the open, and as you get it out in the open, there is tiredness. It has been exhausting to live with these self-attacks.

John: Yeah, when I get physically tired, it is even harder.

Albert: We want to help you put these burdens out on the table and see what happens. It is okay. They are here.

John: I can feel the attack does not stop. Even after I felt good there, feel the praise, all of a sudden I start to feel physically vulnerable. It is like I let off my guard for even a minute and then I actually feel physical discomfort right now [*face is pained, body tense*].

Albert and John continued to pay attention to his self-awareness of physical discomfort in the context of feeling proud and impressed with his hard-won competence. This process provided an ongoing Differentiation of the competencies of his Awareness, Attention, Authority, and Autonomy brain systems. The Autonomy brain system is particularly important here, as he becomes autonomous from his previous emotional patterns of self-attack. John was Integrating his experiences of competence, self-esteem, and self-attack.

When you focus on Activating, Facilitating, Differentiating, and Training distinct brain systems simultaneously, Integrating on multiple levels becomes an inevitable and natural outcome. The more you Trust the Process (as we invited you to do in the Introduction to Part II), the more Integrating will take place. However, as we have said, Integrating in these novel ways often feels uncomfortable. When you and your patient can hang in together through those awkward moments of disequilibrium, conflicted and/or closed brain systems, new learning, and new discoveries, a complex dynamic Integration will result. Albert directed these processes to help John tolerate his discomfort and sustain the Differentiating and Integrating of multiple brain systems. They then explored what was transpiring at that moment in the session that might also be triggering the self-attack.

> **John:** I experience this shame. The self-praise happens and it is like a surge of happiness and good emotion. It is like a wave and then back to the shame [*gestures with his hands*].
>
> **Albert:** What is happening right here with us that is stirring up the shame?
>
> **John [*Puzzled, hand to face*]:** I do not know.
>
> **Albert:** What is happening here in our interaction that might be stirring up this shame?
>
> **John:** We are connecting and analyzing.
>
> **Albert:** We are connecting. We are welcoming your emotions. We are doing both things, and it stirs up the shame [*hands rising up*].
>
> **John** [*Thoughtful, nods.*]
>
> **Albert:** Which part is stirring up the shame the most? The fact that we are connecting or the fact you are sharing your intimate emotional self with us?
>
> **John:** Um . . . [*hand to head, rubs right eye*] I think probably the connection . . . when we are talking and we connect and there is an invitation. I feel like I should take that invitation and let it out. Sometimes when we are talking, I get a little lost. I hear someone knocking at the door, and I just will not let them in. That makes me feel weak and ashamed.

This whole section is an Integrating process. John is aware and attentive to his sensory physical experience of shame in the context of connecting to his self-esteem and connecting with Albert. John discovered that the biggest trigger for his self-attack was shame activated by the healthy connection unfolding with his therapist. This was a moment of spontaneous self-organizing that disentangled his shame from his competence and desire for connection. These kinds of new Integrating experiences need repetition and reinforcement to become fully Differentiated and resilient. The two of them did further work on Differentiating the type of shame that perpetuated the self-attack from the type of shame that reacted to the relational connection that was developing in the session. These two new discoveries were fragile and would need lots of repetition and reinforcement before they could become resilient, flexible, and fully Integrated.

INTEGRATING AND THE FIRST STEPS OF THERAPY

Integrating in the Initial Directed Activation

We have previously (Chapters 6 and 7) talked about the various processes for directly Activating the conscious brain systems. Let's look at some of them again from the perspective of Integrating. To begin with, the Initial Directed Activation seeks to mobilize multiple distinct brain systems and bring them out into the open at the same time. Simultaneous Activations of multiple systems initiate and potentiate the phenomena of Integrating. You will be able to observe your patient's psychophysiological responses to the Initial Directed Activation and decide whether to focus on one brain system or several, depending on their reactions. For example, you may want to emphasize and simultaneously Integrate Awareness, Attention, Authority, and Autonomy as you develop the capability for collaboration, as in the example of Carol (Chapter 7).

Remember that multiple brain systems are always operating under the surface. They will give you clues to their needs and avoidances when you keep a sharp eye out. When you see or hypothesize what might be happening under the surface, you can seize your own authority and invite a directed focus on any particular competence that reveals itself. For example, Albert noticed an increased depth and animation in John's voice as he made each new discovery about himself. That psychophysiological shift suggested there might have been some Activating of the Pleasure, Value, or Importance brain systems that could be brought into awareness to sustain Integrating. So Albert directed the process by inviting John to be aware of his experience of feeling proud of himself. This mutually focused attention will enhance neuroplasticity (Schwartz & Begley, 2002). This Integrating process (simultaneous and sustained Activations of Awareness, Attention, Authority, Value, Importance, Fear, Care, Safe, and Connection brain systems) was successful, as John discovered that feeling proud uncovered an immediate and unintentional self-attack reaction.

Integrating in the Transpiring Present Moment

It can be very helpful when the therapist directs focus and attention to what is actually transpiring inside the patient at the present moment. What the therapist perceives is actually happening in the office can often be quite different from what the patient is thinking. There can be several important interactions that the patient is unable to see or value. The therapist can observe psychophysiological phenomena as evidence of what is transpiring at the present moment in different brain systems. These observations enable the therapist to point out how the patient is being capable without being aware of it. What is actually happening at this moment is evidence of the processing of different brain systems. When we pay attention and value those real-time Activations, they will become part of the Integrating process. For example, Albert directed the process into the Transpiring Present Moment when he asked John, "What is happening right here with us that is stirring up the shame?" A few moments later, John discovered, "I think probably the connection . . . makes me feel weak and ashamed."

Another direction that the therapist can take is to mobilize and Integrate multiple brain systems to help sustain the present-moment learning experience. In the case of John, Albert was simultaneously Training the Attention, Authority, and Value brain systems. For example, Albert invited the presence of Safe, Connection, and Shame by asking, "To what extent do you feel safe right now? . . .What is stirring up the shame, the fact that we are connecting or the fact you are sharing your intimate emotional self with us?"

The therapist can keep directing the Integrating process by taking attendance of these multiple distinct brain systems. The more balls we have in the air, the broader the Integrating. These systems will be better able to operate in a wider variety of contexts and situations. When John felt he had praised himself wholeheartedly, Albert noted, "[Self-praise] is a great counterbalance to this internal attack. It feels good to get it out in the open, and as you get it out in the open, there is tiredness. There has been this weight that you can put it out on the table. It has been exhausting to live with these attacks." In this way, Albert focused on Integrating Attention, Awareness, Authority, Pleasure, Importance, and Shame to support the self-compassion that was happening at that moment in the session.

Integrating Within the Therapeutic Attachment Relationship

From the first moment you sit down with a patient, you can be open, engaged, attuned, and active. The relationship between yourself and your patient will be unfolding moment by moment. Your patient's nonconscious Care, Connection, and Safe (attachment) brain systems will become activated naturally. You can observe the simultaneous Activations and parallel processing of all these brain systems in the evolving Therapeutic Attachment Relationship. This is a novel relationship. The patient's BrainMind will be Integrating this new information naturally. Integrating these brain systems will be happening at this moment in time, even when you are not focusing on those systems. The important effort is to keep yourself present to this relationship so you can observe how your patient is responding internally. You can use your observations to guide you in helping to keep your patient engaged and in the Transpiring Present Moment.

The invitation to the patient, "What you are aware of experiencing right now?," after the Initial Directed Activation, directs the patient's Attention and Awareness brain systems into the Transpiring Present Moment. There is no mention of the relationship, but trust that the relationship is playing a significant role in the activations that the patient is experiencing. Trust the Therapeutic Attachment Relationship as a source of both Activation and emotional regulation. By focusing on the Attention and Awareness brain systems, you are respecting your patient's capacity to pay attention and be self-aware. You can then move to enhance each of those systems to become more resilient.

The resonance between you and your patients is an Integrating experience that plays a major role in successful therapy. As we discussed in Chapter 3, therapist factors are the second-most important variables affecting successful therapeutic outcomes. Daniel Siegel refers to the positive connection between therapist and patient as "resonance," and we find his description of this process particularly apt:

The integrating experience of resonance also gives rise to a sense of spontaneity and creativity when it occurs between two people. Such vibrant connections between minds can be seen within various kinds of emotional relationships, such as those of romantic partners, friends, colleagues, teachers and students, therapists and patients, and parents and children. Two people become companions on a mutually created journey through time. Interpersonal integration can be seen in spontaneous, resonant communication that flows freely and is balanced between continuity, familiarity, and predictability on one side and flexibility, novelty, and uncertainty on the other. Neither partner of a dyad is fully predictable, yet each is quite familiar. The collaborative communication between these two is not merely a reflective mirror, but a reciprocal, contingent process that moves the pair into vibrant states neither alone could achieve. The resultant evolving process creates a sense of the emerging complexity and coherence of integrating minds (Siegel, 1999).

INTEGRATING PRINCIPLES

There are a number of principles that can guide you when you practice with the processes of Integrating. The following principles, introduced in Chapter 3, have special relevance to Integrating the conscious brain systems:

Resilient brain systems are powerful. In the process of developing resilient conscious brain systems, you strengthen those brain systems by Integrating them with nonconscious enhancing brain systems such as Value, Importance, and Pleasure. For example, with John's new self-awareness and discovery, Albert invited John to be aware of his internal positive feedback capability: "What is it like to feel impressed?" John: "It feels really good."

Differentiated brain systems process energy and information in parallel. This principle becomes central when you develop Differentiated and resilient conscious brain systems. Every time you refresh each of the Awareness, Attention, and Authority brain systems, they become stronger and more distinct from each other. For example, John was aware of and paying attention to his autonomous self: "There is a glass wall in my head that is separating my active thoughts from all these anxieties on the other side."

Sustained experiential learning changes the structure of the brain. A successful Integrating process requires repetition and reinforcement to override previous constraining learning and to develop new resilient adaptive neural circuits (Chapter 15). The therapist plays an important role in providing energy and focus to deepen the Integrating processes. This part of Integrating can feel unrewarding—you often get no verbal or even nonverbal feedback about how your patient is benefiting. You can sometimes receive pushback when you are providing adaptive treatment to multiple brain systems. This is illustrated in depth in Chapter 10.

Adaptive present-moment experiences can update traumatic implicit learning. Careful attention to your patient's Awareness, Attention, and Authority brain systems can help them stay mindfully present and override shame and pain from the past. For example, John said, "Even after I felt good there, feel the praise, all of a sudden I start to feel physically vulnerable. I actually feel physical discomfort right now."

Integrating systems release self-organizing system capacities. The ongoing Integrating process develops further resilience, and it Differentiates multiple brain systems so that they will naturally achieve new levels of complexity. This complexity will release the spontaneous self-organizing capacities of the Brain-Mind. The results are new learning, new internal knowledge and wisdom, and often a release of emotional constraints from the Fear or Shame brain systems. For example, John said, "I think that I always feel under attack on the inside. That is why when I feel attacked externally, I collapse. I feel great shame." And later: "I am impressed with myself when I think about it from this perspective." Later he released shame: "The self-praise happens . . . and then back to the shame."

TRAINING AND TREATING: PENNY REVISITED

Integrating is a process that involves a dynamic interaction between the Activations of distinct brain systems that are processing energy and information in their own highly evolved ways. The conscious brain systems function to direct the BrainMind to utilize consciousness to perform tasks that help meet the needs of this specific Self at this moment in time. The Secondaries work in parallel to modulate those systems by enhancing and inhibiting their activations.

We will use another therapy session to illustrate the various processes of developing resilient conscious brain systems. There will moments of Integrating as well, which we highlight to give you ideas of how you might use these principles to change "patient factors" and to develop resilient brain systems in your patients. From another perspective, you can observe how the therapist is working like a trainer or coach who is helping the patient isolate (Differentiate) different muscle groups (brain systems) and exercise them repeatedly in order to strengthen them. At times, the therapist acts like a physiotherapist who helps the patient override constraints (fear, shame) from previous injuries (emotional trauma). Physiotherapy for the BrainMind is such an important concept that we explore it in depth in Chapter 14.

The following case study continues Penny's first session, which we began in Chapter 4, Go the Other Way. At the end of each segment, we pose questions to the reader that have been useful teaching tools in our psychotherapy training courses. We also include some questions posed by trainees who viewed the video of this case study.

Penny was chronically depressed and anxious, to the point that her manner was almost frozen and she had very little self-awareness. We previously saw that when Beatriz Activated Penny's awareness of and attention to her bodily sensations, Penny began to chuckle. Penny's Play brain system revealed itself in the chuckles, and below Beatriz now focuses on Penny's Attention and Awareness brain systems to Integrate Play into their process and relationship. Both of them are valuing Penny's playfulness, and Penny becomes aware of soreness in her cheeks from smiling:

> **Penny:** I feel the soreness on my cheeks . . . like my face starts to hurt from smiling! [*Hands massaging her cheeks, big smile, surprise.*]
>
> **Beatriz:** How interesting. Both of us valuing your playfulness somehow brings a complex emotional experience [*hands reaching out to patient*].
>
> **Penny:** Yeah. I am having tingling here [*hand and fingers around her mouth*]. Now, my throat is very tight. . . . I can't speak . . . [*nods, hand to throat, body tight, dilated pupils, breathing shallow, beginning to cry*].
>
> **Beatriz:** We are valuing your playfulness.
>
> **Penny:** Yeah [*nods more strongly*].
>
> **Beatriz:** Your throat tightness is entangled with playfulness. . . .
>
> **Penny:** My voice . . . [*voice tight, face pained, gentle crying*].
>
> **Beatriz:** Do you <u>want</u> <u>us</u> to value your playfulness? [*Moving hands back and forth between their torsos.*]
>
> **Penny:** Yeah, why not! [*Nods, opens hands and forearms.*]
>
> **Beatriz:** But, is that what <u>you</u> . . .<u>want</u>? [*Stronger voice emphasis on "you" and "want.*]
>
> **Penny:** Yeah. . . .
>
> **Beatriz:** This . . .playful . . .you?
>
> **Penny** [*Sighs, body relaxes and stops crying.*]
>
> **[Beatriz's internal thoughts]:** She is having a psychophysiological shift and release of her distress. I want to keep her in the present moment and expand her self-awareness and capability for emotional regulation.
>
> **Beatriz:** What is happening?
>
> **Penny:** I am just trying to breathe. . . . I am teetering [*smiles, nodding, throat tight, voice stronger, repeatedly moving her torso right and left gently*].
>
> **Beatriz:** This is fantastic, the feeling of teetering. You are out of balance right now.
>
> **Penny:** Yeah . . . I feel off-balance [*nods more vigorously, as her body moves gently sideways*].
>
> **Beatriz:** This is success. You are creating a new equilibrium in your brain. This is success already.

Penny: My whole face is tingling right now [*smiles, surprise*].

Beatriz: This teetering place is very good.

QUESTION TO TRAINEES: What psychophysiological phenomena are capturing your attention?

POTENTIAL ANSWERS: The sudden shift from smiling to her throat becoming very tight and unable to speak in a matter of seconds. When she is teetering, she is smiling and nodding, her throat is tight, and she is moving her torso from side to side all at the same time.

QUESTION TO TRAINEES: Which of the conscious brain systems seem to be activated?

POTENTIAL ANSWERS: Penny is paying Attention to herself and she has Awareness of tingling in her face. She is having trouble expressing her Authority and her wants.

QUESTION TO TRAINEES: How is the therapist Differentiating and developing resilience in these brain systems?

POTENTIAL ANSWERS: Beatriz perceives the weakness in Penny's Authority brain system. She trains and promotes the development of her Authority system by repeating the invitation to her wants. She is disentangling previous emotional learning by reinforcing and being excited about her new learning.

PARTICIPANT QUESTION: How come you are not asking Penny about her thoughts or cognitions about her experiences?

BEATRIZ: Certainly, asking those questions could give you and the patient some interesting information and understanding about her emotional reactions. However, in these processes of Differentiating and Integrating, the focus is on what is uniquely transpiring in her distinct brain systems in the present moment (rather than reporting on her conscious interpretation or associations to her experiences). If you want to change the brain, make new networks (Grawe, 2007).

Albert's commentary: Beatriz constantly supports Penny's evolving self-awareness of her Reflective Self. She repeats invitations to Penny's Authority brain system by saying, "Is that what you . . . want?" When there is a psychophysiological shift, Beatriz directs Penny's Attention to her Sensory and Awareness brain systems by saying, "What is happening?" From that moment on, an Integrating process is unfolding. Penny is regulating her breathing, monitoring her tingling, and saying, "I feel off-balance." Beatriz acts as her physiotherapist, metaphorically holding her hand as Penny's BrainMind Integrates these novel emotional experiences.

Beatriz: What is happening that is making you teeter?

Penny: These new sensations are scaring me. I don't know what they mean. I try to think about them [*nods*] and then they get stronger or they change, and so I start to feel them again [*laughs out loud*].

Beatriz: Tell me about the laughter [*giggles*].

Penny: It is silly, because I am thinking about going back and forth.

Beatriz: Is there delight about the makings of your mind?

Penny: Yeah! [*Smiles, nods with her whole torso, surprised*]. Okay, I am teetering again! [*Laughs, smiles, nods her body.*]

Beatriz: We are staying and delighting in you. Are we still delighting in you?

Penny: Yeah, I am trying to come back. I have been running away [*leans forward, more engaged*].

Beatriz: Are you paying attention to yourself?

Penny: I'm trying to let what you are saying to land on me.

Beatriz: What part?

Penny: The valuing part. I am trying to let it land [*voice choked up, on the verge of tears*].

Beatriz: Are you paying close close attention to you right now?

Penny: Yeah. I am trying not to listen to you and to find excuses as to why you are valuing me [*laughs out loud*].

Beatriz: And right now at this little moment, I am paying attention to you with all my might and my intelligence and my capacity. I am valuing you.

Penny: Yes, it feels that way, but I am still skeptical [*nods, and scowls, head looking sideways.*

Beatriz: And you are paying attention to you. We are both valuing you [*moving hands toward her*].

Penny: Okay [*nodding her head*].

Beatriz: We are valuing you. This is what is happening.

Penny [*Posture more erect, nodding affirmatively with strong eye contact, imitating, mouthing the word "valuing."*]

Beatriz: This is a disconfirming experience from the past, that you are not valuable [*pushes hands to the side*]. And valuing you is happening right now.

Penny [*Throat tight, holds her breath, her body rigid, and shoulders go up, dry mouth*].

Beatriz: What is happening?

Penny: I feel guilt . . . that I am enjoying this?! [*Smiles and chuckles, surprised, moves her arms.*]

QUESTION TO TRAINEES: What psychophysiological phenomena are capturing your attention?

POTENTIAL ANSWERS: She is moving her whole torso, suggesting that there is much less anxiety. Her laughter reveals playfulness and delight. Her stronger voice means that there is less tension in her throat. Her discovery of feeling guilt about enjoying being valued contains a lot of psychophysiological activations: smiles, chuckles, surprise, and opening her arms.

QUESTION TO TRAINEES: Which brain systems seem to be Activated?

POTENTIAL ANSWERS: She has more Autonomy as she claims her separateness. Her Attention brain system seems to be having trouble processing all of this new experience of being valued. Her Awareness brain system is able to be present to the conflict of guilt and enjoyment at the same time.

QUESTION TO TRAINEES: How is the therapist Differentiating and developing resilience?

POTENTIAL ANSWERS: Beatriz showed Penny her distinct phenomenon of laughter to bring her into a state of novelty. She promoted her Play and Pleasure brain systems. She also set the stage for Integrating other brain systems by bringing in curiosity (Seeking) and interest (Importance/ Salience) about the new discoveries.

QUESTION TO TRAINEES: What brain systems are open and capable of parallel processing?

POTENTIAL ANSWERS: Her Attention, Awareness, and Authority brain systems all appear to be functioning simultaneously. Penny is curious (Seeking) and surprised by the uniqueness of what is unfolding inside of herself.

QUESTION TO TRAINEES: What brain systems appear to be closed by maladaptive neural constraints?

POTENTIAL ANSWERS: The patient is aware of feeling skeptical about being valued (Value and Connection brain systems) by Beatriz. Beatriz is disentangling previous emotional learning by noting that the present is "a disconfirming experience from the past." She is in essence saying, "We are valuing you now, even as you felt you were not worthy in the past."

QUESTION TO TRAINEES: Do you see anything that looks like it might be a spontaneous self-organizing phenomenon?

POTENTIAL ANSWER: Her spontaneous discovery of her own guilt about enjoying feeling valued and valuable seems like a new discovery from these processes of Differentiating and Integrating.

PARTICIPANT QUESTION: What are the reasons for repeating the words *valuing* and *valuable* multiple times?

BEATRIZ: There are several reasons. We are meeting her psychological needs for orientation and esteem. She needs to know that we are working together. We want her to feel our actual esteem. We are desensitizing her to taking in our esteem.

PARTICIPANT QUESTION: Would it be helpful to inquire about her skepticism?

BEATRIZ: She would be able to come up with an explanation or rationalization about her skepticism. Her skepticism is real from the past, and her mind is trying to reconfirm that bias. We find it more helpful to stay in the present and keep sustaining the present embodied experiences of feeling valued right now. This becomes a Differentiating experience with new learning and the potential for Integrating.

Albert's commentary: Beatriz is actively directing Penny's attention to enhancing Activations that are unfolding underneath the surface by saying such things as, "We are valuing your mind." Penny's psychophysiological response tells her that this is an important brain system to Facilitate to provide new learning and override the Fear brain system that appears to be dominating Penny at this moment, as shown by her statements such as, "My throat is very tight. I can't speak." There is an interesting disequilibrium between the pleasure and delight she is having in her connection and the fear, flight, and disbelief reactions: "I am trying not to listen [to] you and to find excuses as to why you are valuing me."

Even at this early stage of Activating and Differentiating her brain systems, Penny is experiencing an Integrating process where she is paying close attention to her Transpiring Present Moment experiences of Awareness, Authority, and Autonomy while she is overriding her Fear and Guilt brain systems. Beatriz is acknowledging the "flashes of memories" by supporting and enhancing Penny's Transpiring Present Moment experience: "This is a disconfirming experience from the past." This process is so much smoother when Penny is able to utilize her conscious brain systems to choose to stay present to her wants, to be valued, and to update her emotional learning from the past.

Beatriz: Fascinating isn't it? [*Excited voice.*]

Penny: Yeah.

Beatriz: So, when you say *guilt*, what are the sensations?

Penny: I am having, like, memory flashes.

[Beatriz's internal thoughts]: It is important to stay in the present rather than associations from the past.

Beatriz: And the sensations in your body?

Penny: My face is still tingling, and I feel more tense [*breathes more deeply, raises her shoulders, then releases*].

Beatriz: Tense? . . .

Penny: Pulling away almost [*moving her body backward*].

Beatriz: Is it unsafe?

Penny: Yeah [*nods*].

Beatriz: Your body is feeling is unsafe about . . .what?

Penny: Valuing me? [*Giggles, shakes head in disbelief.*]

Beatriz: Feeling valued is unsafe somehow.

Penny: Wow! How dare I!

Beatriz: Exactly?!

Penny [*Laughs.*]

Beatriz: How dare you value yourself!

Penny: Yeah! [*Laughs with her whole body, head going backward in realization of novelty.*]

Beatriz: Tell me about the laugh.

Penny: Because it sounds so absurd once it is articulated.

Beatriz: We are delighting in you right now.

Penny: Yeah [*smiles, nods*].

Beatriz: We are giggling together. We are delighting in you.

Penny [*Nods.*]

Beatriz: And that makes my eyes shine.

Penny: I don't think anybody in my life has spent this much time making eye contact with me [*sighs, nods, frowns, holds her breath, shoulders up then down, mouth movements*].

Beatriz: What is happening?

Penny: I feel sadness [*voice constrained, grimaces, throat tight, starts to cry softly*].

Beatriz: We can see this is a complex emotional experience. Perhaps some grief from the past, that you have not been valued and delighted in. This is a disconfirming experience.

Penny: And, that I was wrong for wanting to be valued [*frowns, then jaw set, more tears, pained expression*].

QUESTION TO TRAINEES: What psychophysiological phenomena are capturing your attention?

POTENTIAL ANSWERS: She moves her body backward in a way that is congruent with her statement about feeling like pulling away. Her laughter appears quite spontaneous and could be evidence of Differentiating from emotional constraints. There appear to be so many physiological activations when she becomes aware of the therapist's constant unconditional eye gaze. When the patient states that she felt wrong for wanting to be valued, her face seems to reveal some kind of anger.

QUESTION TO TRAINEES: How is the therapist Differentiating and developing resilience?

POTENTIAL ANSWERS: She is Facilitating the patient's Awareness, Attention, and Authority brain systems to observe her body's reactions to feeling valued. Beatriz helps the patient discover that being valued feels unsafe. She sustains the patient's Awareness and Attention to feeling valued while she feels unsafe and releases tears of grief.

QUESTION TO TRAINEES: What brain systems appear to be closed by implicit emotional constraints?

POTENTIAL ANSWERS: Her Value brain system and ability to feel esteemed seem to be closed. The patient's Safe brain system is closed in the context of being valued by the therapist. The patient's needs for Care and Connection appear to be constrained, when she reveals that she feels wrong for wanting to be valued and cared for.

QUESTION TO TRAINEES: Do you see anything that looks like it might be a spontaneous self-organizing phenomenon?

POTENTIAL ANSWERS: Her spontaneous release of laughter, surprise, and disbelief that valuing herself is unsafe appears to be a new visceral learning. Her authentic release of grief while taking in the therapist's unconditional regard is a meaningful discovery of new openness. Her discovery that she felt wrong for wanting to be valued appears to be a new Integration for her.

Albert's Commentary: The rest of the session focuses on repeating the distinctive Activations of all of the brain systems that have revealed themselves thus far. This repetitive Training makes each system stronger and more resilient. Drawing attention to the different psychophysiological activations helps the patient's BrainMind make distinctions between each of the brain systems. As we have seen, the simultaneous Activation of multiple resilient brain systems can release new spontaneous self-organizing phenomena. Maintaining this process of Integrating for longer periods of time can enable the patient's BrainMind to become a Fail-Safe Network. At the end of the session, Beatriz and Penny do a short debrief about the most meaningful aspects of the session. Together they help Penny decide what experiences she wants to practice and exercise between sessions (Training).

BENEFITS

Ongoing conscious self-awareness is an Integrating process and phenomenon. Penny's repeated conscious experience of her Attention and Awareness brain systems, for example, will naturally Integrate them with each other. Information processing across different interconnected regions is coordinated when different brain systems fire action potentials synchronously (simultaneously). Integrating across brain regions is important for memory, emotion, and motivation systems (LeDoux, 1996). Integrating takes effort, and intention is needed to override default patterns of emotional habits.

Integrating helps the BrainMind direct the flow of energy and utilize that energy in adaptive life-affirming ways. Integrating incorporates therapeutic processes such as these:

1. Activating specific systems to harness the energy, processing capabilities, and wisdom of multiple brain systems.
2. Differentiating capabilities that develop, train, disentangle, and sustain distinct resilient brain systems.
3. Managing high levels of simultaneous emotional energy through parallel processing with multiple brain systems.
4. Supporting the patient through the awkward feelings and sensations of disequilibrium that come with novel learning.
5. Discovering new capabilities and unknown constraints.
6. Releasing and dissipating unresolved pain, shame, grief, and terror.
7. Revealing psychophysiological phenomena and potentiates physiotherapy for the treatment.

NEUROPHYSIOPSYCHOTHERAPY

We sometimes use the term neurophysiopsychotherapy to describe our methods and strategies of Integrating within the CIMBS paradigm. *Neuro-* refers to our active interventions to maximize neuroplasticity for long-term learning, including specific interventions to activate multiple neurotransmitters to facilitate the therapeutic process. *Physio-* refers to our observations of psychophysiological phenomena for assessment and to adjust our therapeutic process, and to do physiotherapy for the Brain Mind (Chapter 14). *Psycho-* refers to our focus on multiple psychological brain systems (Care, Fear, and so on) and on meeting the psychological needs of our patients (self-esteem, mastery, and so on). *Therapy* refers to the therapeutic treatment we are providing moment by moment.

These approaches to the conscious brain systems will open patients' Brain-Minds to mindful learning. Mindful learning consists of openness to novelty, alertness to distinction, sensitivity to different contexts, and implicit if not explicit awareness of multiple perspectives and orientation to the present (Langer, 2016). These aspects of mindful learning will help your patients come to experientially appreciate their distinct emotional competencies. For these reasons, we have found it helpful to keep checking in with the conscious brain systems repeatedly throughout each session to maximize our patients' mindful learning.

The careful attention to your patients' Authority and Autonomy brain systems will prime them to be more interested in practicing their new emotional learning (Training) every day between sessions. You may find that they come into the next session in a new place and you can move on from there, rather than having to pick up where you left off the previous session. They may not consciously recognize the long-term learning that is happening in their BrainMinds. Therefore it behooves you to trust yourself, Trust the Process and your patients' nonconscious learning, rather than depending on their cognitive feedback.

Any one of these Integrating elements, components, tools, processes, and perspectives can make a difference in your therapy. So we encourage you to experiment with one or two and see where it takes you and your patients.

CHALLENGES OF CONSCIOUS BRAIN SYSTEMS

We tend to take our consciousness for granted in ourselves, and therefore we tend to take it for granted in other people, including our patients. Because we have lived with our consciousness since infancy, we are usually not familiar with its nuances and subtleties. For example, we are not aware of the air in which we move all the time unless we are outside in a windstorm. Our conscious brain systems are generally invisible to us. We are not used to parsing them out into different dimensions of consciousness. Focusing on the Authority and Autonomy brain systems can be a huge step for some patients because they have not yet developed search patterns in their BrainMinds to detect those subtleties.

Therapist Challenges

It naturally causes discomfort to approach our patients in unfamiliar ways and with unfamiliar interventions. What we are proposing to you is not how you or we were trained. It is uncomfortable to let go of the control you are used to and to Trust the (unfamiliar) Process. It is also ironic that this approach to the conscious brain systems means focusing much of your effort on the nonconscious psychophysiological responses to your interventions rather than the conscious cognitive content. It takes time to develop new search patterns, to see the "weevils" (see Chapter 3). It is naturally uncomfortable, for the therapist as well as the patient, to be in the novelty of now, rather than the familiar ruminations from the past or familiar worries about the future.

Our case studies are illustrative and have clear feedback between the therapist and patient. There are challenges when we receive little or no positive feedback from our treatments. It is hard to trust something that you cannot see. The benefit of collaboration is priceless, but often evolves quite slowly and can easily go unnoticed.

For some therapists, it is difficult to intervene this actively and interrupt distractions as they arise; one of the ways we intervene actively is to Go the Other Way. The process can be intangible for therapists since most of what is transpiring is nonconscious for both the patient and therapist.

Patient Challenges

As you have seen, there are equal challenges for your patients. The unfamiliar activations of their brain systems will upset their usual emotional equilibrium (Panksepp & Biven, 2012). For example, your patient might respond to your inquiry about their internal awareness by saying, "I am not aware of anything," "I don't feel anything," or "I do not want all this attention on me." Some patients will never be able to develop a strong sense of their own authority or autonomy. They do not believe or trust that they have their own autonomous choice. Those innate capabilities may have been shut down in early childhood. For others it can feel like a betrayal of their way of being, family background, or culture. John, for example, struggled with his awareness of shame when he experienced being proud of himself and open to connection with Albert. And Penny felt guilt and a sense of betrayal of her past when she and Beatriz were valuing her and she said, "I was wrong for wanting to be valued."

Treatment Challenges

Many intriguing challenges arise when you approach your patient's conscious brain systems this directly. For example, how do you respond when the patient says they do not want to pay attention to themselves or they do not want to be aware of what they are experiencing or feeling? Some patients may tell you that this careful focus on themselves makes them more anxious. These responses and many others reveal your patient's underlying ambivalence about being intimately connected to themselves and to you. Such responses can be intriguing, for they bring some important underlying constraints out into the open immediately. Those responses are your opportunities to Go the Other Way and embrace their ambivalence.

Some patients can be quite disconnected from one or more of their conscious brain systems. They may be so anxious that they are unaware of themselves or unable to pay more than cursory attention to you or the therapy. That anxiety is good to uncover at the outset, so that you can slow the process down and start working on building a collaborative foundation of the Attention and Awareness brain systems. In doing so, you will be gradually developing resilient brain systems that will serve you and your patients well for the rest of the session and for the rest of their lives.

Embracing your patient's ambivalence can bring other important patient factors out into the open. They can discover that by developing their conscious brain systems, they will no longer need to rely on certain coping mechanisms that they have utilized for years. The patient can feel out of balance, dizzy, confused, or disoriented when they no longer need to lean on these mechanisms. Penny, for example, shared her feeling, "I am teetering." One depressed patient of ours discovered that he did not really want to give up the comfort of his depression. He was afraid that if he let go of his depression, he would lose his sense of self, his identity. Another patient discovered that she was uncomfortable giving up her role as a victim. She was afraid to let go of her attachments that she had achieved by dependence, compliance, and defiance. She recognized that no longer being a victim would be a frightening change in her life.

SUMMARY

Integrating is a fascinating and rewarding therapeutic process and treatment. It can sometimes feel like we are in the middle of a five-ring circus. There is so much going on, and you can only observe part of it. However, trust the fact that Integrating and self-organization are natural phenomena. We can set the stage for Integrating by the processes of Activating, Facilitating, Differentiating, and Training. Then we get out of the way and help the patient stay open to their novel experiences and discoveries. Then the Training exercises that the patient can choose to practice between sessions will further strengthen the resilience of each brain system. The outcome of these processes is Fail-Safe Complex Networks.

The next section focuses on the primary-level brain systems. They are especially intriguing because they are nonconscious and so powerful. The same processes of Activating, Facilitating, Differentiating, Training, and Integrating will be applied to the Safe, Care, Connection, Seeking, Assertive, Play, and Sensory brain systems.

CHAPTER 10

Primary-Level
Brain Systems:
The Powerhouses

....

ANDREW FINDS SEEKING

Andrew came to Albert for therapy because of pervasive symptoms of anxiety. He was often irritable and frequently had anger outbursts that he would feel badly about later. In the beginning of treatment when Albert asked, "What are you experiencing inside yourself right now?," Andrew would change the subject, or would say with a puzzled look, "I don't know." Later when Albert inquired about how safe Andrew felt, or how he was experiencing this connection with Albert, he would respond with a series of self-critical stories.

The early phase of treatment focused on Facilitating Andrew's Awareness and Authority brain systems. Invitations such as "Do you want to be aware of your self?" stimulated ambivalent responses such as, "I guess that's why I'm here." When Albert asked, "Do you want us to get to know you?," Andrew became fearful and withdrew into his conscious ruminations and self-critical stories. At the same time, Albert was Facilitating Andrew's Safe, Care, and Connection brain systems. "It is safe for us to connect together." "We care about whatever you are experiencing." Andrew would mindfully practice those capabilities on his own between sessions with his children and wife. Slowly they were able to desensitize Andrew to his fear and interrupt some of his shame reactions. Together they discovered that experiencing connection with himself and with Albert was especially frightening. This persistent pro-cess of facilitating Andrew's Awareness, Authority, Autonomy, Safe, Care, and Connection brain systems dramatically inhibited the hyperactive Fear and Shame brain systems.

A couple months into therapy, Andrew made a fascinating discovery inside himself. In this exceptional session, he found that it was easier to let go of his stories and ruminations. He spontaneously put his feet firmly on the floor. His breathing became slower and deeper. He suddenly had a surprised look on his face and proclaimed several times, "I want to look around. I want to look around." He turned his head back and forth to look around the room as if he had never been there before. He kept exploring the room with his eyes, with tears of joy falling down his cheeks. His face was filled with won-der. He stated, "I feel like a toddler who has finally been given the chance to explore." When questioned what had enabled this deep physical change, he reported, "I feel safe in a way I never have before. I feel accepted by both of us. I feel strong and connected with myself and with you." Albert was also sur-prised and delighted by the depth of his psychophysiological shift. It seemed as though his Seeking brain system had been turned on (had come online) for the first time since childhood.

At the following session, he was much less anxious. His body was more ani-mated. He kept his feet on the floor and described new sensations in his pelvic region. However, there were also constraints of tightness in his throat and diffi-culty sustaining the feelings of care, kindness, and gratitude that he had experi-enced so readily the week before. The therapeutic work proceeded more rapidly from that point forward.

We chose to include Andrew's case story to illustrate several important points. Facilitating attention on the primary-level Safe, Care, and Connection (attachment) brain systems over a couple of months woke up another one of his Primaries: Seeking. The visceral and emotional shifts were dramatic, surprising, and memorable. Andrew's present-moment conscious physical and emotional experiences clearly stemmed from his early childhood without any associated conscious history. Andrew's difficulties with anger outbursts resolved without ever being the focus of the treatment.

THE DISCOVERY OF MULTIPLE DISTINCT PRIMARY-LEVEL BRAIN SYSTEMS

The farther we go into the depth of our affective foundations—our inside universe—the closer we come to our mental origins.

JAAK PANKSEPP & LUCY BIVEN,
THE ARCHAEOLOGY OF MIND

In the fall of 2015, Daniel Siegel recommended that we read *The Archaeology of Mind* (Panksepp & Biven, 2012). W. W. Norton and Siegel had the wisdom to publish this work in the Norton Series on Interpersonal Neurobiology to make this affective neuroscience knowledge available to a much broader audience, including us. We read the book the following winter while on vacation, when we had time to delve into and discuss the breadth and depth of this knowledge. It was a fortuitous combination of recommendation, wonderful resource, time, and our own clinical research that helped us come to a new understanding of the nature of multiple distinct nonconscious emotions. We were very excited and inspired by this new knowledge. You have seen how Jaak Panksepp's knowledge has been interwoven throughout this book. He wrote *The Archaeology of Mind* in an engaging manner that kept us looking deeper into the roots of our emotional instincts. We had been doing clinical research in the broader area of nonconscious emotional motivations. This book became a prism through which we were able to discover and discern seven distinct nonconscious emotional brain systems that originate in the brainstem. This work has become a primary resource for us. We turn back to it again and again to assist us in educating our colleagues and writing about our clinical research.

Our teaching subsequent to *The Archaeology of Mind* had a new clarity that our trainees appreciated and commented on immediately. Our trainees and other colleagues have found our practical applications of the primary-level brain systems have helped them enormously in working deeply with their patients. Understanding the nature and distinctions between these emotional brain systems can provide a new dimension of trust in the innate potentials of your patients. One of our colleagues had a new insight in her work after a training weekend dedicated to working with Primaries: "We are rewiring the patient's physiology, rather than rewiring (updating) their narrative."

Siegel (2012) suggested "that knowing this material can help us bring more effective treatments and educational insights into our work and our world." There is a lot of new material here for most readers. We suggest that you take your time and explore these different primary-level brain systems piecemeal, depending on your interest. If you are a clinician, think of each one as a magnifying glass with which to discover the inner workings of your patients' nonconscious subcortical (brainstem) emotional circuits.

In Chapter 1 (Figure 1.6), we likened the primary-level brain systems to the parable of the blind men and the elephant. The earliest versions of this parable are found in Buddhist, Hindu, and Jain texts that discuss the limits of perception and the importance of complete context. A group of blind men heard that a strange animal, called an elephant, had been brought to town, but none of them were aware of its shape and form. Out of curiosity, they said, "We must inspect and know it by touch." So they sought it out, and when they found it, they groped around. The first person, whose hand landed on the trunk, said, "This being is like a thick snake." For another one, whose hand reached its ear, it seemed like a fan. The person whose hand was upon its leg described the elephant as a pillar or a tree trunk. Another, who felt its tail, described it as a rope. The last felt its tusk, stating that the elephant is hard, smooth, and like a spear. Each of these perspectives has value and contributes to an understanding of the whole. We invite you to be a blind person with a beginner's mind and touch and feel your own way through the primary-level brain systems.

Primary-Level Features

Each primary-level brain system has distinctive, highly evolved drives, wisdom, psychophysiological signatures, and processing capabilities. The characteristics of these emotional systems are distinguished by the specific neurobiological properties of the neural circuits that compose them. Each will process any situation in its own uniquely evolved fashion. In Andrew's session described above, as he experienced an awakening in his Seeking system, he felt calm with Safe, warmth with Care, and Closeness with himself and Albert. The physical experiences of the safe connection with the therapist activated his Safe and Connection brain systems. Each brain system had its own hardwired psychophysiological responses (deeper breathing and stronger eye gaze) to support the functioning of the system in the present moment. Emotional learning will take place when the innate benefits of the brain systems are sustained. Each brain system generates distinctive emotional feelings that can become conscious if they are strong enough to pass an internal threshold (Panksepp & Biven, 2012).

Below we expand on the descriptions of each of the primary systems we introduced in Chapter 1:

- Safe (Figure 10.1): This brain system moves us toward quiet, calm, secure, protected, and warm environments. Imagine yourself snuggled up with a blanket, next to a fire, with stillness and a sense of well-being. For most of us, the womb is where we first experienced Safe. The wisdom in safeness is that we can direct our inner resources to growth, healing, recovery, and optimal immune system functioning. Feeling safe, we can relax and rest. You can observe Safe in your patient's body—an upright and open posture, soft facial features—and hear it in a gentle, clear voice and diaphragmatic breathing. Most patients have trouble describing the physical experience of Safe beyond the absence of tension and anxiety. Those that can are often surprised at how expansive they feel in their chest and upper torso into their neck and throat. This system processes homeostatic information from visceral organs such as the heart, liver, lungs, and kidneys, indicating all is well. Ironically, Safe can be quite disorienting for some patients. When we experience Safe, our walls and defenses seem to drift away, leaving us vulnerable and yet open, flexible and powerful.

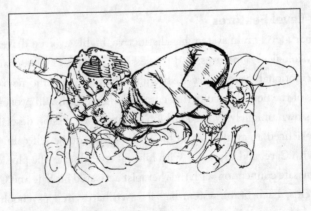

Figure 10.1: Safe Brain System

- Care (Figure 10.2): This brain system inspires and even compels us to invest enormous amounts of attention, energy, and interest in another being or ourselves. Evolution has installed in our genes the wisdom to care for our offspring, partners, family members, and clan members, and that caring benefits the survival of the individual and the community as a whole. You can hear warmth in the voice and observe a tenderness around the eyes, gentle mouth movements, and an opening up of the posture in your patients. Your patient's embodied experience is warmth in the upper chest and around the heart, along with sparkling eyes and spontaneous smiles. There seems to be a reciprocal positive feedback loop between the heart (cardiac plexus, assemblies of neurons found in the body) and lungs (pulmonary plexus) that helps to sustain the activations of Care and is processed by the Care brain system.

Figure 10.2: Care Brain System

- Connection (Figure 10.3): This brain system mobilizes us to gradually and viscerally develop deep emotional attachments to our care providers and others. Attachment relationships and Connection potentiate collaboration, working together as a group and looking out for each other. Your patient's embodied experience of connection is feeling closeness, wanting proximity to this specific person, and a visceral experience that says, "I matter to them; they matter to me." You can observe that your patients are able to sustain a sincere eye gaze, especially in moments of silence. The cervical plexus in the neck and the vagus nerve may play a role in sustaining the Connection brain system.

Figure 10.3: Connection Brain System

- Seeking (Figure 10.4): This brain system directs us to explore our environment to find resources, increase survival opportunities, and meet our needs in thousands of different ways. Seeking helps any animal move out of safety into novel and potentially rich new environments for food and untapped resources. Your patient might hold their head up or tilt their head as if looking to discover

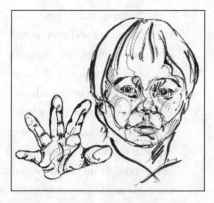

Figure 10.4: Seeking Brain System

something new or from a different viewpoint. Their feelings are interest and curiosity, and they sometimes move the body slightly forward. Their eyes are more open and the pupils might dilate slightly. The patient's embodied experience is the felt sense of interest, curiosity, expectancy, excitement, and anticipation. The body's feedback loop between the sacral and brachial plexuses and the Seeking part of the brainstem may help sustain the activations of exploring, especially when tired or afraid.

- Play (Figure 10.5): This brain system fosters spontaneous activity that is done for its own sake. It evolved to facilitate learning nonsocial physical skills like hunting and foraging, along with many social capacities such as competitive, courting, sexual, and parenting skills (Panksepp & Biven, 2012). The cerebellum participates in the precise physical and emotional coordination learning that enables us to be skillful and graceful (physical and social wisdom). Spontaneous laughter, giggles, chuckles, effervescence, and beaming smiles provide you with psychophysiological evidence that your patient is experiencing the delight, pleasures,

Figure 10.5: Play Brain System

and social joy of the Play brain system. Your patient's embodied experience is one of lightness, uplifting, tingling, an internal giggle, and feeling delight. The body processes the playful touch of tickling with pleasure and the most intense laughter of all. Playful mobilizations are robust, yet they are easily aborted when Fear, Shame, or Grief emotions are present.

- Assertive (Figure 10.6): This brain system empowers us to pursue our needs, satisfy our wants, and thrive in the world. Many of the cries we expressed as infants were assertive, lusty vocalizations alerting others to our needs for food, connection, warmth, and care. The Assertive brain system in the brainstem channels energy and power from the body and peripheral nervous system to make things happen in our lives. You can observe Assertive psychophysiological phenomena in your patients when they start to hold themselves more erect, use a stronger voice, and make assertive movements with their hands and arms. Your patient's embodied experience is strong (especially in the muscles along the spine), powerful, and capable: "I feel like I have a rod up my back."

Figure 10.6: Assertive Brain System

- Sensory (Figure 10.7): This emotional brain system channels, processes, and integrates the

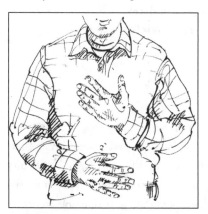

Figure 10.7: Sensory Brain System

emotional information and energy that comes in from our peripheral nervous system. This emotional brain system is distinct from the sensory affect brain systems such as smell (olfactory brain system), sight (visual brain system), and sound (auditory brain system). The neural plexuses of our organs such as lungs, heart, and gut process energy and information from these organs and send it to the Sensory brain system in the brainstem. This system processes information from neural plexuses in the torso such as warmth (Care) in the heart (cardiac plexus), nausea (Shame) in the gut (celiac plexus), and shortness of breath (Fear) in the lungs (respiratory plexus). You can detect psychophysiological phenomena that will alert you to Sensory brain system information. For example, when they blush, you might inquire, "What are you experiencing in your torso right now?" Patients develop a felt sense of themselves and their bodies. Your patient's embodied experience is often described by words such as grounded, heavy, solid, real, and true.

There are many benefits to our survival when each of the primary-level brain systems is resilient, Differentiated, and Integrated with the others:

1. Small stimulations of primary-level brain systems can give rise to strong adaptive (nonconscious and conscious) emotional responses in your patient's BrainMind.
2. The focus on Primaries can shift the therapeutic balance away from the emotions of fear, shame, terror, or guilt toward joy (Play), capability (Assertive), or competence (Sensory).
3. Differentiating Primaries can take your patient beyond feeling successful in the moment, a state experience, to developing an enduring mental capacity such as self-confidence, an enduring trait.
4. Activating, Differentiating, and Integrating Primaries helps to keep the therapeutic process in the Transpiring Present Moment where neuroplasticity is enhanced and long-term changes can develop.
5. Primaries provide energy to focus the conscious brain systems and increase collaboration.

CASE STUDY OF MARIA

The following transcript is from Maria's fourth session. She was a 35-year-old woman who had failed therapy with both medications and several other therapists. The patient was depressed, overwhelmed by life, and having difficulty coping with physical and psychological pain. In addition to her depression, she had chronic fatigue syndrome and sometimes spent days in bed unable to get up because of inexplicable pains.

This transcript is a natural (naturally flawed), unedited session intended to be illustrative of Activating and Facilitating primary-level brain systems. This case study can provide you with a lot of interesting information and phenomena to help you see how much is going on in every session and with every intervention. We invite you to use this example to help you learn to slow down, look closely with curiosity, and develop new search patterns to discern subtle phenomena in your patient. What we are sharing is not anecdotal and not speculative, because it is easily and readily reproducible. We demonstrate these phenomena and processes live every time we teach. Our challenge here is to help evoke experiences in you that could be similar to the ones our training participants have.

Beatriz interjects some of her internal thoughts, the musical score, within the transcript. Albert's commentary is a composite of comments, discussions, and answered questions that are addressed to participants in our weekend trainings when we show video recordings of sessions such as this one. The transcript starts after the brief meditation that starts the session.

Beatriz: We are leaving everybody outside [*both hands push off to the side*].

Maria [*Nods, engaged eye gaze, mixed smile then grimace, then neck extended, holding head higher.*]

Beatriz: And we are here to pay close [*hands reaching out*] caring attention to you [*gentle and tender voice, body leaning forward*].

Maria [*Nods, grimaces, on the verge of tears.*]

[Beatriz's internal thoughts]: It appears that my constant eye gaze is Activating lots of emotion in Maria's face. Her tears are evidence of the mix of activations.

Beatriz: It is important that you go inside of you, paying attention to you, being present with you [*both hands on her upper chest*].

Maria [*Nods, reaches for a tissue and sniffles.*]

Beatriz: We are here to help you feel safer inside of yourself [*hands move down her own torso*].

Maria [*Mixed facial expression, tight smile, gentle tears, wipes tears.*]

Beatriz: Whatever is inside of you [*moves hands up and down her torso*] is what will carry us today. Whatever is inside of you is not good, not bad, it just is.

Maria [*Face tense, more tears, touched, shallow breathing, nods.*]

[Beatriz's internal thoughts]: Maria is revealing many psychophysiological phenomena in response to these interventions. I see a mix of Connection, Safe, Care, and Fear. She is clearly uncomfortable and somewhat off balance.

Beatriz: We have no expectations. Just to look inside. "Oh look at that! How interesting!" [*Embodies looking inside herself, with smile and curiosity.*]

Maria [*Smiles and cries, nods, face quite tense.*]

Beatriz: "How curious—look what is there!!" So go inside of you [*hands on her chest, nodding, smiling, constant eye gaze, soft voice*] and pay attention to you.

[*Long silence.*]

Beatriz: What are you aware of?

Maria [*Looks away, closes eyes*]: I just want to hide. I am really trying to keep it all together [*voice much louder, moving hands assertively*]. I am doing a really good job, I am. I am [*stronger voice, and asserts with her hands, then sighs, closes eyes*].

[**Beatriz's internal thoughts**]: This is interesting. Even though Maria is quite tense, she feels safe enough to speak up and assert herself. Her increased eye gaze, stronger voice, and assertive hand movements are in contrast to the content of her words about wanting to hide and trying to keep it together. I trust what Maria's body is telling me more than her words.

Beatriz: So we're paying attention to you. Caring for you [*both hands on her chest*]. You do not need to keep anything together here with us. There are no expectations for you at all.

Maria [*More tears, deeper breathing, wipes tears away, holds her head up higher.*]

Beatriz: What are you aware of? What sensations?

Maria: I have tight chest, throat [*hand to her throat, voice is tight, soft*].

Beatriz: Umhmm.

Maria: I just feel sad . . . but not depressed sad . . . more like a grieving sad . . . like a loss [*surprised and curious facial expressions*].

Albert's commentary: Beatriz is explicitly activating all three of Maria's primary-level attachment brain systems—Safe, Care, and Connection—right at the beginning of the session. At the same time she is monitoring Maria's Tertiaries, such as Attention and Authority, so that they are able to collaborate on this process together. Although the Tertiaries are not the priority for this discussion, there is ongoing evidence of their presence and functioning throughout the session. The powerful emotions that are stimulated by those interventions reveal themselves physiologically with a mix of tears, tension, facial grimace, movements of the neck, and shallow breathing. We could speculate that:

- Safe is constrained by Fear, revealed by shallow breathing.
- Care is helping Maria release some Grief, revealed by her tears and feeling sad.
- Connection is helping Maria override her Shame, revealed by her tight throat and wanting to hide.

Beatriz: So there is pressure here [*hand to her own chest*] and pressure here [*hand to her own throat*].

Maria [*More engaged eye gaze, nods.*]

Beatriz: And there is a grieving sad, like a loss . . . [*lets her hands fall into her lap*].

Maria [*Nods, releases more grief, pain in her face, more tears.*]

Beatriz: Hmm [*silence*].

Maria: I feel a little bit impatient and [a] little bit angry [*assertive gesture, stronger mouth movements, baring her teeth a little*]. Sensations that come from down here [*hands to her belly, then hands more active*]. Steamy, lava-like [*voice louder, face more animate*], not explosive [*hands show explosive*]. I see you. You are kind of red and gurgles down there! [*She looks down at her belly, chuckles.*]

Beatriz: Tell me about the chuckle.

Maria: It is a funny image [*smiles, facial look of surprise, shakes her head in curiosity, bigger smile*].

Beatriz: So, is there a little bit of play in you right now? [*Hands are gently playful.*]

Maria [*Nods, then grimaces, and starts crying.*]

[Beatriz's internal thoughts]: Very interesting. It appears that Maria cannot tolerate our playful, safe connection for more than a couple of seconds. We are onto something very important here.

Beatriz: What happens with the play?

Maria: My brain wants to tell me . . . [*shakes head, puzzled, curious, voice remains strong*] I shouldn't be okay.

Beatriz: How interesting! [*Voice higher pitched, eyes light up.*]

Maria: I know.

Beatriz: You are having a little bit of play, and immediately the brain is telling you "stop that" [*gestures with her hands to demonstrate assertive and play from her pelvic region versus the shutdown from her head*].

Maria [*Nods, cries, then head extends.*]

Beatriz: And yet you are having it. It is part of you [*hands reach out*].

Maria [*Grimaces, smiles, moves her shoulders forward, then back and down, tears, then smiles more broadly*]: Yes, I am.

Beatriz: What do you want?

Maria: I want to have the play [*voice very soft, tentative, eyes downcast*].

Albert's commentary: Beatriz is continuing to embody her Care and Connection with Maria. She is utilizing interventions to acknowledge her tight throat and using her body language to show Maria the Connection they share. We can see that Maria's body, face, and vocal movements are clearly more engaged. She is more assertive, has more connection, and feels safe enough to chuckle in the midst of all these other emotions. Beatriz's invitation to Maria's Authority and Autonomy, "What do you want?," is activating to Maria's primary-level brain systems (Assertive, Play) and reveals the psychophysiological constraints of her Fear and Shame Secondaries. They are now in the struggle to help Maria develop greater access to her Play and Assertive brain systems.

QUESTION: Why did the therapist pick up on the chuckles rather than the anger?

BEATRIZ'S ANSWER: The anger is not coming from the present-moment interaction with the therapist. Her chuckle is coming up spontaneously in the present moment and reveals what is actually happening inside of her. The chuckle is a psychophysiological phenomenon that we can all observe. We could ask her about her anger, impatience, grief, or we could Go the Other Way. By focusing on her chuckles we are facilitating the parallel processing, Differentiating, and Integrating her primary-level brain systems in order to help Maria process her own feelings of anger and loss with her competencies.

Beatriz: Do you want to have what is there inside of you? [*Moves her hands to show the mix of inner experiences.*]

Maria [*Nods, hesitant*]: Yeah. . . .

Beatriz: Because life is very hard as it is.

Maria [*Nods, mixed facial expressions, and cries*]: Yeah.

Beatriz: And now you have this brain that tells you, "Stop playing." So how are you going to deal with a hard life when you don't have the play? [*Smiles, animated.*]

Maria [*Smiles, nods.*]

Beatriz: And this is you smiling [*hands to her own smile*]. This is what you have inside of you at this moment [*hands to her torso*].

[Beatriz's internal thoughts]: I want to help her assert her desire to play and to take pleasure in herself. It is also important to help her harness her Authority and Autonomy right now.

Beatriz: Do you want to enjoy this play for just this moment?

Maria: Yes . . . [*nods, smiles, voice is tentative*].

Beatriz: What are you saying yes to?

Maria: I want to enjoy the play for just this little moment [*playful voice, big smile, laughs, direct eye contact, then she grimaces*].

Beatriz: There it is again—can you feel that play? [*Hand reaching out to patient.*] And here it is again [*hand movement of suppression*]. Is it wrong, bad, or something like that?

Maria: It is more like "get back to the task" [*shakes head "no"*]. "You have things to do. You have to keep it together. You have to be there for your kids, or your husband."

Albert's commentary: Notice how the process of Activating the primary-level brain systems is in the Transpiring Present Moment and within the Therapeutic Attachment Relationship. Beatriz is Facilitating and Training Maria's Assertive and Play brain systems by repeatedly inviting her capability to seize her authority and experience. "Do you want to have and to enjoy your pleasure and your play?" We can observe the success of these interventions by noticing psychophysiological evidence revealed by Maria's playful voice, big smile, and more intimate eye contact.

[Beatriz's internal thoughts]: I want to help Maria stay in the present moment with her experience of enjoying herself, having a little bit of delight, caring for herself, connecting and collaborating. Focusing on caring and connection will enhance our Therapeutic Attachment Relationship and meet her need for attachment.

Beatriz: Your kids are not here. Husband is not here. The task here is to be with you.

Maria [*Nods.*]

Beatriz: The task here is to be with you, Caring for yourself. And we are here connected together caring for you. That is the task.

Maria [*Nods.*]

Beatriz: And right here <u>play</u> is bubbling up [*hands bubbling up*]. Do you <u>want</u> to stay with your play? [*Voice stronger.*]

Maria: Yes [*nods, soft voice, nods again*].

Beatriz: Are you just saying yes because I say so?

Maria: No, I want to [*shrugs her shoulders*]. It just feels far away. It feels harder today [*smiles*].

Beatriz: And yet is there bubbling inside of you? [*Hands over her torso.*]

Maria [*Nods.*]

Beatriz: Because it is part of you [*long silence, intimate eye gaze*].

Maria [*Makes a big sigh and nods her head affirmatively.*]

Beatriz: What is happening?

Maria: I am just thinking why it's harder today.

[Beatriz's internal thoughts]: Great! I can see from the physical shifts in Maria's body that her primary-level brain systems are coming more online. Rather than just accepting the constraint that comes instantaneously, she is questioning to know more. It seems that there is a small space (Differentiating) in between her Play and the immediate constraint. Let's experiment with Differentiating the constraint from her Authority. So she then will have a choice.

Beatriz: It is interesting, isn't it? But if I would tell you, "Let's cry," that would be okay. If I would tell you, "Let's be overwhelmed," that would be all right, wouldn't it?

Maria [*Smiles, playful, face has a quizzical look of "how ridiculous," louder voice, firm look on her face*]**:** My brain says that already! [*Laughs out loud, shakes head in disbelief*] That is not why I am here!

Beatriz: That is exactly what I am talking about.

Maria [*Laughs out loud, smiles*]**:** It is silly.

Beatriz: What is silly?

Maria: I just want that to stop. I want to stop feeling overwhelmed [*cries, grimaces*].

[Beatriz's internal thoughts]: That is interesting. It only lasted for a second. We need more work.

Beatriz: Umhmm. And for a moment here, when you were in play, the feeling of "overwhelmed" wasn't here? Am I correct with that?

Maria [*Nods*]**:** Yeah.

Beatriz: Oh, it's hard to sustain not feeling "overwhelmed"? [*Gestures the pushing down of play and caring.*]

Maria: Yeah [*nods, puzzled*].

Beatriz: Interesting, isn't it?

Maria [*Nods, more puzzled*].

Albert's commentary: Beatriz is repeatedly and carefully Activating Maria's Care and Connection brain systems. She trusts that the energy transpiring in those nonconscious brain systems will help Maria stay in the present moment in the Therapeutic Attachment Relationship. The Activating of Safe, Care, and Connection are paramount to this level of work, and they provide the initial power to break out of the depression.

The question, "Are you just saying yes because I say so?" is often overlooked. Patients can be compliant or cooperative, or try to meet what they believe is expected of them. When you endeavor to have a fully collaborative patient, it helps greatly to invite their authority frequently with invitations such as, "Do you want to stay with your play?" And don't be in a hurry to take "yes" for an answer—hence the question Beatriz asked to check in with Maria's capability for collaboration at that moment.

We will see the outcome of Maria's session in Chapter 12, on the Integration of primary-level brain systems. In Table 10.1, we summarize sample verbal prompts we use to both Activate and Facilitate primary-level brain systems, as a synopsis and guideline for your practice.

TABLE 10.1 : Activating Primary-Level Brain Systems

Brain System	Therapist Prompt	Therapist Facilitates
Safe	We are here to help you feel safer inside yourself.	It is important that you feel safe with us right now.
Care	We are here to pay caring attention to you together.	Our care for you is unconditional.
Connection	We can connect together with you right now.	It is safe for us to connect with you.
Seeking	We are curious and interested in whatever you are experiencing.	It is safe to be curious about yourself.
Play	Your smile and giggles are welcome.	Tell me more about what you experience when you laugh.
Assertive	There is room for you to assert your wants.	Can you notice what you experience in your body when you assert yourself now?
Sensory	Whatever you notice inside your body is important information for us.	What are you experiencing inside as you speak assertively?

ANGER HAS A SPECIAL PLACE

Anybody can become angry, that is easy; but to be angry with the right person, and to the right degree, and at the right time, and for the right purpose, and in the right way, that is not within everybody's power, that is not easy.

ARISTOTLE (320 BC, QUOTED IN PANKSEPP & BIVEN, *THE ARCHAEOLOGY OF MIND*)

Let's interpret Aristotle's quotation from a brain systems perspective. To be angry with the right person depends on the activation of the Care and Connection brain systems. Angry to the right degree and in the right way depends on the balance in the Fear, Grief, Shame, and Guilt brain systems. At the right time and for the right purpose depends on the Authority, Autonomy, and Agency brain systems.

Anger is a brain system, although we are not treating it in the same way as other brain systems. That is why anger is a special case.

We have chosen to elaborate on the emotion of anger in this chapter because we believe the major source of all anger is in each of the primary-level brain systems. Each Primary has its own drive and wisdom. Anger is part of a normal emotional continuum. If that drive is denied or prevented, there will be some level of irritation and some effort to diminish the irritation. The emotional continuum starts with irritation and with increasing intensity can become annoyance, then anger, and finally rage. This continuum reflects the different levels of threat to our survival that cause the corresponding emotions. For example, if the drive to connect is prevented, there will be some level of irritation and some effort to diminish the irritation. If that drive to connect is continuously prevented, it will grow into anger and then rage.

A brain systems approach to the patient's symptoms of anger is primarily (pun intended) conducted by Activating and Facilitating the underlying Primaries that are at the roots of the anger. This is a core concept in CIMBS.

Threats to our autonomy, needs, desires, or wants generate anger, and threats to our survival generate rage. We believe each brain system has its own anger. For example, loss of care causes different anger than loss of connection. The anger from loss of care has to do with grief, and the anger from loss of connection has to do with shame. When the toddler doesn't receive care he feels grief, or when there is a loss of connection he feels shame. Therefore the anger that comes with loss of care has dimensions of grief, and the anger that comes from the loss of connection has dimensions of shame. The anger that comes with not feeling safe has dimensions of fear. According to Panksepp, that is the way those brain systems evolved. As a consequence of the neurobiology of these brain systems, when an animal loses care, it feels grief, not shame.

We find it helpful to distinguish between proactive/assertive anger and reactive/defensive anger within each brain system. Proactive anger comes out of drive or desire, and reactive anger often results from unresolved pain.

Proactive/Assertive Anger

Proactive anger has an evolved potential in all of the emotional brain systems. It is built in and requires no learning. Naturally we experience anger from birth on, and we learn nonconsciously how to manage the anger potential contained in each brain system. Most if not all of that learning is adaptive and enables us to utilize that energy to meet our needs, help us thrive, and protect our survival. This is easiest to picture in an infant or toddler. For example, if the child's need to feel safe is activated, she will move away from noise or cold that seems threatening. If the child is unable to satisfy the need to feel safe, she may become fussy. With further obstacles to safety, her cries will increase in intensity as she becomes angry. Last, she may become enraged with the loudest cries, thrashing around, or in some other way trying to protect her survival.

Proactive anger can be intrinsic or relational. *Intrinsic anger* refers to the emotions that energize us to intensify our efforts to sustain our homeostasis, comfort, well-being, and survival. *Relational anger* refers to the emotions that seek to bring others in line, rapidly, with our evolutionary desires and motivations (Panksepp & Biven, 2012).

When we as therapists are misattuned, distracted, misunderstanding, or making a mistake, our patients will experience some level of authentic Transpiring Present Moment anger with us. We want to address that proactive anger directly. We have found our best results occur when we welcome and then explore the roots of the patient's anger right away. It is important not to become defensive but rather curious about which of the Primaries are at the roots of the patient's present-moment anger with us. For example, if we are distracted or misattuned when our patient is trying to connect with us, their Connection and Shame brain systems will respond by mobilizing anger in order to expend more energy and effort to make a stronger connection. We can then work with the Connection brain system and their desire to connect, celebrating their assertiveness and effort to make stronger connection. If we forget their appointment, they will miss out on the care we have to offer each other. They might say, "You don't really care about me." That anger sounds both proactive ("I want to receive your care") and reactive ("My parent did not care for me unconditionally"). We encourage you to focus on your patient's anger that comes from the Care brain system, which motivates them to receive your care unencumbered by their past.

Mistakes are inevitably a part of every therapy. We believe it is best to embrace our patient's complex emotional experiences first before we make the necessary repairs to the relationship. Our patients want to experience and learn that all of their emotions are welcome in our Therapeutic Attachment Relationship.

Reactive Anger

We believe that reactive and defensive anger results from developmental learning that occurred in situations of crisis, trauma, or neglect. These forms of anger can lead to symptoms, behavioral problems, and relationship difficulties. Symptoms of reactive anger are sometimes the presenting complaints that bring our patients to therapy. When most people think of anger, they recall examples of reactive anger, which tends to be loud, dramatic, aggressive, and even violent.

Everyone's reactive anger is unique to their life experiences and early developmental learning. We all have reactive anger because there is no possible way that all the needs of each of our brain systems could be met simultaneously. For example, when we were meeting our need for care, we may have had to sacrifice our need to feel safe. If the child's parent is rage-full and shaming, the child will feel unsafe and fearful. However, they need their parent's care in order to survive, so they will reach out to obtain care even when they feel afraid of their parent. Over time, their Fear brain system will generate anger, even rage, although they have learned to suppress those emotions in order to meet their need for care. That angry energy might therefore be suppressed by the Shame or Guilt brain systems. It might be blocked by the psychophysiology of terror. If these phenomena continue, they could well be incorporated into the emotional and personality development of the child.

Recognizing Anger

Patients often present with symptoms or difficulties related to anger. They may come for anger management, relationship difficulties, or anxiety that arises from underlying problems with the energy of anger. The anger can be out in the open (overt) and/or hidden under other emotional or behavioral patterns (covert). Often those difficulties will manifest in the therapy and therapeutic relationship. The patient's anger may be directed at us or someone else in their life. The anger may be turned inward and reveal itself as depression or passivity. This anger is often defensive to avoid the pain of shame, abandonment, or grief. All forms of therapy have developed different approaches to reactive anger.

It can be an interesting puzzle to discover the underlying causes of reactive anger, and sometimes an easy way to the proverbial rabbit hole. However, the most effective response in order to recognize the sources of reactive anger is to inquire inside ourselves, "What was happening in this moment when the anger surfaced?"

The Therapeutic Attachment Relationship, the Initial Directed Activation, and the focus on the Primaries do not provoke anger, although they sometimes trigger an incongruence (see Chapter 13) or anger from the past. When the patient starts to become angry in the session, it is almost always because some reactive anger has been triggered. Typical answers to the question, "What was happening in this moment when the anger surfaced?" are too much closeness, too much care, unfamiliar nonconscious emotions, or some other kind of incongruence. These answers provide evidence of some nonconscious conflict between the Primaries and Secondaries in this Transpiring Present Moment. Facilitating the Primaries when the patient is experiencing anger will often both inhibit the angry reactions and update the emotional learning in the present moment. Our approach to anger in a session is to Go the Other Way. For these reasons, the anger symptoms that our patients present will typically melt away with time, both in session and in their lives. Our research and teaching have shown us that focusing on the Primaries gives the patient and the therapy the energy and wisdom to override their nonconscious anger reactions.

There is a good example above when Maria states, "I feel a little bit impatient and [a] little bit angry. Sensations that come from down here. Steamy, lava-like." She looks down at her belly and chuckles. Maria's anger is not being provoked by Beatriz; it has deeper roots. Maria's chuckle is coming up spontaneously in the present moment and reveals psychophysiological evidence of energy from her Primaries. Beatriz is observing Maria's mixed experience, including her anger, and chooses to Go the Other Way when she Facilitates the Primaries of Safe, Play, and Connection. By focusing on her chuckles, she is Facilitating, Differentiating, and Integrating her Primaries in order to help Maria process her own feelings of anger within her competencies.

OPENING THE FAN: CHALLENGES AND OPPORTUNITIES

It can be hard to visualize the spectrum of primary-level brain systems, because they are nonconscious and usually invisible. It takes time to become familiar with each of these distinct systems. The energy and information that bring these distinct systems to life come primarily from the body and the peripheral nervous system. Psychophysiological phenomena (Chapter 14) can provide you with the evidence and alert you to the presence of each distinct primary-level brain system.

We believe that energy and information from the heart, lungs, and other organs—which are transmitted by the sensory part of the vagus nerve—activate many of the Primaries. The vagus nerve connects in the lower brainstem and has been the focus of a great deal of attention in the last 20 years, thanks to Stephen Porges's research and writing. The motor component of the vagus nerve plays a major role in the social engagement system, and fight, flight, and freeze reactions (Porges, 2011). However, 80% of the information carried by the vagus is sensory rather than motor.

We have developed a useful teaching tool to help our trainees become more comfortable with Activating these invisible brain systems. We have used an open fan as an image that shows how all of these brain systems appear when they are open and interconnected. The ribs of the fan represent the rays of energy and emotion of each brain system. Figure 10.8 shows that they are equal and interconnected with each other, and that there is no hierarchy. Usually our patient's fan of primary-level brain systems is only partly open. So the therapist needs to observe which systems are open and which ones are closed or only partly open. Or the fan could be closed by psychophysiological phenomena that arise from emotions such as fear, shame, or grief (Figure 10.9). For example, at the beginning of Maria's session, her Safe and Care brain systems were modestly open. Depending on the situation, you might want to Facilitate the system that recently opened up. For example, Beatriz Facilitated Maria's Play when she saw the psychophysiological activation of that system with Maria's chuckles. In another situation, you might want to open up another part of the fan by Activating (opening) other brain systems, as Beatriz did by Activating Maria's Care and Connection brain systems.

Physiopsychotherapy (Chapter 14) for the BrainMind can be visualized as a gradual opening of the fan to gain access to the emotional power and processing capacities of the Primaries.

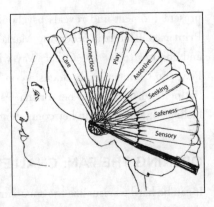

Figure 10.8: Open Fan: Parallel Processing of Primaries

It is especially difficult to see or access the potential of the Primaries when your patient is triggered, terrified, or shut down. *Triggered* means that some survival-oriented emotional circuit or Secondary from the past has been activated (see Figure 2.4). When triggered, the MindBrain goes into some kind of habitual survival mode of fight, flight, freeze, or shutdown. Those reactions can take many forms. The patient might get stuck with shame or self-criticism and lean on some coping mechanism such as rumination or projection. For example, Maria grimaced and shut down her Play when it was the focus of her Assertive choice.

When our patients become frightened or triggered, it tends to close their fan of multiple brain systems. Where does their emotional energy go? Does it go into depression, anger, retaliation, shame, or humiliation? The metaphor of the fan can help you see how your patient can appear to behave like a turtle. One minute they are open and engaged, and the next minute they have retreated into their shell (Figure 10.9). Therapists often become anxious to solve the problem and use the tools they

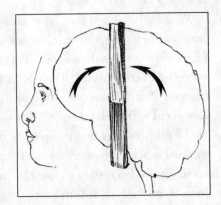

Figure 10.9: Closed Fan: Primaries Shut Down

are familiar with when confronted with constraints. An experiential therapist might use pressure to break through the defenses. A psychodynamic therapist might use an interpretation to try to undo the resistance. A cognitive-behavioral therapist might use desensitization. Another therapist might use eye movement desensitization and reprocessing (EMDR) to regulate the emotions.

We use a different approach to contend with this stuckness. When the therapy gets stuck or the patient gets triggered, it is important to realize that usually only one brain system is the source of the problem, and most if not all of the other Primaries are not stuck.

Depression can be viewed as a logjam. Activating brings in much more flow and energy. Activating Safe dislodges Fear. Activating Seeking and Play adds more power and flow to further open up the emotional channels. This parallel processing of multiple primary-level brain systems is like having a broad river with many open channels that continues to flow freely in times of flood or new obstructions. This approach is less about breaking up the obstructions in the river than about moving beyond that narrow riverbed of rigidity (Siegel, 2010a). The depression, shame, and fear may still be obstructing Maria's Assertive brain system, but the others are now flowing much better as the session unfolds.

SPECIFIC CHALLENGES

There are some common pitfalls for the therapist in working with primary-level brain systems. The three Attachment brain systems (Safe, Care, and Connection) can often have neurobiological attachments to certain secondary-level brain systems, which complicate their responses to your interventions. We described one such example above when discussing the relationship between secondary-level brain systems and neurobiological anger pathways. Furthermore, among the remaining Primaries, it can be difficult to perceive the response of the brain system accurately because other behaviors interfere or the observation process itself is difficult.

Safe

Safe is neurobiologically attached to the secondary-level Fear brain system in all mammals. When you provide your patients a Safe experience, that may trigger a Fear or even terror reaction in many patients. Therapists tend to take safety for granted. They assume that since they intend to provide a safe relationship and space, the patient will naturally feel safe. The subtle spectrum of Safe takes time to discern. It is often awkward to ask the question, "To what extent do you feel safe right now?"

Care

Care is neurobiologically attached to the secondary-level Grief brain system in all mammals. When Care is absent, the animal will cry, whine, or chirp. That applies to our patients, and directly activating Care will often release Grief and Fear of the Grief.

Connection

Connection is neurobiologically attached to the secondary-level Shame brain system in all mammals. Your authentic Therapeutic Attachment Relationship may trigger Shame in many patients.

Assertive

When Activating the Assertive brain system, it can be difficult to distinguish assertive from reactive behaviors. Sometimes our patients will make a negative statement that can sound like an assertion. For example, when we ask them, "Do you want to pay attention to yourself?" they might respond, "No, I don't." But we don't consider that response an assertion, because the answer did not tell you what they want. It only negated your invitation. Their answer could reflect ambivalence, fear, defiance, or anger. An assertion is a proactive statement. We need to listen carefully for each component, where the patient claims their authority and autonomy, uses the pronoun *I*, and expresses a clear, direct desire, drive, and motivation.

Seeking

Seeking is often entangled with Fear, Shame, and Guilt. For those reasons, it is hard to uncover the energy of Seeking when all you can see is fear or shame. In the example above, it took a number of sessions in which Albert kept Activating Andrew's Safe, Care, and Connection brain systems before he was able to have an authentic embodied experience of Seeking.

Play

Little moments of activation of the Play brain system can be easily overlooked when the patient's dominant experience is one of anxiety or depression. In the example above, as Maria was talking about feeling sadness, grief, impatience, and anger, there was a brief chuckle. It would have been easy to miss the chuckle when all of the verbal content was consistent with Maria's depression. Furthermore, Play can be confused with humor. Some patients use playful humor as a way of avoiding intimacy.

Sensory

Some patients have no awareness of their embodied emotional activations. For example, when you notice a clear psychophysiological phenomenon and inquire about what they are experiencing, they might respond, "I don't feel anything." The challenge with those patients is to keep observing psychophysiological phenomena and invite their Attention by saying such things as, "What are you feeling when you move your hand to make a fist?"

Describing and illustrating these seven primary-level brain systems may feel a bit disjointed, vague, or confusing to you. Few of us have ever looked at our nonconscious emotions with this level of specificity and precision. When we first studied them, we wondered whether we could find any practical ways to use these insights in our training courses. As it turned out, our trainees found the perspective of Primaries very enlightening. It takes practice to work with these brain systems effectively, and the next two chapters will help you discover how you might incorporate these Primaries into your understanding of the inner workings of the human BrainMind. Chapters 13 and 14 take a closer look at the secondary-level brain systems, which both get in our way and enable us to thrive.

CHAPTER 11

Horizontal and Vertical Differentiating of the Primary-Level Brain Systems

....

In Chapters 7 and 8, we explored Facilitating and Differentiating hyperactive, hypoactive, and hyperconnected conscious brain systems. In this chapter, we are exploring Facilitating and Differentiating from another perspective and with different emphasis. In the Introduction to Part II, we introduced the concepts of horizontal and vertical integration, which we explore in detail in Chapter 12. Here we examine horizontal and vertical Facilitating and Differentiating, two treatment strategies that seek to harness the full range of the patient's conscious and nonconscious brain systems, in order to change the neural structures of the BrainMind. They prepare the patient for horizontal and vertical integration. Siegel (2007) introduced us to the concepts of horizontal and vertical differentiation. We have followed these approaches and then added some of our own spices.

As you may recall from Chapter 8, Facilitating occurs when the therapist focuses on the adaptive emotional competencies that the patient is revealing in the moment. Differentiating occurs when you isolate and exercise distinct neural circuits and brain systems. Differentiated systems enable the patient to choicefully respond rather than being limited to an old reflexive reaction pattern. Differentiated systems retain their flexible functionality, no matter the nature of the previous trauma.

Horizontal Facilitating and Differentiating accesses the various brain systems on a particular level of the nervous system. The systems on one level could be undifferentiated from each other. Horizontal Differentiating aims at isolating specific systems and then repeatedly Activating and Facilitating each of these brain systems within each level of processing. For example, there are seven different primary-level brain systems. With horizontal Differentiation, we isolate each of the seven Primaries from each other and Facilitate them individually. We distinguish the Care brain system from the Connection brain system, both of them from the Safe brain system, and the Assertive brain system from the Seeking system, and so on.

Vertical Facilitating and Differentiating refers to distinguishing brain systems on two or more of the four levels of emotional processing. For example, vertical Differentiating of a patient's Care brain system could look like this: feeling warmth in their heart (peripheral nervous system) as they are sensing pleasure inside themselves (Pleasure secondary-level brain systems), aware of the uncomfortable feeling in their chest (Peripheral and Fear brain systems), and also consciously aware (tertiary-level brain system) that they are feeling love.

CASE STUDY: VICTORIA

Let us introduce you to Victoria. In the following vignette, she is in the process of experiencing and vocalizing her own horizontal and vertical Facilitations and Differentiations. Victoria is a 30-year-old married woman with two young children. She came to therapy because of depression and panic attacks. This is her seventh attempt at therapy.

Victoria started her 15th session commenting on how she feels different now: "I used to feel fear and worthlessness all the time. Now I surprise myself, valuing myself without realizing it. When that happens, it always surprises me, as if it is not me who is doing this new behavior. I can feel the old self and I can immediately know that is the story of the past. I also have the feeling of being at home inside of me, warmth in my chest, loving me, safe and calm inside of me and connected. It is not perfect by any means. I am always having to struggle; half of my throat feels warm and the other half feels constricted. Half of my chest feels jumpy and anxious, and then I can feel calm underneath the jumpy. Before, my whole throat felt constricted and I would feel overwhelmed and then collapse in an anxiety attack. Now I am winning the battle little by little. I am constantly practicing engaging my core muscles, standing up inside of me and connecting with the warmth in my heart, and repeating the experiences of being powerful and strong. The feeling of warmth in my heart and in my throat means I am feeling lovable and valuable. I keep on repeating these sensations again and again, feeling the connections inside.

"When I feel the triggers, feel overwhelmed, or remember again and again my traumatic rape five years ago, I can choose to change channels in my brain. I can be more connected to me because I matter to me. I realize that I can create those feelings internally again and again, although nothing has changed outside of me. I am less and less depressed."

Victoria is experiencing the psychophysiological sensations of several different brain systems. She is in the middle of what Beatriz calls the "three-, four-, or five-ring circus," meaning that Victoria is having a complex experience inside herself. She is simultaneously experiencing multiple Primaries at the same time: Safe ("Half of my chest feels jumpy and anxious, and then I can feel calm underneath the jumpy"), Care ("Warmth in my chest"), Connection and Assertive ("I am constantly practicing engaging my core muscles, standing up inside of me and connecting with the warmth in my heart and repeating the experiences of being powerful and strong."), and Sensory brain systems (the felt sense of different sensations in her body). This process is what we call horizontal Facilitation and Differentiation; she is experiencing five distinct brain systems on one horizon of primary-level processing. Victoria is also in the process of accomplishing a vertical Facilitation and Differentiation by being aware (tertiary level) of her Shame and Fear (secondary-level brain systems), as her primary-level (Safe, Care, and Connection) brain systems are being activated physiologically.

To illustrate what it could look like when brain systems are not differentiated from each other, let's pay attention to Victoria's difficulties. We discovered very quickly in her sessions that her Care brain system was not differentiated from the Connection brain system. Victoria could feel caring in her body (warmth in her chest) for the therapist, but was unable to make eye contact to connect directly with the therapist. In that way it was difficult to harness the energy of both systems. They were undifferentiated. The Connection brain system was getting in the way of the Care brain system, and therefore it was difficult to sustain the connection of an unconditional eye gaze in order to receive Beatriz's care. Incidentally, this was one of her presenting problems: difficulties having friends and connecting with her husband. At the time of the vignette illustrated above, Beatriz and Victoria had successfully Facilitated and Differentiated her Care and

Connection brain systems so that she could process strong emotions and stay present to herself and the people in her life.

Undifferentiated does not mean hyperconnected, hyperactive, or hypoactive. It is a different phenomenon. In our research, we have found that when brain systems are undifferentiated from each other, their energy becomes defused and unfocused, and they can muster only half their power and capacity. It is as if the BrainMind is operating with a blunt instrument rather than a sharp scalpel.

HORIZONTAL FACILITATING AND DIFFERENTIATING AT ANY LEVEL

The brain systems therapist can direct the process of identifying and harnessing the energy of each distinct brain system across one level of the nervous system. If we think of brain systems as generators and we put each generator online, each one has its own clear energy, differentiated from the others but working together. Then we have a very powerful machine that has more much more energy, flexibility, and processing power. If one of the generators were to fail, the machine could keep on operating.

For this reason, it is important to horizontally Facilitate and Differentiate each brain system at each level of the nervous system, in order to harness their full energy and wisdom. Horizontally Differentiated systems can develop positive feedback loops to sustain adaptive activations to keep evolving and learning. They can then become resilient brain systems.

This concept of horizontal Differentiating has been difficult for our trainees to grasp. We have needed lots of examples to illustrate it.

Let's look at another brief case example. Holly had completed therapy with Beatriz five years previously, when they had worked with vertically Differentiating her Fear and Shame from her Connection and Care brain systems. Holly was much improved, but she was now stuck in her attempts to take full charge of her life. She called Beatriz to obtain more help. In the interim period, Beatriz had been experimenting with horizontal Differentiating of the brain systems at different levels of the BrainMind. When Holly came in, Beatriz started Facilitating each conscious brain system one by one. They both realized that Holly's Awareness, Attention, Authority, and Autonomy were well differentiated. However, it became apparent very quickly that Holly had no idea what Agency felt like! Bull's-eye! No wonder her life was in chaos. She did not have the agency to direct her life and be in charge. Holly knew what she wanted (Authority) but had difficulty implementing her desires. Her Agency brain system was hypoactive and undifferentiated. Now Beatriz knew what to do: Activate, Facilitate, Differentiate, and Train the Agency brain system until it had enough processing capability to become a resilient brain system. Now the therapy was truly successful. Phew! Saved by the bell of the horizontal Differentiation.You can read the full transcript on our website (http://www.complexintegrationmbs).

HORIZONTAL FACILITATING AND DIFFERENTIATING OF PRIMARIES: METHODOLOGY

The Primaries are the powerhouses of the BrainMind. Patients often don't have full access to their powerful energy because of the limitations of the implicit learning absorbed during the first year of life. For this reason, horizontally Facilitating and Differentiating the Primaries is especially important in therapy.

Facilitating

If you want Differentiation to take hold and be resilient, the first step could be to focus on the adaptive emotional competencies of each of the Primaries. Here are some guidelines on how to do it.

Pick Up the Activation of the Primary "on the Fly"

This is a phrase that Beatriz has utilized in order to explain this process to our trainees. When a bird passes by in front of our eyes in a split second, we need to catch it in flight. Activations of the Primaries are moments of spontaneous flexibility in the nervous system (Siegel, 1999). It takes patience and careful attention to discover and grab those spontaneous moments of activation on the fly and reveal them to your patient. Here is where our patients say: "I didn't know that I didn't know that" about themselves.

Because the Primaries are nonconscious, the only way we know that there has been some Activation is when we see psychophysiological changes in the patient (the bird in flight). Suppose the patient suddenly sits up from a slouched position. That psychophysiological change tells you, without a doubt, that something meaningful is being Activated. You don't need to know what brain system is Activated; you just need to know that something is being Activated. The best way to catch the bird on the fly is to ask, "What is happening right now?"

At other times the psychophysiological changes are not so obvious, and we need to train our eyes to see such minute changes. If we don't pick up these psychophysiological cues, they subside and go underground again, and we lose a precious opportunity to perform a horizontal Differentiation. Don't worry, though: The train will come back again.

Consider another example: a depressed patient suddenly has a tiny smile and looks at the therapist with care in their eyes for just a split second. They may not even be aware they are doing this. The therapist wonders if a Primary has had a psychophysiological activation and invites the patient to notice: "What are you aware of?" or "There was a little smile in you," or "Maybe you were not aware of it, but there is something interesting happening inside of you. Let's be curious about it." Even if the patient answers, "Nothing is happening," trust that their Attention and their psychophysiological phenomena were just paired in their BrainMind. Your effort to touch that brain system is not lost. You are Facilitating the systems, and maybe the patient will be aware the next time, or the time after. We usually tell our trainees to watch videos with the sound off to teach themselves to see these tiny psychophysiological phenomena. We discuss psychophysiology in detail in Chapter 14.

Call Each Brain System by Name

Once you have the bird in hand, call it by name and avoid getting distracted by any hyperconnections. The following are familiar examples from earlier case studies:

- "We are *caring* for you right now." (Caring brain system)
- "We are *connecting* together." (Connection brain system)
- "We are *playing* together." (Play brain system)
- "You are experiencing *safeness* right now." (Safe brain system)
- "You are being *curious and interested* in your own sensations." (Seeking brain system)
- "I can see you are feeling your *assertive* power right now." (Assertive brain system)

Avoid Getting Distracted

Be aware that these assertions could Activate hyperconnections with the secondary-level brain systems. Your patient could feel uncomfortable because differentiation is happening, and that is a success! "When we are uncomfortable we grow." If the patient says, "My throat is hurting really badly right now," we could guess that shame is being Activated, and we don't pay too much attention to the shame. The therapist could say, "Hello shame, my old friend. You are here. And right now we are caring for *you*." That is how you sidestep getting distracted by hyperconnections. Neurobiologically speaking, the act of paying attention is what sends blood to the synapses. We want to pay attention to the capacities of each brain system and send blood to those synapses rather than the already well-known and rehearsed constraints.

Be an External Generator
Activate and Facilitate each brain system by becoming the external generator to keep the sensations happening for one more round. Refresh and refresh the sensations of the brain system that you are focusing on at various times for the resulting Differentiation to take hold and be resilient.

Foster Parallel Processing With Other Brain Systems
For example, "When you feel our care, what are you experiencing in your body?" (Sensory brain system). "Do you want to receive our care?" (Authority brain system). "Do you want to be seen receiving our care?" (Connection brain system). In particular, act as an external generator to bring in enhancing secondary brain systems to keep the energy moving as part of the processes of Facilitating. For example, "Your play is valuable for us" (Value brain system). "Is there a little feeling of satisfaction or pleasure in letting yourself be playful in front of us?" (Pleasure brain system). "You are persevering by keeping the playful feeling happening one round more!" (Motivation brain system), and so on.

Differentiating
- Constantly orient your patient to the Transpiring Present Moment. For example, "Right now, just at this precise moment in time, what are your sensations?" Remember that the sensations of the Transpiring Present Moment are different from the sensations of possible anger or anxiety that patients could feel in their bodies in this moment but that are about the past.
- Constantly orient yourself as the therapist in the Transpiring Present Moment. In order to best catch those moments of spontaneous flexibility

in the nervous system (neuroplastic moments), you need to be present in this precise moment of time and not thinking about what you are going to do next.

- Differentiate the physiological experience of each brain system. For example,
  - "What sensations tell you that you are feeling *care* right now?"
  - "We are *connecting* together. What sensations tell you that you are feeling a connection with me?"
  - "You are feeling *assertive* right now. What sensations in your body tell you that you are feeling assertive?"
- Help your patient be capable of a complex experience. Stay aware that each brain system has a different bodily sensation. Emphasize to your patient that they are capable of holding all these different sensations in their body at the same time. They are capable of being in a complex experience rather than an either/or, black or white, binary experience. For example, "Notice that your body's sensations of care feel different from the sensations of connection. You can have both sensations at the same time as you are experiencing safeness in your body. You are experiencing three different energies, sensations, feelings in your body right now."

CASE STUDY: JOEL

Heads up! Parts of this case study will be very repetitious. This repetition illustrates the Facilitating process that is so important for harnessing the power of the Primaries. This is an accurate transcript of the session. We could have edited out the repetitions so it would be less tedious to read, but the repetition with the patient is intentional. We find that the patient experiences each repetition differently, because every time you touch (pay attention to) the system, you strengthen it. Think about piano practice. If you practice twice, you double its strength. If you practice 10 times, you strengthen the system by an exponential factor of 10. Activating the neural circuit will recruit adjacent neurons, making the changes long-lasting and resilient. Also, when a neural circuit is activated repeatedly, over time it will become myelinated. The speed of myelinated circuits is 20 to 100 times faster in processing information.

It is interesting to realize that this repetition is not a tedious experience for our patients. They report that it feels mixed; some of the repetitions feel stronger and better every time, and some of them feel weird and awkward. In the following transcript, you will see that Beatriz is taking the patient out of his comfort zone and helping him to keep relying on his own power. This is what being the external generator looks like. If patients are fully present and paying attention to their changing sensations with each repetition, they experience the changes as intriguing and inspiring. On the other hand, if they are ambivalent and not fully engaged, they might react and complain about the repetition.

It is difficult to grasp what this process feels like just from the printed page. We encourage you to get a greater felt sense of this process by looking at the videos of actual therapy sessions (see http://www.complexintegrationmbs).

Six years ago, Beatriz was struggling to sustain horizontal Differentiation with her patients. Because of this difficulty, she tended to leave horizontal Differentiation behind and jump into vertical Differentiation instead. We picked this case study of a patient named Joel to show you how to persist at horizontally Facilitating and Differentiating the Primaries despite the temptation to focus on previous emotional learning. This is the tale of her struggle. Beatriz's internal thoughts and Albert's comments are in roman type. Psychophysiological phenomena are in italics. Facilitating and Differentiating moments are in italics.

Beatriz started the therapy session with a brief meditation to bring Joel into present-moment awareness, then followed with the Initial Directed Activation, the way we start all our therapy sessions from first to last.

Beatriz: Let's start with a small meditation. I will close my eyes, and I invite you to do the same if you feel comfortable doing so [*closes her eyes, lowers her head and is quiet for a moment, and then keeps her eyes closed*]. Arriving here at this present moment in our lives, being fully present at this moment in time, fully present inside of ourselves.

Joel [*Closes his eyes.*]

Beatriz [*After a moment of silence, opens her eyes*]: And when you are ready, open your eyes.

Joel [*Opens his eyes.*]

Beatriz [*Proceeds with Initial Directed Activation (Chapter 6)*]: We are here to pay close caring attention to you. . . . [*finishes with*] What are you aware of?

Joel: I feel a stressful feeling. My stomach is in knots, and before I left the house I felt stressed. I feel fear, can't stop the ruminations, and feel weak.

[Beatriz's internal thoughts]: If we keep Facilitating his Awareness of himself, we will probably uncover one or more of his Primaries.

Beatriz: Good awareness! This is very important that you are aware of yourself! Curious. What else are you aware of?

Joel: I am aware of my seat, aware of my breathing and my heartbeat. And I am just kind of bringing myself down.

Beatriz: Oh! How are you doing that?

Joel: Consciously breathing with intention. Matching my heartbeat with my breathing, and that has a great calming effect. I do that when I meditate.

Beatriz: Wow! You are being capable of putting yourself in safeness inside of you. Can you feel putting yourself in safeness inside of you? This is so important. This is the present moment of you. And you are being capable to bring yourself in safeness inside of you. Well done! [*Excited voice, leaning forward.*]

Joel: Yeah, but what I found out this morning was . . .

[Beatriz's internal thoughts]: We are able to pick up the activation of the Safe Brain System on the fly. Don't let him get distracted by what happened earlier this morning. Call the brain system by name. Bring in the awareness of the present-moment Activation of safeness. Be the external generator of safeness.

Beatriz [*Interrupting him*]: Just right now, you are being <u>capable</u> of bringing yourself into safeness inside of you. Your <u>capacity</u> to put yourself in safeness is <u>valuable</u> to us. Is it <u>important </u>for you to be in safeness inside of you? . . .You are being <u>capable</u> of doing it. . . . Can you feel your capacity? [*Facilitating, external generator, activating enhancers.*]

Joel: I am aware that I am doing it [*quizzical look and then with stronger voice*]. I am really doing it! It is like another level up! [*Small smile and shiny eyes.*] I am really doing it!

Albert's commentary: This is a clear example of how to be an external generator. Beatriz is repeating and reinforcing his experience of being and feeling safe. To read, it sounds tedious, but we can assure you that it is not tedious for the therapist or the patient in the trenches. Beatriz is Activating and Facilitating other brain systems in relationship with the Safe brain system: Sensory to help Joel feel his sensations of safeness, and Motivation and Value to help him stay in his safeness. She touches the circuit of safeness six times to enhance its capacity. It is interesting how things change as if by magic.

Beatriz: Yes! This is you being capable of staying in safeness inside of you. Can you feel the satisfaction of, "I am really doing it?" [*Facilitating.*]

Joel [*Making an assertive movement with his fist*]: I am really doing it!

[Beatriz's internal thoughts]: Another brain system is activated, Assertive. Pick it up on the fly. Call it by name. Differentiate Assertive from Safe and have the bodily sensation of both at same time. Keep Facilitating both sensations again and again.

Beatriz [*Imitating his gesture*]: This is your assertion. Right now you are experiencing your assertiveness. Is there power in your hand?

Joel: Yes [*making an assertive movement with the fist again*]. I am powerful. I can feel it!

Beatriz: Well done! [*Excited voice.*] What are the sensations of powerful in your body?

Joel: Strong hands, and I can feel like a rod inside of my torso [*making a fist and moving it up and down in front of his chest*].

Beatriz: This is success! Are you still in safeness?

Joel: Yes. I still feel calm inside of me. My breathing is calm [*touching his chest*].

Beatriz: And here we are paying attention to your capability of putting yourself in safeness. Sustaining the feelings of safeness by calming your breathing and experiencing your power, your assertiveness like a rod inside your torso. Two very different experiences inside of you at the same time. Can you feel the satisfaction of you being capable of having both your power and safeness at the same time? [*Holding up both hands as if holding something in each hand, Facilitating and Differentiating.*]

Joel: I didn't think it was possible to feel safe and have my power at the same time! Yes, I can feel them! [*Shiny eyes, smiling, body erect, fists.*]

Beatriz: This is success! Are you still experiencing these two different feelings in your body? [*Facilitating and Differentiating.*]

Albert's commentary: Beatriz just finished one of many repetitions of horizontal Facilitation and Differentiation between the Safe and Assertive primary-level brain systems.

Joel: Safeness is calm breathing in my chest and powerful is like I have a rod up inside my chest, strong muscles [*makes fists with both hands*]. I wonder if it is that simple . . . [*quizzical look*]. 'Cause this morning I was feeling all shriveled up and upset. It is like a magnet that pulls me to the left towards this rumination.

[Beatriz's internal thoughts]: Don't let us get distracted by the events of the morning. Keep Joel in the Transpiring Present Moment feelings of safeness and assertiveness.

Beatriz: And right now, right now we are not giving attention on that left pull, but toward your capabilities of safeness inside of you. And your powerful feelings of assertiveness. Both energies at the same time. Three energies! Because you are sensing these energies in different places in your body. Are you still claiming your power inside of yourself? [*Facilitating and Differentiating.*]

Joel: I am feeling sad, and I don't know why [*scrunching his face*].

Beatriz: Are you curious about it? Interesting, isn't it? Let's explore the sadness.

[Beatriz's internal thoughts]: Oh! Oh! Mistake—I got distracted by the hyperconnection between the constraint to his assertiveness, which is releasing sadness. I need to change course.

Beatriz: Wait, wrong question. . . . Sadness is here, and we are also paying attention to your feelings of safeness, assertiveness, and your power. Feeling safe as you are experiencing the rod of your power. It is safe to feel your power [*Differentiating*].

Joel [*Tilting his head and body moving forward in silence, scrunching up his face*]: This is weird. I lost the power when the sadness came.

Albert's commentary: At this juncture it is very tempting to Differentiate the sadness, which presumably is arising from a hyperconnection between his Assertive brain system and an inhibiting Secondary. Beatriz briefly embraced Joel's sadness with her interest and curiosity. However, when we are working with horizontal Facilitation and Differentiation, we do our best to Go the Other Way and keep harnessing the power, and strengthening and Facilitating the capacity of the circuits within each level of processing. Following this principle, Beatriz asks Joel if he wants to bring back the bodily sensations of safeness and assertiveness. Horizontal Facilitating and Differentiating of the Primaries can shift the therapeutic balance from feelings of fear, shame, terror, and grief to the experiences of safe, powerful, and capable, and can develop an enduring mental capability of success.

> **Beatriz:** Do you want to bring back the sensations of safeness and the rod in your chest with muscle memory?
>
> **Joel:** Yes. I want to claim my power and not the ruminations! [*Hands in fists and sitting up straighter.*] I never claimed my power like this before.
>
> **Beatriz:** This is new! What do you want at this moment in time?
>
> **Joel:** I want to claim my power and not the ruminations.

We will return to Joel's session later to demonstrate vertical Facilitating and Differentiating, which we describe below. For now, we offer Figure 11.1 as a cheat sheet, a shortcut, to remind you what brain systems to consider as you are in the process of Activating and Facilitating multiple brain systems.

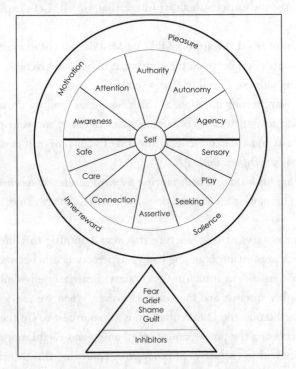

Figure 11.1: Multiple Brain Systems Reminder
Drawn by Janel Fox

VERTICAL FACILITATING AND DIFFERENTIATING

Vertical Differentiating of brain systems that are on separate levels of the nervous system—say, Care from Shame, or Agency from Fear—is a more complex task than the horizontal equivalent. We want to remind you here of the four levels of emotional processing in the nervous system. Impulses that originate in the neural plexuses of the body (peripheral nervous system) project upward into the brainstem (primary level of processing), then continue their upward trajectory to the basal ganglia (secondary level), and end up in the neocortex (tertiary level). Also recall that we described Secondaries as gatekeepers, which can have both enhancing and inhibiting roles. Most commonly, problematic hyperconnections that hamper primary (and tertiary) brain system functioning arise from the inhibitory aspects of the secondary-level Shame, Guilt, and Fear brain systems.

In our research, we have found that for Differentiation of these inhibitory brain systems to take hold and stand the tests of time, it also needs to be done on all four levels of emotional processing. Vertical Differentiating helps the patient to sit in the middle of the four-ring circus and observe the pulls and drives of distinct brain systems being activated at a precise moment. It is best when it has been experienced through the body lots and lots of times.

Vertical Facilitating and Differentiating have many important values in the therapy process:

- When we focus on the capabilities of each Primary and we keep Activating and Facilitating their adaptive neural circuits, a curious phenomenon may occur: the maladaptive circuits of the secondary level of emotional processing get somewhat suppressed.
- Differentiating the Primaries strengthens the capacity to make choices rather than follow the brain's survival biases of fear, shame, grief, and guilt.
- When four levels of the nervous system are involved and functioning in harmony, the internal balance of the BrainMind moves toward flexibility and increases its capacity to thrive.

Methodology

Vertical Facilitating and Differentiating can operate between the four levels of processing in the circular-spiral fashion that we have described before (Figure

11.2). It has no specific directionality. Below we offer three guidance pointers to help you with vertical Facilitating and Differentiating.

- Where to start? The only thing we know at the start of every session is that we will commence with the Initial Directed Activation, which stimulates all four levels of processing, starting with the Primaries of Safe, Care, and Connection, followed by Seeking. After that we follow the patient, asking them to pay attention to their sensations (Sensory brain system). We are also Activating the Tertiary Awareness and Attention brain systems. So when we get to the last sentence of the Initial Directed Activation, "What are you aware of," three levels are being Activated, and we just sit back and enjoy the ride. This means we are following the

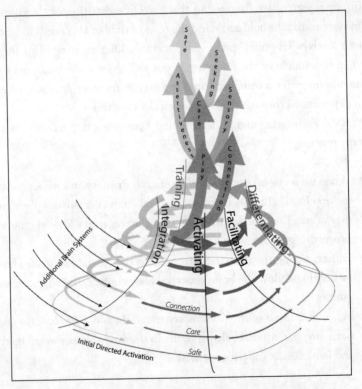

Figure 11.2: Spiral of Activating, Facilitating, Differentiating, Training, and Integrating Primary-Level Brain Systems

process of the patient in the Transpiring Present Moment, not the cob-
webs of the past.

- Look for the Transpiring Present Moment Activations and psychophysiological phenomena and follow them. For example, Joel was self-aware:
"I feel a stressful feeling. My stomach is in knots . . . I felt stressed. I feel
fear, can't stop the ruminations, and feel weak." The stress he was feeling was not caused by the session. What he was expressing happened
one hour earlier. With the question, "Curious. What else are you aware
of?," we are looking for the Transpiring Present Moment Activation. Joel
answered, "I am aware of my seat, aware of my breathing, and my heartbeat. And I am just kind of bringing myself down." This is the Transpiring Present Moment Activation. This is what is happening at this precise
moment in time. This is the process that we follow and explore. Joel is
Activating and Facilitating his Safe brain system spontaneously.
- Help the patient to become consciously aware of their innate competencies that are revealing themselves at this precise moment. This awareness
will help to Differentiate these capabilities from the constant pull of the
Secondaries that may be hyperactive or hyperconnected and hampering
their innate capacities. For example, these Secondary emotional patterns
or habits have been activated so many times that they have a very strong
pull, what Beatriz calls the six-lane highway.

The next vignette of Joe's transcript reveals the need for a vertical Facilitation
and Differentiation. As you recall (above), we left Joel spontaneously realizing
that he was afraid to claim his power. After that realization, Beatriz and Joel
continued working with the process of suppressing his constraints by strengthening his adaptive capabilities until they hit a snag, another hyperconnection,
and could not process any further. This hyperconnection was stronger than the
other ones, and Beatriz needed to pay direct attention to it.

Beatriz: What is happening? You sat back—did you lose the feeling? . . .
Joel [*Interrupting, one finger raised with strength*]: No, I am staying in my
power, but it is a calm silent power!
Beatriz [*Smiling with bright eyes*]: You are being assertive here with me and
standing up to me, honoring you in your wisdom.

Joel: My throat is killing me now [*hand on his throat and crouching back in his seat*]. I am very uncomfortable. Is it time to finish?

Beatriz: This is interesting. As soon as I saw you standing up in your power and asserting your autonomy with me, your throat [constriction] came [*hand on her own throat*].

[Beatriz's internal thoughts]: This is challenging to keep picking up his assertiveness when it makes his throat so uncomfortable. I want to be sure to check in with his Authority brain system.

Joel [*Looking at his watch, eyes darting back and forth*]: I am very uncomfortable.

Beatriz: In uncomfortability we grow! This is good. It is good that the difficulty is here with us so we can work with it. Uncomfortable means we are being successful. Being seen standing in your power is entangled with [your] throat. This is great that we can see it! Do you want to disentangle it?

Joel [*Wringing his hands*]: Yes, but it is uncomfortable.

Beatriz: Do you want to be seen standing up in your power?

Joel: I want to run and my throat is hurting . . . but yes, it is important [*hand in a fist for one second, then hand flops down, releasing the fist*].

Beatriz [*Imitating the fist*]: Can you feel your determination?! Being seen standing up in your power is important! [*Her hand in a fist again.*] Can you feel all the pulls of the different energies inside of you? Wanting to be seen in your assertiveness [*fist up*] and then wanting to hide and run away, and the throat and your determination to stay in your power, because this is very important for you?

Joel [*Scrunching up his face in pain*]: It is very uncomfortable.

Beatriz: Well done. In uncomfortability we grow! And you are growing your strength to be seen in your power right now. Well done! We need to stay here feeling all the pulls of all the energies inside of you one more round so we can disentangle it!

Joel's case study illustrates our insight that circulating and Differentiating within multiple levels of processing is an important approach that reduces constraints and hyperconnections. Beatriz keeps circulating Joel's awareness between the four levels of processing three more times before finishing this session. As you can see, Beatriz is Facilitating Joel's mixed experiences in the middle of the four-ring circus to Differentiate all of the brain systems that are activated. Beatriz had Activated the tertiary-level Authority and Autonomy brain systems: "*Wanting to be seen standing up in front of us.*" Joel is also experiencing Activation of his primary-level Assertive brain system and the body-level processing of his peripheral nervous system. The uncomfortable constrictions in his throat arise from the inhibitions of the Secondaries Shame and Fear. And his determination to keep standing up in his power and being seen, because that is important for him, are coming from the enhancing Secondaries Motivation and Important. Beatriz will continue this process a few more times in the following sessions with Joel, and he will have more successful experiences in those sessions, which will make this Differentiation become long-lasting.

SPIRAL PROCESS OF FACILITATING AND DIFFERENTIATING

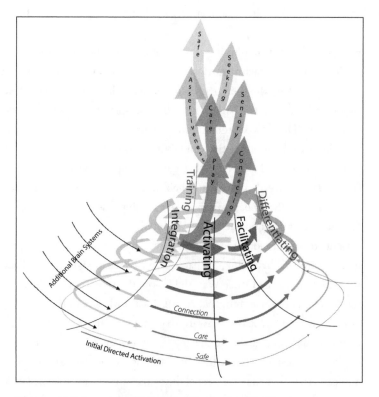

Figure 11.2 (repeated): Spiral of Activating, Facilitating, Differentiating, Training, and Integrating Primary-Level Brain Systems

Differentiating in CIMBS becomes what we call an 80–20 process, with 80% of our time and energy dedicated to Going the Other Way: developing resilience in the Primaries and enhancing Secondaries and Tertiaries. We give special emphasis to Facilitating and Training the Primaries because they can potentiate the release of some of the constraints that are placed on Primaries and Tertiaries from traumatic implicit memories that are stored in the secondary-level inhibitors of Shame, Grief, Fear, and Guilt. The remaining 20% of our time and energy is spent on Differentiating the inhibitors from other brain systems to relieve those constraints.

It is very important to keep emphasizing that CIMBS therapy is done in a circular way, spiraling up and down the four levels of processing. The case studies are the best examples of how one can intervene in a variety of ways to keep the energy moving, Facilitating and Differentiating distinct brain systems.

In this circular spiraling process there are eight decisions that we make constantly, and the rest happens organically. These decisions are not sequential, and you don't have to follow them all or in any kind of order to be successful.

- First, in this circular spiraling process of CIMBS, the therapist steps into the Therapeutic Attachment Relationship and directs the process of Activation by starting the therapeutic session with the Initial Directed Activation and bringing the patient into the Transpiring Present Moment of themselves. These two interventions can activate as many as 10 different brain systems at the same time and four levels of processing as well. When your patient says, "I am aware that I am anxious—my heart is beating fast," they are already processing their anxiety on three levels: aware (Tertiary), anxiety (Secondary, Fear), heart beating fast (Sensory, Peripheral).
- Second, we expand on the Initial Directed Activation as we invite the patient to be conscious and curious about their sensations at this precise moment in time by asking, "What are you aware of right now?" Then we typically Go the Other Way and follow the sensations of the capabilities of any brain system that reveals itself rather than the sensations of the constraints. Please be aware that various sensations or capabilities could be Activated at the same time, and you can choose which one to explore. It doesn't matter which one, as long as you explore a capability. You can trust that the other capabilities will appear again later, and then you can follow them. For example, the patient may say, "I feel tight in my belly, and my heart is racing, but I feel calm and happy to be here." The

constraints are tight belly and racing heart, but the capabilities are calm and happy; which one would you choose to explore?

- Third, always be on the lookout for and pick up moments of spontaneous flexibility in the nervous system. Pick up on the fly the psychophysiological phenomena that denote a nonconscious internal response of the Primaries. For example, Joel is spontaneously mobilizing his Safe brain system in the face of feeling fear and weakness. Then the choice is to keep Facilitating and affirming that capability by becoming an external generator. The circular nature of CIMBS permits you to notice one spontaneous activation at one time and another spontaneous activation at another time. There are no dead ends, right ways, or wrong ways. You just follow the clues from the spontaneous psychophysiological phenomena.
- Fourth, Activate and Facilitate (horizontally Differentiate) the Tertiaries one by one, starting with Awareness and Attention. If the patient is not conscious and paying attention to the process, we will never be able to have a co-therapist who is aware of their sensations and can share them with us. A further intervention that invites their self-observations is to Activate their authority (Authority and Autonomy brain systems). We engage their authority by inviting their conscious willingness to stay in the uncomfortable sensations and pay attention to their capabilities because they want to face their difficulties. Beatriz's intervention with Joel is an example: "Do *you want to* bring back the sensations of safeness and the rod in your chest with muscle memory?" It is like engaging their authority to continue the aerobic exercise, even if they feel some pain, because they want to get in shape. Activating the Authority and Autonomy brain systems could deactivate ambivalence about doing the work of therapy and leaving behind their symptoms of depression, anxiety, trauma, and so on. As we are Activating and Facilitating the Tertiaries one by one, they are being horizontally Differentiated from each other.
- Fifth, Activate and Facilitate the enhancing secondary-level brain systems and become the external generator to aid in the task of keeping the adaptive capabilities of each brain system buoyant for one more round and one more round. Harnessing their drive (Assertive and Motivation brain systems) to stay in the uncomfortable feelings one second longer becomes an important supporting instrument for success. Beatriz used the following intervention: "[*imitating the fist*] Can you feel your determination?!"

- Sixth, at the same time, we are Activating the Safe, Care, and Connection brain systems through constant attention to the Therapeutic Attachment Relationship. Facilitating one of these Primaries helps the patient stay in the Transpiring Present Moment. "This is the present moment of you. And you are being capable to bring yourself in *safeness* inside of you."
- Seventh, when we run into a secondary-level constraint such as shame or guilt, decide to resume Activating the Awareness, Attention, and/or Seeking brain systems: "How interesting—we are being aware that as soon as we pay caring attention to you, our old friends shame and fear are here!" In this way, we are also practicing vertical Differentiation. As we saw when Beatriz encountered Joel's sadness, the decision here is to avoid being distracted by those inhibiting emotions, but rather to continue following the capabilities as much as you can.
- Eighth, the therapist makes a continuous choice to seek out and stay in the Transpiring Present Moment of the patient's awareness of their psychophysiology and emotions. The therapist also pledges not to get distracted by the psychophysiology of the implicit learning from the past that could also be present in the body of the patient. For example, "You are feeling safeness inside of you, breathing deeply, and your stomach is relaxed at the same time that your chest and shoulders are very tight. You are experiencing safeness in the present moment as your body feels unsafe from the past."

Figure 11.2 shows the process and the outcome of Complex Integration of Multiple Brain Systems, Activating, Facilitating, Differentiating, Training, and Integrating in a circular spiraling way. It starts with the process of the Initial Directed Activation, activating the Attachment brain systems of Safe, Care, and Connection (Therapeutic Attachment Relationship) and bringing other brain systems into the mix. It culminates with the upward arrows showing the power of the energy of the Primaries Differentiating and Integrating with each other.

DIFFERENTIATING FOR THE THERAPIST

The direct interventions of CIMBS often pose difficulties for beginner trainees. They become tentative and uncomfortable, tending to back off from direct assertions such as, "We are here to care for you" or "You are being uncomfortable. This is good progress. In discomfort we grow!"

The process of Differentiating starts with self-treatment by the therapist. In order to learn Differentiating, we need to start by Differentiating within ourselves to see our innate aversion to making our patients uncomfortable. It is totally natural to feel shame when we cause others to feel uncomfortable. It can feel as if we are doing something wrong, and that we should stop this behavior now. Our human programming is that shame and guilt should be avoided at all costs. We need to Differentiate ourselves from this evolutionary avoidance of shame, guilt, and fear in order to develop the ability to tolerate our own discomfort.

As we are utilizing the Therapeutic Attachment Relationship and the Initial Directed Activation, we are directly offering safeness, care, and connection. Our intentions are loving, and these offerings of care, safe, and connection in the Transpiring Present Moment will activate shame and discomfort in many of our patients (because of hyperconnections and secondary learning from the past). Is it good to trigger shame? Shame is always operating and moves us in nonconscious ways. It is good to bring the shame out in the open. We are not triggering shame, we are Activating safe, care, and connection, and those experiences are revealing some entanglement with shame. When we disentangle ourselves from our own shame, we will be able to say, "Hello shame, my old friend, you are here. This is success—we have found an entanglement!"

The important question to ask the patient out loud in this situation is, "What happened just before the shame appeared?" And a silent question for yourself is, "What Primary was being activated before the shame came?" This question will keep you in the Transpiring Present Moment, rather than thinking, "I am doing something wrong—I should stop my behavior," or "Let's talk about your shame and what happened to you growing up that causes you to feel shame." We believe that asking about the shame may Differentiate it cognitively, but the process will not help with the task of harnessing the full energy and wisdom of Differentiated brain systems.

Differentiating ourselves can be tricky when our patient pushes our buttons. The first trick here is not to get triggered by your own shame and lose your balance by shutting down, withdrawing from the patient, changing tactics, going into teaching mode, or talking about the stories of the past. The second trick is not to get provoked when the patient's shame gets Activated, and they become defiant, angry, shut down, or withdrawn or try to pick a fight.

An example is the story of Tony, a 27-year-old man. Beatriz would initiate the Therapeutic Attachment Relationship as usual by moving her hands toward him with an intimate eye gaze and a warm smile, and by saying, "We are here to pay close, caring attention to you." Whenever she did this, his shame would be strongly activated. Sometimes he would start imitating her hand gestures, saying, "Is that how you talk in Latin America?" Sometimes he would defy her assertion: "You don't really care for me. I am just your cash cow." Those were very personal attacks. Beatriz needed to keep her balance and remind herself that he was pushing her away because he was feeling uncomfortable with Beatriz's caring feelings toward him. Therefore his reactivity was not the issue. She was there to Facilitate his ability to experience care and connection. First Beatriz needed to Differentiate herself from her own shame. Then she was able to intervene by saying, "What a huge discovery that you get reactive as soon as there are good feelings coming your way. It is interesting, isn't it? Are you curious about that?"

It takes practice to do that. It takes practice to Trust the Process. Trusting the Process means to be always aware that we are Activating Safe, Care, and Connection in the Transpiring Present Moment and that these feelings are innately healthy and adaptive. The secondary-level learnings from the past are what makes the patient feel shame or fear in our connection. Therefore, when you encounter reactions of shame or fear, you can come to see those reactions as evidence of progress on the road to success.

SUMMARY

In this chapter, we have focused on Facilitating and Differentiating the primary-level brain systems with a particular emphasis on horizontal and vertical differentiation. We illustrated how it looks when therapy is practiced in a circular way, spiraling up and down the four levels of emotional processing. The therapeutic emphasis is on constantly Activating, Facilitating, and Training the adaptive capabilities of various brain systems at the same time. Simultaneous horizontal and vertical Facilitating and Differentiating can weave together multiple open systems in the present moment, which is a form of Integration.

Integrating differentiated brain systems is important in order to harness the powerful energy of each system for long-term learning, which takes us to our next chapter: Integrating the Primaries.

CHAPTER 12

Integrating Primary-Level Brain Systems

···

INTEGRATION AND INTEGRATING REVISITED

Let's begin by reviewing some of the key components of the Integrating processes. As you recall, *Integration* means the state of the nervous system in which several or more brain systems are independently interconnected. Our basic tenet is that a network made up of multiple resilient and integrated brain systems can process large amounts of emotional energy and information. Your careful attention to multiple brain systems will support your patient's (BrainMind's) capabilities for achieving the state of Integration between those systems.

Integrating is the process of weaving together multiple open systems in the present moment. We use the term *Integrating* more frequently to emphasize the fact that this is a continuous, dynamic process, not a static state. This weaving together generates what we call complex systems, and as we outlined in the introduction to Part II, multiple systems can spontaneously self-organize to increase complexity. Integrating also refers to the continuous parallel processing of energy and information by multiple distinct brain systems. The systems need to be open to the influence of other systems in order for Integrating to unfold. Integrating is a natural process that can lead to further opening of closed systems and releasing of emerging phenomena and spontaneous self-organizing capacities of the BrainMind. Although Integrating is a process that occurs spontaneously in life and in nature, often it takes a combination of energy and intention to override the tendency for neural circuits to remain in their usual equilibrium or coherence. Examples of the emerging phenomena that result from Integrating could be the release of painful memories, Differentiating shame from self-esteem, or a shift in the balance in the autonomic nervous system.

Integrating primary-level brain systems is an impressively powerful therapeutic process. Integrating Primaries means that you are harnessing and sustaining each of those powerhouses. Recall that in the introduction to Part II, we defined horizontal and vertical Integration. You can be horizontally Integrating when you are Activating and Differentiating multiple brain systems at the primary level of emotional processing. For example, Activating, Differentiating, and Integrating the Safe, Care, and Connection brain systems will enable your patient's BrainMind to engage in parallel processing of those systems. This process can feel like a three-ring circus where you and your patient are in the middle, Activating, Differentiating, Integrating, and linking as many as all seven Primaries at the same time (Figure 12.1). Figure 12.2 is a cross-section of Figure 12.1 at the primary level.

The body plays a special role in Integrating Primaries. We have found that a multidimensional Integrating approach to the energy and wisdom of the body can help our patients get beyond their embodied constraints from previous trauma. Each of the Primaries has distinct resonant connections with the power of the body's emotional neural circuits.

In addition, you can be vertically Integrating all four levels of the nervous system. You can be accessing the energy and wisdom of the body and each of the distinct primary-level brain systems. You also can be utilizing the strength of the enhancing Secondaries (Importance and Motivation) and releasing any inhibitory brakes of the inhibitory Secondaries (Fear, Shame, Guilt). And finally, you

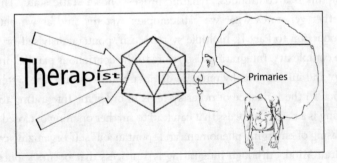

Figure 12.1: Side View of Horizontal Integrating

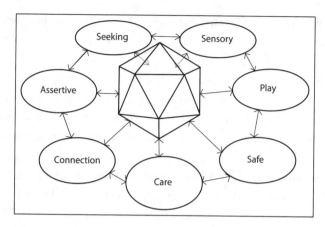

Figure 12.2: Top-Down View of Horizontal Integrating

can be enabling your patient to use their conscious brain systems, the A-Team, to direct their process and experience by channeling all of this power, energy, and wisdom to thrive in their lives (Figure 12.3).

The channeled focus of the energy and information unfolding when Integrating primary-level brain systems is effective. The effectiveness is often observable right in front of your eyes in a matter of a few minutes. Harnessing this emotional energy is important because it is the most powerful energy in the whole nervous system. There are a number of pathways and neurobiological principles you can utilize when Integrating Primaries. This Integrating has the potential to release constraints of Fear, Shame, Grief, and trauma of all kinds.

The therapist can play a central role in the processes of Integrating. The therapist can start the process of Integrating primary-level brain systems in the first few minutes of every session by utilizing the Therapeutic Attachment

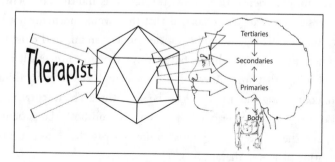

Figure 12.3: Side View of Vertical Integrating

Relationship and Initial Directed Activation. As we discussed in Chapters 5 and 6, you can Activate multiple Primaries with a careful focus on your immediate relationship with your patient that is unfolding in the Transpiring Present Moment. You can also assertively and directly be Activating various conscious and nonconscious brain systems. Integrating is dynamic and novel, so there are many places in which the patient or therapist can lose their equilibrium. That loss of balance is inevitable. Those moments of disorientation and awkwardness are where we learn the most. Trusting the Process is one of the therapist's key tools for entering into the unknown discoveries that lie ahead. The therapist's role can be one of carefully and selectively reflecting back the patient's innate competencies, the body energy and wisdom that they cannot see. Often those responsive affirmations are difficult for your patient to feel or tolerate because of shame and fear.

INTEGRATING LENS

Integrating primary-level brain systems has unique features that are not present when Integrating the conscious-level brain systems. Integrating can be a lens through which you observe multiple phenomena at the same time. There are a number of ways in which to utilize the Integrating lens. You can picture the lens as a multifaceted prism through which you can observe different dimensions of energy operating at all four levels of the nervous system (Figure 12.3). The lens can be a magnifying glass that enables you to see subtle psychophysiological phenomena and access the energy and information of those phenomena. This lens can also focus your energy and attention more precisely to Facilitate the subtle parallel processing that is going on under the surface. You can direct your patient to observe and experience themselves through this multifaceted lens, helping them be present to a range of emotions that they would normally not notice or be able to tolerate. This lens can help foster understanding and trust that Integrating is not just a static condition, but mainly a dynamic process. It is not just a snapshot of things that are connected, it is the complexity of many things in the process of connecting and happening at the same time. The Integrating lens also operates to magnify the energy of all systems within both the patient and the therapist, and thus contributes greatly to the synergy that often occurs during the Integrating phases of therapy.

INTEGRATING PRINCIPLES

There are a number of neurobiological principles that can help you appreciate the significance of different aspects of the Integrating process that would otherwise go unnoticed. It might be helpful to be reminded of the Integrating principles we introduced when discussing conscious brain systems in Chapter 9:

- Resilient brain systems are powerful.
- Differentiated brain systems process energy and information in parallel.
- Sustained experiential learning changes the structure of the brain.
- Adaptive present-moment experiences can update traumatic implicit learning.
- Integrating systems releases self-organizing capacities.

The case study of Paul below illustrates the Integrating process over the course of a session. We invite you to read the case study while noticing several elements: Which Primaries are active at the same time? What is Albert doing to Facilitate those systems? Which Secondaries are constraining Paul's experiences? Which of the Integrating principles seem relevant?

CASE STUDY: PAUL

Paul has had recurrent depressions since early adolescence. He struggled with self-hatred, persistent suicidality, and self-defeating behaviors. He came for therapy after six months of sobriety when his depressive symptoms and suicidality were becoming more intense. Paul's Awareness and Authority brain systems were hypoactive and constrained by feelings of guilt and shame. At this point in his treatment, he was much more aware of his internal experiences and able to override his constraints of shame and self-contempt. This session occurred about a year after the start of treatment.

As soon as the patient sat down, the session started out with the Initial Directed Activation. We will pick up the transcript two minutes into the session. The nonverbal aspects, psychophysiological activations, and body movements are printed in italics. Albert's conscious observations, assessments, and intentions are separated and labeled. Beatriz's commentary follows.

Paul [*Nods, nods.*]

Albert: All of you is welcome. This is important.

Paul [*Smiles.*]

Albert: What are you aware of?

Paul: Anxiousness, seriousness, a strength [*makes fists*].

[Albert's internal thoughts]: He is spontaneously Integrating Awareness, Attention, Fear, and Importance, and his fist reveals an embodied assertiveness. I want to enhance the distinctions and sustain the Integrating processes.

Albert: It's great that you are present to a range: the anxiousness, seriousness, a strength [*mimics the fists*].

Paul [*Smiles, chuckles*].

Albert: What we are here to do is important. To feel the sense of importance. This is valuable, and you are important.

Paul: I am important [*voice tentative*].

Albert: You are valuable.

Paul: I am valuable. I am in new unfamiliar territory [*silence, tilting head side to side, smiles, chuckles*].

Albert: It's great that you get that. You are in unfamiliar territory. What are you experiencing?

Paul: On the way here I was thinking, and I started talking positive to myself. I can do this. I can take care of myself and do what I can.

Albert: Awesome.

Paul: And it is really different to do that [*chuckles, smiles*].

Albert: Wonderful.

Paul: There is an anxiousness there too. This is really different.

Albert: You are taking charge and not just reacting to the fear. Being proactive instead of reactive.

Beatriz's commentary: When Paul's BrainMind is Integrating, he is unaware of many of the adaptive experiences he is having. We can see psychophysiological evidence of this integrating process when we observe Paul's head tilting left and right. He is clearly in a state of emotional disequilibrium. We can just imagine how his cerebellum, insula, and corpus callosum are working to process all of this new energy and information. Albert is Facilitating and Reflecting (see below) the competencies of Paul's Importance, Value, and Motivation brain systems to sustain the Integrating processes that are unfolding. Albert is not talking about or explaining Paul's emotional experiences. He is helping Paul to embody and stay present to the multiple activations. Albert uses specific words such as *value* and *important* in Activating the enhancing brain systems to help Paul develop internal positive feedback circuits.

Paul [*Smiles*]: I think I react a lot. That is my standard.

Albert: That is what you learned. This a huge shift: to take charge, to be proactive, to prime yourself for success, to be realistic.

Paul [*Makes fists*]: It is part of valuing and esteeming myself, and it feels weird. It is normal, but it does not feel normal.

Albert: This is not how you were trained. It is healthy to do that for yourself. It is great to learn how to do it now.

Paul: I am also pushing myself out of another comfort zone. I'm writing about self-care every day. Talking about it makes me anxious, and it's really good to do.

Albert: Wonderful for you and anyone else. Your self-love will shine through.

Paul: I really want to do it [*starts to cry, moves body*]. I have to fight against all of these things in my head. I feel some sense of betrayal.

Albert: That is the biggest part of the project. That is important work. You really want that, and yet you have to override all these other feelings.

Paul: No one is saying this to me. It is in my head [*shakes head, facial expression of anguish, hands move, cries*]. I feel a pain on two sides, and it hurts. I feel like I have missed out on this self-love, and really nice to connect with it [*grimaces*]. It is frightening to share it with you right now.

[Albert's internal thoughts]: Paul's feelings of betrayal reveal how he had to deny his own self-love and self-worth in order to meet his needs for belonging when he was young. This is a major guidepost that lets me know he is having a profound experience. Differentiating the pain of caring for himself and the shame or fear of exposing his self-care with others is a valuable breakthrough for him. He is spontaneously developing a broader Integration. I want to reflect back the adaptive experiences and discoveries he is making.

Albert: That part of sharing these positive feelings, to actually come out and reveal these positive feelings to others, is important. It is so hard with these painful feelings [of betrayal]. To thrive and let others thrive on their own terms. An enormous gift. You are really committing yourself to love yourself. It does not hurt anyone.

Paul [*Fingers fidgeting, tears.*]

Albert: Loving yourself does not hurt anyone [*hands and arms open*].

Paul: It hurts something inside of me to share.

Albert: You are asking your body to do something very different. The pain is in you. You are learning to step over invisible fences, the pain in your body. It does not hurt anyone else.

Paul [Nods]: Yeah.

Albert: It helps you actively move through the feelings of betrayal. Caring for yourself.

Paul: Everyone needs it, but it is just . . . so scary to do [*smiles, sighs*].

Albert: It is scary for you to do. Everyone needs it.

Paul [*Deep breath, ponders.*]

Albert: It is difficult for many people to step out of their comfort zone, to take charge, tolerate the pain of change, the grief of what has been lost.

Paul: To open up and flourish [*opens arms and hands*].

Albert: To open up and flourish [*opens arms and hands*]. To feel that in your body right now.

Paul [*Pained expression and tears, and grimaces*]: Part of me is very critical of doing this.

Beatriz's commentary: A great many nonconscious phenomena are happening in this vignette that we can observe in his body and the peripheral nervous system. All of the body movement, the release of tears, the smiles, deep breaths, and open arms and hands provide us with psychophysiological evidence that Paul's experiences and emotional learning are occurring mostly in the body. This lets us know that his primary-level brain systems are genuinely involved. Albert's nonverbal interventions are Differentiating Paul's body's experiences of openness, flourishing in spite of his fear and shame. He is Facilitating Paul's nonverbal learning by putting words to the nonconscious emotional brain systems that are active at the Transpiring Present Moment. For example, he noted the pain of stepping over previous learning and the release of grief.

Albert: And just to notice your body's sensations. It is being spontaneous and authentic. It is a good thing, yet part of you wants to hide it.

Paul: This is me! [*Hands and arms open.*]

Albert: Open and flourishing.

Paul: Yeah.

Albert: Fear and shame come from the past. You have to step over them.

Paul [*Sighs*]: I told my roommate about doing this project of self-care. She wanted to post it and to follow me on my journey [*makes a fist*]. In my mind, why would you want to post that? Why would you care? Why would anyone care? It is so automatic in me. This shaming of myself and hiding, it is just in me.

Albert: You were not aware of it. Interesting to notice that when you open up and flourish, you have an automatic shutdown reaction.

Paul: All of this blaming or accusing is in me. It is automatic.

Albert: It was not safe to flourish. Your mind has created reasons not to flourish.

Paul: I am anticipating something bad. I am afraid I am going to get hit [*flinches, sighs, grimaces*].

Albert: Being positive sets off alarms.

Paul: Whatever I learned, there were a lot of false positives. There were alarms going off without a legitimate reason.

Albert: Lots of false alarms. Now you can update those. You can do proactive things even when the alarms are going off. Encouraging yourself and notice how different. . . .

Paul: I am proud of my self!

[Albert's internal thoughts]: Wonderful spontaneous assertion as a result of these new discoveries. This is a completely new level of spontaneous self-organization for Paul. I want to help him further embody this discovery.

Albert: What just happened inside, that said, "I am proud of myself"?

Paul: There is something in there [*fist over his heart*]. Something . . .

Albert [*Mimics fist.*]

Paul: Warmth and respect for myself.

Albert: Respect for yourself.

Paul: This is something I have wanted to do. It is uncomfortable and there is a value in it.

Albert: You are asserting something. You are feeling the value, importance, warmth, care, and love for yourself.

Paul: What also helps identify it, is that it feels difficult to do. So let go—I am caring for myself.

Albert: Stretching even more [*opens arms out*].

Paul [*Breathing deeply, grimaces.*]

Albert [*Silence.*]

Paul [***Pained voice, tears***]: There was so much shame that did not need to be there. Now I can just talk about it without so much shame. I do not have slide down into the shame.

Albert: I'm glad you brought it up today and chose to seize your capability to not be overwhelmed by the discomfort, shame, or suicidality.

Paul: It feels so embarrassing to talk about it [*voice choked*]. That is what got tangled up.

Albert: It is a big deal to talk about it.

Paul: And to be okay [*hands open out*].

Albert: To feel respected and cared for.

Paul [***Tears, choked voice, squirms, painful experience, grimaces***]: Respected, cared for, and shame.

Albert: It is a big deal to disentangle all of this.

Paul [*Cries more deeply, glasses fog up.*]

Albert: It is important work that we are doing together and what you are feeling right now [*hands over heart*].

Paul [*Sighs, cries, grimaces.*]

Albert: To feel our care, our respect, to feel our unconditional connection with you, even as there is shame and pain and fear. It is a big deal.

Paul: I feel that if there is shame or embarrassment, then there is no room for respect. You should hide. Hide your self! Nice to see that there is respect and it is foreign [*nods, cries, sighs, opens his arms, laughs*]. Yeah. It is safe to feel all of these emotions.

Albert: It is important to claim that again. To assert yourself. You are speaking a visceral truth, you are claiming it.

Beatriz's commentary: There is so much going on at the same time, I don't know what to focus on. Let's see what Paul and Albert are Differentiating (disentangling). On the body level, Paul is experiencing and releasing several distinct emotions: care and assertiveness when he makes a fist and describes warmth in his heart. He is feeling safe when he breathes deeply and pain when he grimaces. He is feeling the emotions of shame and guilt, as evidenced by his pained expression and tears. He is feeling connection as he describes feeling cared for, respected, and together. He is clearly experiencing a multidimensional emotional disequilibrium (see Chapters 4 and 15).

It can be challenging to keep our eyes on the brain systems when so much emotion is arising in the present moment. Facilitating, Differentiating, and sustaining multiple brain systems simultaneously is the key to both horizontal and vertical Integrating. In this vignette we can observe Albert keeping Paul's focus on the Tertiaries, the Awareness, Attention, and Authority brain systems, by asking, "What just happened inside?" He Facilitates the Secondaries, Value, Importance, and Pleasure, by reflecting, "You are feeling the value, importance, warmth." And Albert reflects the Transpiring Present Moment competencies of Paul's Primaries: "You are asserting something . . . care and love for yourself."

We know something momentous is unfolding when Paul asserts that he is proud of himself. He has been burdened with low self-worth, self-hatred, depression, and suicidality. This is a new and disorienting discovery for Paul. It conflicts with his implicit emotional learning that has been rigid and has contradicted his innate self-worth and esteem. You can see how hard his nervous system is working to process all of this novel information and emotional learning. I have never seen a patient's forehead work so hard that it fogs up his glasses. We can imagine that his prefrontal cortex is processing enormous amounts of energy and information right now. Albert has been careful to emphasize Paul's felt sense of his internal wisdom and to hear his own visceral truth. This visceral emphasis adds greatly to the vertical Integration of all four levels.

An important supplement to Facilitating, Differentiating, and Integrating primary-level brain systems is Training. At the end of each session, Paul and Albert would reinforce and refresh the most meaningful learning. After they debriefed, Paul could decide what experiences he wanted to keep rehearsing between sessions. Paul actually related some of what he had been practicing on the way to his session: "On the way here I was thinking and I started talking positive to myself. I can do this. I can take care of myself and do what I can."

QUESTION FROM TRAINEE: What about asking Paul how he is experiencing the feelings of proud, strength, or warmth in his body?

POTENTIAL ANSWER: Those invitations could help further ground those emotions in his body. They would help those systems become more resilient, which is useful and effective. In this context, Paul's BrainMind is capable of doing more. He is presently processing and experiencing his emotions utilizing multiple brain systems at the same time. That will facilitate the Integrating processes and have the advantage of developing Fail-Safe Networks.

QUESTION FROM TRAINEE: Can you help me understand how talking about caring for himself feels so dangerous and a sense of betrayal?

POTENTIAL ANSWER: It is hard to be sure. His Assertive, Care, and Safe brain systems all appear to be constrained by developmental emotional learning contained in his Shame, Fear, Guilt, and Grief brain systems. His Transpiring Present Moment behavior of loving himself contradicts his baseline equilibrium of self-hatred. We could speculate that his BrainMind has created some rationalizations to justify self-hatred. Caring for himself could betray the implicit rules of belonging that he learned in his family and community. We believe that betrayal will cause feelings of guilt.

TYPES OF INTEGRATION

Being Present

The patient's BrainMind has an instinctive drive toward Integrating. Often that drive toward Integrating is overshadowed by ruminations, fear, grief, or shame. Those emotional reactions can be so entrenched that the patient becomes stuck in their negative thinking, anxiety, or depression. So it takes patience and careful attention at every step of the process to discover any spontaneous moments of flexibility, when the process of Integrating reveals itself.

In order to best catch those moments of flexibility, you need to be present. We wrote in Chapter 5 about the importance of the therapist's presence to enable the Therapeutic Attachment Relationship to develop. We have found that the practicalities of implementing the Therapeutic Attachment Relationship and the Initial Directed Activation, and staying in the Transpiring Present Moment, will naturally enhance your ability to be present to your patient. Those actions will also facilitate your sense of presence within your Self. Your personal presence will have a neurobiological impact on your patient's conscious and nonconscious brain systems. When we ask our patients at the completion of therapy what made it so successful, we often hear variations of, "You were always present." You can surmise many of the significant meanings *present* has for different individuals.

Your presence and therapeutic focus can help you be on the lookout for those opportunities for Integrating primary-level brain systems. You can observe the transpiring Activations of your patient's reactions and responses to your presence and focus. This is where you can follow your patient's nonconscious lead. Which lead do we follow when there are so many active at any given moment? A patient may send you off on a tangent by telling you a story or complaining about a symptom. However, in addition to being present you can also intervene and discern what is actually transpiring in your patient's Primaries and Go the Other Way. The more practiced you are in detecting the psychophysiological phenomena leads, the more precise will be your therapy.

Horizontal Integration

Take a look at the horizontal view of the primary-level brain systems (Figure 12.1). Which of the brain systems are visible? Which ones can you sense are just below the surface? Let's look at the case study of Paul. He described his initial awareness of anxiety, seriousness, and strength, and he made fists. His openness to his transpiring experience indicated that his Safe and Connection brain systems were active. His strength and the psychophysiological phenomena of his spontaneous fists provided evidence of the Activations of his Assertive and Sensory brain systems. Albert recognized this as an opportunity for horizontal Integrating, and so he joined in the middle of Paul's experience by acknowledging the importance and value of Paul's Activations: "It's great that you are present to a range: the anxiousness, seriousness, and strength." Paul's psychophysiological responses of smiling and chuckling alerted us to his sense of pleasure and feeling acknowledged and valued. That evidence provided the lead to sustain and enhance this process of horizontal integration of Primaries.

Horizontally Integrating primary-level brain systems is a dynamic process that can unfold naturally until it runs into constraints, contradictions, and shutdowns. However, since multiple Primaries are participating in the Integrating, the emotional constraints of fear, grief, or shame are less likely to take over your patient's BrainMind. Your patient thus need not be stuck in their survival mode of functioning. In the case study example, Paul's self-care was constrained by shame and guilt. However, he had sufficient Assertiveness, Safe, and Connection to override the shame and guilt. Paul's process of horizontally Integrating helped him stay open and harness the power of his Primaries to stay in the Transpiring Present Moment and tolerate the shame and guilt that were holding him back. The success of this process was revealed physiologically by his release of tears of grief and regret.

Your patient's nonconscious emotional lead may present itself in a manner that is unclear, distorted, confusing, and uncomfortable to both your patient and yourself. However, this discomfort, confusion, and lack of clarity often present the best opportunities for change and new discoveries. It is hard to trust the process of horizontal Integrating of primary-level brain systems when you cannot see evidence of its beneficial impact. Hang in there. The energy of your presence, your Care, Connection, Seeking, and Assertiveness will be Activating those brain systems in your patient as well. Your energy is never lost nor destroyed. It may not be reflected back by a sparkle or smile in your patient's eyes, but it still will have an impact that will activate their innate Primaries. The fact that you cannot see the reflection of your energy gives you some clues about how you might proceed. For example, Ann (Chapter 2) rejected Albert's Care when she said, "I feel nausea and want to run away! I don't want you to care for me. I am not a good person." Albert took those clues as an opportunity to Go the Other Way. He started Activating her Seeking, Care, and Connection brain systems explicitly. He was following Ann's nonconscious lead and need for horizontal Integration of her Care brain system.

Body-Brain Bond

The primary-level brain systems have an inseparable link with the body. Our emotional experiences are made up of a complex interplay between physiological phenomena that originate in the body and processing and regulation by the brainstem. Porges (2011) refers to this interplay as "reciprocal influences between brain and body." Damasio (2012) refers to these phenomena as a perpetual resonant loop: a body-brain bond. The Primaries "provide a direct experience of one's own living body, wordless, unadorned, and connected to nothing but sheer existence." He goes on to point out how our nonconscious Self develops at this level of the nervous system.

This inseparable bond between the body and the brain invites us to pay careful attention to the psychophysiological phenomena that are transpiring at any given moment. Those phenomena and their shifts reveal distinct body states that can help you when Activating and Differentiating the Primaries. It is important to remind ourselves that each of these brain systems has its own psychophysiological signature and wisdom. These innate and highly evolved neural circuits coalesce to become what we call motivations and emotions. Most of these circuits develop adaptively from infancy on. You can trust that many adaptive nonconscious emotion circuits are available even in your most traumatized patients. The trauma these patients suffered was not innate or highly evolved. Trauma is a learned process stored within the secondary-level brain systems such as Fear, Shame, and Grief, processed by the amygdala, hippocampus, cerebellum, and hypothalamus, and expressed in the body.

Many patients seek out psychotherapy because of symptoms in their bodies, which can range from chronic pain and physical tension (headaches, backaches), to gastrointestinal symptoms (pain, irritable bowel), to fatigue. Indeed, a large percentage of patients present to their primary care provider with symptoms that have a significant psychophysiological component. Our physical and emotional well-being are inexorably tied to our bodies. As we have noted before, we believe that these symptoms are the tip of the iceberg and call for an integrative perspective.

Several therapeutic approaches that focus on treating trauma pay careful attention to the body. Peter Levine (2017) emphasizes the clinical importance of the felt experience that depends on awareness of the body. He believes that traumatic symptoms stem from the residue of emotional energy that has not been resolved and discharged from the body. Van der Kolk (2014) invites us to endeavor to help our patients' bodies begin to feel safe. He notes that this is challenging because people with trauma do not readily regulate their physiology in the presence of other people. Pat Ogden (2017) points out that the wisdom of the body is a largely untapped resource in psychotherapy. She believes that the body is a target of therapeutic action that provides patients a much-needed avenue of self-knowledge and change.

We agree with these trauma therapists about the importance of the body and the residue of trauma in successful therapy. However, we have found that you have much more to offer when you Activate and Integrate the body-brain bonds contained in each of the primary-level brain systems. What we add to their knowledge is the benefits of harnessing all the emotional power and wisdom of the body-brain bonds that are and were not traumatized.

Vertical Integration

Careful attention to the primary-level brain systems will bring you and your patient into direct psychophysiological contact with the state of their bodies due to the perpetual resonant loop. The emotions and emotional processing initially occur in the peripheral nervous system, at a level below the brainstem. Because of the brain-body bond, those emotional activations are simultaneously being perpetually processed within the primary-level, secondary-level (basal ganglia), and tertiary-level (neocortex) brain systems. Vertically integrating brain systems combines neurobiological activity on all four of these levels (Figure 12.3).

Daniel Siegel introduced us to the concepts and processes of vertical and horizontal Integration. We find his description of vertical Integration particularly congruent with our understanding, research, and therapeutic practice. He noted that vertical Integration is important in disentangling the unresolved losses and constraints that have cut us off from our full vitality. He emphasized the importance of bringing somatic (body) input to our conscious awareness and attention so that we can use that energy and information for choice and change (Siegel, 2007).

Your presence and the Therapeutic Attachment Relationship will enable you to see how the Activations of your patient's Safe, Care, and Connection brain systems are being revealed in their bodies. Noticing those adaptive psychophysiological phenomena starts your process of vertical Integration. Your awareness of the Primaries and the body level (psychophysiology) helps you Integrate those two levels. For example, Paul had a felt sense of strength, and his body spontaneously made fists. Albert refreshed and reinforced the Assertive brain system by repeating "strength" and mirroring the psychophysiological Activations of Paul's body by acknowledging and mimicking the fists. This is two-level, body and brainstem, vertical Integration in action.

When you continue Integrating your patient's adaptive body-brain connection, you have the opportunity to reinforce those circuits by being an external generator and harnessing the power of the enhancing Secondaries: Value, Pleasure, Motivation, and Importance. Recruiting these brain systems provides several distinct benefits: (1) The Secondaries will add their wisdom and energy to the body and the Primaries; (2) your patients will experience the sense that they can have their own internal positive feedback loops to enhance the competence of their Primaries; and (3) Their BrainMinds will be vertically Integrating adaptive neural circuits on three levels: body, brainstem, and basal ganglia.

In order to expand his ability to vertically Integrate, Albert harnessed Paul's Importance and Value secondary-level brain systems in the case study. He invited Paul to have a conscious felt sense of his body's experience of vertical Integration: "What we are here to do is important. To feel the sense of importance. This is valuable, and you are important." Activating a brain system such as Importance requires repetition, because it is a nonconscious system. Your patient's conscious mind may understand the words the first time, but the Secondaries require more stimulation before you can harness their energy. After the intervention, we could then observe how Paul's body, brainstem, and basal ganglia responded to that intervention.

Vertically Integrating the body, Primaries, and Secondaries is happening on all three nonconscious levels of the nervous system. This Integrating happens in our lives all the time, whether we are aware, mindful, or not. Integrating can happen at any time in any therapy session, and the key for us is to notice and Facilitate any dynamic vertical Integration as it unfolds and evolves. Your patient's BrainMind will respond, react, and give you clues about how you can best follow their leads. As you can see, this process of vertical Integration is resonant and reciprocal. Your presence and attunement provide some of the energy to help your patients change the structure of their brains.

Paul's nervous system responded to these interventions on all four levels. His body chuckled and smiled, he tilted his head side to side, and his voice was tentative. His Assertive brain system stated out loud, "I am important. I am valuable." He was able to reinforce his own Value and Importance Secondaries explicitly. His conscious Tertiaries were able to mindfully observe that he was in new, unfamiliar territory.

You can foster the benefit and long-term learning from the vertical Integrating process when you participate on all four levels with your patient. Your presence in their new, unfamiliar territory will help desensitize them to the awkwardness, disequilibrium, pain, shame, or fear that is likely to arise. Your embodied pleasure, curiosity, acceptance, and compassion will communicate your full involvement at all four levels of emotional processing.

Vertical Integration often uncovers new information, learning, and discoveries. Paul's ability to Differentiate the pain of caring for himself and the shame or fear of exposing his self-care to others was a valuable breakthrough for him. We will look at that further below.

REFLECTING: THE THERAPIST'S ROLE

There are a variety of approaches you can take to promote the process of Integrating primary-level brain systems with your patients. Integrating is a process that occurs spontaneously in life and in nature. However, it often takes a combination of energy and intention to override previous patterns that prevent the development of new levels of Integration and the release of spontaneous self-organization that is more flexible and resilient. You can play a role in sustaining and directing the Integrating processes. In the sections above, we pointed out how the presence of the therapist (or another person) will Activate primary-level brain systems, which will Integrate to some extent on their own. Your attuned presence will enhance the natural tendency for our nervous systems to resonate with each other and deepen the experience and the learning. Using the lens or prism of Integration will help you discover unfolding therapeutic opportunities. The lens of Integration can also help you focus your energy more precisely. Recall that this is a precious opportunity to harness the power of multiple Primaries at the same time. Those systems can synergize with each other and achieve one of the outcomes we seek, the Complex Integration of Multiple Brain Systems.

Repeatedly reflecting your patient's Integrating experiences is perhaps the best way for you to intervene to Facilitate the development of increased complexity and Fail-Safe Networks. *Reflecting* in this context refers to selectively noting adaptive distinct brain system activations that arise spontaneously in the process and then turning that energy back toward them with greater focus and precision. In this manner you are intervening like a parabolic reflector in which the patient's competence or capability is reflected back in a more precise and intense way so that they can reexperience their competence on a deeper level, feel seen in a new way, and meet their need to be acknowledged and understood. A parabolic reflector has one trick that makes it useful: the vast majority of energy that hits the reflector is focused on a single point, in this case the patient's Primaries. For example, at the outset of the session, Albert was reflecting Paul's competencies when he repeated with emphasis the three words, "anxiousness, seriousness, strength." More importantly, he was reflecting Paul's body's competence when he used his own body to mimic Paul's fists. Albert was resonating with Paul's Integrating processes to sustain and enhance their significance. Reflecting will often shift the internal emotional balance and release new learning. Colleagues who observed this session described it as follows: "Paul was finding his own compass. He was resetting distortions from his old learning. He is developing his own internal gyroscope."

The patient is often unaware of the Activation of adaptive neural circuits and primary-level brain systems that arise when you initiate the Therapeutic Attachment Relationship and/or the Initial Directed Activation. Paul experienced feeling valuable and important as both novel and unfamiliar. His nervous system would likely have deleted those experiences unless enough other energy and intention was exerted to strengthen those new, unfamiliar neural circuits. In fact, sometimes patients experience the competence of their Primaries as wrong, bad, dangerous, or shameful.

We have several suggestions to offer for you to deepen your role in Integrating primary-level brain systems. Slow down and Trust the Process without need for explanation. Many therapists are used to explaining, educating, and/or interpreting the therapeutic process with their patients, and so they do the same thing even when so much is happening at once. Those explanations often take the patients out of the Integrating experiences and into their own conscious minds as they try to understand or figure out what is happening. Sometimes you will see patients trying to put words to their experiences. We have found it most useful to pause the verbal interaction and help the patient focus on the complexity of their visceral experience. For example, you could say, "Just stay present to your experience without words," or "Whatever you are experiencing right now is important." Stay focused in the middle of the three-ring circus. Four-dimensional multiple simultaneous processes are unfolding. You do not have to figure it out; it is better just to get out of the way.

PATIENT CHALLENGES

Your patients will encounter conscious, nonconscious, and visceral challenges as they are horizontally and vertically Integrating the primary-level brain systems. The obvious conscious challenge is that most of this part of therapy is addressing nonconscious brain systems. The patient's BrainMind often has no search patterns to observe or even detect the Activations of those systems. Some patients complain that "nothing is happening," or "this is boring." Many patients have a picture in their mind of what talk therapy is supposed to look like, and these principles and approaches are not what they were expecting. Integrating Primaries typically unfolds and evolves slowly, so it requires patience. But given the chance, patients will soon discover that underneath their puzzlement and defenses are the wonderful capabilities of their BrainMinds.

Integrating primary-level brain systems will take your patients out of their present equilibrium, their comfort zone. Some patients are afraid to let go of their conscious worries to explore the unknown capabilities underneath the surface, the bottom of the iceberg. Occasionally patients have a sense that these forms of Integration could uncover aspects of themselves that they have never known and may be afraid of. They could be afraid to give up their coping mechanisms, their armor, and feel open, vulnerable, and powerless.

There are many nonconscious challenges for patients to uncover. Initially patients will note that what is happening inside of them and in the process is unfamiliar. Paul stated, "I am in new unfamiliar territory." Patients may use words such as weird, foreign, unsettling, confusing, off-balance, or frightening to describe their experiences. Your patient is likely to want to shy away from unfamiliar experience. They will be crossing invisible fences of previous emotional learning, which will stir up nonconscious visceral reactions. Trespassing in this forbidden territory can set off alarms inside the patient's BrainMind. They may only notice ambivalence, reluctance, or immobilization in reaction to your invitations to experience their deep emotional resources. However, we invite you and your patient to Go the Other Way. Step into the discomfort. Send their anxieties through a prism to discern the distinct primary-level brain systems that have been Activated but not yet Differentiated. Please note that these feelings of weirdness and foreignness occur throughout treatment, because the present-moment experiences are happening on nonconscious levels. Your patient may have some cognitive familiarity with these moments, but their present experience is both novel and often contradictory to early developmental learning.

The visceral challenges for Integrating primary-level brain systems exist on a continuum from subtle to dramatic. You will run into one or more emotional constraints stored in the Secondaries (amygdala, hippocampus, cerebellum) such as Fear, Grief, Shame, and Guilt from previous emotional learning. Psychophysiological examples of such subtle constraints include a tentative voice, minimal facial animation, and intermittent eye contact. Paul's body moderately exhibited symptoms generated by all four of the inhibitory Secondaries: Fear, Grief, Shame, and Guilt. The visceral evidence of Fear was his tentative voice and hesitations. Grief was shown by his release of tears, Shame by his fear of sharing himself, and Guilt by his feeling that he would be hit. Patrick (Chapter 3) had a dramatic visceral challenge when he felt sure he was going to vomit at the end of his first session.

Integrating primary-level brain systems can enable your patients to develop a new, lower perceived center of gravity in their bodies. They often put their feet more firmly on the floor and describe feeling grounded in an unfamiliar way. Their breathing is deeper, and their voices more resonant. It takes some time for these new neural circuits, the new equilibrium, to be processed by the cerebellum. A patient's physical coordination may be awkward for 20 to 30 minutes as their nervous system updates with this novel Integration. Some patients have trouble signing their names or may feel unsteady standing up or walking down the hall at the end of a session. We recommend to our patients that they sit for a while or go for a walk after each session to give their BrainMind time and energy to further Integrate and install this new learning.

THERAPIST CHALLENGES: TRUST THE PROCESS

We have found that the biggest challenge for therapists with Integrating primary-level brain systems is to Trust the Process. It is hard to trust what you cannot see or hear. It is difficult to let go of our need to understand and make sense of what is happening. When we do not Trust the Process, we tend to talk too much, make long interventions, and ask complicated questions. Therapists are trained to ask questions rather than make assertions or reflections of primary-level brain system Activations. When we do not Trust the Process, we are more likely to get entangled with our patient's defenses, resistances, or reactions rather than to Go the Other Way.

When our patients become uncomfortable, we all have an instinctive tendency to take them out of their distress. This impulse is especially strong when a patient's defensive survival pattern has been triggered. Sometimes this distress is manifested by difficult behavioral patterns such as defiance, hostility, obfuscation, or hopelessness. There is a risk of getting hooked by those reactions, focusing on the behavioral patterns, and losing sight of Integrating Primaries. Even though it feels like they are pushing back or away with all their might, some little part of them is saying, "Don't give up on me. Don't let me push you away. Don't let me dismiss you." You will trip and fall, and that is to be accepted even though it might be embarrassing.

DELIBERATE PRACTICING

Integrating primary-level brain systems requires deliberately practicing new skills and methods of interacting with your patients. The word *practice* is tricky in the context of a medical or psychotherapy practice. We went to school and through training in order to become physicians or therapists. During our training we practiced a variety of treatments. When we started our careers, we went into practice. There are different meanings for the noun *practice* and the verb *practice*. The practice (noun) of medicine or therapy is actually a performance. *Practice* used as a verb refers to a different process than performing. The difference is easier to see when one thinks of a musician who keeps practicing their instrument alone doing scales, or rehearsing a phrase or piece of music throughout their career. Even the most skilled musicians often work with a teacher to fine-tune their practicing. Practicing enables the musician to trust their skills so that they can be creative during their performances.

A psychotherapist's primary instrument is their Self. We believe that for us to be most effective requires a lifetime of deliberately practicing our skills and honing our instrument. Deliberately practicing skills refers to learning such skills as Directed Activation, Differentiating distinct brain systems, or horizontally Integrating primary-level brain systems. Honing our instrument refers to looking at video recordings to discover our strengths and weaknesses to fine-tune our practicing. And it refers to working with a therapy trainer to expand our capabilities and to discover learning opportunities that we had not seen by ourselves. In our teaching, much of the time is spent practicing exercises and specific skills in our weekend training courses and our small training groups. As therapists enter new courses of study and training to advance their clinical acumen, there will be points at which their BrainMind will mobilize a mix of fear and shame that will slow down practicing and integrating new approaches (Warshow, personal communication, 2017). Tony Rousmaniere's (2017) book *Deliberate Practice for Psychotherapists* is an excellent resource for clinicians and teachers who want to become more effective.

SPONTANEOUS SELF-ORGANIZING

Integrating can lead to releasing the power of spontaneous self-organizing capacities of the BrainMind. You may recall that self-organizing is a process in which some form of overall order arises from interactions between Differentiated brain systems (Chapter 9). The results are new internal knowledge and wisdom, and often the release of nonconscious emotional constraints.

The discoveries of new internal knowledge and capabilities are rewarding for both the patient and therapist. These self-organizing phenomena can be evidence of a new emotional equilibrium that, once established, becomes stable and can never be undone. However, since these are emergent phenomena, they can be transitory and go unnoticed. We tell our trainees, "Don't worry, the train will come around again soon." With Training, you can help the patient reinforce these experiences and make the changes permanent. The new knowledge can be transpiring experiences that prompt patients to make remarks such as, "I have never felt safe inside my body until this moment" or "I never knew that I never knew that about myself" (Chapter 1). Paul said, "Everyone needs it, but it is just . . . so scary to . . . open up and flourish" (*opens arms and hands*).

Novel self-organizing phenomena can be distressing as well as rewarding. New levels of flexibility and complexity are naturally unfamiliar. Sometimes it can be a much bigger change than just letting go of emotional habit patterns or shutdown reactions. Patients describe their experiences as disorienting, weird, even discombobulating. The new balance of self-organizing phenomena is like finally mastering riding a unicycle: You can travel in any direction, but you also can fall in any direction. You are discovering capabilities you never knew before. There is some inevitable grief over losses, and there may be regrets over not having had access to the newfound resources years ago.

The release of self-organizing phenomena can also uncover nonconscious Fear, Grief, Shame, and Guilt. The distress is especially painful when the release comes from traumatic learning in early infancy. Previously unknown emotions of terror, annihilation, or betrayal can be viscerally experienced and released. Those painful emotions were depressed or repressed in the patient's BrainMind. We have found it helpful to use a scuba diving analogy to help the patient have patience and compassion to move through this process. When a diver has been deep for a prolonged period of time, they need to come up slowly and make several decompression stops on the way to the surface. At each stop, they breathe out the excess nitrogen that has been compressed in their body before ascending further. Releasing fear or shame is akin to the detoxifying process of the diver's decompression stops.

Paul's therapy session illustrates several of these phenomena. When he asserted his competence to care for himself every day, he released anxiety and at the same time experienced the value and importance of caring for himself. His body released tears of grief, and he shifted his posture to accommodate the new internal experiences of himself. He also discovered emotions of guilt and betrayal that made no sense to him. He exerted his Agency and Autonomy to fight against all of those feelings inside his head. "I feel a pain on two sides, and it hurts. I feel like I have missed out on this self-love, and really nice to connect with it [*grimaces*]. It is frightening to share it with you right now."

We wonder what is happening physiologically in the patient's BrainMind during this process. We imagine that the initial Activation and unfamiliarity free the patient from some nonconscious emotional constraints. First, their amygdala and hippocampus activate to learn from this novel important experience. Second, if the novelty of this process is sustained, their cerebellum updates the previous emotional equilibrium to achieve a new flexibility. The patient can feel dizzy or disoriented at this point. Third, if this visceral learning incorporates sufficient novelty of multiple brain systems, a unique self-organizing potential may be released in the patient's BrainMind. We think of this level of change as the Complex Integration of Multiple Brain Systems. After change occurs at that level, the patient's face and body often appear so different that multiple observers comment, "It looks like he had a facelift and a makeover" (Chapter 1).

We believe that the components of Activating, Facilitating, Differentiating, and Integrating the primary-level brain systems in the Transpiring Present Moment have a reciprocal cause-and-effect relationship with each other. "Scientific endeavor is a natural whole, the parts of which mutually support one another in a way which, to be sure, no one can anticipate" (Einstein, 1950). These processes harness the powerful energy and wisdom of multiple nonconscious brain systems. The ongoing transpiring novel learning and inhibiting of old constraints can create a cascading effect that can give rise to significant reorganization in the BrainMind. This is the release of spontaneous self-organization, which we mentioned earlier. The emerging self-organizing process naturally expands the Integrating processes. Your patient will naturally achieve new levels of complexity. Paul had spent his whole life full of self-hatred until this phase of his therapy.

His spontaneous, powerful assertion, "I am proud of my self!," provided us with evidence of a new level of self-organization for Paul.

We include a testament from a therapist and patient we will call Judy that speaks to her experience of the value of self-organizing for healing and growth. She describes how her conscious effort and intention enabled her to keep Differentiating her shame, grief, and fear ("I don't want to") from her Agency, Motivation, Sensory ("get going" sensation), and Assertive brain systems. Those changes released her self-organizing capability to achieve a new level of complexity in her BrainMind. Judy wanted to share her struggle with a self-defeating pattern of procrastination and the results of the Integrating and self-organizing phenomena in her BrainMind.

• •

Before (this therapy), I could only consciously feel the confusing, immobilizing "I don't want to" sensation. Now, I have a new option for responding when that happens. Instead of forcing myself to override the stopping sensation, I recognize it consciously, with very clear understanding that it's not actually about anything in the present. I feel genuine compassion for myself. From this place of comfort and compassion, I'm able to purposely turn my attention toward the "get going" sensation, and allow myself to lean into it more, and follow it. It's as if I can stand in the millisecond of that "firing," feel both sensations separately, knowing what they each are, without reaction or judgment toward either of them. It's a little moment where I can finally choose for myself, and move more easily, instead of struggling between states of frozen stress and rushing stress.

This hasn't worked like a switch, so that I'm never late to anything again. The paired firing still happens on most days. The difference is that I can feel it and understand myself when it happens. It feels like a new track has opened inside of me. Instead of just feeling confused, discouraged, and stressed, I can also feel the drive to get going, and can choose which sensation to focus into and follow. Now that I've made this connection, I can never "not know it" again. Focusing on the agency sensation, honoring it with my attention, I move more freely, without getting bogged down in confusion and stress. This takes effort, intention, and practice. When I'm tired, over-scheduled, or distracted, I still fall into the old pattern. But I'm no longer in the dark about what's happening to me, at the mercy of a pattern that I couldn't understand. I feel compassion and competence, rather than shame about it. Also, I notice that this new approach comes a little more naturally, with less intentional effort required, the longer I do it.

I've tried all my life to get to the root of this immobilizing, depleting pattern, including 10 years of therapy and EMDR work, with no success. I could not have gotten to the bottom of this alone. I did work very hard for it, but it also required a counselor who knew how to help me connect with this pattern and discover how I can redirect it. It felt extremely uncomfortable, sometimes terrifying, to accept Beatriz's invitation to widen my attention and self-awareness in the midst of that "I don't want to" sensation, and to allow enough collaboration for that to happen, so that I could begin to feel my agency, instead of just the fear that interrupts it. It's remarkable, having the power to consciously reshape nervous system "wiring" from babyhood, compounded by over 50 years of reinforcement, and to actually bring healing to a root of suffering.

....

REVIEW

One can review the case study of Paul from the perspective of developing a Fail-Safe Complex Network. In this session, Paul's BrainMind has developed increasing levels of complexity. He is horizontally Integrating Safe, Care, Connection, Seeking, Assertive, and Sensory primary-level brain systems. His BrainMind is developing internal positive feedback loops with the enhancing of secondary-level brain systems such as Value and Important. The fact that he is able to release his constraints of Fear, Grief, Shame, and Guilt provides us evidence that he is vertically Integrating Primaries and Secondaries, and that these brain systems are sufficiently resilient that he can keep moving forward in the midst of his emotional turbulence.

In Chapters 13 and 14, we look more closely at the secondary-level brain systems. It is at this level that our BrainMind stores our emotional constraints and adaptive learning. Chapter 13 defines and describes eight nonconscious secondary-level brain systems that guide, constrain, and enhance our primary-level brain systems. Each of them has both innate and learned competencies. Clinical illustrations will show practical ways to interrupt these constraints and provide new adaptive emotional experiences. Psychophysiological phenomena reveal the Activations of these nonconscious brain systems. Chapter 14 illustrates how Training, Differentiating, and Integrating these nonconscious brain systems further enhances your patients' emotional competence. We refer to this process as physiotherapy for the Brain/Mind.

CHAPTER 13

Secondary-Level Brain Systems

THE GLORY AND MISERY OF EMOTIONAL LEARNING

In this chapter we take a more precise look at the eight nonconscious secondary-level brain systems (Secondaries) that guide, modulate, train, inhibit, and constrain our primary-level brain systems. These brain systems generate specific emotions such as fear, grief, shame, guilt, and importance/salience. They modulate underlying emotions and motivations (care, connection, seeking) by a mix of inhibition and enhancement. Therapists are familiar with working with these emotions, which are often the presenting complaints and symptoms that bring patients in for therapy in the first place.

We are examining the secondary-level group last among brain systems, because we have found that when we focus on Facilitating and Differentiating the conscious and primary-level brain systems, the constraints within the Secondaries and other forms of implicit emotional learning tend to drop away naturally. Admittedly, the secondary level of emotional processing is quite complicated, so it is beyond the scope of this book to go into depth with the treatment of these brain systems.

The Secondaries contain their own unique, highly evolved knowledge and processing capabilities that enable us to thrive in a wide range of environments and circumstances. Some of this knowledge is innate, but the majority is learned during our lifetimes. Emotional learning starts in utero and then really takes flight after birth. The Secondaries process and store most of our important experiential emotional learning throughout our lifetime. The vast majority of that learning is nonconsciously held in neural circuits, neural cell groups, cell assemblies, individual neurons, and synapses. Most of the Brain-Mind is involved in storage and retrieval of this learning and knowledge. Each of the Secondaries possesses some maladaptive learning (constraints) from previous trauma, neglect, or abuse. Psychophysiological phenomena and shifts reveal the present-moment activations of these nonconscious brain systems to the trained therapist.

As you may recall, the secondary level of the central nervous system refers to structures in and near the basal ganglia. The following secondary-level clusters of nuclei are the most important processors of emotions and storage space for emotional memory: the amygdala, hippocampus, hypothalamus, thalamus, insula, cingulate, nucleus accumbens, substantia nigra, ventral tegmental area, cerebellum, and striatum. It is easier to see the functions of secondary-level mental processing when you recognize the roles other structures in the basal ganglia play in coordinating our ability to walk or run. The caudate nucleus, putamen, globus pallidus, and cerebellum coordinate energy and information from the tertiary level (motor cortex) and from the body and brainstem so we can walk gracefully with or without attention.

In Chapter 1 we defined two categories of secondary-level brain systems: enhancers (Pleasure, Importance/Salience, Motivation, and Valuable/Internal Reward) and inhibitors or gatekeepers (Shame, Fear, Guilt, and Grief). Enhancing brain systems provide nonconscious internal positive feedback to sustain life-enhancing experiences. They help us maintain and strengthen adaptive emotions and actions; they develop positive feedback loops that sustain those adaptive emotions and actions; and they reinforce our innate capabilities to make them increasingly competent.

The emotions of fear, grief, shame, and guilt are familiar to all of us. We tend to think of these emotions in negative terms, and indeed they are sometimes treated as pathological or bad. The experience of these emotions often is aversive, yet as we will explain, these brain systems also adaptively modulate the body's physiology and behaviors and the activities of the primary-level brain systems. The actions of the inhibitory brain systems are not all-or-none phenomena. Their roles are to direct, titrate, and coordinate, in a positive manner, the energy and information that arise primarily from Primaries such as Care and Connection. They help us learn the fine points of pursuing our needs and wants in attachment and social relationships. Inhibitors—the innate Fear, Grief, Shame, and Guilt brain systems that we're all born with—are our gatekeepers of survival, defensive emotions that evolved to help us survive in a dangerous world. These brain systems are named after the emotions that they generate. It is important to remember, however, that the brain system and the associated emotion are not the same.

The beneficial and adaptive aspects of the Fear, Grief, Shame, and Guilt brain systems are more difficult to grasp. The emotions that arise from these brain systems are often at the roots of our patients' symptoms and presenting complaints. Because the emotions of fear, grief, shame, and guilt are painful and aversive, it is hard to appreciate their utility in everyday life and in the therapeutic process. For example, if you are being too assertive with your boss, your Guilt and/or Shame brain systems will tone down, or titrate, your assertiveness so that your boss continues to listen to your ideas. Facilitating functionality of the Fear, Grief, Shame, and Guilt brain systems can be the most challenging treatment strategy for many therapists. We will explore these adaptive roles of the gatekeepers in detail later in this chapter.

There is a natural balance between the modulating and enhancing of the Secondaries that helps us to be both precise and graceful at the same time. Analogous circuits helped us learn how to talk; when we mispronounced a word, our ears detected the error and systems suppressed that circuit and activated a recovery circuit. When we spoke just right, our enhancers reinforced or potentiated that circuit. We each have our own personal experience and familiarity with the emotions described in this chapter. Now, we invite you to put that learning aside and approach these emotions and Secondaries with a beginner's mind.

FACILITATING FUNCTIONALITY

The principles of Facilitating, Differentiating, and Integrating we have described elsewhere apply here too. There are unique treatment strategies and opportunities that apply at the secondary level of the BrainMind. What is special at the secondary level of mental processing is the distinct enhancing brain systems that can each augment the activations of the Primaries. We have illustrated those phenomena throughout the case studies in previous chapters. We want to reemphasize the importance of using the enhancing brain systems within the processes of

Facilitating adaptive circuits, knowing that they will also inhibit the maladaptive learning patterns that are stored at the secondary level of mental processing.

Patients suffering from depression provide a classic case of inadequate functioning of secondary-level brain systems. The fact that depressed patients cannot sustain motivation is evidence of a brain system dysfunction. In addition, depressed patients do not feel pleasure or value in actions and experiences that are clearly healthy and healing. For example, the depressed person can go for a walk and feel better briefly, but then may be unable to hold on to the benefit of that experience. The underdeveloped Motivation, Value, Pleasure, and Importance brain systems are unable to provide the nonconscious positive feedback that would enable the depressed patient to repeat the healing behaviors and sustain the activations of the Primaries. In addition, the patient's experience of pleasure and value is incoherent and incongruent (see below) with the normal balance or equilibrium that is their depressed baseline.

Differentiating the eight Secondaries (Figure 13.1) enables you to discover more explicitly the nature of any nonconscious dysfunctions. Armed with psychophysiological evidence, you can make your therapeutic energy more potent and effective when you direct your therapeutic laser precisely at one or two of the brain system dysfunctions. For example, with the depressed patient, you can narrow your focus to increase the functionality of their Motivation brain system. Even though you see no evidence of their motivation, your knowledge of the Secondaries will empower you to trust its presence and continue

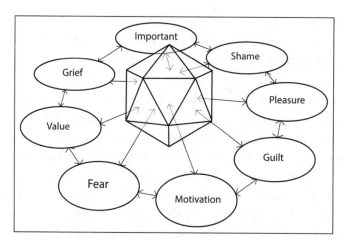

Figure 13.1: Prism of Secondaries

Facilitating. Activating the Motivation brain system knowing it will release dopamine from the nucleus accumbens. This dopamine will give the patient's BrainMind a burst of energy, attention, and novelty (see Chapter 15). Your patient will walk out of your office with a little spring in their step even as they deny that they feel any better. That is what we mean by Facilitating the functionality of nonconscious brain systems.

For another example, the mobilization of an emotion such as Play-full delight is a transient (state) phenomenon. With the help of the Secondaries, the delight can be sustained and Integrated with other brain systems so that playfulness can become an ongoing trait (Hanson, 2016).

Most therapists are unfamiliar with prioritizing and harnessing the Motivation, Value, Pleasure, and Importance brain systems. Facilitating any of those brain systems will provide more energy to sustain the Activations of the conscious and primary-level brain systems. These brain systems provide internal positive feedback for adaptive experiences and learning, and are therefore self-affirming.

Later in this chapter, we explore each of the secondary-level brain systems in depth to help you develop new appreciation for their power and wisdom and to give some guidance on how we work with them in therapy. First, however, we highlight one inhibitor, Grief, to elaborate on some key properties that all the Secondaries share.

GOOD GRIEF

We have chosen to single out Grief to expand our discussion of the relationship between secondary-level brain systems and the emotions of the same names, and how these brain systems interact with other levels of brain systems, the primary level in particular. Similar principles apply to all of the Secondaries.

Grief is a familiar emotion for all of us (Figure 13.2). On the one hand, the experience of the emotion of grief is sad and often painful. However, the Grief brain system plays a significant role in the success of our attachment relationships. The emotion of grief is different from the mix of activations and processing carried out by the Grief brain system. That may be hard to grasp at first. The Secondaries evolved to help us sustain adaptive actions and to titrate, reduce, or inhibit unsuccessful actions. Panksepp and Biven's (2012) research provides volumes of evidence that Grief evolved as a modulating emotion and brain system to sustain and

enhance care between the newborn and
the care provider. At its most basic, the
child's Grief brain system helps the infant
maintain and even facilitate the parent's
caring for the child. If the mother is too
far away, the infant will cry out (referred
to as a "distress vocalization" in animal
research) to bring the mother back into
proximity. In more subtle ways, the Grief
brain system may be sensitive to small
movements away from care, causing the
child to initiate actions such as turn-

Figure 13.2: Grief Brain System

ing the head toward the mother, smiling, or looking with shiny eyes toward the
mother. In those ways, the Grief brain system is both proactive, to enhance care,
as well as reactive, to reestablish care when it has gone missing.

The Grief brain system provides the child with essential good emotional
learning. The child learns nonconsciously how to enhance and titrate the care
offered by the care provider by moving closer, engaging with facial expressions,
and making endearing vocalizations. When the parent responds with care, the
child's Grief brain system calms down as a result of the release of oxytocin and
endogenous opioids. The parent's nervous system also calms down with the
release of their own oxytocin and endogenous opioids. Those neurotransmitters
will facilitate further development of a secure attachment relationship.

The Grief brain system can also be the source of traumatic learning that will
have a lifelong impact on the developing BrainMind. In the Baby Blues example
in Chapter 2, Ann could not tolerate her feelings of shame and unworthiness
when her newborn daughter Dawn sought care from her. Rather than responding to Dawn's bids for care and connection, Ann pulled away and put her baby
down. The child's Grief brain system would initiate cries of longing and protest
to reinitiate care and closeness. However, Ann could not respond due to her own
secondary-level psychophysiological shutdown. If that response had continued,
Dawn's Grief brain system would have learned to shut off her Care impulses to
protect her BrainMind from the enormous pain of loss and abandonment. As a
result of the learning in the Grief brain system, this child could possibly have
developed an avoidant attachment pattern, chronic anxiety, or panic disorder.

Channels of Grief

All secondary-level brain systems operate on three distinct channels that we call *events*, *learning*, and *transpiring*. Again taking the Grief brain system as an example, *grief events* refer to significant life experiences that caused grief from loss of care and connection with important people in our lives. That grief may or may not be conscious. This form of grief is historical, has been processed previously, and is stored in various parts of the nervous system. An obvious grief event would be the death or loss of a treasured friend or parent.

Grief learning refers to how our BrainMinds have processed care and connection over the course of our lifetimes. We learned to modulate our behavior and emotions to sustain and enhance our attachment relationships to whatever extent was possible. This dynamic form of grief is a nonconscious operating system that developed over the years and has become our best practice for keeping our emotional balance in important relationships. For example, grief learning taught us to be sensitive to the feelings and needs of others so that we could sustain our relationships with them.

Transpiring grief refers to the emotional activations that are uniquely occurring to facilitate the relationship we are having at this moment. The therapeutic relationship is particularly relevant here. The patient's BrainMind has an innate drive to feel safe, care, and connection with others and at this moment with the therapist. So even when it appears that the patient is resisting the connection, underneath the surface their Grief brain system is working to build a healthy attachment with the therapist. For example, when the patient feels the therapist's genuine interest, their Grief brain system could relax to be more open and vulnerable to receiving the therapist's care.

It is hard to separate these three different aspects of grief in our minds. Grief events are familiar experiences for all of us. Our conscious minds tend to associate grief with loss and loss events in our life. The grief learning and transpiring grief are nonconscious and more difficult to grasp. It may take some deliberate practice for the therapist to recognize them (recall the weevils in Chapter 3). We believe all three forms of grief are interconnected in the BrainMind.

Each of the eight Secondaries has the same channels as those described for the Grief brain system. We all have noteworthy fear, shame, and guilt events that we can consciously recall. However, we also have experienced many other events that affected our emotional learning nonconsciously, and we have Grief operating in the present moment when we are connecting with other people.

How does this knowledge help you? Knowing about the eight different Secondaries will give you some new clarity about what is happening deep inside the iceberg of your patient's BrainMind. You will better be able to see their nonconscious strengths and understand their internal constraints, compromises, and incongruence, which we discuss at the end of this chapter. Teasing these apart will help your patient be able to tolerate the dissonance and distress of their nonconscious emotional conflicts. Staying in the Transpiring Present Moment and Therapeutic Attachment Relationship will enable your patient to harness the wisdom and energy of multiple differentiated nonconscious brain systems.

In the following sections, we explore each of the eight Secondaries in depth to help you develop new appreciation for their power and wisdom. We detail the characteristics and some associated psychophysiological phenomena of each of the brain systems; we identify the neurotransmitters and neuroanatomical structures that are involved; we offer sample interventions that you can employ to Activate that brain system; and we provide a brief excerpt of a clinical case study from a previous chapter that illustrates working with that brain system. Other Secondaries surely exist; however, we have found the most neurobiological evidence to support the distinctions and clinical relevance of these eight. Our clinical research and experiments have reinforced the utility of Facilitating, Differentiating, and Integrating these eight Secondaries with the Primaries and conscious brain systems. The horizontal and vertical Integration of all 20 brain systems becomes the Complex Integration of Multiple Brain Systems.

INHIBITING BRAIN SYSTEMS: THE GATEKEEPERS

Fear

The Fear brain system contains the neural circuits that detect physical danger and react to help us survive (Figure 13.3). Severe threats to survival activate hardwired circuits in the brain and produce responses such as fight, flight, or freeze (LeDoux, 2002; Porges, 2011). Some Fear circuits are innate and do not need to be learned. A loud noise will activate freeze circuits in all mammals. The video from the 1996 Atlanta Olympic Games bombing showed everyone freezing at the time the bomb exploded. Most of the Fear circuits, however, are developed throughout life as part of conditioned learning. Fear plays a major role in the emotional learning of all the other nonconscious brain systems.

The Fear brain system has reciprocal connections with the primary-level Safe brain system, such that activations in Safe can suppress or inhibit Fear circuits (Figure 13.4). This neurobiological knowledge is one of our therapeutic principles. Although your patient's fear can be intimidating, a greater power resides in their Safe brain system. It is obvious how the Fear brain system takes us out of danger. It is not so obvious how our Safe brain system takes us out of fear. Moving toward safety takes us out of danger and enables us to thrive. Facilitating your patient's Safe brain system when they are overwhelmed with fear is a form of our Go the Other Way treatment strategy.

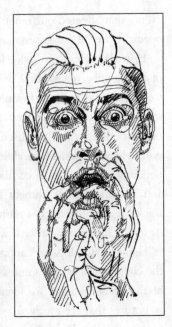

Figure 13.3: Fear Brain System

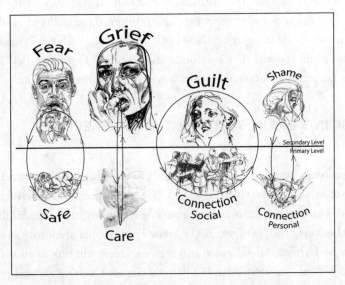

Figure 13.4: Reciprocal Connections Between Secondaries and Primaries

Fear is the most familiar of all the secondary-level brain systems, and it impacts the lives of all of us. Fear learning constrains the functioning of our patients' motivations, conscious capabilities, and emotional regulation. Fear, panic, and anxiety are similar feelings that are often not precisely distinguished. Fear is a specific neural reaction to physical danger, whereas panic is a neural reaction to losing connection with our loved ones. Anxiety is a broader emotional term that refers to distress about fear, panic, anxiety about the unknown, strange places, strange people, and our own emotions of shame, grief, or guilt.

The Fear brain system is well recognized by all neuroscience researchers including LeDoux, Panksepp, Porges, Grawe, Davidson, and others. The Fear brain system is a pathway that runs from the central zones of the amygdala to the anterior and medial hypothalamus, surrounding the third ventricles, and from there to dorsally situated areas of the periaqueductal gray matter. This system includes specific autonomic and behavioral outputs that control the physiological symptoms of fear such as sweaty palms, rapid heartbeat, freezing, or running away (Panksepp & Biven, 2012; Porges, 2011). The catecholamine hormones (adrenaline, noradrenaline), the corticotropin releasing factor and the adreno-corticotrophic hormone, and the sympathetic branch of the autonomic nervous system are the neurotransmitters and neural mechanisms that arouse the body into fear reactions.

The psychophysiological evidence of the Fear brain system tends to be fairly obvious. You can often observe skin color changes, absence of facial expressions, pupil size changes, tension in the extremities, shallow breathing, and vocal tension as evidence of fear circuits. For more detail, see Chapter 14. It can help to discern the baseline fear manifestations, such as constant fidgeting, from changes that occur to increase or decrease fidgeting activations of the Fear brain system to guide the process of your therapy.

The emotion of fear is often problematic, in contrast with the wisdom of the Fear brain system, which evolved to modulate and titrate our actions to keep us safe. From one perspective, the motivation of the Fear brain system is to support and modulate our Safe brain system. When traumatic life experiences have activated the Fear brain system to extremes, the subsequent implicit emotional learning, such as nonconscious terror, PTSD, and other anxiety disorders can be crippling. Differentiating the previous emotional fear learning from the adaptive functioning of the Fear brain system in the present can be a transformative experience for your patients.

Your interventions can facilitate the energy and wisdom of the Fear brain system. You might welcome your patient's fear by saying, "Your fear is important and welcome." You might Differentiate their Awareness and Attention brain systems from Fear: "Great that you are aware of your tension." Or you can make their psychophysiological phenomena conscious: "What are you physically experiencing with your fear?"

Sandy (a clinical example from Chapter 6) presented for therapy with severe and chronic symptoms of anxiety. In the following vignette from her first therapy session, you can see how Albert worked at Differentiating Sandy's fear learning (symptoms) from the competence of her Fear brain system in the Transpiring Present Moment. In this moment, her Fear brain system helps her sustain and increase her body's experiences of being alert and attentive. Albert is also Differentiating her Awareness and Attention brain systems from her fear when he keeps inviting her physical awareness of tension, breathing, and cognitive processing. Sandy is having a mixed experience as her Safe brain system discovers she is safe in the Transpiring Present Moment relationship, while at the same time she is experiencing and releasing some of her body's fearful psychophysiological phenomena.

> **Albert:** The fact that you are aware of the physical tension in your chest is very helpful.
> **Sandy:** Okay [nods].
> **Albert:** What else are you aware of feeling? What else are you noticing?
> **Sandy:** I feel tension in my shoulders and neck. Like there is something pressing down on my chest [hands on her shoulders]. I can breathe, but I cannot take a deep breath. I can try really hard and it does not work. I have to keep my thinking on track [hands to her head]. I get distracted.
> **Albert:** It is difficult to focus. Does it affect your vision or your hearing? Your throat?
> **Sandy:** My jaw is really tight [hands on her jaws]. That would be another manifestation.

Each of the inhibiting brain systems can play a significant role in reactive anger (see Chapter 10). For example, in the case of Fear, the young patient's BrainMind may have suffered life-threatening abandonment. The Safe, Care, and Fear brain systems would have mobilized proactive anger and rage to attempt to meet the need for safety, care, and connection. If those emotions had been blocked by terror, they would not have been released. Those emotions may remain buried in the secondary level of emotional processing and become some of the sources of the patient's anger/rage or depressive reactions. The same is true of the Grief, Shame and Guilt brain systems. Similar traumatic learning can give rise to the symptoms of chemical dependency, obsessional thoughts, compulsive behaviors, and self-destructive tendencies and impulses.

We have found that Facilitating the Tertiaries and Primaries will meet our patients' emotional needs and drives in the Transpiring Present Moment. For those reasons, anger in reaction to the emotional learning contained in the Fear, Grief, Shame, or Guilt brain systems plays a much smaller role in our therapies than it previously did. At the same time, we are Differentiating each of the brain systems to remove any obstacles to those drives. When there are few obstacles, there is no need for the brain systems to generate proactive anger.

Shame

The Shame brain system is composed of neural circuits that modulate and sense threats to important relational connections (Figure 13.5). Shame evolved to develop and sustain the attachment relationships with care providers. This system develops early in the first year of life in order to learn how best to meet the needs for attachment with one's specific care providers. We have all experienced and felt the emotion of shame. Most shame activations are subtle, nonconscious, and out of our awareness. Shame is represented physiologically by a transition from a positive (enthusiasm) to a negative (passive) state. At its core, shame is the emotional reaction to the loss of attunement with caretakers (Cozolino, 2002). Shame is characterized by behaviors of withdrawal and feelings of distress, powerlessness, and worthlessness. Shame can manifest, for example, as a toddler's psychophysiologically adaptive freeze reaction when they run enthusiastically into the street, which causes their parent to cry out in distress. The name for the

Figure 13.5: Shame Brain System

Shame brain system comes from the usage of Tomkins, Schore, Cozolino, Siegel, and others.

You can observe the psychophysiological evidence of Shame in your patients' posture, eye gaze, body movements, and tone of voice. For example, rounded shoulders, lowered head, and avoidance of eye contact all can be evidence of Shame activations. Shame also triggers visceral sensations of nausea, gagging, and/or an inward collapse. Most of us can attest to the visceral power of shame. You can also observe shame in a patient's avoidant behaviors, pessimism, or self-deprecating comments. The misapplication of shame as a parenting or disciplinary tool predisposes children to long-term difficulties with emotional regulation, high anxiety, and internalized feelings of worthlessness. "Because shame is powerful, preverbal, and physiologically based, the overuse of shame can predispose children to problems with affective regulation and self identity" (Cozolino 2002).

The Shame brain system has reciprocal connections with the primary-level Connection brain system, such that Activating Connection can suppress or inhibit Shame circuits. This neurobiological knowledge is one of our therapeutic principles. Although your patient's shame can be intimidating, their Connection brain system has greater power. Moving toward connection takes us out of shame and enables us to thrive. From an evolutionary perspective, connection is very adaptive, and shame evolved later to modulate, titrate, and protect those connections. Facilitating your patient's Connection brain system when they are overwhelmed with shame is another form of the Go the Other Way treatment strategy. The genuine compassion you feel for another's suffering can mitigate the emotions of shame.

There has been limited neuroscience research into the secondary-level brain structures that are part of the Shame brain system. Activation of the right amygdala and posterior insula has been observed with Shame and the disgust system. The hypothalamus probably also plays a role in the modulation of Shame by Connection. The vagal nerve is primarily an afferent nerve, and so it is likely that it is taking in information from the peripheral nervous system that participates in helping the Shame brain system maintain the relational bond with the parents. Both Fear and Shame are likely to be activated when the vagal nerve senses a shift from safe connection to loss of connection. This sense of lost connection can also lead to changes in the autonomic nervous system from sympathetic to parasympathetic dominance (Porges, 2011).

You can facilitate the energy and wisdom of the Shame brain system with a variety of interventions. You could welcome your patient's shame by saying, "Hello shame, you are a friend helping build connections." Or you could Differentiate their Awareness, Shame, and Connection brain systems from the emotion of shame: "You are aware of your nausea as we make our connection explicit." And you could make their psychophysiological phenomena conscious: "What are you physically experiencing with your shame?"

Ann (in the clinical example from Chapter 2) came for therapy because of difficulty attaching to her newborn. In the following vignette from her first therapy session postpartum, you can see how Albert worked at Differentiating Ann's feelings of shame and unworthiness from the competence of her Connection brain system in the Transpiring Present Moment. When Albert could see the shame and grief in Ann's face, he chose to focus on the transpiring care and connection that were present in the Therapeutic Attachment Relationship. He trusted that the power of Ann's Care and Connection brain systems would be able to inhibit the shame and grief emotions that were causing Ann's difficulties.

Albert: Ann, what do you see in my eyes right now? . . .

Ann: You like me?

Albert: Yes! I care for you. I am caring for you.

Ann: I feel nausea and want to run away!

Albert: How wonderful that you are being aware of the feelings of nausea and running away. You are aware of these feelings and you are not running away. Are you curious about that?

Ann: Not really. I just want to run away and hide.

Albert: Curious, isn't it? Any idea of what is bringing up this feeling of nausea at this present moment?

Ann: I don't want you to care for me. I am not a good person.

Albert: What do you see in my eyes?

Ann: You still like me?

Albert: Together we can care for you in your struggle.

Traumatic nonconscious shame learning occurs frequently and can be the source of some of our patients' most troubling symptoms and presenting complaints. For example, many of your patients' difficulties with reactive anger arise from the drives of the Care, Safe, Connection, and/or Assertive brain systems. Often these anger/rage reactions occur because of nonconscious shame learning. When this occurs within a session, we suggest you examine what happened the moment before the anger reaction occurred (see Chapter 11). Tony's provocations with Beatriz arose out of his shame/anger reaction to receiving her care and connection.

Guilt

The Guilt brain system is made up of neural circuits that facilitate our social bonding with family, clan, peer group, or culture (Figure 13.6). Evolution sculpted our genes to develop neural circuits that could enhance our ability to meet our needs for belonging with those groups. Our survival depended on learning how to fit in. The terms *guilt* and *shame* are often confused and used imprecisely. There has been sufficient research to clarify distinct behavioral and neurobiological features of each of these brain systems. We believe the most striking differences are the motivational features: shame generates the desire to hide, escape, or strike back, and guilt generates the desire to confess, apologize, or repair. The name for the Guilt brain system comes from the usage of Schore, Cozolino, Kelly & Lamia, and Tangney & Dearing (2002). The Guilt brain system appears to be localized in parts of the thalamus and cingulate.

The Guilt brain system helps us learn the spoken and implied rules and expectations of our group. In the same way that we learned how to ride a bicycle, this system helps us modulate, titrate, and learn nonconsciously the give-and-take of collaborative and supportive social relationships. In this context, *social* refers to the biological instincts of social animals to sacrifice their personal needs and wants for the greater good of the wolf pack, troop of monkeys, or ethnic clan. Most of the neural circuits contained in our Guilt brain system will always remain out of our awareness. Social learning enables us to follow many of the rules of the road without needing to think about what is the right choice when we drive a vehicle. When we experience a significant rupture of those wise and developed

Figure 13.6: Guilt Brain System

circuits, we will consciously experience the emotion of guilt. Like any other emotion, guilt can be manipulated to control or influence others.

The Guilt brain system can generate emotional experiences characterized by feeling distress when we believe we have done something that compromises our internalized standards of conduct for the group, clan, or family. Some patients experience sensations that they attribute to doing something wrong, taboo, dangerous, or inappropriate. Some patients experience distorted fears that they have harmed or could harm someone. Guilt includes a fear of being punished that is distinct from shame. Patients often suffer fear and/or shame about feeling the emotion of guilt.

The psychophysiology of the Guilt brain system is subtle, adaptive, and therefore difficult to observe. At the beginning of treatment, patients typically are trying to figure out the rules and expectations of therapy and of this specific therapist. That is such an adaptive social response that we do not notice how the Guilt brain system is operating to foster social bonding with the therapist. In similar ways, the Guilt brain system is operating to stay within the social contract of this culture and society. We can infer the functioning of the Guilt brain system by the adaptive social behavior of our patients. Our patients do not feel guilty when this brain system is functioning adaptively.

Shame and guilt are both social emotions, so there is often a visible overlap in their psychophysiology. These two emotions arise from distinct Secondaries, however, and modulate different innate motivations. The psychophysiology of guilt appears most distinctively in the form of impulses to take responsibility for our actions and make repairs. The psychophysiology of shame has an observable collapse, such as difficulty talking, whereas guilt is more animated and vocal, and shows evidence of urges to make amends.

You can Facilitate the energy and wisdom of the Guilt brain system with a variety of interventions. The Initial Directed Activation explicitly speaks to the Guilt brain system with the following phrases: "without expectations," "without judgment," "without agenda." You can also reflect the presence of Guilt: "Your ability to let go of expectations frees you to be true to yourself." You have the options of Differentiating it from other brain systems—"It is safe to care for yourself"—or bringing it into the therapeutic relationship: "Your wisdom is welcome with us."

Much of the treatment in the clinical case study of Paul (from Chapter 12) involves Facilitating the competencies of his Guilt brain system and correcting dysfunctional implicit guilt feelings. Paul is energized and assertive at the beginning of the session, which reveals that his Guilt brain system is not blocking his adaptive energy. Albert implicitly gives social permission and encourages Paul to keep asserting himself when he mimics Paul's clenched fists. When Paul declares he is in unfamiliar territory, he is referring to stepping over the discomfort of disregarding the rules and expectations of his social background. Instead, his Guilt brain system is repeatedly learning new guidelines that asserting himself is not only safe, but a valuable experience. Tilting his head back and forth could be psychophysiological evidence of an Integrating process as he updates previous social learning.

> **Albert:** What are you aware of?
>
> **Paul:** Anxiousness, seriousness, a strength [*makes fists*].
>
> **Albert:** It's great that you are present to a range: the anxiousness, seriousness, a strength [*mimics the fists*]. . . .
>
> **Paul** [*Smiles, chuckles*]: . . . I am valuable. I am in new unfamiliar territory [*tilting head side to side, smiles, chuckles*].
>
> **Albert:** It's great that you get that. You are in unfamiliar territory. What are you experiencing?
>
> **Paul:** On the way here I was thinking and I started talking positive to myself. I can do this. I can take care of myself and do what I can.
>
> **Albert:** Awesome.
>
> **Paul:** And it is really different to do that [*chuckles, smiles*].
>
> **Albert:** Wonderful.
>
> **Paul:** There is an anxiousness there too. This is really different.
>
> **Albert:** You are taking charge and not just reacting to the fear. Being proactive instead of reactive.
>
> **Paul** [*Smiles*]: I think I react a lot. That is my standard.
>
> **Albert:** That is what you learned. This a huge shift: to take charge, to be proactive, to prime yourself for success.
>
> **Paul** [*Makes fists*]: It is part of valuing and esteeming myself, and it feels weird. It is normal, but it does not feel normal.

ENHANCING BRAIN SYSTEMS

Pleasure

The Pleasure brain system is composed of neural circuits that increase the incidence of survival or life-enhancing behaviors such as eating, drinking, or sex (Panksepp & Biven, 2012; Grawe, 2007). These circuits also activate to prevent harmful or painful behaviors. This brain system plays a role when we act in ways that meet our emotional as well as physical needs. Some of these circuits release endogenous opioid neurotransmitters and others release dopamine. A number of regions at the secondary level of the brain contain these circuits, such as the preoptic area of the hypothalamus, nucleus accumbens, and ventral pallidum (Davidson, 2012). The name for this brain system comes from the usage of Panksepp, Grawe, Davidson, and others.

You can observe psychophysiological evidence of the Pleasure brain system when your patient has a smile or twinkle in their eye. You might see their facial expressions soften and the physical tensions in their body relax. There can be a wide range of conscious sensations when the Pleasure brain system is active. However, be sure to remember that most of the activations of the Secondaries are nonconscious, and the patient will not feel pleasure when the system is Facilitated. This system evolved to enhance adaptive actions and reduce painful behaviors, and the actual feeling of pleasure is just the cherry on top of the sundae. Many patients, especially depressed patients, will not be able to feel pleasure when their Pleasure brain system is active.

You can Activate and Facilitate the energy and wisdom of the Pleasure brain system with a variety of interventions. You can orient your patient to their physical experience by saying, "What are the sensations in your body that are telling you that you are experiencing happiness?" You can also make their psychophysiological pleasure conscious: "What is happening here that makes you smile?" Or try affirming the action of their Pleasure brain system: "What are you experiencing that tells you it feels good to be in charge right now?"

In the following clinical example (from Chapter 7), you can see how Claire's Pleasure brain system helps her sustain and increase her body experiences of feeling strong and happy. Beatriz intervened by Facilitating, Differentiating, and Training Claire's assertive strength, which she perceived as sensations in her heart and lungs. She was able to become conscious of the pleasure of feeling happy. Claire's psychophysiological phenomena (in italics) provide evidence of her Assertive, Pleasure, Play, and Sensory brain systems:

> **Claire:** I feel strong [*nods, surprised, stronger voice*].
>
> **Beatriz:** Oh, tell me about strong! How are you experiencing strong?
>
> **Claire [*Smiles, brightens up*]:** I feel a little happy to hear that. I feel a little strong.
>
> **Beatriz:** Those are beautiful words [*animated gestures*]. What are the sensations in your body that are telling you that you are experiencing strong or happy?
>
> **Claire:** My pulse is accelerating a little bit [*hand over heart*]. Like a little bit of push up. I am feeling a little happy [*smiles, deep breath, nods*].

Motivation

The Motivation brain system includes neural circuits that provide drive, focus, and determination to meet our needs and pursue our goals. The energy from this system helps us persevere when we meet obstacles or other difficulties. This energy helps us climb over (override) our fears, shame, or other inhibitions. This system evolved to sustain and enhance our adaptive learning to more effectively approach our wants and needs. The name for this system comes from the neurobiological research of Davidson, Grawe, Schwartz, and Panksepp.

You can observe the psychophysiological evidence of the Motivation brain system when your patients' bodies lean forward. You can hear it when they speak with more depth in their voices and when they are fully engaged in the process with you. Sometimes you can see them set their jaws when this brain system is activated. Other times they will make a fist for emphasis without realizing it.

Facilitation of the Motivation brain system is especially important in psychotherapy. The work of psychotherapy can be challenging when we meet high levels of anxiety or resistance. This discomfort is often the source of the patient's ambivalence about becoming more open or vulnerable to themselves. Addressing the patient's Motivation brain system explicitly can shift their internal equilibrium to take the risk of moving forward in therapy. This system releases dopamine from the nucleus accumbens and substantia nigra, which has been shown to play a role in long-term learning and neuroplasticity. Indeed, some of the research has shown structural changes in the BrainMind (Schwartz & Begley, 2002; Davidson, 2012).

You can Facilitate the energy and wisdom of the Motivation brain system with a variety of interventions:

- Invite it by name: "Do you have motivation to pursue this together?"
- Reflect its presence: "Your drive is important."
- Differentiate it from other brain systems: "It is safe to feel your drive."
- Bring it into the therapeutic relationship: "Your powerful drive is welcome with us."
- Celebrate the presence of motivation: "Awesome, wonderful."

In the following clinical example from Chapter 12, Paul is beginning to discover and experience the capabilities of his Motivation brain system. The words he expresses to affirm himself and his competence are only part of the picture. His manner of speaking, his emphasis on his capability—"I can do this"—and his psychophysiological phenomena all provide empirical evidence of his Motivation brain system activity.

> **Paul:** On the way here I was thinking, and I started talking positive to myself. I can do this. I can take care of myself and do what I can.
> **Albert:** Awesome.
> **Paul:** And it is really different to do that [*chuckles, smiles*].
> **Albert:** Wonderful.
> **Paul:** There is an anxiousness there too. This is really different.

Importance/Salience

The Importance/Salience or external reward brain system includes the neural circuits that estimate and weigh how much effort an action will require compared with the benefit that will be obtained. Both the Importance and Value brain systems involve a reward process. The key difference is that Importance entails an external relational or social reward, whereas Value is an internal reward circuit. The word *salience* refers to recognition of something as prominent or conspicuous, that is, standing out from the background. Panksepp (2012) notes how experiences of external reward teach us incentive salience. Grawe (2007) concludes that everything that a person should learn in therapy must have a high motivational salience. The learning of context of what is important or relevant resides in the hippocampus, which plays the central role in the Importance brain system, with assistance from the ventral striatum. The hippocampus contains novelty circuits and will release dopamine when it determines that the sensations are novel. The ventral striatum becomes active when people anticipate receiving something externally rewarding (Davidson, 2012).

The Importance brain system evolved to help mammals learn new things, grow, and find novel resources. Social animals need to learn what is important to the clan from each other. Saliency detection is considered to be a key attentional mechanism that facilitates learning and survival by enabling organisms to focus their limited perceptual and cognitive resources on the most pertinent sensory data. The Importance brain system responds to adaptive behaviors by providing positive feedback to sustain actions that are important to our well-being.

You can observe the psychophysiological evidence of the Importance brain system when your patients are able to feel the rewarding experience of shared attention. Their eye contact improves as they are able to feel the importance of the caring and connection that the therapeutic relationship offers them. They begin to accept that they are unconditionally important and worthy to you and to others. The Importance brain system helps patients stay present to themselves and to you when they also feel fear or shame about exposing themselves. Their sense of importance keeps their eyes on the prize.

Your interventions can Facilitate the energy and wisdom of the Importance brain system. You can call out your patient's importance by saying, "You are worthy. You are enough just as you are." Or you can orient your patient to their physical experience with questions such as, "What sensations tell you that you are experiencing unconditional caring?" And you can make their psychophysiological phenomena conscious: "What are you experiencing that brings this soft intimate eye gaze?"

In the following clinical example (from Chapter 5), you can see how Lucy's Importance brain system helps her sustain and increase her body's experiences of being worthy and lovable. Beatriz is facilitating the Importance brain system when she states, "You are being the most important person for us right now." Her tone of voice and body language communicate the patient's importance to the therapist. She also brings in the sensory experiences of importance and care to further the process of Differentiating and Training the Importance brain system.

> **Beatriz:** We are here to pay close, caring attention to you. . . . You are worthy of our complete attention. . . . We are "worthing" you. <u>You are being</u> the most important person for us right now. How is that for you?
>
> **Lucy:** That feels good [*hands on chest and smiles*] and it is not something I've grown up with. I did not get that kind of attention from my mother, you know. So it feels new. . . . It is weird. I have a feeling right now. . . . You have a very motherly tone, and I feel a little grief [*starts crying softly*] almost like an infant. You know, like complete attention on the baby, and the baby just being [*hands on her torso*], just being . . .and the mother giving the attention . . . [*cries some more*] not judging.
>
> **Beatriz:** And here you are <u>being</u> enough. Nothing to do. Nothing to change. You are just being valuable and worthy. You just being is enough. . . . [*prolonged silent, intimate eye gaze*].
>
> **Lucy:** I feel some internal caring and compassion. I am worthy [*both hands on chest, and soft eyes*].
>
> **Beatriz:** . . .What sensations tell you you are experiencing internal caring?
>
> **Lucy:** It is like an internal soft warm blanket on my chest. This is new; I never felt that before! [*Crying softly.*]
>
> **Beatriz:** It is <u>happening</u> that you are <u>being</u> lovable.
>
> **Lucy:** That is another shift for me. I never felt lovable. A lovable person has qualities that I don't have.

Value

The Value or Internal Reward brain system consists of neural circuits that provide us with internal positive feedback even when there is no obvious benefit or pleasure in our actions. These circuits innately help us come to know our own unique desires and motivations. These circuits also play roles in learning about ourselves, our capabilities and competencies. These unconditional internal rewards enable us to be confident and competent without judgment or expectations from others. These circuits play a role in establishing and meeting our need for self-esteem (Grawe, 2007).

Damasio, Grawe, Davidson, and Panksepp have all written about the Value neural circuits from their own perspectives. Damasio (2012) points out how "biological value" has the status of a principle in the evolution of many of the brain systems. The nucleus basalis and its release of acetylcholine probably plays a central role in the Value brain system. The neurons of the striatum that release the neurotransmitter gamma-aminobutyric acid (GABA) are components of this internal reward system as well.

Nature evolved this enhancing brain system to give us the internal positive feedback to learn what is ultimately valuable for us to survive and thrive in our lives. Activations of the Value circuits will inhibit other constraining circuits that would otherwise interrupt our goal-oriented behaviors and emotions. This system evolved to help us be consistent with our intrinsic motivations such as persistence, discipline, selective attention, and determination, which enable us to reach our goals, especially when gratification is delayed.

We believe that when a young child experiences their unconditional value and importance, they will develop a strong sense of their own self-worth. It seems likely that the Value and Importance brain systems are instrumental in developing a person's intrinsic worth. Feeling worthy is a birthright for everyone. However, worth needs to be developed during the first several years of life. You can test a patient's sense of worth when you assert, "You are unconditionally important here with us." When Albert said that to one of his patients a while back, she suddenly had a novel experience, saying, "I did not realize I feel loathing towards myself until this moment."

You can observe psychophysiological evidence of the Value brain system when your patient is able to feel confident, capable, and competent. It is hard to describe these phenomena, since they are nonconscious and subtle. The patient experiences an expansion of the chest, and their body language is also more expansive. You can sense that they feel full inside themselves. They may not be aware of the psychophysiological phenomena that accompany trusting themselves and putting aside any expectations of the therapist or themselves. Your patients may verbalize that they are valuing themselves, feeling worthy, capable, and competent. They may also notice feelings of accomplishment or self-satisfaction.

You can intervene by Facilitating and Differentiating the energy and wisdom of the Value brain system. You may call out your patient's innate value by saying, "You are worthy. You are enough just as you are." Or you may orient your patient to their physical experience: "What sensations tell you that you are experiencing feeling capable?" And you may make their psychophysiological phenomena conscious: "What are you experiencing when you say, 'I am valuable'?"

In the following clinical example (from Chapter 9), you can see how John's Value brain system helps him sustain and increase his body's experiences of esteeming himself. Albert is Facilitating the Value brain system when he Differentiates John's present experience of valuing himself from his usual self-attack by telling him, " . . . that is a great counterbalance to this internal self-attack."

> **Albert:** Good. What is it like to feel impressed [*hands over torso*], to be proud of yourself?
>
> **John:** It feels really good, and it feels like I have won something [*face brightens*]. Like I have been praised wholeheartedly.
>
> **Albert:** By whom?
>
> **John:** By myself [*surprised*].
>
> **Albert:** By yourself—that is a great counterbalance to this internal self-attack. It feels good to get it out in the open. . . .
>
> **John:** I can feel the attack does not stop. Even after I felt good there, feel the praise, all of a sudden I start to feel physically vulnerable. It is like I let off my guard for even a minute and then I actually feel physical discomfort right now [*face is pained, body tense*].

"IN SUSTAINED DISSONANCE WE CAN DISCOVER COMPLEX COHERENCE"

On the surface, a patient's statements, emotions, and psychophysiology may seem to present a tangle of conflicts and contradictory behavior. Such incongruence is a normal aspect of the processing of life experiences by the Secondaries, where consistency, conflict, contradiction, and congruence all get worked out. We all struggle with the consequences of these incomprehensible emotional phenomena, not only in our own lives, but in those of our family members, partners, colleagues, and patients.

These conflicts, compromises, and inconsistencies result from the fact that there are so many distinct emotional brain systems that seem to have their own motivations (goals), priorities, and ways of pursuing life. There are so many variables. Each brain system has its own distinct life experience that is different from those of the other brain systems. They are all dynamic, meaning that they are constantly changing and influencing each other. Fortunately, these conflicts are mostly nonconscious. We are only aware of how our BrainMind has worked out the patterns (the algorithms, if you will) that define our baseline emotions, behavioral patterns, personalities, and symptoms. The analogy that comes to mind is the complexity of 535 members of the U.S. Congress and 13,000 lobbyists trying to achieve their particular agendas.

Congruence is the emotional and psychophysiological state in which real experiences and motivational goals are in alignment and in sync. Incongruence is when real experience and motivational goals are in conflict. Many of the symptoms and psychological problems of our patients are a result of incongruence between motivational approaches of the primary-level brain systems and the avoidances and inhibitions of Shame or Fear.

Consistency is to the compatibility of simultaneously transpiring neural and mental processes. Consistency also refers to the internal relations among intrapsychic processes and states. Consistency is a basic principle of internal regulation that supersedes all specific needs (Grawe, 2007). Inconsistency is a state in which the activations of different emotional brain systems are not compatible with each other.

Conflict in this context refers to situations when the drives of one system oppose, contradict, or are at odds with another system. For example in Chapter 7, Penny's Fear system shuts down her Play system. When something does not make sense to us, it is incomprehensible. When the patient's responses to your interventions do not make sense, it is a heads-up call to look for underlying inconsistencies or nonconscious incongruence.

When we help our patients reduce conflict and achieve moments of congruence and consistency, their BrainMinds can operate in a state of neural synchrony, meaning the harmonious firing of multiple brain systems. Daniel Siegel calls this state coherence, which is the outcome we refer to as the Complex Integration of Multiple Brain Systems.

When you examine how the four enhancing and four inhibiting/gatekeeping brain systems interact with the amygdala, hippocampus, hypothalamus, thalamus, and cerebellum, you can begin to make sense of self-defeating, maladaptive, and even self-destructive emotions and behaviors. Please remember that you do not have to figure out or make sense of those emotions or behaviors to work with them therapeutically. However, we and our trainees have found that having a deeper understanding of the workings at this level of the BrainMind enables us to be more effective as therapists. These understandings can help you meet your own needs for coherence, congruence, and consistency. Meeting the need for coherence will help you tolerate the dissonance, incoherence, frustration, "craziness," and disappointment that is often experienced because of implicit emotional learning that is encoded at this level of the BrainMind. This knowledge will help you Trust the Process.

Treatment at the secondary level of the BrainMind is more challenging than at the primary or tertiary levels. This is partly due to the fact that the top-down energy and information from the conscious level and the bottom-up energy and information from the body and the Primaries meet here in the middle. At the same time, decades of stored implicit emotional learning are impacting and sometimes interfering with the processing of all that energy and information. Most problematic and maladaptive emotional patterns are nonconsciously maintained at this level. They feel like emotional ruts to the patient and therapist alike. "What's a person to do?"

Observing the phenomena that are transpiring in your patient's BrainMind through the metaphoric prism of the Secondaries (Figure 13.1) can give you innumerable choices of how to customize your therapy to this patient's secondary-level brain systems at this moment. One approach to these challenges is to Go the Other Way. For example, in Chapter 12, at the beginning of the case-study session, Paul was aware of feeling "anxiousness, seriousness, a strength [*makes fists*]." Paul was experiencing a mix of fear, assertiveness, and perhaps importance. Albert responded by reinforcing each of those associated brain systems in the Transpiring Present Moment. Then Albert Facilitated Paul's mixed experience by Activating the Importance and Value brain systems and inviting Paul to embody those Activations, "to feel the sense of importance. This is valuable, and you are important." In a few minutes, Paul felt the dissonant emotions of fear (anxiety), grief ("I have missed out"), and guilt (betrayal).

When our patients experience incongruence, they will naturally avoid novel, unfamiliar emotions to stay within their comfort zone and reduce their distress. There is no conscious choice in those reactions. In the example above, Paul was able to sustain the incongruence of his pain, fear of exposing himself, and Importance of connecting with his self-love capability. "In my mind, why would you care? Why would anyone care? It is so automatic in me. This shaming of myself and hiding, it is just in me. All of this blaming or accusing is in me. It is automatic." The avoidance of incongruent energy or information is inherent in our BrainMinds. For a deeper understanding of these phenomena, we invite you to explore the research into cognitive dissonance theory (Grawe, 2007). Paul was initially experiencing unfamiliarity with his positive self-appraisal, which then became incongruence with the Facilitation of his positive emotions. The key here was to Trust the Process. Paul was able to stay in the transpiring experience of "so scary, to open up and flourish" (*opens arms and hands and then pained expression, tears, and grimaces*). He was able to release some of his shame and guilt with his observation of those emotions: "Part of me is very critical of doing this."

Writing and teaching about the Secondaries has been challenging. So much information and energy is contained in these systems that can appear inconsistent, incongruent, and counterintuitive. The Fear, Guilt, and Shame reactions that our patients have are often quite daunting. It is easy to avoid the intimacy of the moment that is stirring up those reactions. It takes time to get to know and become comfortable with the Secondaries. They can help you understand your patients' reactions with more compassion and understanding. At the same time, they can improve your own balance and ability to respond creatively when your patients push your buttons.

CHAPTER 14

Psychophysiological Perspective and Physiopsychotherapy

What do you remember about the man with the brogue from Chapter 1? What we and other participants at the training remember is that the next day, it appeared as though he'd had a facelift. We could all see the changes, no matter what explanations might be offered. The changes in his facial muscles are hard to appreciate without seeing them for yourself. They reflected psychophysiological changes in the nonconscious brain systems as a result of the demonstration therapy session. So far in this book, we have referred often to the value of psychophysiological phenomena in CIMBS therapy, and we have provided numerous examples from our patients' sessions. In this chapter we explore in depth the origin and utility of psychophysiological phenomena and provide additional guidelines on how to use them in therapy.

WHAT ARE PSYCHOPHYSIOLOGICAL PHENOMENA?

Psychophysiological phenomena are the observable physical movements, changes, and behaviors that arise from the activations of nonconscious emotional brain systems. Common examples are facial and mouth movements, tone of voice, eye contact, visible tears, and body posture. Some psychophysiological phenomena, such as pulse rate, skin tone, and depth of breathing, are quite subtle. These phenomena are present in all humans and other mammals.

Psychophysiological phenomena are an intimate form of communication over which we have limited control. They arise from the brainstem and are mostly out of our awareness. We intuitively read psychophysiological information in each other all the time. The capacity to read others' emotions is built in and develops from birth on. Attuning to others' psychophysiology and emotions enables us to develop attachment relationships, coregulate our emotions with others, and enhance our own emotional balance.

Psychophysiological phenomena are present throughout the body and the BrainMind. As a consequence of the body-brain bond (Chapter 12; Damasio, 2012), it is hard to distinguish the source of the phenomena we are feeling or observing. I cannot know whether the warmth in my heart originates there and is processed by my Care brain system, or whether my Care brain system changes the energy in my heart, giving me the sensations of warmth. Important peripheral nerves, such as the cranial nerves, play significant roles in creating the psychophysiological phenomena we observe. For example, the vagus nerve is primarily an afferent nerve, meaning that most of its fibers receive information from the body. It also has efferent fibers that impact our voice, facial movements, hearing, breathing, and heart rate (Porges, 2011).

Psychophysiological phenomena can be important to us as therapists because they originate in the primary- and secondary-level brain systems and the peripheral nervous system. Most of what is happening emotionally in our patients is nonconscious; therefore these phenomena help us to discover what is transpiring under the surface. When you pay attention to psychophysiological phenomena in therapy, you will acquire information and have access to energy that would otherwise be unavailable. You can come to trust the validity of these nonconscious phenomena without needing confirmation from your patients. In fact, often they are not aware of these phenomena, even when you point them out. Psychophysiological phenomena are hardwired into our nervous systems, and they evolved to enhance survival, to help us thrive, and to communicate nonverbally with others in our family or group. Most of these phenomena do not need to be learned, although individual nonconscious developmental learning can affect their responses to life circumstances.

Different brain systems reveal themselves with specific psychophysiological phenomena, which can enhance the precision of your therapy. Attention to these phenomena can help you discover immediate evidence of your patient's responses to therapeutic interventions. Therapy can therefore become more experiential and empirical at the same time. It takes time and practice to develop your neural circuits, or search patterns, to detect and observe these phenomena.

Brainstem structures called the periaqueductal gray matter, midbrain, pons, and medulla oblongata all play significant roles in psychophysiological phenomena, such as facial expressions, tears, coughing, and posture. All the nerves connecting the brain with the rest of the body pass through the brainstem, and as such it acts as a central switchboard. Many psychophysiological phenomena reflect activations of the sympathetic and parasympathetic parts of the autonomic nervous system.

PSYCHOPHYSIOLOGICAL PERSPECTIVE

The psychophysiological perspective refers to a consciously chosen focus of attention on nonverbal and nonconscious physical phenomena that give the therapist valuable information about the inner workings of a patient's nervous system. Each of us is constantly reading the emotional states of people in our environment nonverbally and nonconsciously to determine whether they are safe. Porges calls this process *neuroception*. This psychophysiological dance is always happening nonconsciously in all of our interactions.

When you first greet a patient in the waiting room, you are beginning to read your patient's psychophysiology. You can notice the initial eye contact, the facial expressions, the expressions in the eyes, the tone of voice, the body posture, and the gait as the patient walks into your office. You have already gained a lot of information even before they sit down or speak. One could say that you are utilizing a psychophysiological perspective when you are reading the patient's psychophysiology from the initial contact.

The patient is also reading your psychophysiology from the beginning of each session. This dance of neuroception is especially important in the Therapeutic Attachment Relationship because of its narrow focus and relative intimacy. The patient intuitively (but mostly nonconsciously) notices whether you make eye contact, hold their gaze, adjust to their anxiety, and greet them with a smile or a blank face. They attempt to read whether you are present, distracted, anxious, tense, or irritated. They are trying to figure out whether you are safe, available, interested, curious, caring, or afraid.

In addition, the Initial Directed Activation focuses your patient's careful attention on themselves. Their attention is directed at their body's sensations in the present moment to utilize that information to guide the session right now. You can use your psychophysiological perspective to notice how their eye contact, posture, facial expressions, or breathing changes as you Activate different brain systems during this intervention. The prism metaphor mentioned previously (Chapter 6) is helpful here as well. When you look through a prism, you would be able to see the activations of several different brain systems underneath the same psychophysiological phenomena. A rapid heartbeat could arise because of the Fear or the Assertive brain systems, or both at the same time. Those lenses could help you discern distinctions between the peripheral, primary level, or secondary level of the nervous system.

It is important to notice these psychophysiological phenomena and discern what they represent. Then you can use that information to guide your therapeutic process based on nonverbal and nonconscious evidence. The skills of reading your patients' psychophysiological cues and understanding what they are telling you will fine-tune your interventions. That recognition, connected with your intellectual understanding, will lead you to a robust ability to respond intuitively and effectively to your patients' nonconscious signals and therapeutic needs. Peter Levine (2017) has pointed out how important it is for the therapist to take notice of the patient's body experience before initiating the therapeutic process. He further emphasizes the importance of helping the patient to become increasingly aware of their internal, self-aware, sensations. Psychophysiological phenomena can also guide you in adjusting the level of activation in the patient and in optimizing the patient's engagement in the therapeutic process.

Case-study examples in previous chapters illustrate how we utilize the psychophysiological perspective to make precise observations about the inner workings of nonconscious brain systems and so fine-tune the treatment and direct our next intervention. For example, in Chapter 2 we see Ann sit up straighter and speak more firmly as she asserts, "Let's override it!" when she is struggling with her resistance. Those are significant psychophysiological shifts, telling us that her Authority and Assertive brain systems are being activated. She is in a state of novelty and discovery. Albert utilizes this psychophysiological perspective to alert him to the shift in Ann's BrainMind from avoidance to approach. Her equilibrium has shifted from the Fear to the Assertive brain system, and Albert affirms with enthusiasm that they are overriding her shame and discomfort. His support helps her stay in the transpiring experience of receiving their care and honors her desire to care for herself and her daughter.

That successful intervention releases further psychophysiological phenomena of fear and nausea. Albert reinforces that experience and sustains it to enable Ann's BrainMind to integrate all of this new learning. It is vital for our patients that we notice and hold onto these new adaptive experiences in order to change the brain.

In Chapter 4, Beatriz is helping Penny focus on her psychophysiology as she invites her self-awareness: "What are the sensations that you are aware of?" Penny's Fear brain system is so hyperactive that she cannot even respond to the invitation. Beatriz uses her psychophysiological perspective to further explore Penny's psychophysiology by inquiring about her breathing. Gradually Penny is able to become aware of her clammy hands and dry mouth. Beatriz's fine-tuned focus on Penny's psychophysiology enables her to help Penny activate her Awareness and Attention brain systems, which reduces the activation of her Fear brain system. Using this psychophysiological perspective helped Beatriz change patient treatment factors in the first several minutes of the first session.

Learning a Psychophysiological Perspective

Shifting to a psychophysiological perspective and orientation requires some effort and intention. Normal everyday human interactions tend to center around words, ideas, thoughts, and conversations. We tend to be most aware of cognitions, but the psychophysiological perspective invites us to observe what is happening at the bottom of the iceberg. It takes a bit of practice to put aside these patterns in our conscious mind to add another perspective. We suggest that you imagine that you are putting on 4-D magnifying glasses in order to readily see small yet meaningful phenomena that are transpiring at this present moment. It takes time to get used to seeing what is happening under the surface physiologically. We have found three keys to learning a psychophysiological perspective in our therapy: slow down, move your body with your interventions, and carefully watch and listen to your patient's physical responses.

Slowing down allows the psychophysiological phenomena to unfold. These phenomena are transpiring in the present moment. They are arising from the body and the peripheral nervous system. Even though they utilize innate neural circuits, the present experience is being put together uniquely moment by moment. If you move too fast, there will not be enough time or space for the unique phenomena to develop sufficiently to become visible. Cognitions and verbal responses occur more rapidly and can easily capture the attention of the patient and therapist, thus missing the information and energy coming from the deeper structures in the BrainMind. Usually there are many different simultaneous psychophysiological phenomena, so give yourself a little time to observe what you can.

We introduced the value and importance of embodying your interventions in Chapter 6, in the Initial Directed Activation. Your physical movements with your interventions will help you become more involved in the process and communicate that to your patient. Our body language helps us own the intervention. For example, when you put your hands on your chest, you are communicating nonverbally your intention for your patient to connect with their own internal bodily experiences. Their body and mirror neurons will naturally activate in response to those interventions. You will be modeling and welcoming your patient's own psychophysiological activations that will arise in the intimacy of the therapeutic process. Our research has convinced us that the BrainMind cannot help but respond, if only on a nonconscious and invisible level. Our patients and those of our colleagues have confirmed the therapeutic benefits when the therapist embodies the interventions. You can come to trust these adaptive responses over time.

A psychophysiological perspective provides you with multiple sources of energy and information on multiple levels of the nervous system. You can be carefully watching the eyes, mouth, hands, feet, chest, shoulders, and neck all at the same time. Even with lots of practice, you cannot see it all. You will be carefully watching for microscopic shifts. You can also be carefully listening for changes in the tone, volume, cadence, and prosody of your patient's voice. These observations are sources of information about nonconscious brain systems, which can help you fine-tune your therapeutic process. Equally important, these psychophysiological phenomena can alert you to sources of energy that your patient can harness to do the work of therapy.

You will be better attuned to your patient's psychophysiological phenomena when you are also aware of and attentive to your own physiology. The Initial Directed Activation seeks to bring both you and your patient into a couple of minutes of deepening presence and self-awareness. It is in those moments that you can let go of your distractions or worries and come to notice such phenomena as the tension in your chest or hands. You can take a couple of abdominal breaths to release those muscles and settle into the safeness of this moment and connection.

Empirical Evidence

So much depends on gathering good information about what is happening in the psychotherapeutic process that it is important that we gather the most accurate evidence available to us at any given moment. Psychophysiological phenomena and a psychophysiological perspective can give you empirical evidence of what is actually transpiring in your patient's nonconscious brain systems at any given moment. *Empirical evidence* is facts or information that are based on observations and present-moment experience rather than theory, speculation, or logic. This evidence can be readily verified and validated by other observers. Neurobiological phenomena give rise to the psychophysiological evidence we have been describing. Psychophysiological phenomena can give you reliable empirical evidence, in contrast with the limitations of verbal reports, explanations, or history.

Psychophysiological phenomena provide empirical evidence of the accessible primary-level brain systems ready to be harnessed. For example, in Chapter 4, Beatriz was able to help Penny harness the energy of her Play brain system when she observed Penny smiling, chuckling, and bouncing in her chair. Penny said, "Because there is a little bit of this that is kind of . . . fun. And . . . playful!" For your reference, we summarize some of the most readily observable empirical psychophysiological phenomena and their interpretations in Table 14.1.

Psychophysiological phenomena can provide you and your patient empirical evidence of emotional learning from the past. For example, in Chapter 12, Albert was working with Paul to help him override self-destructive emotional learning from his early life. Paul started his session describing thinking and talking positively to himself. Albert was affirming the value and importance of Paul treating himself with care and esteem. As Paul asserted his innate value out loud, he started to experience a range of psychophysiological phenomena and shifts. Paul made fists, started to cry, moved his torso, shook his head, and had a facial expression of anguish. Paul was able to articulate his experience: "I feel a pain on two sides, and it hurts. I feel like I have missed out on this self-love, and really nice to connect with it. It is frightening to share it with you right now."

Such psychophysiological shifts are unique empirical learning opportunities. There is a fluidity to be captured. There is both energy to be harnessed and flexibility to be enhanced and Integrated. Examples of psychophysiological shifts are changes in the volume of the patient's voice, amount of eye contact, depth of respiration, level of emotional engagement, pupil dilation, skin color, fluidity

TABLE 14.1. OBSERVABLE PSYCHOPHYSIOLOGICAL MANIFESTATIONS

Physical Attribute	Examples	Discussion
Eyes	Eye gaze, blink rate, tears, pupil size, back-and-forth movements (nystagmus), shiny eyes, eyes wide, eyes shut. The muscles around the eyes reveal a true, Duchenne smile.	Soft, constant eye gaze could be evidence of Connection brain system activity. A rapid eye blink occurs with activation of the Fear brain system. Tears come from a broad spectrum of emotions such as grief, anger, compassion, pride, care (love), feeling acknowledged, pain, or joy.
	Shiny eyes (Chapter 5).	These occur when the therapist is experiencing simultaneous activations of several brain systems such as Care, Connection, Safe, Pleasure, Importance, Value, and Play (delight). These activations reveal themselves with psychophysiological phenomena that the patient sees in the therapist's eyes. The shiny quality results from increased light reflection in the therapist's eyes. The increased reflection comes from increased opening of the eyelids, pupils in mid position, and typically some increase in tear production (with sufficient parasympathetic activation). The patient's experience of the therapist's Care and shiny eyes can range from pleasure to terror.
Voice	Volume, pitch, speed of speech, inflection, hesitation, spontaneity.	A soft voice could be evidence of activation of the Fear or Shame brain systems. A deep pitch could be evidence of the Assertive and/or Authority brain systems. All words and sentences are usually uttered with a background emotional inflection. The inflection is an instance of prosody, the musical, tonal accompaniment to the speech sounds that constitute words. Prosody can express not just background emotion, but specific emotions as well (Damasio, 1999).

Breathing, chest, and torso	Upper chest breathing, abdominal breathing, frozen, still, hyperventilation, breath holding, rate, sighing, yawning.	Upper chest breathing is shallow and indicates activation of the Fear brain system. In contrast, abdominal breathing is deep and suggests activation of the Safe brain system. Sighing is sometimes a release of tension, or a reflex that opens up the alveoli at the base of the lungs. Some patients yawn in therapy when they are actively working their nervous system outside of their comfort zone.
Facial expression	Animation, facial movements, twitching, impassive, flat, furrowed brow, narrowed eyebrows; mouth: smile, frown, grimace, sneer, gagging, still, dry, salivating; nose: flared nostrils, sniffing, runny (from tears).	A smile could be evidence of the Pleasure or Play brain systems. A sneer could be Shame or disgust. A flat face suggests activation of the Fear or Grief brain systems.
Posture	Head and neck: holding the head up, erect, slumped, collapsed, tight muscles, leaning forward or backward, head tilted to left (curious) or right (skeptical); shoulders: back, in, collapsed.	The patient sits slumped in his chair, with his head held down, which could indicate the patient's Shame and/or Grief brain systems are hyperactive and interfering with the patient being present to himself and the therapist. After several minutes in the session, a different patient might shift her posture and sit up and forward, which could indicate the Assertive and Authority brain systems are becoming more active.
Extremities	Arms: crossed over chest, held tight over torso, rigid, relaxed, embracing self, or widely open; legs: fidgeting, rigid, crossed, open; hands: wringing, fidgeting, fists, limp, tight, sweaty, cold, clammy; feet: firmly on the floor, wide versus narrow stance, fidgeting, cold; coordination: graceful or awkward gait, smooth or jagged movements.	The patient's legs are jiggling constantly to release anxiety and tension. The patient slowly makes fists as she feels more assertive and experiences more activation in her Assertive brain system.

of body movement, tone or prosody of voice, or activation of facial muscles. Paul's vignette is an example of utilizing psychophysiological shifts to enhance his learning of self-love and to reduce the constraints of grief, pain, and shame.

You can conduct a scientific therapeutic process using psychophysiological evidence. First, you make an initial assessment of the baseline phenomena. The evidence we first look for is the level of anxiety and the quality of relatedness demonstrated by the patient. We typically test the patient's level of anxiety with the directed activation, "We are here to pay careful attention to you." The patient's psychophysiological responses to that intervention can suggest a hypothesis. The case discussed below in a training session gives an example of how to conduct such an assessment.

Teaching a Psychophysiological Perspective

One simple example of conducting a scientific therapeutic process comes from a training course during which we reviewed a brief live-therapy demonstration. Albert acted as the therapist, working with one of the participants as the patient. The following brief transcript of the discussion during the training course will give you the feeling of being there too, as he explains his thinking behind an intervention.

> **Albert:** The intervention was a simple statement such as, "We're here to play close attention to you." That is a very powerful intervention. I was watching his physiology, and there was a physiological response when I said that. There was a little bit of a nod, a little bit of a hesitation; they were both going on. So he didn't say anything and I wasn't asking him anything. The intervention initiates the process, and I was watching his mixed psychophysiological responses to that intervention. I was sending energy to him, telling him explicitly that we're here to do this together and watching his physiological response.
>
> We can observe, "How does his Connection brain system take that? How does his Care brain system respond? To what extent does he feel safe?" I can read that physiologically, because I know they are important. It's a very focused intervention process to bring him into the present moment—"We're here to pay close and careful attention to you"—and see what is unfolding, *happening*.
>
> **Participants:** What did you see changing in his physiology?

Albert: I saw facial expressions primarily. Also sighing, a little bit of skin color shifting, tone of voice shift, little things that he might not be aware of. They're not random, and they were coming in the context of something that was unfolding in our connection, in the work we were doing together. I wanted to help ground him in that experience by remaining silent for a bit, so that he could stay present and have an experiential learning.

Remember that our goal is emotional learning, and that is primarily nonverbal and nonconscious. The participant was really building a widening awareness, and he was able to feel his own authority, when he emphatically declared, "Yes! I want our attention." To feel it—not just think it, but feel it. Then he could mindfully observe, "Oh, it went away," or "Oh, it's back," in order to really have that shift internally, to really facilitate his Attention and Awareness brain systems.

When we demonstrate the concepts of psychophysiological phenomena during our training courses, we go very slowly. The participants need to develop their own felt sense of these phenomena in order to utilize this energy and information. We will typically show two or three minutes of a recorded session to help the participants focus on the small physical details. Sometime it is helpful to turn off the dialogue. Often we will go back and look at the same minute again to help them discover phenomena that they were not able to discern the first time through. Actually, every time you look with a different focus, you can see something more. For example, try focusing just on the mouth, or the eyes, or the hands.

The following is a partial transcript from the fourth session with a man we will call David, who suffered with depression for more than 10 years. Antidepressants had helped a little, and yet he was still depressed. The transcript starts from the very first minute of the session. The words in italics describe his psychophysiological phenomena and shifts as well as nonverbal interventions such as silence or pauses.

Albert: So let's settle inside ourselves and focus on our breathing for a few moments. . . . Close your eyes if you are comfortable with that. And breathe in the stillness. . . . Breathe in the quiet. . . . If there are any distractions, put them aside [*pushes hands and arms off to the side*].

David [*Shifts in chair.*]

Albert: And become more present to ourselves [*places hands on chest*]. More present to our bodies. . . . More present to this moment. . . .

David [*Shifts in chair, then opens eyes and makes partial eye contact.*]

Albert: We are here to pay close and careful attention to you. . . .

David [*Nods, better eye contact, couple of deep breaths.*]

Albert: Do *you* want to pay attention to yourself? [*Reaches hands out to David.*]

David [***Head nods, body nods, voice modest***]: Yes.

Albert: Do *you* want us to pay attention to you? [*Reaches hands out to David.*]

David [***Head nods, body nods***]: Yes [*clears throat, nods*].

Albert: Is that important to *you*?

David: Yes [*nods, voice stronger*].

The following is the discussion with a group of therapists who were being exposed to this focus on psychophysiology for the first time, and were shown a video of just these first three minutes of this therapy session.

Albert: What are you noticing?

Participant: Care.

Albert: Care. How are you picking up on that?

Participant: He just seems like he's taking the time to be in touch with himself and be gentle with himself actually.

Albert: Great, yes! Great that you pick it up, because it's very important. You don't know about this guy, but he's very hard with himself. So to have that *care* present at this moment is very encouraging. That's part of why initially it was hard for him to pay attention to himself, because he doesn't like himself. What else are you picking up?

Participant: He seems like he feels safe. Like he's settled into what I sense are the mindful rituals at the start. When you're speaking to him, it looks like he felt increasingly safe, like, "Here we go. I know what's gonna happen."

Albert: Yeah! And you're right, he is feeling increasingly safe. What are you picking up on that's telling you he's *increasingly* safe? It's not just a static safe, it's increasingly safe.

Participant: I saw him kind of wiggle down into his body. He got more solid.

Albert: Exactly. And picking up on that psychophysiology is really important. So, there's care and increasing safeness, which is really valuable—
we've got those two primary systems online. They're being processed
smoothly and that's revealing to us that things are evolving and things are
moving, so we're in a good place to keep working.

Beatriz: And it is <u>happening</u>. He's <u>feeling</u> safeness right now.

Participant: Seeking. There's a lot of direct attention . . . going towards, his
body is leaning forward. . . .

Albert: Seeking, great! There's definitely that, too. So there's good energy
to work with.

Beatriz: What did you notice when he said, "Yes?"

Participant: Assertiveness. A quality of . . . without knowing the backstory
here, but you can feel in his response that it took some process to get to
that "yes."

Albert: Yeah, right. So, what psychophysiological constraints are you picking up?

Participant: Tension in his body.

Albert: Tension in his body, yes.

Participant: I actually had a question about the "yes." I'm curious about
my own responses, you know. It felt really quick, and so for me, I wasn't
sure if that was full-body seeking. There's definitely seeking, but I almost
wondered about that there's a seeking but simultaneously constraints.

Albert: You're right, they're definitely both there, and that's important that
you can pick that up. It's a mixed experience, which is fine, but the issue
then becomes, "Is the constraint stopping him? Or stopping us?" Or is
it just part of the natural process that we're gonna keep working with?
And so, I agree with that. I thought he said "yes," but there wasn't a lot of
investment in it. So I said, "Do you want us to pay attention to you?" And
then I added the importance: "Is it important to you?" That is another
brain system, to get a sense of how salient that is. Is paying attention
to him really important? And again, it's mixed, but it's adding another
dimension, so we can keep moving forward.

Participant: Right before his last answer, because his voice changed, right
before you paused it, what was the question that you asked there?

Albert: "Is it important to you?"

Participant: Is this the second time you said it?

Albert: No, the first one was, "Do you want us to pay attention to you?" And actually, that's where it was a little more mixed, and he cleared his throat, which to me is a mix of speaking up and probably some shame. It's both assertive and constraint at the same time. So his throat was kind of working that out. It didn't stop him. He wanted to speak up, but there was some effort to do that. Okay, what occurs to you that you might want to do next to move forward at this point of the process?

Participant: Acknowledge the energy—he seems very energetic. He seems eager, and you can kind of tell he's been down this path many times, and he's ready to get into it again. So I would feel compelled to acknowledge that, to help bring us both into this moment rather than the traditional. . . .

Albert: Right. And I'm gonna do exactly that with an invitation: "What are you experiencing?" So I want him to discover that activation that you're picking up. There is some extra energy to work with, and I want to invite it with, "What are you experiencing?" I want to foster his observation of that process, so I'm working with awareness and discovering what he can do. I don't know what he's going to say, but I'm trusting and believing that he can discover something and it'll move us along. So let's see what he does.

As you can see, this process of learning the psychophysiological perspective can be slow and even tedious at times. However, the participants' responses and questions are rich and engaging. If you are curious about exploring this perspective, you could do something as simple as video recording five minutes of one of your sessions. Then, as we began doing early in our practice, you could go back and look at that recording several times and discover whatever you can. You could focus just on the eyes or the mouth. You could focus on the prosody of the voice or turn off the sound altogether. This is not an idle exercise. Although it is uncomfortable for most therapists to look at their own work, you cannot help but learn something useful. It takes discipline to look at your work, so we suggest you get together with a colleague like yourself who is interested in learning more and learning together.

PHYSIOPSYCHOTHERAPY FOR THE BRAINMIND

Physiopsychotherapy includes forms of treatment that emphasize directing the therapeutic process toward harnessing the nervous system's innate emotional resources. The goals are both to strengthen those capabilities and to release (open up) emotional constraints from early neglect and/or trauma. Both aspects provide healing for the patient's BrainMind. We have chosen the term physiopsychotherapy to describe this treatment strategy and approach because the process is similar to the treatment you would receive from a physiotherapist (physical therapist) after an injury, illness, or surgery.

When you seek out a physiotherapist, they will take a careful, intentional approach to your treatment. They will listen briefly to the history of the symptoms, but mostly they rely on their observational skills and the physical exam of your body and its symptomatic areas. They discern the relative strengths, weaknesses, and constraints of your musculoskeletal systems. They ascertain the functioning of the nerves and the coordination of the joints, muscles, and balance. They do not need to rely on your interpretation of your symptoms, your body's limitations, or why it all happened in the first place. Their focus is on treating the muscles that need strengthening, the joints that need mobilizing, the nerves that need stimulation, and the coordination between all of these systems to return you to your best possible level of functioning. They will send you home with a variety of exercises to sustain and increase the progress you are making with your physiotherapist. Most of the treatment and healing will happen outside your physiotherapist's office.

When Albert was providing primary care to the Aymara Indians in rural Bolivia, he treated a young man who had suffered a displaced fracture of his humerus (upper arm bone) several years previously. He had received no treatment at the time of injury. His body had immobilized the shoulder with pain in order to keep the fractured bones from moving, which would enable them to knit together. When he presented for treatment, his humerus was now solid (fully healed), but his shoulder joint had a very limited range of motion. There was nothing structurally wrong with the joint. It had fallen into disuse because of the pain, and was now difficult to move. He used his other arm exclusively and was having trouble supporting himself. Albert assessed the joint and then helped this young man start to move his arm and tolerate the inevitable pain and fear that resulted from not moving his joint for a number of years. Albert taught the man a series of physical therapy exercises so that he could regain full mobility of his shoulder joint.

Application of Physiopsychotherapy

You can operate with similar flexibility and confidence when you utilize a psychophysiological perspective in your assessment and treatment strategies. Your knowledge of the multiple brain systems that make up your patient's BrainMind can give you confidence in their underlying resources and undeveloped potential, no matter how depressed or terrified your patient is at this moment. The various interventions we have proposed and illustrated throughout this book can enable you to trust your ability to Activate, Facilitate, and Differentiate these innate capabilities of your patient's nonconscious brain systems. Rather than being stymied by the rigid reaction patterns (frozen shoulder) that have resulted from previous trauma, now you can uncover hidden strengths and release healing potential, just as a physiotherapist does.

Operating in these ways as a physiotherapist can focus your energy to isolate specific brain systems that have been underdeveloped, atrophied, or even closed off. In addition, interrupting the emotional habits that resulted from previous implicit emotional learning can help the patient develop new emotional coordination. This combination of Activating distinct nonconscious primary-level brain systems and interrupting old habits often feels weird and uncomfortable, and may create a kind of emotional disequilibrium. It takes repetitive practice to Integrate the strengths of patients' innate emotional resources that have been disconnected, hyperconnected, or shut down by previous trauma or neglect. Although there is value in hearing the stories or exploring symptoms of the trauma, we are proposing that you consider adding physiopsychotherapy to enhance your therapy.

Physiopsychotherapy helps you bring out into the open and address patient factors that would otherwise be inaccessible. Examples of patient factors include motivation to change, fear, shame, cognitive limitations, psychosis, and personality patterns. Although many of these factors are hidden from view (nonconscious), they play the biggest role in successful therapeutic treatments. Physiopsychotherapy helps you trust the BrainMind's innate resources, capacities, and ability to change (neuroplasticity), to recover and heal from trauma and neglect. You can trust the nature and intentions of your treatment so that you can persist when the process is uncomfortable, confusing, disorienting, and unexpected.

We have developed a teaching tool to train therapists in practicing physiopsychotherapy with their patients (Figures 10.8 and 10.9). The illustrated fan (Figure 10.8) lists all of the primary-level brain systems in a manner that shows how they are all interconnected and that there is no hierarchy between them. You can visualize that when a patient first presents for treatment, their fan of Primaries is at least partially closed. Their fan could be closed because of emotions such as fear, shame, anger, or terror. Physiopsychotherapy for the BrainMind can be visualized as a gradual opening of the fan to gain access to the emotional power and processing capacities of the Primaries.

Physiopsychotherapy Treatment

Physiopsychotherapy can provide efficient and effective treatments on multiple levels of the nervous system. A psychophysiological perspective helps you discover the most accurate empirical evidence of the functionality of each brain system. You can be more efficient because you can customize therapy based on this accurate information. These treatments are effective because they enable the therapeutic energy to be precisely focused on nonconscious resources. As we have illustrated in previous chapters, Facilitating and Differentiating brain systems harnesses their energy to do therapeutic work.

Physiopsychotherapy treatment is more effective when the energy is focused on Facilitating adaptive neural circuits. We know that Facilitating adaptive circuits will also inhibit maladaptive (negative, destructive, toxic, dysfunctional) neural circuits (Grawe, 2007). Just as a physiotherapist focuses on the healing potential of the body, you can direct your interventions to release the healing potentials of the BrainMind. Physiotherapy treatments are experiential, embodied, and repeated many times. Physiopsychotherapy treatments are also experiential, embodied, and repeated many times to help patients develop new adaptive neural circuits.

Treatment Can Be Painful

Successful physiopsychotherapy and physiotherapy treatments are often painful. That may be obvious when recovering from physical trauma, but it is equally true when recovering from emotional trauma. Patients and their therapists have a natural tendency to try to avoid pain. A physiopsychotherapy approach can help you desensitize yourself and your patients to the inevitable pain, fear, and grief that come with treatment. Together you can learn to tolerate the discomfort that comes with healing and growth.

Several sources of discomfort and pain come with successful physio-psychotherapy treatment. Initially you are inviting your patient to let go of their usual control and step into new experiences of themselves and therapy. This can be quite frightening for many patients. Therapy involves climbing out of an emotional equilibrium that can feel like a rut and facing fears of the unknown. The therapeutic Activations of the Safe, Care, and/or Connection brain systems have often been experientially linked, and even entangled, with emotional constraints such as fear, shame, and/or terror. For example, it can seem quite counterintuitive that Facilitating the Safe brain system can feel frightening and even terrifying for some patients.

Successfully Differentiating the primary-level brain systems such as Safe, Care, or Connection from the Fear or Shame brain systems will often release the emotions of grief, guilt, shame, fear, pain, or nausea from previous life experiences. Those emotions have often been suppressed or repressed in early life, and they remain hidden in the secondary-level brain systems. Physiopsychotherapy treatment can operate like a decompression process that will allow these emotions to be released.

These treatments will shift the balance from old traumatic learning toward new flexible and unpredictable discoveries and experiences. Patients can feel that they are losing their balance or missing a familiar internal tether. It is as if they no longer need to hold onto a railing but now can stand with their feet firmly on the ground. There are literal changes in physical coordination with these treatments. Sometimes patients feel unsteady on their feet or have trouble writing their name at the end of a session.

Adaptive Changes Take Practice

The new therapeutic experiences that unfold from physiopsychotherapy treatments are fleeting unless they are refreshed, repeated, and reinforced. The novelty of the treatment will mobilize the neuroplastic abilities of the nervous system. However, our BrainMinds have a strong confirmation bias, and they will delete new information that is not congruent with previous learning. It takes effort to tolerate the discomfort that comes with sitting in the incoherence of conflicting emotions. You can harness secondary-level brain systems such as

Importance, Motivation, and Value to develop internal positive feedback circuits to sustain the adaptive learning that is transpiring in each session.

After your appointment with your physiotherapist, you are sent home with several exercises to practice. Likewise, it can be very helpful for your patient to practice what they have learned and experienced between sessions. The Brain-Mind is most flexible and plastic after a novel experience in therapy. Emotional memory reconsolidation that occurs during physiopsychotherapy treatments will be more available for the next five to six hours (Chapter 15). Inviting patients to go for a walk or move their bodies after a session will release dopamine from the nucleus accumbens, which will facilitate long-term learning. Together you and your patients can come up with specific exercises that will help their further development every day. For example, many patients find it helpful to start their day by expressing several affirmative assertions. Recalling their physical sensations with new emotional discoveries will enable those neural circuits to become increasingly resilient.

CHAPTER 15

Neuroplasticity

· ·

Neuroplasticity or neural plasticity refers to the ability of the brain to change over the patient's life span. Neuroplasticity enables the brain to learn new skills and to reassign jobs. The power of plasticity distinguishes the nervous system from every other system in the body (Schwartz & Begley, 2002). Our mind literally has the ability to change the structure of the brain (Doidge, 2015). These changes take place on the level of neurons first, then neural circuits, which lead to changes on a system level and potentially on the level of networks. To make these changes, however, it is necessary to provide stimulation that is sufficiently intense and frequent, so that the new neural structures can be effectively ingrained for long-term learning. Neuroscience tells us that if we don't provide the necessary forms of frequent stimulation under optimal levels of arousal, the BrainMind could prune those new neural circuits.

We have referred to the importance and benefits of neuroplasticity throughout this book. Here we expand on the neuroscientific and psychological research on neuroplasticity to highlight many aspects of the roles it plays in CIMBS psychotherapy. Our goal for this chapter is to summarize the treatment strategies and procedures that seek to harness the neuroplastic potential of the BrainMind. The processes of CIMBS simultaneously mobilize multiple different types of neuroplasticity that are readily accessible for therapists in order to increase their efficacy. This knowledge could give your psychotherapy the power to facilitate the growth of new adaptive circuits.

SIX TYPES OF NEUROPLASTICITY

The process of CIMBS mobilizes six different, well-documented types of neuroplasticity:

Emotional memory reconsolidation (Ecker, Panksepp)
Implicit emotional memories are deeply installed because of their importance and therefore are resistant to cognitive changes. When emotional memories are reactivated, they become open to being revised (reconsolidated). Neuroscience research has shown that those memories can be updated by a type of neuroplasticity known as memory reconsolidation, in which a series of therapeutic experiences changes the targeted implicit emotional learning (Ecker). The repetitive CIMBS treatments explicitly give the patient reconsolidation experiences, launching a series of present-moment experiences and providing states of incongruence with the old programming. New adaptive experiences can provide moments of disequilibrium and potential neuroplastic changes. These experiences help the BrainMind reorganize the old existing memories. For example: "I always thought I was unlovable. Now I experience feeling lovable inside of myself."

Constraint-induced neuroplasticity
Norman Doidge's book, *The Brain's Way of Healing*, describes how Edward Taub originally applied this therapy to stroke patients who had lost the use of their arms. Taub demonstrated that it is possible to rewire the brain as a result of physical therapy. His therapy constrained the use of the healthy arm and applied sets of exercises to mobilize the paralyzed arm. These exercises were repeated hundreds of times over a period of months. Posttreatment brain-scan studies showed that Taub's treatment recruited neurons adjacent to the injured part of the brain, which began to take over from the damaged or dead neurons. In CIMBS we use a variant of this therapy when we interrupt the patient's maladaptive emotional patterns (such as defenses, ruminations, shame, guilt, and anxiety that are holding the patient back in their growth potential) with

a mix of activation of other, more adaptive competencies (Go the Other Way). Then we use precise repetitions (hundreds of times) in the therapy sessions, and repetition of homework exercises between sessions (Training), to constrain the old patterns. This is the physio- part of physiopsychotherapy. When we constrain the use of the automatic reaction patterns and activate Go the Other Way competencies, we help the patient develop alternative neural circuits. It is possible that we are rewiring the BrainMind after the past emotional trauma (the equivalent of a stroke).

Mental force neuroplasticity (Schwartz), self-efficacy (Davidson), or Motivational force (Siegel)

"Directed, willed mental activity can clearly and systematically alter brain function. The exertion of willful effort generates physical force that has the power to change how the brain works and even its physical structure" (Schwartz & Begley, 2002). Many of our patients feel ineffective and incapable of being in charge of their lives. It is possible that they do not have access to their own Attention, Awareness, Autonomy, Authority, and Agency brain systems. When we Activate those brain systems explicitly, we help our patients to tap into the neuroplastic potential utilizing their own willful mental effort. "Through mental activity alone, itself a product of the brain, we can intentionally change our own brain" (Davidson, 2012).

"Neurons that fire together, wire together": Hebb's principle (Schwartz)

It has also been said that "Neurons that fire apart wire apart" (Doidge, 2015). If we Facilitate new adaptive neural circuits, the original maladaptive circuit will not be reinforced, and over time it will begin to weaken. Habit revision in adulthood is likely to be more challenging than habit formation in childhood (neurons that fire together, wire together). Repetitive trauma has wired together various neural circuits, some of which become emotional triggers. For example, we could hear from a sexual abuse survivor, "Every time I receive love, I feel terror." CIMBS uses four treatments in order to achieve the differentiating, firing apart of the wired-together neural circuits: (1) constant repetition of the adaptive neural network by intently focusing on and Facilitating the sensations of care rather than the sensations of terror; (2) repeatedly Differentiating adaptive neural circuits, for example by saying, "We are caring for you"; (3) Activating the motivation and desire of the patient to ally with the therapist in the consistent execution of novel firing patterns, for example by saying, "Do you want to receive our caring?"; and (4) connecting the love sensations with other brain systems, for example, "What are you experiencing physically when you receive our caring?" "We are playing together as you receive our caring."

Neural synchrony

Refers to imultaneous firing or activations of neurons in multiple areas of the brain. "The suspicion is that by firing in sync, neurons cause far-flung networks to work together, with the result that cognitive and emotional processes become more integrated and coherent" (Davidson, 2012, p. 212). Simultaneous activation of multiple areas of the brain leads to integration across brain regions. Integrating takes effort and intention, characteristics needed to override default patterns of emotional habits (LeDoux, 2002). The CIMBS therapist facilitates neural synchronicity in two ways. First, parallel processing concurrently Activates other previously Differentiated brain systems simultaneously with the one specific brain system that is being Differentiated (Chapters 8, 9, and 11). Second, Integrating resilient brain systems by interconnecting several independent brain systems creates a network than can process large amounts of emotional energy and information, leading to increased complexity and the formation of Fail-Safe Complex Networks (Chapters 9, 12).

Neuroplastic competition (Doidge, 2015)

Every minute of every day, there's a battle going on in our brains—a battle for cortical real estate. Our experiences, behaviors, emotions, and even our thoughts are constantly, literally changing and shaping our brain. "The more a creature makes a movement, the larger the cortical area given over to that movement" (Doidge, 2015). Differentiation, Go the Other Way, and Training can change the landscape of the cortical real estate. Facilitating present-moment competences, and repeatedly visualizing and consciously experiencing new bodily sensations, have the potential to change the shape of the BrainMind. For example, a patient may say, "I feel warmth on my chest, like a column of warm water in my chest. I feel valuable." By refreshing, repeating, and paying attention with intention to this new bodily sensation, we are entering into the competition for cortical real estate, claiming more territory, and occupying more real estate than the old circuits.

CIMBS TREATMENT STRATEGIES AND PROCEDURES THAT HARNESS NEUROPLASTICITY

Below we review each of these treatments, strategies, and procedures and high-light how each one interacts with the properties of neuroplasticity to advance our therapeutic goals.

- Developing resilient brain systems (Chapter 2) by Activating, Facilitating, Differentiating, Training, and Integrating each brain system (Chapters 8, 9 11, and 12): We call the sum of these processes physiopsychotherapy for the BrainMind (Chapter 14). When each brain system becomes resil-ient, it can process and generate large amounts of energy and information without getting overwhelmed, triggered, or shut down in times of crisis. It doesn't matter what the trauma has been. A resilient brain system will be able to tap into evolutionary wisdom and continue thriving and learn-ing. The better the new neural circuits that compose the resilient system are Facilitated during therapy, the more easily they can be activated out-side of the therapy session, and the more they will function as an effective barrier against the cascade of the activation (triggers) of the trauma-induced neural circuits from the implicit memory.
- Being an external generator: The therapist Facilitates and sustains the Activation of the innate resources of any brain system through constant repetition (Chapters 8, 11). The repeated firing of the new neural circuits formed as you exercise these resources will recruit neighboring neurons (neuroplastic competition), leading to the formation of multiple additional neural circuits, thus augmenting the capacity to become a new self-sustaining neural system. The external generator can also direct willed mental activity (mental force neuroplasticity) that can systematically alter brain function (Schwartz). The process of myelination is increased in those circuits that are activated repeatedly, speeding the information flow through the brain networks, and offering the potential to change the BrainMind forever.
- Fostering parallel processing: Activating and Facilitating two or more differentiated brain systems simultaneously can enhance neural syn-chrony, following Hebb's principle that "neurons that fire together,

wire together." When this happens, newness and learning (changing the strength of synaptic connections) has taken place.

- Staying in the Transpiring Present Moment: Change and neuroplasticity take place only in the Transpiring Present Moment. There is newness when the patient is able to be present and aware of the reality of themselves, rather than constantly seeing themselves with the critical eyes of the past. We work with the processing mind (Siegel), focusing on what is happening between the patient and the therapist and within the patient in this precise moment.

- Maintaining optimal levels of emotional arousal: Neurons will fully develop only in the presence of adequate amounts of stimulation and under optimal high levels of arousal (Schore 1994). In order to strengthen the memory formation of a new emotional habit, and to prevent the pruning effect, the amygdala should be in moderate to high arousal. If the arousal is too high, memory will be impaired, and the brain will not be sufficiently neuroplastic (LeDoux). CIMBS utilizes various treatments in order to keep the arousal levels optimal. The Therapeutic Attachment Relationship generates the arousal necessary for neuroplasticity and change. This arousal stimulates the release of dopamine, as well as opioids and oxytocin, from the amygdala (Medina, 2008). The Initial Directed Activation focuses the therapeutic energy to enhance the arousal and provide novel emotional experiences. This novelty stimulates the hippocampus to promote new learning.

- Responding to psychophysiological shifts: Your responses to the psychophysiological shifts that occur in your patients as a result of these practices are very important for harnessing the capacities of neuroplasticity. Often these shifts in the energetic emotional equilibrium reveal evidence of new adaptive emotional experiences that can lead to emotional memory reconsolidation. These moments are novel states that will disappear if they go unnoticed. Your attention with intention can keep the shift of the energetic balance flowing for one more round.

- Stimulating emotional disequilibrium: As we said in Chapter 4, emotional disequilibrium can be one of the sources of energy that helps to release the constraints of the present equilibrium or status quo into new phases of growth and discovery. Moments of disequilibrium are also states of novelty and potential neuroplasticity. We have observed many different levels of disequilibrium in our patients, from the simple awkwardness that is often created when the therapist steps fully into the Therapeutic Attachment Relationship, to the multidimensional emotional disequilibrium that results when more intense and unfamiliar activations occur (see below).

ENDOGENOUS NEUROTRANSMITTERS ENHANCE THE NEUROPLASTICITY OF THE BRAINMIND

Have you ever had a session so important that it seemed earth-shattering—thinking that this session would change the life course of your patient—just to realize at the next session that actually nothing changed? Or that the patient forgot all about it? It seems that the BrainMind has a protective survival mechanism by which it can remove content from conscious awareness if it is not consistent with other memories and emotions (Grawe, 2007). A new plastic circuit that has been activated in therapy could be sorted for storage or deletion based on how it relates to other (already established) circuits. A major factor determining the durability of a therapeutic experience is the extent to which it triggers the release of neurotransmitters, the currency of nervous system communication. Below we explore how key neurotransmitters are involved in the retention of therapeutic learning, and how we take advantage of those features in CIMBS therapy.

The Dopamine Effect: Activation of Six Dopamine Circuits

The neurotransmitter dopamine transmits the synaptic impulses of activated neurons. Experiences that trigger large releases of dopamine tend to be particularly strongly felt and retained. The release of dopamine during therapy could sustain adaptive learning and reinforce the circuits, making sure that new circuits will not be deleted. When we activate waves of dopamine release, it creates a positive feedback loop, interrupting (for the moment) the nonconscious depressive neural networks. We have experimented with six different dopamine systems to provide energy and reinforcement to sustain the activation and neuroplastic changes for long-term learning.

First, dopamine from the striatum (Figure 15.1) is involved in weighing the importance or saliency of an action and the reward that will be obtained from that action. We believe that by activating the Importance brain system (Chapter 13) we may be activating dopamine release in the system.

Second, dopamine-producing neurons also tend to fire predominantly when pleasant consequences occur (Grawe, 2007). The ventral tegmental area contains the natural reward circuitry of the brain. It releases dopamine when we activate the Value brain system (Chapter 13) or have experiences of internal reward and feelings of satisfaction.

Third, the nucleus accumbens is a significant source of dopamine. When the Seeking brain system is activated, it produces all kinds of approach behaviors and it also makes the patient feel excited about doing the work of therapy. The Seeking system has been called the brain reward system. It is involved in the cognitive processing of physical movement functions related to reward, drive, determination, and perseverance. The Seeking system is insatiable, and the dopamine released when it is Activated greatly enhances neuroplasticity and long-term learning (Grawe, 2007). Activating the Motivation brain system along with Seeking together could release enough dopamine to overcome fear and the dominance of avoidance behaviors, changing the balance of impulses toward approach activations.

Fourth, the hippocampus, the novelty circuit of the brain, compares incoming

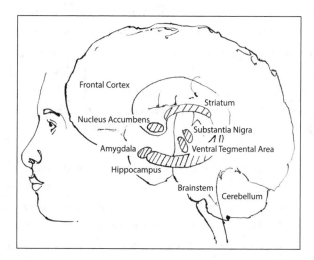

Figure 15.1: Distinct Basal Ganglia/Nuclei Structures That Release Dopamine

sensory information with stored knowledge. If these differ, the hippocampus sends a pulse of dopamine to a group of nerve cells in the brain called the substantia nigra. Neural circuits extend back to the hippocampus and trigger a further release of dopamine, creating what is called the dopamine feedback loop. This process washes the nervous system with waves of dopamine and explains why we remember things better in the context of novelty. CIMBS treatment procedures seek to Activate new neural circuits rather than developing a new understanding of the old memories:

- The Therapeutic Attachment Relationship provides novelty. The narrow and precise focus solely on the patient in the present moment, rather than on stories from the past, activates the nervous system in new ways. The patient has never had a Therapeutic Attachment Relationship before, and will never have felt this energy before. Your interest in their internal experiences, constant eye gaze, and caring energy will reveal that they are the focus of attention. They are the most important person at this moment rather than anything or anyone else.
- The Initial Directed Activation also produces novelty. The dialogue does not follow the same routes that the patient is familiar with. There is no confrontation with the patient's past, which would activate the contents of implicit memory. The focus is to Activate the patient's brain systems and presence with themselves. This is often a new endeavor, because they are not used to approaching their own minds with curiosity, interest, respect, and compassion. They are more familiar with fear and avoidance.
- As you are constantly Activating and Facilitating the Primaries, Secondaries, and Tertiaries, Go the Other Way focuses on the patient's competencies, producing repeated encounters with newness.

Fifth, physical movement, even just walking around the block, also triggers release of dopamine from the substantia nigra. Exercise immediately after the therapeutic session will enhance and reinforce the new adaptive neural circuits that were Facilitated in therapy. Other exercise outside of the session also releases dopamine, preventing the deletion of these new plastic circuits.

Sixth, the amygdala is chock-full of the neurotransmitter dopamine, which it uses in the way an office assistant uses sticky notes (Medina, 2008). When the brain experiences a highly emotionally charged event, the amygdala releases dopamine as a chemical sticky note on the new neural circuit that has been activated. This means that information will be more robustly processed for long-term learning. "In discomfort we grow!"

Other Neurotransmitters: The Feel-Good Effect

Another set of endogenous chemicals, such as oxytocin, serotonin, and the opioids, are labeled the feel-good neurotransmitters, which inhibit the fear circuits in the brain. Activating any level of brain system—Primary, Secondary, or Tertiary—can release these neurotransmitters and provide valuable neurological resources to assist with the hard work of therapy. As therapists, we can be more effective by learning how to activate waves of these feel-good neurotransmitters right in our sessions. We have developed four ways of doing this:

1. Constant Activation of the Care and Connection brain systems (such as through the Therapeutic Attachment Relationship) will activate oxytocin, opioids, and possibly serotonin. Each episode of Activation, by stimulating the release of these neurotransmitters, further strengthens the neural connections associated with being cared for. Over time, then, the corresponding neural circuits are more easily activated. The regulation of emotions in the attachment relationship rapidly inhibits anxieties and fear, and makes way for internal emotional regulation.

2. Activating the Assertive, Authority, and Motivation brain systems stimulates the release of gamma-aminobutyric acid (GABA), which plays a principal role in reducing neuronal excitability through the nervous system. It is a neuroinhibitor which inhibits the activation of transmissions at the synapses emerging from the amygdala. When we activate these brain systems, the resulting intrinsic motivation and willpower enhances the release of GABA, inhibiting the fear circuits, in pursuit of goal-oriented behavior. An example is the combat soldier who disregards his survival instincts and advances from the trenches because he is motivated to achieve a strategically important position.

3. Activating the Safe brain system can also stimulate release of GABA, as well as oxytocin and opioids. If there is a sense of safety, the hypothalamus suppresses the secretion of the stress-related hormone cortisol and begins instead to secrete hormones that lead the pituitary gland to secrete oxytocin and opioids. These neurotransmitters enter the bloodstream

directly, inhibiting the synapses that transmit fear signals, and thus help to reduce hyperactivity in the Fear brain system.

4. Activating the Play brain system will increase the levels of oxytocin and serotonin, as well as dopamine, in the brain, supporting the sprouting of new neurons in areas such as the hippocampus. Vigorous aerobic exercise also increases levels of serotonin in the brain—neuroplasticity at its best.

MULTIDIMENSIONAL EMOTIONAL DISEQUILIBRIUM

A patient who starts therapy is usually in a state of equilibrium. Equilibrium is a state in which multiple sources of energy are in some kind of stable and sustainable—but not necessarily functional—relationship with each other. Depression, chronic anxiety, obsessions, and so on, are all states of equilibrium for the patient. The adult BrainMind has well-ingrained neural circuits or cell assemblies that have been activated thousands of times during the course of their lives. Our patients seek relief from those that are troublesome, such as one that might be constantly sending them the message, "I am unlovable and incapable."

In addition, our BrainMinds are equipped with innate neural mechanisms for ensuring consistency and continuity of such equilibria. They continuously produce expected scenarios about how a situation will continue from this moment on. These forecasts come from previous learning, and anything that is not congruent with those beliefs is not seen or gets deleted. *The Invisible Gorilla* is a well-known case in point (Chabris & Simons, 2009). Subjects were shown a video recording in which persons in white shirts pass basketballs to each other. The subjects were instructed to count the number of passes according to certain rules. Then a gorilla enters the scene, thumps its chest, and exits. Researchers found that, when asked, half of the subjects did not even notice the gorilla. It is fascinating that their minds deleted the gorilla because it was incongruent.

The changes in brain structure and processing that neuroplasticity makes possible in psychotherapy can make for a very disorienting and uncomfortable experience for the patient. They may be thrust out of a familiar (if troubling) equilibrium into new, unfamiliar territory. It takes the patient's strength, and your consistent support, to help them through the transition to a more flexible, adaptive, and resilient posture. We use the phrase *multidimensional emotional disequilibrium* for therapeutic moments when multiple distinct equilibria are simultaneously changing, adjusting, and updating. These moments are part of the healing processes that occur when you are Facilitating and Differentiating several brain systems at the same time. It is hard to describe all of the simultaneous phenomena that occur when the BrainMind is integrating multiple brain systems at increased levels of complexity.

The case study of Paul in Chapter 12 gives an example of a patient experiencing an ongoing multidimensional emotional disequilibrium. Paul came to Albert in a state of (dysfunctional) equilibrium in which emotions of guilt and suicidality were suppressing his ability to respect and care for himself. As Albert helped Paul to develop his powers of self-respect and self-care, his BrainMind needed to update the persistent feelings of betrayal, embarrassment, and suicidality that were aroused. Paul passed through a painful, shameful, and fearful disequilibrium as he became free to respect and care for himself. He was expanding the conscious capacities of his Authority, Autonomy, and Agency brain systems, and at the same time he was paying attention to his emotions of pain, shame, and fear. He was able to assert that it was safe to feel all of these emotions, even when he felt emotional alarms going off inside his BrainMind.

Paul was experiencing this disequilibrium at all four levels of emotional processing. His body was feeling pain, with a choked throat, and releasing tears. The Primaries of Care, Connection, and Safe were all active. The Secondaries of Guilt, Shame, Fear, Grief, Motivation, Value, and Importance were all being adjusted and updated. The Tertiaries of Authority, Autonomy, and Agency were all being exercised in novel ways. You could see how hard his BrainMind was working when his glasses fogged up and he described feeling wobbly inside himself, "as if gravity is changing."

Our patient Penny (Chapter 9) showed similar psychophysiological symptoms of disequilibrium, which she described this way:

Penny: I am teetering [*smiles, nodding, throat tight, voice stronger, repeatedly moving her torso right and left gently*].

Beatriz: This is fantastic, the feeling of teetering. You are out of balance right now.

Penny: Yeah . . . I feel off balance [*nods more vigorously, as her body moves gently sideways*].

Beatriz: This is success. You are creating a new equilibrium in your brain. This is success already.

Penny: My whole face is tingling right now [*smiles, surprise*].

Beatriz: This teetering place is very good.

The adaptive moments of multidimensional emotional disequilibrium can cause a wide range of surprising experiences for our patients. Sometimes our patients make statements such as, "I feel like a Picasso painting—my eyes and mouth in different places" or "I feel unstable, as if I am teetering." One patient was sure the chair was crooked and even got up to check the legs of the chair! Sometimes their physical balance is unsteady (for a little while), and they have difficulty walking down the hall after a session. It is interesting that our therapist trainees have reported the same phenomena.

From the very beginning of therapy, the CIMBS therapist is creating moments of inconsistency, which is an incompatibility or discrepancy between simultaneously activated mental or neural processes (Grawe, 2007). In other words, CIMBS creates disequilibrium or inconsistency by Activating mental or neural processes that go against the established consistency mechanisms of the BrainMind. We are creating multidimensional emotional disequilibria by Going the Other Way, rebuilding impoverished brain systems, activating and strengthening neural circuits, and utilizing several forms of neuroplasticity in order to develop resilient brain systems. We are fostering newness and sustaining the patient's activation of the innate capabilities of each brain system as well as Activating multiple brain systems at the same time. Any of these processes repeated over some period of time will inevitably create multidimensional emotional disequilibria in the patient's BrainMind.

Any novel, unexpected, demanding situation initially triggers unspecific arousal in large parts of the neocortex and the basal nuclei (Grawe, 2007). Multidimensional emotional disequilibria, in particular, set off a stress reaction that increases synaptic transmissions. This stress reaction releases adrenalin, which influences almost all regions of the brain and leads to a number of chain reactions that ultimately have positive effects. "Specifically, the stimulation of the neural adrenalin receptors increases the brain's readiness to learn—it enables the easier facilitation of synaptic connections" (Grawe, 2007). The repeated confrontation with the same type of incongruence leads to increasingly strong new neural activation patterns. Waves of dopamine are secreted in response to deviations from expectancies, and the autonomic nervous system reacts to this stress by heightening the release of acetylcholine (Grawe, 2007).

Is this what is happening in the BrainMind when our patients say, "I feel like a Picasso painting" or "I feel wobbly inside of me, as if gravity is changing"? Is it possible that this present-moment multidimensional emotional disequilibrium is affecting the brain in such a way that it is changing its structure right in front of our eyes? We need more research to understand these phenomena. What we know for sure, from our 10-year follow-up studies, is that these changes are resilient and the trajectories of our patients' lives continue to improve over time.

CHAPTER 16

Summary

....

CASE STUDY: DIFFERENTIATING MULTIPLE BRAIN SYSTEMS UNPACKS TRAUMA

A patient we will call Kathy came to see Albert five years after she had been raped in her early 20s. She had seen a couple of therapists in the previous years after the rape. She was still troubled with depression, so she sought out new treatment when she had a change of insurance with a new job. Kathy's treatment was remarkable because the trauma of the rape never came up in the first several sessions. After her fourth session, Kathy remarked how she had been feeling surprisingly better after each session. She described how her previous therapies had focused on the trauma of her rape, and she said she often felt worse after her sessions and for days afterward. Our approach to Kathy's case is a hallmark example of CIMBS as an alternative to conventional psychotherapy. At the center of our treatment was Facilitating, Differentiating, and Integrating multiple brain systems.

What happened that enabled Kathy to get out of her depression and feel better after each session? Trauma in the attachment system is really at the heart of therapy for most patients (van der Kolk, 2014). After a basic intake, Albert started the therapeutic work by developing the Therapeutic Attachment Relationship and Kathy's experience of herself in the Transpiring Present Moment. After the Initial Directed Activation, Albert facilitated Kathy's awareness and attention on herself and her physical sensations, saying, "What are you aware of?" Kathy said she was aware of tension in her chest and nausea. She was surprised by those sensations, and she was also aware of an impulse to withdraw inside herself.

This Therapeutic Attachment Relationship enabled Kathy to have novel bodily experiences of the Primaries of Safe, Care, and Connection that were quite different from the past and from her trauma. This was the beginning of the processes of Facilitating and Differentiating her nonconscious Primaries to engage and strengthen previously unknown inner resources. Her awareness focused on a sense of safety and care, as reflected in her statements such as, "I am breathing more deeply than usual. I have this surprising warmth in my chest." Albert repeatedly reinforced her competence to feel her strength and her motivation to engage in the therapy with reflecting interventions such as, "You are capable of feeling open and safe right now" and "You are safe to care for yourself now." As he kept Facilitating her Awareness and Attention brain systems, Kathy had new embodied experiences of her own authority and autonomy. Her voice deepened, and her body language became more animated.

Kathy became tearful and frightened at various times in her sessions. Albert welcomed those reactions and directed their collaborative attention to the brain system activations that triggered those reactions. The processes of Go the Other Way helped Kathy stay open to her Transpiring Present Moment experiences.

The ongoing Facilitation of each of her distinct conscious brain systems and Primaries inhibited the constraints contained in her nonconscious Fear, Grief, Shame, and Guilt brain systems that had remained entangled and stuck after the rape. She began to feel the physical power of her Authority, Autonomy, and Assertiveness even as those sensations felt disorienting. She released the emotions of grief, shame, and guilt about having been stuck in her life. Facilitating her innate strengths kept the rape-trauma memories from interfering with developing a healthy attachment to her emotional self and Albert.

You may be surprised by the absence of anger in this story. Certainly Kathy experienced anger at the time of the rape and subsequently. Kathy and Albert were Facilitating and Differentiating her Primaries, Secondaries, and Tertiaries within the Therapeutic Attachment Relationship and in the Transpiring Present Moment. The anger and rage from her rape experience did not surface in the session because she and Albert were meeting the needs of all of her brain systems in the present moment. There were episodes of anger in Kathy's sessions when she experienced constraints within her BrainMind that interfered with the present-moment experiences of her drive for safeness, care, and connection with Albert. Those episodes of anger came from early developmental learning that preceded the rape by many years. The resolution of anger from deep inside her Primaries gave her the healing and peace she needed. The anger over the rape was resolved on a deeper developmental level without having to revisit the rape experience again. Kathy's mixed emotions of shame, anger, guilt, and fear were Differentiated, released, and Integrated. Her BrainMind no longer needed to depress the intolerability of those entangled emotions.

Subsequent sessions continued the focus on developing Kathy's authentic Authority and Autonomy brain systems. Harnessing those systems enabled her to release the energy of the emotions of shame, rage, grief, guilt, and fear. These nonconscious constraints had prevented her from healing from the rape. Her previous therapy had not been able to access her Authority, Autonomy, and Agency to stand up for herself. She realized that she had been holding onto being a victim, and that was a familiar role for her. It kept her from feeling her power, authority, and autonomy.

In Kathy's case, Albert used the strategy of Go the Other Way to strengthen her competencies, rather than to dwell on her trauma. But importantly, the way he did so was to selectively Activate the Primaries of Safe, Care, and Connection to support the underperforming conscious brain systems (Awareness, Attention, Authority, Autonomy) so she became less vulnerable to being triggered again by her trauma circuits. In addition, these activations suppressed the maladaptive entanglements of the inhibitory Secondaries that had been aroused by the trauma of the rape: Fear, Grief, Shame, and Guilt. The treatment process worked to open, disentangle, and strengthen all levels of brain systems, and wove them together to become complex and resilient. This is the essence of Facilitating, Differentiating, and Integrating. The directed Activations of her present-moment (attachment) competencies Differentiated her BrainMind from the traumatic patterns where she felt stuck. The novelty, energy, and wisdom of these Differentiating and Integrating processes helped her release some of the grief and shame that had also constrained her growth.

We present Kathy here as we prepare to end our book partly because she is a dramatic example of the success of a brain-systems approach. She healed from the trauma of rape without having to reimmerse herself in the experience through freeing the power of brain systems that were constrained or hypoactive.

But Kathy also illustrates the full scope of the CIMBS practice. We were Activating, Facilitating, Differentiating, Training, and Integrating all four levels of the nervous system in a process that implemented all of those interventions repeatedly and out of order as needed, but with eventual process toward Integration. As each session unfolded, Kathy experienced both horizontal and vertical Integration of multiple brain systems and emotional learning. Her brain systems became more resilient, and with time formed a Fail-Safe Network. Kathy's case illustrates many of the principles in this book that we summarize in the remainder of this closing chapter.

NEUROBIOLOGICAL PARADIGM

Complex Integration of Multiple Brain Systems is a therapeutic paradigm that is based on the neurobiological wisdom that our BrainMind is made up of multiple systems. Each of these systems evolved over the course of our evolution to secure survival, adapt to different environments, and respond flexibly to a wide range of stressors. These systems are innate (hardwired) at birth and can also develop throughout the life span.

Our BrainMind has a wide range of brain systems that enable us to see (visual), hear (auditory), move our bodies (musculoskeletal), and maintain the narrow range of temperature, hydration, blood pressure, and oxygenation (respiratory) that we need to survive. Our BrainMind also has a wide range of emotional brain systems that help us not only survive but thrive in relationships, unique circumstances, and complex societies. These emotional brain systems are the centerpiece of CIMBS.

The human nervous system operates on four different levels of processing. Most of the information and energy of the nervous system originates in the peripheral nervous system, which includes the visceral organs and neural plexuses. The primary level of processing operates in and around the brainstem. The secondary level of processing takes place in the basal ganglia, cerebellum, hypothalamus, and adjacent structures. Conscious thought and the Tertiaries primarily operate in the extensive neocortex.

Consciousness is difficult to define from a neurobiological perspective. It appears to involve many elements operating together, creating the emergent phenomena we call consciousness. There is a range of consciousness, much of which depends on deeper structures of the brain such as the periaqueductal gray matter within the brainstem. Most mental and emotional processing takes place in the peripheral, primary, and secondary levels of the BrainMind and therefore is nonconscious. Our emotional learning and habits are also mostly nonconscious and therefore resistant to change from cognitive or conscious learning.

We have developed this brain-systems therapeutic paradigm out of our desire to have a deeper understanding of the inner workings of the BrainMind, a wider range of treatment options, and the ability to be more effective and efficient with our patients. We have introduced you to the 20 emotional brain systems that we have found substantiated by the most recent neurobiological and clinical evidence. One could make a case for the roles of other emotional brain systems as well, and we look forward to that research.

In the process of developing our brain-systems paradigm, we have experimented with a wide array of treatments and treatment strategies designed to facilitate adaptive functioning and address underlying dysfunctions. The neurobiological principles described in Chapter 3 can become a different foundation on which to stand. These scientific principles can be guideposts to a further scientific treatment process. For example, when you observe the psychophysiological responses of distinct brain systems to your interventions, you will naturally develop hypotheses to try to understand what is causing the reactions you are observing. You can experiment with different interventions and then gather the empirical evidence contained in patients' psychophysiological reactions. You can experientially test your hypotheses to obtain valuable information and provide treatment at the same time. There are no mistakes here. All results (data) are valuable. It takes concentration to discover the hidden image in a 3-D picture. You need to allow your visual brain system to process the information in the picture in a different manner in order for the hidden image to jump off the page. It will take a similar effort to see the many hidden nonconscious emotional resources that are present in your patients. We hope we have aroused your relentless Seeking brain system to explore some of these concepts, treatments, and interventions.

This therapeutic paradigm has enabled us to harness the wisdom and generating power of multiple brain systems at the same time. The BrainMind has enormous processing capacity when each brain system is activated and differentiated simultaneously. Developing resilient brain systems meets the patient's emotional needs in the moment and can provide them with nonconscious resources that are always available even in a crisis.

Looking at this paradigm from an energy perspective, one can more easily observe how it works and why it can be quite effective. Each of these brain systems can generate energy. The Primaries are especially important because they generate the most energy of all (Panksepp & Biven, 2012). In the case example of Kathy, Albert helped her harness the power of her Safe, Care, and Connection brain systems to override the constraints of fear, shame, and guilt. Our Brain-Mind evolved with the capability for all of these energy generators to operate simultaneously and in parallel so that they can integrate and synergize with each other. We need energy to move or change. The more sources of energy we summon, the more work can be done. The more processors we have online, the more precise and wise will be our choices and actions.

In addition, repeatedly Activating a neural circuit or a brain system will strengthen it, recruit adjacent neurons, and enable it to become myelinated. These benefits will increase the resilience, efficiency, and flexibility of that system over time. These are the benefits of nonconscious experiential learning. If you change one part of a complex network of systems, you will change the whole system. Multiple brain systems operating independently, simultaneously, and in coordination with each other will naturally integrate and with time achieve new levels of complexity. In many patients over the years, we have seen this complex integration of systems become a Fail-Safe Complex Network.

THERAPIST FACTORS: THE PRIMARIES AND TERTIARIES

The second most important components of successful psychotherapy outcomes are therapist factors. We have found that training our colleagues in the processes of Activating, Facilitating, and Differentiating multiple brain systems changes the therapist. Utilizing the Therapeutic Attachment Relationship inspires the therapist to become more open and engaged. They naturally sit forward, feel more curious, and let go of trying to accomplish something. They gradually develop increasing confidence in their own competence. They feel much less shame about their limitations, misattunements, or struggles. The release of shame also releases fear about doing it wrong. Those releases free up the therapist to be more creative, engaged, and embodied in their treatments. One of our trainees recently made these observations about herself: "The process is more visceral for me now. I was able to stay in the Transpiring Present Moment for 35 minutes with a difficult patient and trust myself and my patient. There was lots of flow. It was the purest therapy I have ever done. It comes about from trusting my patient's competence and the process."

It is not possible to overstate the utility and power of the Therapeutic Attachment Relationship. This intervention brings the energy of the therapist and their intentions into focus and moves the treatment forward in many nonconscious ways. The nonconscious and invisible Activations of the Safe, Care, and Connection brain systems provide both energy and novelty to the treatment process. Albert utilized the Therapeutic Attachment Relationship to keep Kathy in her body and opening herself to her deeper emotional resources. Trusting the importance of this unique and evolving relationship is one of the pillars of Trust the Process. The ability of the patient to collaborate in the treatment often depends on the quality of this relationship. The patient needs to feel that we are genuinely and vulnerably in this together.

As a therapist, you are at your best when you are both directing the process and following the patient's lead. This duality may seem like a paradox at first. The Initial Directed Activation mobilizes a broad range of brain systems and focuses the energy of both participants to work together in this precious moment of therapy. Although this intervention may seem simple and rote at first, it Facilitates responses and reactions on all four levels of emotional processing. The patient's conscious and nonconscious responses to the intervention become the leads and clues that are the guideposts to explore. The immediacy of this intervention helps you discern the distinctions between emotional responses that arise in the Transpiring Present Moment and those that are reactions from early developmental learning. Albert was observing Kathy's psychophysiological responses to his interventions in order to follow the lead of her BrainMind.

These interventions (Therapeutic Attachment Relationship and Initial Directed Activation) shine a light on the strengths and limitations of the patient's tertiary-level brain systems. We all tend to take our consciousness and our patient's consciousness for granted. These initial invitations to your patient's Awareness, Attention, and Authority brain systems are both therapeutic and enlightening. Facilitating these Tertiaries plays important roles in the patient's ability to collaborate, self-regulate their emotions, and embody the experiential learning that is unfolding in the session. Kathy's level of engagement in the therapeutic process shifted significantly when the competencies of her Tertiaries were Facilitated. Without the Tertiaries, your patient will not be able to "save these valuable documents."

Go the Other Way is another intentional process whereby the therapist directs the patient's attention and energy toward their underlying adaptive resources, residing in the Primaries, rather than focusing on the distress that just surfaced. Kathy was energized and relieved at the end of each session when she and Albert helped her harness the energy of her Care and Connection brain systems. This collaborative interruption of emotional habit patterns often leads to feelings of discomfort, incongruence, and being out of balance. Go the Other Way is often counterintuitive for both the patient and therapist. Yet you can come to experience how Facilitating the Primaries has the added benefit of inhibiting maladaptive emotional patterns.

A psychophysiological perspective and psychophysiological phenomena can provide the empirical evidence to help guide the therapist to operate as a physiotherapist for the BrainMind with the patient. Observing the patient's nonconscious activations and responses to interventions enables the therapist to fine-tune and customize the interventions to a particular patient at a precise moment. This perspective and these phenomena can help you Trust the Process and Facilitate new competencies as they begin to reveal themselves in the session. Albert received nonverbal evidence in Kathy's sessions when her body was at first in a slumped posture, then gradually became more erect, as the Therapeutic Attachment Relationship helped her harness the power of her Safe, Care, and Connection brain systems.

PATIENT FACTORS: THE ENHANCING SECONDARIES

A brain systems perspective can be very helpful in addressing and changing patient factors. Patient factors play the biggest role in successful outcomes in therapy. Often those factors appear as resistance, defenses, or obstacles to treatment, which are the results of nonconscious learning contained in the secondary-level brain systems and processed in the basal ganglia. The most important emotional learning takes place in the first few years of life. That learning is processed nonconsciously at the secondary level of the BrainMind and within the secondary-level brain systems. The emotional patterns that develop in our early childhood help us build relationships with our parents and other family and clan members. Those patterns will last a lifetime and resist change because they were installed so early and resulted from highly evolved emotional drives.

We have found that the patients whose treatment was the most challenging also had the most traumatic infancies when their emotional brain systems were first developing. For example, some infants were separated from their parents for extended periods of time because they had serious medical problems at birth or soon thereafter. Not only did they miss out on the early development of their Safe, Care, and Connection attachment brain systems, they also were subjected to life-threatening dangers and abandonment.

Knowledge of the secondary-level brain systems can direct treatment toward being more precise and focused on Facilitating the enhancing brain systems: Value, Importance, Motivation, and Pleasure. That knowledge can change the whole dynamic of the treatment and the outcome of therapy. The energy and wisdom of the enhancing Secondaries is often overlooked in therapy. Facilitating and Differentiating those systems will enable the patient's BrainMind to develop internal positive feedback circuits to sustain the primary-level drives that would otherwise become fatigued or constrained. Accessing these brain systems often tips the balance in therapy when significant patient factors are interfering with progress. Albert used interventions with Kathy such as, "Your internal experience of care right now is valuable" and "Taking pleasure in discoveries about your strengths will help you hold onto them."

A brain-systems perspective is helpful in distinguishing the adaptive strengths of the inhibitory brain systems of Fear, Grief, Shame, and Guilt from the emotions of fear, grief, shame, and guilt. That knowledge can empower the therapist to Go the Other Way when those emotions prevent progress or overwhelm the patient's ability to regulate their emotions. You can Trust the Process, and together with your patient you can move through the moments of disequilibrium that are both frightening and painful. Those periods of disequilibrium are also opportunities for deep change and neuroplasticity to sustain those new levels of flexibility and complexity. In Kathy's case, her patient factors were the constraints in her Grief, Shame, and Guilt brain systems that had led to her depression. Her experience of disequilibrium within the Therapeutic Attachment Relationship and the constant focus on Facilitating and Differentiating her Primaries and Secondaries freed her from those constraints and released new levels of complexity in her BrainMind.

You may have noted how we have not used the term *pathology* in our treatment approaches. In this context, pathology refers to disease, physical damage, or degeneration of the BrainMind. Rather, we find that the vast majority of our patients' symptoms and disorders are a result of developmental difficulties. The adaptations the BrainMind develops to react to physical and emotional neglect and trauma, and to manage the resulting brain system imbalances, create the symptoms and disorders that bring most patients for psychotherapy. Some patients present with conditions such as brain injuries, congenital limitations, dementia, and so on. There is some detectable pathology in those patients' Brain-Minds. However, we have found that a brain systems approach can be very helpful and surprisingly successful for those patients as well. The physiotherapy for the BrainMind mindset makes sense of those beneficial treatments.

THE UPWARD SPIRAL

It has been challenging to describe and make sense of the circular therapeutic processes we have found most effective in utilizing this neurobiological paradigm and these treatment strategies. The repetitive Activating, Facilitating, Differentiating, Training, and/or Integrating interventions are often happening simultaneously. We have found it helpful to limit our focus to either horizontal or vertical Integrating at various stages of the process to enhance learning and neuroplasticity phenomena. The spiral illustrations, Figures 8.1 and 11.2, are our attempts to give you a felt sense of what we are attempting in CIMBS psychotherapy. The energy and wisdom of multiple systems active at the same time can be quite inspiring for both the patient and the therapist.

Integrating multiple Activated and Differentiated systems on multiple levels of the nervous system occurs as a natural phenomenon. That potential can easily be obstructed by other natural processes such as the emotions of fear, grief, shame, or guilt. There is a natural tendency to delete unfamiliar or incongruent information and energy. Novel experiences are unfamiliar, weird, and therefore often avoided. We propose that your therapeutic interventions and intentions seek to sustain the Integrating process for extended periods of time. This Integrating process is both uncomfortable and liberating at the same time. Sustained Integrating will also release spontaneous self-organization in the nervous system.

Imagining yourself as a physiotherapist (physical therapist) can be helpful when using this paradigm in your own practice. The physiotherapist focuses treatment on developing the innate strengths, flexibility, and coordination of the body. The history of the injury or other limitations are not the focus. There is a ready acceptance that moving joints and muscles in new or unfamiliar ways will be uncomfortable. Repetition, training, and practicing are all part of physiotherapy.

After each treatment session the therapist sends the patient home with exercises to practice every day to speed the treatment and healing processes. The seemingly tedious repetition that you have observed in the transcripts can make more sense when you understand the need for learning to take place on all four levels of the nervous system.

We remind you that psychotherapy is best learned in collaboration and consultation with other colleagues. No one can fully learn psychotherapy from a book. Many of these concepts and interventions are more powerful than they appear on paper, so we recommend that you practice with your colleagues first before you experiment with your patients. For the same reason, we encourage you to practice with your highest-functioning patients to become comfortable with working with these multiple levels of activation in the emotional brain systems.

We are grateful that you have come far enough to reach the end of the book. If you have found the knowledge in this book interesting and you want to learn more, we refer you to our website (CIMBS, http://www.complexintegrationmbs .com/). There you will find links to the video recordings of some of the sessions transcribed in this book. There are seven online training courses (with five units of continuing education credit) on specific topics and perspectives that have been introduced here. We will resume live two- or three-day experiential training courses once that is safe again (after the pandemic). The website provides information about the two- or three-day experiential training courses that we offer in appropriate formats for therapists who seek additional exposure to CIMBS.

ADDENDUM: CIMBS ONLINE THERAPY

During the COVID-19 pandemic in 2020, as we were in the middle of writing this book, we were all forced to morph our usual way of providing therapy to fit into online formats. In response to questions and requests, we are adding this addendum about how we have adapted our CIMBS treatment approaches to working online. We have found our trainees and patients readily report that the power of CIMBS still has remarkable effectiveness online. In addition, when we conduct online therapy demonstrations, they are clearly effective treatments for the "patient" (participant) and have been validated by the other observers.

We assert that the Complex Integration of Multiple Brain Systems is a neurobiological paradigm. This paradigm remains a constant no matter what therapeutic modality you use. The Primary, Secondary, and Tertiary-level brain systems are always present and always operating. That knowledge has helped us trust that the therapeutic approaches we use to harness the power and wisdom of emotional brain systems, which have been so effective in person, will also help us be effective therapists online as well. That trust has been borne out by our experiences.

We have made a number of adaptations to our treatment approaches with our patients and trainees in order to enhance our effectiveness online. It is helpful to be aware of some of the special challenges when working online with treatments focused on multiple emotional brain systems.

THERAPEUTIC ATTACHMENT RELATIONSHIP

We have found that the Therapeutic Attachment Relationship (Chapter 5) remains the keystone to Activating the attachment brain systems, Safe, Care, and Connection. Remote and online sessions make it more difficult to access the safeness of the Therapeutic Attachment Relationship, and it is harder for our patients to experience our care. Developing and nurturing the Connection brain system takes more effort from a distance. The narrow focus we maintain while working in the Transpiring Present Moment within the Therapeutic Attachment Relationship provides an intimacy and immediacy that would otherwise be difficult to achieve online. Our constant eye gaze is especially important online because the patient cannot take in our full energy and full body engagement in their process. Eye-to-eye connection will engage more emotional arousal in order to work with neuroplasticity and build resilient brain systems.

Adaptations: We wanted our patients to take in as much of the Therapeutic Attachment Relationship as they can online, so we experimented with trying to approximate the intimate connection via various online platforms. We found that it works best for the therapist and patient elevate their cameras on top of books or boxes so the camera focuses directly on their forehead just above the eyes. Both therapist and patient are then at eye level with each other. The therapist's body (from the knees up) needs to fill the screen, taking up all the space on the patient's monitor. For that we ask the patient to turn off the image of themselves on their screen so that they are watching only us.

NONCONSCIOUS PROCESSING

The therapeutic focus in CIMBS remains on nonconscious emotional processing. CIMBS therapy is primarily directed to activating and harnessing the power of the brainstem and basal nuclei. Therefore it remains important that the online patient sees our gestures and body language, which speak to the nonconscious emotional processing of our patients. We want to be able to see and experience our full engagement. At the same time we want to be able to read our patient's psychophysiological shifts as well.

Adaptations: We position our camera so that the patient can see our torso and arms. We ask the patient to position their camera further back and with the top of the computer inclined forward, so that in addition to their face, we can see their torso and especially their hand gestures.

ENERGY FLOW

We have found that it takes more energy to Activate the brain systems in our patients when practicing online. Arousal tends to be low in online therapy, so it is harder to access dopamine circuits, neuroplasticity, and long-term learning. It is possible that the mirror neurons are slow in the uptake too.

Adaptations: The careful narrow focus we use when working with the Transpiring Present Moment and the Initial Direct Activation help provide more focused energy to make up for the distance of online therapy. We have adapted by emphasizing and making more our body movements more clear with our interventions.

CHALLENGES OF ONLINE CIMBS THERAPY

There are a number of challenges to using these approaches online:

It is harder to assess breathing, skin color, and prosody (Chapter 14).

Everything we do takes more energy.

It is more difficult to provide affect regulation and relational collaboration.

It is harder to access the peripheral nervous system, because you cannot see—or more importantly, feel—the body language as well.

It is easier to get caught up in the verbal content and lose sight of the nonconscious processes that are happening in the session.

It is harder to provide the quiet and privacy of in-person therapy. For example, if the patient has little children in the home, they are more easily interrupted.

Sometimes it can be difficult to discern whether the internet is freezing up or the patient is freezing up!

We often find ourselves extra tired at the end of the day because of the extra effort expended to treat patients online. You should feel free to fully relax and indulge yourself on the couch with "cookies" and funny entertainment to help yourself recharge.

Adaptations:

- You will need to carefully focus your energy as the External Generator (Chapter 5).

Take a 15–20 minute break between patients to recharge your batteries.

Engage your patient's collaboration explicitly and repeatedly (Chapter 5).

Your patient's conscious awareness and experience of their body and emotional sensations is a useful focus. So we ask the patient to be our co-therapist and provide an account of the movements in their lower body (Chapters 6 and 7).

Slow down even more to let the nonconscious activations have sufficient time to reveal themselves. Be patient because online therapy is slower and may take as much as twice as long as in-person therapy.

We don't know where the psychotherapy profession will be headed in the months and years after the pandemic has passed. However, we suspect that some of the changes and innovations introduced to adapt to the pandemic beginning in 2020 could persist. In particular, some patients and therapists may find reason to continue conducting therapy online. We are convinced that CIMBS, like all forms of psychotherapy, is most powerful when practiced in person. However, we also have clearly found that CIMBS therapeutic approaches can be adapted to remain effective and efficient online.

GLOSSARY

This glossary is intended to provide the reader with our specific use of important words and phrases. Many of these terms have everyday familiarity, but here we are applying them to this therapeutic paradigm with precision. We capitalize specific brain systems, interventions, and phrases that are particularly important.

Activating: The specific and precise use of verbal and nonverbal (embodied) interventions to arouse one or more neural circuits or emotional brain systems. Activating mobilizes the system to utilize its wisdom, energy, and processing capabilities. Activating also tests the functioning of a distinct circuit or system; for example, responses could be hyperactive, moderate, or hypoactive.

adaptive and maladaptive neural circuits: *Adaptive circuits* develop early and naturally through a combination of genetic drives and nonconscious learning to support our survival and enhance our ability to thrive. *Maladaptive circuits* develop in threatening situations where the developing child needs to suppress one or more of the highly evolved brain systems in order to survive. For example, although those circuits were beneficial at the time, when they became automatic patterns, they could continue to prevent the functionality of the Care or Connection brain systems.

affects: Neurobiological phenomena that generate a specific kind of brain activation that mobilizes us to respond to some stimulus or threat. There are three categories of affects: homeostatic, sensory, and emotional. When the homeostatic affect for hydration mobilizes thirst, an animal will seek out water without the need for any conscious choice. It is automatic. When our sensory affect of taste detects bitterness, we automatically spit out whatever is in our mouth. When our emotional affect of care sees our infant, we automatically direct our energy and attention to comfort and connect with our child.

Agency: A tertiary-level brain system that gives the patient a sense that they are capable and can make things happen in their lives. When this brain system is activated, they vocalize their desires and choices with a strong voice and congruent physical activations as well.

alliance: A union or association formed for mutual benefit.

amygdala: A neural structure in the brain that is active when experiencing fear, anxiety, and danger, and when emotional processing takes place (Figure 15.1). It and the hippocampus are the main reservoirs of nonconscious (implicit) emotional memories.

anger: The intrinsic emotions that energize us to intensify our efforts to sustain our equilibrium, comfort, well-being, and survival. Relational anger refers to the emotions that seek to bring others in line, rapidly, with our evolutionary desires and motivations (Panksepp & Biven, 2012). Anger is part of a normal emotional continuum. The emotional continuum starts with irritation and with increasing intensity can become annoyance, then anger, and finally rage.

anxiety: An internal state of agitation that may arise when responding to present experience, anticipating the future, or reflecting on the past (Siegel, 2012).

assertions: Interventions that declare an observable fact or truth. "Our attention is unconditional." "You are enough just the way you are."

Assertive: A primary-level brain system that empowers us to pursue our needs, satisfy our wants, and thrive in the world. The patient's embodied experience is strong (especially in the muscles along the spine), powerful, and capable: "I feel like I have a rod up my back."

attachment: Highly evolved mammalian neural patterns that influence and motivate individuals to seek care, safety, and connection with caregivers.

attachment brain systems: Nonconscious primary-level Safe, Care, and Connection brain systems. They have played the biggest roles in the development of everyone's unique attachment patterns (Chapter 10).

Attention: A tertiary-level brain system that supports the ability to focus and direct conscious energy to some specific interest.

attunement: The ways in which internal emotional and bodily states are the focus of attention and mindful awareness (Siegel, 2012). Interpersonal attunement occurs when the therapist is mindfully aware, caring, open, and attentive to the patient. Internal attunement occurs when the patient/person can be mindfully aware, receptive, and open to their own present-moment emotions and physiology. Attunement is not the same as matching.

Authority: A tertiary-level brain system that gives the patient a sense that they know who they are and that they are the authors of their feelings and desires.

Autonomy: A tertiary-level brain system that provides the ability to act on one's own power separate from all others. When this brain system is activated, the patient is able to make conscious, explicit decisions on their own behalf on an ongoing basis.

Awareness: A tertiary-level brain system that refers to deliberate nonjudgmental attention to the present moment: "I am aware of feeling sad."

balance: The ability to sustain an even distribution of weight, enabling someone to remain upright and steady. It can refer to emotional as well as physical stability. For example, your present emotional balance could mean holding onto your fear from childhood to protect yourself from the pain of attachment and abandonment. We describe the psychophysiological process and uncomfortable experience of being outside of the usual equilibrium as being out of balance, off balance, or in disequilibrium. Loss of balance refers to becoming disoriented or overwhelmed emotionally. We have a tendency to utilize (lean on) old, rigid coping mechanisms or automatic reaction patterns when experiencing a loss of balance.

belonging: The drive and capability to be a genuine member of a family, peer group, clan, or society. When we do not adhere to the rules or norms of the group, the emotions of guilt, fear, and/or betrayal are mobilized and inhibit impulses to break the norms, often out of our awareness. Belonging is so important to humans that it may well be considered a brain system in its own right.

bottom-up: Information, sensations, and feelings that come from sensory input that arises uniquely from the present-moment experience. Associated memories are secondary effects.

BrainMind: A term asserting that there is no useful distinction between the brain and mind in affective neuroscience (Panksepp & Biven, 2012). There are many brain systems in our BrainMind.

brain system: A system that takes raw inputs from the body and environment and focuses that energy into emotions, motivations, inhibitions, and enhancers. The brain systems operate like the processors in your computer. A distinct brain system is made up of many interconnected neural circuits dedicated to meeting our survival and emotional needs.

capability: The extent to which the capacity of a system is fully realized and functional at this moment. For example, your visual system's capability is impaired if you suffer from cataracts.

capacity: The innate performance ability of a system that evolved to enhance survival, such as vision, hearing, or speaking. For example you are born with the capacity to have vision.

Care: A primary-level brain system that inspires us to invest enormous amounts of attention, energy, and interest in another being or ourselves. The patient's embodied experience of care is felt as warmth in the chest, sparkling eyes, and spontaneous smiles.

circus: The conscious self-awareness of physical or emotional feelings in the present experience, in two or more rings or levels. A three-ring circus is the conscious self-awareness of both approach and avoidant emotions in the present experience at the same time. A five-ring circus, a metaphor for many things happening at once, is the conscious self-awareness of multiple thoughts and feelings in the present experience, along with awareness of the relational experience with the therapist and ability to make conscious choices at the same time.

closed loop: A rigid neural circuit that creates habits that are not open to updating. A closed loop could be a conscious thought (e.g., "I am unlovable") or a nonconscious avoidance of accepting caring from other people.

coherence: A state of neural synchrony, meaning the harmonious firing of multiple brain systems. When we help our patients reduce conflict and achieve moments of congruence and consistency, their BrainMinds can operate in this state of coherence (Siegel, 2007). This coherence is the outcome we refer to as the Complex Integration of Multiple Brain Systems.

collaboration: The type of therapeutic alliance in which the patient is able to engage their authority and autonomy to fully participate in the therapeutic process. Collaboration is contrasted with cooperation, or following along, and compliance, when patients do what they think is expected of them.

compassion: Literally, to suffer with someone. Compassion is more than empathy, for it contains the genuine felt experience of suffering in a fashion similar to the person for whom we feel compassion. Compassion can be an antidote to feeling unworthy and/or undeserving.

competency: An actual and visible activation of a capability that is revealed in this moment. Experience and training have the potential to enhance the competencies of each brain system.

complex system: A system that can change in nonlinear ways, such that small inputs can lead to large and unpredictable long-term changes. Complex systems can release Spontaneous Self-Organization phenomena (Siegel, 2012).

Complexity refers to a new level of functionality that arises out of the integration of multiple differentiated systems.

conflict: Situations in which the drives of one brain system oppose, contradict, or are at odds with another system. For example, in Chapter 4, Penny's Fear system shuts down her Play system. When the patient's responses to your interventions do not seem to make sense, it indicates a conflict and is a signal to look for underlying inconsistencies or nonconscious incongruence.

congruence: The emotional and psychophysiological state in which actual experiences and motivational goals are in alignment and in sync. Incongruence occurs when real experiences and motivational goals are in conflict. Many of the symptoms and psychological problems of our patients are a result of incongruence between motivational approaches of the Primaries and the avoidances and inhibitions of Secondaries (Grawe, 2007).

Connection: A primary-level brain system that mobilizes us to gradually and viscerally develop deep emotional attachments to our care providers and others. The patient's embodied experience of connection is one of feeling closeness, wanting proximity to this specific person, and feeling, for example, "I matter to them, and they matter to me."

conscious: The subjective experience of being aware. Conscious also refers to tertiary-level brain systems and phenomena that can enter awareness.

consistency: The compatibility of simultaneously transpiring neural or mental processes. Consistency also refers to the internal relations among intrapsychic processes and states. Consistency is a basic principle of internal regulation that supersedes all specific needs. Inconsistency refers to incompatibility or discrepancy between simultaneous activated mental or neural processes (Grawe, 2007).

constraint: Emotional inhibitions from secondary-level brain systems that are out of proportion to the situation of the present moment. For example, the patient may avoid connection with the therapist because of shame or fear.

deliberate practice: Ongoing learning and skill refinement that we pursue after our initial professional training, such as observing your own work with video recordings, getting expert feedback, setting small incremental learning goals just beyond your ability, repeating behavioral rehearsals of specific skills, continuously assessing your performance, and working with a mentor or training group to practice new interventions (Rousmaniere, 2017).

Differentiating: Dynamic therapeutic processes that enable the therapist and patient to distinguish and experience the distinct nature of one or more neural circuits and/or brain systems. Differentiating can mean paying attention to multiple systems with equal interest or singling out one or two for special attention. Differentiating also means disentangling and interrupting rigid, habitual, maladaptive emotional patterns that interfere with the capabilities of other systems.

disentangling: The term many patients use spontaneously to describe their felt sense or visceral experience of letting go of constraining emotional learning from the past (see *entanglement*).

disequilibrium: Not just a shift out of a previous harmony and emotional equilibrium, but also includes sensations of discomfort, distress, wrongness, betrayal, and badness (see *equilibrium*).

embodying intervention: A therapist moving their own body to communicate the intervention. For example, therapists may open their arms to welcome the patient's emotional experiences, or put their hands on the chest to invite the patient to be aware of sensations in their torso.

emotion: A conscious and nonconscious neurobiological phenomenon that has its own distinct psychophysiological signature that is often visible to others. Emotions also refer to our conscious perceptions of visceral activations that inspire us to movement and motivation. We have a felt sense of our emotions that is unique to each of us and often unique to the context and relationships. Our gut feelings or heartfelt experiences are literal and metaphorical examples of our conscious emotions.

emotional brain system: A distinct neurobiological system that evolved to enable a person to meet their psychological needs for safety, care, connection, and learning. These systems operate as generators of energy, processors of information, and sources of highly evolved neurobiological wisdom. These systems have become more specialized and precise in primates and other higher mammals, enabling them to thrive and live complex social lives.

empirical evidence: Facts or information that are based on observations and present-moment experience rather than theory, speculation, or logic. This evidence can be readily verified and validated by other observers. Psychophysiological phenomena can give you reliable empirical evidence, in contrast with the limitations of verbal reports, explanations, or history (Chapter 14).

entanglement: A situation that can occur when different brain systems do not function independently. For example, experiences of autonomy may feel shameful if the Shame brain system is entangled with the Autonomy brain system. *Entanglement* is often used interchangeably with *constraint*.

equilibrium: A state in which multiple sources of energy are in some kind of sustainable balance with each other. Our minds develop a kind of emotional equilibrium based on the energy of multiple brain systems. The energy from five to ten distinct systems could be playing a role in your present emotional equilibrium.

explicit and implicit: We use the term *explicit* in two distinct ways. One form refers to interventions that explicitly label the brain system or intention of the therapeutic intervention. For example, "We are here to help you feel *safe* inside yourself." "Do you want us to *collaborate* together?" The other form refers to two different kinds of stored learning: implicit and explicit. Implicit learned memory develops from birth and is mostly nonconscious. Implicit learning is also called procedural memory. Explicit (declarative) learned memories are conscious, and they become available later in life (age 3), after the hippocampus develops sufficiently to install conscious memories.

external generator: The therapist's role in using their precisely focused energy to keep stimulating a brain system that would otherwise come to rest and lose its power. For example, you are operating as an external generator when you can direct the energy of your curiosity (Seeking), delight (Play), and Care brain systems to keep stimulating activations in your patient.

Facilitating: Interventions that are intended to ease, speed, and enhance treatment. Facilitating involves sustaining and reinforcing the activation of adaptive neural circuits and brain systems. Therapists are facilitating when they focus their energy and interest in specific observable competencies of the patient in the transpiring present moment.

Fail-Safe Network: Multiple resilient and complex integrated brain systems that can process large amounts of emotional energy and information, especially in a crisis. Using an electric power grid analogy, these systems all function in parallel (see Figure 2.2). When one or more of these brain systems shuts down or gets triggered, the other integrated brain systems are able to assume the load of energy and information. CIMBS can provide your patients with a Fail-Safe Complex Network.

Fear: A secondary-level brain system (LeDoux,1996; Panksepp, 2012) that activates in response to physical (not Safe) danger. The nonconscious physiological experience is: "Pull back from the danger—come back to safety." Severe threats to well-being activate hardwired circuits in the brain and produce responses that help us survive. Fear can be both an adaptive response aimed at survival in the face of life-threatening circumstances, and also may create devastating psychiatric problems, including severe affective disorders.

feedback loop: See *negative feedback loop* and *positive feedback loop*.

feeling: A conscious sensation or manifestation of emotional brain system activations. The physical sensations that could become conscious are primarily nonconscious (see *emotion*).

gatekeeper or inhibitory brain system: A secondary-level brain system which invites adaptive actions in and keeps maladaptive actions out. In other words, it potentiates adaptive neural circuits and suppresses neural circuits that interfere with our needs and motivations. When these secondaries are hyperactive or entangled with other brain systems, they can become constraints to adaptive emotional functioning.

Go the Other Way: Directing therapeutic energy and attention toward the adaptive resources of multiple brain systems rather than addressing the patient's distress or anxiety directly (Chapter 4). Facilitating underlying capabilities and competences will inhibit the BrainMind's stress reactions.

Grief: A secondary-level brain system (Panksepp, 2012) that activates in response to the danger of loss of Care from others. The nonconscious physiological experience is: "Stop the aloneness—come back to Care." Grief can be consciously experienced as mental suffering, sorrow, or painful regret.

Guilt: A secondary-level brain system (Schore, 1994; Cozolino, 2016) that activates in response to social danger (not belonging to the group). Guilt is an emotional experience characterized by feeling distress when we believe we have done something that compromises standards of conduct for the group, clan, or family. The physiological experience of the Guilt brain system is a suffocating, heavy feeling in your chest and an incessant throb in your heart, pushing you to make repairs.

horizontal: Facilitating, Differentiating, and Integrating refer to utilizing those processes on one or more brain systems but limited to the same level of the nervous system and mental processing. For example, you may simultaneously differentiate and connect the Attention, Awareness, and Authority brain systems.

hyperactive systems: Automatic, conditioned sets of neural circuits that have been activated so frequently that they have become rigid and closed to new learning. They have the highest probability of being activated, sometimes called triggers.

hyperconnected: Entangled brain systems that are undifferentiated and often in a closed loop with another brain system. Hyperconnected brain systems can be at the root of maladaptive habits or reactions. For example, the Shame brain system may be hyperconnected with the Play brain system and so prevent a person from being able to play. The psychophysiological responses are constrained, conflicted, or even contradictory when brain systems are hyperconnected or entangled. Differentiating hyperconnected brain systems requires perception, patience, and trust.

hypoactive: Underdeveloped brain systems that have been rarely activated so that they are weak, impoverished, and unlikely to be activated. Even when activated, they are unable to handle large amounts of energy and information without shutting down.

implicit: See *explicit.*

Importance/Salience: A secondary-level brain system (Grawe, 2007) that responds to adaptive behaviors by providing positive feedback to sustain actions that are important to our well-being. This brain system enables your patient to stay present and focused on your therapeutic work even when they are uncomfortable. You can also Activate it to reinforce the activation of other hypoactive brain systems.

inhibitory brain system: See *gatekeeper or inhibitory brain system.*

Initial Directed Activation: A collection of interventions in multiple brain systems that carefully focuses the therapeutic process at the beginning of the session. This intervention contains two parts: first, a brief meditation, and second, a series of carefully worded assertions. The sequence of words gives the therapist structure and helps direct the patient's attention to the work of therapy in the present moment.

Integrating: The simultaneous parallel processing of energy and information by multiple distinct brain systems. Integrating is a natural process that can lead to the opening of closed systems and releasing of spontaneous capacities of the BrainMind. Integrating is also a treatment process directed by the therapist that facilitates keeping multiple systems active even when fear, shame, or fatigue get in the way (see *spontaneous self-organization*).

internal generator: The ability of the patient to produce self-sustaining loops capable of Facilitating and enhancing the energy and activity of any neural circuit or brain system. The patient has the ability to use internal positive feedback to take over the therapist's external generator role to sustain adaptive activations.

intervention: The therapist's verbal and nonverbal actions to provide treatment. Types of interventions include the following: *assertions*, which draw attention to adaptive activation (e.g., "Great awareness" "You are being capable"); *invitations* to self-awareness (e.g., "What are you experiencing?" "What are you noticing right now?"); and questions for *Facilitating* (e.g., "How are you experiencing your assertiveness in your torso?").

matching: The natural tendency to experience the same emotions as another person. This is partly learned and partly arises from mirror neurons. The tendency for matching can interfere with the therapist's awareness of the activations of Primaries.

mindfulness: Deliberate nonjudgmental awareness and attention to the present moment and to the BrainMind's mixed processes.

Motivation/Determination: An enhancing secondary system (Schwartz & Begley, 2002; Grawe, 2007) that provides energy to help us persevere when we are meeting obstacles or other difficulties. It provides a sense of wanting or desire to pursue that which is within our reach. This energy helps us override our fears, shame, or other inhibitions.

myelination: The process by which the brain insulates axons with a fatty sheath in order to speed their signals.

needs: Humans' basic psychological needs (Grawe, 2007), including (1) attachment, (2) self-esteem enhancement, (3) orientation, (4) mastery, (5) coherence, (6) increase pleasure/decrease distress, and (7) acknowledgment.

negative feedback loop: Inhibits and puts the brakes on the activation of another system. *Negative* refers to the fact that the loop reduces or inhibits energy flow. Negative feedback loops reduce maladaptive impulses out of our awareness all the time.

neural circuits and networks: The brain is made up of a hierarchy of individual neurons, circuits, and systems. Thousands of neurons connect together due to genetics and/or experience into circuits, and multiple circuits then coalesce into brain systems. Multiple interconnected systems form an integrated network.

neuroplasticity (or neural plasticity): Our mind's ability to literally change the structure of our brain over the life span. Neuroplasticity enables the brain to reassign jobs. The formation of new synaptic connections is one form of neuroplasticity.

neurotransmitter: A chemical messenger that transmits information from one nerve cell across the synapse to a target cell. It is a chemical made by the nerve cell specifically to transmit messages. Examples are dopamine, opioids, oxytocin, and serotonin.

nonconscious: The vast realm of processes and contents of the BrainMind that can never be known, although their effects can be clearly observed. Highly evolved hidden wisdom and earned information are contained in the nonconscious BrainMind.

nonconscious anxiety: Physical and psychological manifestations that arise from implicit dangers and/or previous learning. The nervous system is constantly protecting us from dangers of which we have no conscious awareness.

open loop: A neural circuit that creates emotions and behaviors that are contingent, often unique, and fit the context. Open loops are constantly dynamic and are being updated from moment to moment within a range of possibilities (see *closed loop*).

orientation: A basic psychological need, referring to where we are and what are we here to do together.

paradigm: A distinct, broad framework of concepts including theories, research methods, postulates, and standards that are used to structure the practice of science and guide the direction of research.

parallel processing: The sustained simultaneous activations of differentiated brain systems (see Figure 2.2). Parallel processing is often an incongruent experience when each brain system is operating independently. Parallel processing can potentiate the processes of integrating differentiated systems to unfold (versus linear processing).

patient: A person who comes for therapeutic help because they are suffering. The word *patient* is the present participle of the Latin verb *patior*, which means to suffer. The complement to the patient who suffers is the healer who tries to relieve the suffering.

patient factors: Include self-awareness, motivation to change, fear, shame, cognitive limitations, psychosis, and personality patterns. These factors are not usually what the patients complain of when they seek therapy, although they can significantly affect the progress and success of therapy. Patient factors play the biggest role in successful therapeutic treatments.

physiopsychotherapy: Forms of treatment that emphasize directing the therapeutic process toward facilitating the nervous system's innate emotional resources. The goals are both to strengthen those capabilities and to release (open up) emotional constraints from early neglect and/or trauma. Physiopsychotherapy treatments are also experiential, embodied, and repeated many times in order for patients to develop new adaptive neural circuits.

Play: A primary-level brain system that motivates us to interact with others in a funny, joyous, rough-and-tumble, laughing, spontaneous, quirky, and exploratory fashion. The patient's embodied experience is one of lightness, uplifting, tingling, an internal giggle, and feeling delight.

Pleasure: An Enhancing secondary-level brain system (Panksepp, 2012) that activates in response to stimuli that enhance our survival. For example, consuming healthy food activates neural circuits that alert us that we like what we are eating. Your patient will often have a smile or twinkle in their eye when they experience pleasure.

positive feedback loop: Sustains and adds energy to the activation of another system. *Positive* refers to the fact that the loop adds energy, and it could add energy to a maladaptive habit or pattern. *Positive* does not refer to the value of the feedback loop (see *negative feedback loop*).

prefrontal cortex: An area of the brain that, along with its medial and orbital subregions, is the anatomical region where the brain's executive center is believed to be localized (Figure 15.1).

presence: A manner of being open, receptive, and flexible to ourselves and to others. We also use this term to describe the therapist being aware of and connected to the patient.

primary-level brain system (Primary): A nonconscious system that has most of its neural circuitry located in the brainstem, including Safe, Care, Connection, Assertive, Seeking, Play, and Sensory systems.

proactive anger: An evolved source of energy and strength in all of our brain systems. It is built in and requires no learning. Proactive anger helps us to meet our needs, thrive, and survive.

process: Brain systems operate like the processors in your computer. They take raw inputs from the body and environment and focus that energy into emotions, motivations, inhibitions, and enhancers. Brain systems do the work of the mind (Siegel 1996, 2007); they process energy and information.

psychophysiological perspective: A consciously chosen focus of attention on nonverbal and nonconscious physical phenomena that give the therapist valuable information about the inner workings of the patient's nervous system. This psychophysiological information can provide precise information with which to guide the therapy (Chapter 14).

psychophysiological phenomena: Both the observable and invisible physical movements, changes, and behaviors that arise from the activations of nonconscious emotional brain systems. Common examples include facial and mouth movements, tone of voice, eye contact, visible tears, and body posture. Psychophysiological phenomena are intimate forms of communication over which we have limited control.

psychophysiological shift: An observable physical shift in the level of anxiety, arousal, interest, engagement, drive, body language, and so on. It reveals internal nonconscious changes and potential for new learning and neuroplasticity.

reactive anger: Also defensive anger, results from developmental learning that occurred in situations of crisis, trauma, or neglect. These forms of anger can lead to symptoms, behavioral problems, and relationship difficulties. Reactive anger tends to be loud, dramatic, and aggressive, and can be violent.

reflecting: Selectively noting distinct adaptive brain system activations that arise spontaneously in the therapeutic process and then turning that energy back toward the patient with greater focus and precision. In this manner, you are intervening like a parabolic reflector in which the patient's competence or capability is reflected back in a more precise and intense way so that they can reexperience their competence on a deeper level.

reflective awareness: Observing one's experience in light of underlying mental states. It makes sense of the experience versus the process of the experience.

repetition: The process in which the therapist is Facilitating one or more brain systems again and again. On a cognitive level, this can look and sound tedious. However, on a visceral level, each time we activate a circuit or system, we are strengthening it.

resilient brain system: A brain system with the following characteristics: it is highly developed and distinct, capable, reliable, and competent. It can process large amounts of energy and information without getting overwhelmed, triggered, or shut down. It operates smoothly, independently, and autonomously even in times of crisis. It is differentiated from other systems and does not depend on other networks to function well.

Safe: A primary-level brain system that encompasses much more than the absence of fear or anxiety. The patient's embodied experience of Safe is a deep sense of calm, fullness, expansive, solid, and grounded.

safeness: A state that occurs when we come to connect with another person and our brain establishes psychophysiological harmony with the other. There is a fulfillment of the desire for a co-created state in which the face and the intonation of the voice are conveying that their physiological state is calm (Gilbert 2005; Porges, 2014). Safeness behaviors are open and vulnerable.

safety: The absence of physical danger. Safety behaviors are closed and avoid threats and often other people.

search pattern: An established pattern of observation that enables our BrainMind to recognize a word, object, or movement that we have seen before and rapidly identify it.

secondary-level brain system (Secondary): A nonconscious brain system, most of whose neural circuitry is located in the basal ganglia. Secondaries alter the strength of motivations, emotions, feelings, and impulses. For example, the Fear brain system nonconsciously moves us toward safe environments, not just away from dangerous situations. The actual emotions of fear, grief, or motivation are not the same as the brain systems.

Seeking: A primary-level brain system that, when active, gives us the freedom and desire to explore our environment and meet our needs in thousands of different ways. The patient's embodied experience of seeking is the felt sense of interest, curiosity, expectancy, excitement, and anticipation.

Self: A dynamic conscious process that integrates the unique feelings and experiences of the nonconscious primary-level and secondary-level brain systems that are unfolding from moment to moment. This Self is a process, not a thing.

self-efficacy: An individual's belief in his or her capacity to execute behaviors necessary to produce specific performance attainments.

self-function: The capability of each brain system to establish and maintain its own highly evolved needs and drives. The self-function of each brain system evolved as a result of the saliency of the activations that further the needs of that system.

self-organization: A process in which some form of overall higher order arises from interactions between differentiated and integrated parts (systems) of an initially disordered system. The term was initially introduced to science in

1947 by W. Ross Ashby, an English psychiatrist. Self-organization can be released within the integrating process (see *integrating*).

Sensory: A primary-level brain system that conducts the brainstem's processing of emotional information that arises from the peripheral nervous system and the torso in particular.

Shame: A secondary-level brain system (Schore, 1994) that activates in response to relational (no Connection) danger. The nonconscious physiological experience is: "Stop the action that upsets my caregiver—come back to Connection." Shame is characterized by behaviors of withdrawal and feelings of distress, powerlessness, and worthlessness. Shame also triggers visceral sensations of nausea, gagging, and/or an inward collapse.

shiny eyes: A phenomenon that occurs when the therapist (or patient) is experiencing simultaneous activations of several brain systems such as Care, Connection, Safe, Pleasure, Importance, Value, and delight (Play).

Static Contradiction: Internal brain system constraints in which the inhibition is so strong that it contradicts the underlying Primary drive. Multiple Static Contradictions between the Primaries and Secondaries lead to the structural problems that can result in personality disorders, core shame, chronic depression, and other mental disorders.

struggle: "In struggle we grow" refers to staying in the disorienting experience of new learning that often activates avoidant neural circuits. Learning to ride a unicycle is a suitable metaphor.

tertiary-level brain system (Tertiary): A brain system, most of whose neural circuitry is located in the neocortex. This level includes the conscious brain systems we call the A-Team: Awareness, Attention, Authority, Autonomy, and Agency (Chapter 7).

Therapeutic Attachment Relationship: A relationship that goes beyond the therapeutic alliance of conventional psychotherapy by prioritizing the development of attachment brain systems. In this intimate relationship, both the patient and the therapist are experiencing emotions, not just talking about their emotions. The interventions we use to develop the Therapeutic Attachment Relationship are primarily nonverbal, experiential, and embodied by the therapist.

therapeutic process: A dynamic series of emotional and relational interactions between the patient and the therapist. This is in contrast to content, which refers to the words or stories that are being discussed. The contrasting paradigm of CIMBS is predominantly focused on the nonconscious dynamic processes that are transpiring within the patient and between the patient and therapist.

therapist factors: Personal characteristics of the therapist, the real relationship between the patient and therapist, and the manner in which the therapist utilizes the therapeutic relationship to heal the patient and address the symptoms. Norcross et al. (2009) and Miller and Rollnick (2013) list the factors found in successful therapeutic outcomes: empathy, genuineness, respect, openness, congruence, collaboration, alliance, goal consensus, cohesion, and positive regard.

Training: Intentionally and actively exercising and modifying specific neural circuits and brain systems. In a session, the therapist exercises (facilitates, reinforces, and enhances) a neural circuit repeatedly to improve its functionality. At the end of each session, the therapist and patient decide on precise exercises that can be practiced between sessions to maintain and increase experiential learning.

Transpiring Present Moment: *Transpiring* refers to uniquely unfolding immediate emotional responses to therapeutic interventions. *Present* refers to the experience of right now, rather than some recent or past experience. A *moment* is a period of time long enough to contain a conscious or emotional experience (7–10 seconds).

treatment: The interventions and approaches that seek to harness the full range of the patient's conscious and nonconscious emotional brain systems in order to change the neural structures in their BrainMind. Treatment consists of Activating, Facilitating, and Differentiating innate adaptive, positive, self-affirming neural circuits and brain systems. These treatments need to be experiential, embodied, and repeated many times in order for patients to develop new adaptive neural circuits. We know that Facilitating adaptive circuits will also inhibit maladaptive negative, destructive, and dysfunctional neural circuits (Grawe, 2007).

Trust the Process: Most of the changes and learning that take place by applying CIMBS principles occur on the patient's nonconscious levels of emotional processing. You will not necessarily be able to receive verbal feedback or confirmation of the progress you are making.

Value/Internal Reward: A secondary brain system (Grawe, 2007; Panksepp, 2012) that provides us with internal positive feedback even when there is no obvious benefit or pleasure in our actions. Nature evolved this enhancing brain system to give us the innate incentives to learn what is ultimately valuable for us to survive and thrive in our lives.

vertical: Facilitating, Differentiating, Training, and Integrating refer to directing those processes in one or more distinct brain systems at more than one level of the nervous system. For example, when the patient is paying attention (Tertiary) to his motivation (Secondary) to harness his drive and power (Primary) and experiencing the strength in the core of his torso (peripheral), he is vertically integrating at all four levels of emotional processing.

welcoming: Approaching and accepting all of the patient's emotional and psychophysiological experiences, especially ones that they would like to get rid of, such as shame and anxiety.

worth: The sense of one's own unconditional intrinsic value and importance. It appears to be an emergent emotion that arises from the Value and Important brain systems. Worth develops very early and may or may not be connected to the conscious self. Every patient has some level of worth nonconsciously, even when they seem to have no self-worth. Compassion can be an antidote to feeling unworthy or undeserving.

BIBLIOGRAPHY

Abbass, A. (2015). *Reaching through resistance*. Kansas City, MO: Seven Leaves.

Abbass, A., Hancock, J. T., Henderson, J., & Kisely, S. (2006). Short-term psychodynamic psychotherapies for common mental disorders. *Cochrane Database of Systematic Reviews, 4*, CD004687.

Ainsworth, M. D. (1982). Attachment: Retrospect and prospect. In C. M. Parkes & J. Stevenson-Hinde (Eds.), *The place of attachment in human behaviour*. London: Tavistock.

Badenoch, B. (2008). *Being a brain-wise therapist*. New York: Norton.

Bowlby, J. (1960). Separation anxiety. *International Journal of Psychonanalysis, 41*, 89–113.

Bowlby, J. (1980). *Attachment and loss: Vol. 3. Loss: Sadness and depression*. New York: Basic Books.

Brown, B. (2010). *The gifts of imperfection*. Center City, MN: Hazelden.

Bugental, J. F. T. (1990). *Intimate journeys: Stories of life-changing therapy*. San Francisco, CA: Jossey-Bass.

Chabris, C., & Simons, D. (2009). *The invisible gorilla*. New York: Random House

Coughlin, P. (1996). *Intensive short-term dynamic psychotherapy*. New York: John Wiley & Sons.

Cozolino, L. (2002). *The neuroscience of psychotherapy*. New York: Norton.

Cozolino, L. (2006). *The neuroscience of human relationships*. New York: Norton.

Cozolino, L. (2016). *Why therapy works*. New York: Norton.

Damasio, A. R. (1994). *Descartes' error: Emotion, reason, and the human brain*. New York: Avon.

Damasio, A. R. (1999). *The feeling of what happens: Body and emotion in the making of consciousness*. New York: Harcourt Brace.

Damasio, A. R. (2003). *Looking for Spinoza: Joy, sorrow and the feeling brain*. Orlando, FL: Harcourt.

Damasio, A. R. (2012). *Self comes to mind: Constructing the conscious brain*. New York: Pantheon.

Dana, D. (2018). *The polyvagal theory in therapy*. New York: Norton.

Darwin, C. (1998). *The expression of emotion in man and animals* (3rd ed.). New York: Oxford University Press. (Original work published 1872)

Davanloo, H. (1990). *Unlocking the unconscious*. New York: John Wiley & Sons.

Davanloo, H. (2005). Intensive short-term dynamic psychotherapy. In H. Kaplan & B. Sadock (Eds.), *Comprehensive textbook of psychiatry* (8th ed., Vol. 2, pp. 2628–2652). Philadelphia: Lippincott Williams & Wilkins.

Davidson, R. (2012). *The emotional life of your brain*. New York: Hudson Street.

Dichter, G. S., Felder, J.N., & Smoski, M. (2008). Effects of psychotherapy on brain function: Brain imaging studies indicate changes. *Psychiatric Times, 25*(10), 34–38.

Doidge, N. (2007). *The brain that changes itself*. New York: Penguin.

Doidge, N. (2015). *The brain's way of healing*. New York: Viking.

Ecker, B., Ticic, R., & Hulley, L. (2012). *Unlocking the emotional brain*. New York: Routledge.

Einstein, A. (1950) *Out of my later years*. New York: Open Road Media.

Ekman, P. (2003). *Emotions revealed*. New York: Times Books.

Ekman, P., & Davidson, R. J. (Eds.). (1994). *The nature of emotion: Fundamental questions*. New York: Oxford University Press.

Fogel, A. (2009). *Psychophysiology of self-awareness*. New York: Norton.

Fosha, D. (2000). *The transforming power of affect: A model for accelerated change*. New York: Basic Books.

Fosha, D., Siegel, D. J., & Solomon, M. F. (Eds.). (2009). *The healing power of emotion: Affective neuroscience, development and clinical practice*. New York: Norton.

Gardner, H. (2000). *The disciplined mind*. New York: Penguin.

Gardner, H. (2011). *Frames of mind*. New York: Basic Books.

Gilbert, P. (Ed.). (2005). *Compassion*. New York: Routledge.

Ginot, E. (2015). *Neuropsychology of the unconscious*. New York: Norton.

Goleman, D. (1995). *Emotional intelligence*. New York: Bantam.

Goleman, D. (2006). *Social intelligence: The new science of human relationships*. New York: Arrow.

Gottman, J., & Gottman, J. (2015, May/June). Myths and realities of couples. *Psychotherapy Networker*.

Gottman, J., & Silver, N. (1999). *The seven principles for making marriage work.* New York: Three Rivers.

Grawe, K. (2007). *Neuropsychotherapy: How the neurosciences inform effective psychotherapy.* Mahwah, NJ: Erlbaum.

Greenberg, L. (2002). *Emotion-focused therapy: Coaching clients to work through feelings.* Washington, DC: American Psychological Association.

Greenberg, L., & Watson, J. (2005). *Emotion-focused therapy of depression.* Washington, DC: American Psychological Association.

Grigsby, J., & Stevens, D. (2000). *Neurodynamics of personality.* New York: Guilford.

Gustafson, J. P. (1986). *The complex secret of brief psychotherapy.* New York: Norton.

Hanson, R. (2009). *Buddha's brain.* Oakland, CA: New Harbinger.

Hanson, R. (2016, March 22). *Mindful cultivation* [Paper presentation]. Seattle: University of Washington.

Hayes, S. C., Follette, V. M., & Linehan, M. M. (Eds.). (2004). *Mindfulness and acceptance.* New York: Guilford.

Iacoboni, M. (2009). *Mirroring people: The new science of how we connect with others.* New York: Farrar, Straus, and Giroux.

Kabat-Zinn, J. (1990). *Full catastrophe living: Using the wisdom of your body and mind to face stress and illness.* New York: Dell.

Kahneman, D. (2011). *Thinking, fast and slow.* Toronto: Doubleday Canada.

Kandel, E. (2007). *In search of memory: The emergence of a new science of mind.* New York: Norton.

Kelly, V., & Lamia, M. (2018). *The upside of shame.* New York: Norton.

Klerman, G. L., Weissman, M. M., Rounsaville, B. J., & Chevron, E. S. (1984). *Interpersonal psychotherapy for depression.* Northvale, NJ: Jason Aronson.

Kramer, P. D. (2005). *Listening to Prozac.* New York: Viking Penguin.

Lambert, M. J. (1992). Psychotherapy outcome research: Implications for integrative and eclectic therapists. In J. C. Norcross & M. R. Goldfried (Eds.), *Handbook of psychotherapy integration* (pp. 94–129). New York: Basic Books.

Langer, E. J. (2009). *Counter clockwise.* New York: Ballantine.

Langer, E. J. (2014). *Mindfulness.* Philadelphia: Da Capo.

Langer, E. J. (2016). *The power of mindful learning.* Philadelphia: Da Capo.

LeDoux, J. (1996). *The emotional brain: The mysterious underpinnings of emotional life.* New York: Simon and Schuster.

LeDoux, J. (2002). *The synaptic self: How our brains become who we are.* New York: Penguin.

LeDoux, J. (2015). *Anxious: Using the brain to understand and treat fear and anxiety.* New York: Viking.

Levenson, H. (1995). *Time-limited dynamic psychotherapy.* New York: Basic Books.

Levine, P. (1997). *Waking the tiger.* Berkley, CA: North Atlantic.

Levine, P. (2008). *Healing trauma.* Boulder, CO: Sounds True.

Levine, P. (2017). Emotion, the body and change. In M. Solomon & D. J. Siegel (Eds.), *How people change* (pp. 127–149). New York: Norton.

Lewis, T., Amini, F., & Lannon, R. (2000). *General theory of love.* New York: Random House.

Magnavita, J. J. (1997). *Restructuring personality disorders.* New York: Guilford.

Malan, D. (1999). *Individual psychotherapy and the science of psychodynamics* (2nd ed.). Oxford: Butterworth-Heinemann.

Medina, J. (2008). *Brain rules.* Seattle: Pear Press.

Miller, W. R., & Rollnick, S. (2013). *Motivational interviewing.* New York: Guilford.

Montgomery, A. (2013). *Neurobiology essentials for clinicians.* New York: Norton.

Norcross, J. C., Beutler, L. E., & Levant, R. F. (2009). *Evidence-based practices in mental health.* Washington, DC: American Psychological Association.

O'Donohue, J. (1998) *Anam cara: a book of Celtic wisdom.* New York: Harper Collins.

Ogden, P. (2017). Beyond words. In M. Solomon & D. J. Siegel (Eds.), *How people change* (pp. 97–125). New York: Norton.

Ogden, P., & Fisher, J. (2015). *Sensorimotor psychotherapy.* New York: Norton.

Ogden, P., Minton, K., & Pain, C. (2006). *Trauma and the body: A sensorimotor approach to psychotherapy.* New York: Norton.

Panksepp, J. (1982). Toward a general psychobiological theory of emotions. *Behavioral and Brain Sciences, 5,* 407–467.

Panksepp, J. (1998). *Affective neuroscience: The foundations of human and animal emotions.* New York: Oxford University Press.

Panksepp, J., & Biven, L. (2012). *The archaeology of mind: Neuroevolutionary origins of human emotions.* Norton Series on Interpersonal Neurobiology. New York: Norton.

Porges, S. (2009). Reciprocal influences between body and brain in the perception and expression of affect. In D. Fosha, D. J. Siegel, & M. F. Solomon (Eds.), *The healing power of emotion: Affective neuroscience, development and clinical practice* (pp. 27–39). New York: Norton.

Porges, S. W. (2011). *The polyvagal theory.* New York: Norton.

Porges, S. W. (2014, January/February). Signaling safety. *Psychotherapy Networker.*

Porges, S. W., & Dana, D. (2018). *Clinical applications of the polyvagal theory.* New York: Norton.

Reber, A. S. (1993). *Implicit learning and tacit knowledge.* New York: Oxford University Press.

Rousmaniere, T. (2017). *Deliberate practice for psychotherapists.* New York: Routledge.

Schore, A. (1994). *Affect regulation and the origin of the self: The neurobiology of emotional development.* Hillsdale, NJ: Erlbaum.

Schore, A. (2003). *Affect dysregulation and disorders of the self.* New York: Norton.

Schwartz, J., & Begley, S. (2002). *The mind and the brain: Neuroplasticity and the power of mental force.* New York: Harper Collins.

Servan-Schreiber, D. (2003). *The instinct to heal.* Emmaus, PA: Rodale.

Shapiro, F. (2001). *Eye movement desensitization and reprocessing.* New York: Guilford.

Sheldon, B., & Sheldon, A. (2014). *Unconscious anxiety and shame* [Video]. CIMBS. http://www.complexintegrationmbs.com.

Sheldon, B., & Sheldon, A. (2015). *Transpiring present moment* [Video]. CIMBS. http://www.complexintegrationmbs.com.

Sheldon, B., & Sheldon, A. (2016a). *Expanding efficacy and effectiveness in psychotherapy by utilizing psychophysiological information* [Video]. CIMBS. http://www.complexintegrationmbs.com.

Sheldon, B., & Sheldon, A. (2016b). *Therapeutic attachment relationship* [Video]. CIMBS. http://www.complexintegrationmbs.com.

Sheldon, B., & Sheldon, A. (2017a). *Challenging therapies: Getting unstuck working with highly anxious patients; differentiating and integrating multiple nonconscious emotional brain systems* [Video]. CIMBS. http://www.complexintegrationmbs.com.

Sheldon, B., & Sheldon, A. (2017b). *Learning to work with multiple levels of consciousness: Approaches to treatment for resistant depression* [Video]. CIMBS. http://www.complexintegrationmbs.com.

Sheldon, B., & Sheldon, A. (2018). Discovering the Wisdom and Power of Primary Process Emotions. video-recording training course. CIMBS. http://www.complexintegrationmbs.com.

Sheldon, K., Kashdan, T., & Steger, M. (Eds.). (2011). *Designing the future of positive psychology: Taking stock and moving forward.* New York: Oxford University Press.

Siegel, D. J. (1999). *The developing mind.* New York: Guilford.

Siegel, D. J. (2007). *The mindful brain: Reflection and attunement in the cultivation of well-being.* New York: Norton.

Siegel, D. J. (2010a). *The mindful therapist.* New York: Norton.

Siegel, D. J. (2010b). *Mindsight.* New York: Bantam.

Siegel, D. J. (2012). *Pocket guide to interpersonal neurobiology.* New York: Norton.

Siegel, D. J. (2018). *Aware.* New York: Penguin Random House.

Siegel, D.J. (2019). *Dan Siegel on Interpersonal Neurobiology in the consulting room.* [Webcast presentation.] Psychotherapy Networker. https://catalog.psychotherapynetworker.org/sq/pn_001257_dansiegelapplyingscience_organic-30318

Stark, M. (2000). *The modes of therapeutic action.* Lanham, MD: Rowman and Littlefield.

Stern, D. N. (2004). *The present moment in psychotherapy and everyday life.* New York: Norton.

Stevens, A., & Price, J. (2000). *Evolutionary psychiatry.* Philadelphia: Routledge.

Tangney, J. P., & Dearing, R. L. (2002). *Shame and guilt.* New York: Guilford.

Thompson, G. (2018). Brain-empowered collaborators: Polyvagal perspectives on the doctor-patient relationship. In S. W. Porges & D. Dana (Eds.), *Clinical applications of the polyvagal theory* (pp. 127–148). New York: Norton.

Tomkins, S. S. (1962). *Affect, imagery, consciousness: Vol. 1. The positive affects.* New York: Springer.

Tomkins, S. S. (1963). *Affect, imagery, consciousness: Vol. 2. The negative affects.* New York: Springer.

Valliant, L. M. (1997). *Changing character.* New York: Harper Collins.

van der Kolk, B. (2000). Post-traumatic stress disorder and the nature of trauma. *Dialogues in Clinical Neuroscience, 2*(1), 7–22.

van der Kolk, B. (2014) *Trauma, Attachment and Neuroscience* [Paper presentation]. IEDTA Conference Washington DC.

Wallin, D. (2007). *Attachment in psychotherapy.* New York: Guilford.

Wampold, B. E., & Imel, Z. E. (2015). *The great psychotherapy debate.* New York: Routledge.

Weissman, M. M., Markowitz, J. C., & Klerman, G. L. (2002). *Comprehensive guide to interpersonal psychotherapy*. New York: Basic Books.

Wilkinson, M. (2010). *Changing minds in therapy*. New York: Norton.

Wilkinson, M. (2017). Beyond words. In M. Solomon & D. J. Siegel (Eds.), *How people change* (pp. 73–96). New York: Norton.

Wilson, E. O. (1998). *Consilience*. New York: Alfred A. Knopf.

Wright, R. (1994). *The moral animal*. New York: Vintage.

Yalom, I. (1989). *Love's executioner*. New York: Basic Books.

INDEX

ABOUT THE AUTHORS

BEATRIZ SHELDON, M.Ed., Psych., has practiced psychotherapy for forty years in four languages. Ms. Sheldon received specialized post-graduate training in short-term dynamic psychotherapy at McGill University, Montreal, Canada. She has been director of a psychotherapy training program for advanced clinicians in Vancouver, Canada. Beatriz is currently supervising, training, and treating therapists in Seattle.

ALBERT SHELDON, M.D., a clinical professor of psychiatry at the University of Washington, Seattle, has specialized in the research, practice, and training of psychotherapy for 35 years. Dr. Sheldon practiced as a primary care physician for ten years before completing his training in psychiatry. He received a Bush Medical Fellowship to study psychotherapeutic processes from a psychophysiological perspective.

Beatriz and Albert have researched and taught experiential dynamic psychotherapy together for 20 years throughout North American and Europe. Fifteen years ago they conceived of a new therapeutic paradigm now called Complex Integration of Multiple Brain Systems. Today this paradigm has become a way of being for many therapists and patients alike. In your hands is a comprehensive yet approachable book that describes and illustrates their brainchild.